Conducting the Reference Interview:

A How-To-Do-It Manual for Librarians®

Second Edition

Catherine Sheldrick Ross
Kirsti Nilsen
and
Marie L. Radford

HOW-TO-DO-IT MANUALS®

NUMBER 166

Neal-Schuman Publishers, Inc.
New York   London

Preface

We wrote *Conducting the Reference Interview: A How-To-Do-It Manual for Librarians*, Second Edition, for the many librarians, educators, and students who have asked us, "Where can we read about skills for the reference interview?" or "I have to develop a training package for my staff/ my course, and I need any help I can get." Although knowing the sources and how to navigate information systems is crucially important, this book is *not* about reference sources or about where to look for information. It is about understanding the user's information needs to the extent that the librarian knows quite specifically what to look for.

Whether the transaction occurs face-to-face or virtually, the process of finding out what the user really wants is the bedrock of successful reference service upon which everything else depends. The most comprehensive understanding of the sources is wasted if the information intermediary is looking for the wrong thing. The need to understand what the user really wants to know remains the same, whether the reference transaction is face-to-face, over the telephone, or online.

This book brings together in one convenient place the results of two decades of research on the reference interview conducted by Patricia Dewdney, Catherine Ross, and Kirsti Nilsen, co-authors of the first edition, and Marie L. Radford, who brings to the second edition her expertise on communication theory, interpersonal communication, and virtual reference (VR). Our goal in this latest edition is to translate research findings about the reference transaction into practical guidelines and exercises that can be used by professionals who work in information settings. The second edition offers a wholly updated chapter on virtual reference, together with updates and additions throughout the book that acknowledge changes in the reference and research landscape over the past seven years. The constant theme that unites everything we say is the crucial importance of taking a user-centered rather than a system-centered approach to thinking about reference service. In this second edition, we consolidate research findings—our own and that of others— from many different books, articles, and other sources.

Since the publication of the first edition of *Conducting the Reference Interview* (2002), some things haven't changed. Reference librarians still need to understand how to find out, quickly and efficiently, what users really want to know. And because the basics of human communication remain the same, we have retained the microskills training approach, developed by Allen Ivey and adapted for the library context in *Communicating Professionally: A How-To-Do-It Manual*, Second Edition, by Ross and Dewdney (Neal-Schuman, 1998). However, developments in technology have changed the context in which the reference transaction happens. Libraries have been early adopters of technologies that have turned reference into a multichannel activity where librarians are connecting with users both face-to-face (FtF) and through telephone, e-mail, text messaging, and chat. But as Joe Janes has said, "It's all reference." In this second edition, we have given expanded scope to VR to reflect current practice in libraries.

The seed for the first edition of *Conducting the Reference Interview: A How-To-Do-It Manual for Librarians* was a workshop that Patricia Dewdney and Catherine Ross developed to teach the skills required for effective reference interviews. Over the years, Dewdney and Ross presented this workshop to thousands of information professionals in Canada and the United States. They called the workshop "How to Find Out What People Really Want to Know," although privately they thought of it as "Why Didn't You Say So in the First Place?" Anyone who has ever worked in any kind of information setting will instantly recognize the problem—"everything you have on travel" turns out to be a request for information about how to get a visa for travel to Russia. A person asking for "information on allergies" turns out to want specific information about side effects for a particular antihistamine.

This second edition is the fruit of a happy intersection of two research programs: the Library Visit Study, conducted by Pat Dewdney, Catherine Ross, and Kirsti Nilsen at The University of Western Ontario, and the Seeking Synchronicity study conducted by Marie L. Radford at Rutgers University and Lynn Silipigni Connaway from OCLC. All of us involved in the two editions of *Conducting the Reference Interview* have taught reference courses in graduate professional programs. This educational setting has allowed us to recruit students as participants in our various research programs on the reference transaction as it happens in the field. In the Library Visit Study, for example, we asked MLIS students to go to a library of their choice, ask a question that matters to them personally, and write a step-by-step account of what happened. They also evaluated the experience, describing what they found helpful and not helpful about the service provided. Successive classes of students over some fifteen years have provided accounts of about 250 face-to-face reference transactions, 150 VR transactions, and 500 readers' advisory transactions.

To complement this material based on users' perceptions, we have drawn extensively on the verbatim transcripts of 332 reference interviews that Patricia Dewdney tape-recorded in public libraries. We also have analyzed the data from the Mental Models study, in which Patricia Dewdney and Gillian Michell observed reference transactions in three different public library settings and afterward interviewed the librarians and thirty-three users about their perceptions of the transactions. With these rich sources, we are able to illustrate particular aspects of the reference interview—the physical environment of the library, communication accidents, ill-formed queries, appropriate use of specific skills such as open questions, what happens when appropriate skills are not used, etc.—with specific examples drawn from real reference transactions and real statements from users.

But what about the reference interview in the virtual environment? Is it the same or a whole different animal? Speculation abounds, but it is useful to have empirical data of real reference transactions in virtual settings. Phase 3 of the Library Visit Study provided 150 detailed descriptions of what happened when users posed a question virtually, either through e-mail or chat. Another rich source of data was Radford and Connaway's (2005–10) IMLS-funded Seeking Synchronicity project (2005–2008) that included a large number of phone and online surveys of virtual reference services (VRS) librarians, VRS users, and VRS non-users. They also analyzed an international sample of over 750 verbatim transcripts of chat reference, 434 of which were found to have evidence of query clarification. This corpus of transcripts and survey results has allowed us to analyze types of questions asked, communication behavior of users and librarians, and barriers and facilitators of chat reference. The Library Visit Study accounts provide rich-grained evidence about the users' experiences. Empirical data from these various complementary research projects have provided sources from which we have drawn real examples as the basis for the thirty-six cases included in this book.

In this second edition, we have added many more examples, especially new examples of chat reference. We hope you find it useful to see the points we make about communication in the reference interview illustrated with real examples taken from the field. Although the challenge of finding out what the user really wants to know is the same in public, academic, governmental, and other special libraries, we have tended to illustrate our discussion with straightforward examples drawn from public libraries, so that a specialized subject background is not needed to understand the context of the user's question.

Because we believe in the integration of theory and praxis, and are convinced that a useful book on reference must be informed by relevant theory and research while also being purposefully practical, this book had its genesis in both the teaching environment of workshop and classroom and in our research. The reference workshop, though rooted in a sense-making theory of information and based on current research in reference, was essentially practical in emphasis. Through a combination of methods, including small lectures, modeling, group exercises, role-plays, and discussion, the workshop explored communication problems occurring between library users and library staff and presented some skills for coping with these problems. Workshop participants over the years shared with us their experiences of reference interviews gone right and wrong, and we fed this material back into the workshops.

Organization

In Chapter 1, "Why Bother with a Reference Interview?," we describe the theoretical foundations for this book and review perspectives on the need for conducting a reference interview. We argue that taking questions at "face value" does not work because the initial question rarely reflects three essential aspects of the user's information need as defined in Brenda Dervin's sense-making theory—the situation (how the need arose), the gap (what is missing in the user's understanding), and the uses to which the user hopes to put the information. Chapter 1 also introduces mental models theory (with previously unpublished examples) to explain why users do not always present their questions clearly and completely. If librarians want to provide helpful answers beyond "the 55 percent rule," they must hone their communication skills to perform "the art of translation."

In the next three chapters we use Allen Ivey's microtraining approach to identify those communication skills most helpful in the reference interview. We illustrate these with examples, both positive and negative, from our own research and training programs. Chapter 2, "Setting the Stage for the Reference Interview," covers the basic skills needed for the crucial first seconds of contact—nonverbal, listening, and verbal skills that establish a positive communication climate.

Chapter 3, "Finding Out What They Really Want to Know," begins with some common problems observed in reference interviews, such as negative closure and unmonitored referrals, and then sets out the major skills for the reference interview—asking open and sense-making questions, avoiding premature diagnosis, paraphrasing, summarizing, and achieving closure. Chapter 4, "Beyond Negative Closure," includes skills useful for later stages of the interview—inclusion, one-to-one library use instruction, and essential follow-up techniques. We also give tried-and-true tips for practicing and integrating skills into everyday behavior.

Chapters 5, 6, and 7 cover a variety of special contexts in which librarians must adapt these skills for particular purposes and user groups. Chapter 5, "Special Contexts for the Reference Interview," includes telephone reference service, voicemail, and handling imposed queries (when one user presents a question on behalf of another). Sections are devoted to working with children and young adults, with so-called problematic people, and with adults who have special language-related needs. This chapter also brings together the many communication problems arising from medical and legal reference questions, as well as those arising in collaborative reference. Chapter 6, "The Reference Encounter in Virtual Environments," has been almost entirely rewritten since the first edition to take into account the rapid expansion of mediated forms of reference in libraries. Here we deal with the principles of communicating effectively in the VR interview, specifically reference conducted through e-mail, instant messaging, chat, and emerging initiatives such as Short Message Service (SMS) and reference in Second Life. The readers' advisory interview, covered previously in a chapter section, has been expanded to become Chapter 7. Finally, in Chapter 8, "Establishing Policy and Training for the Reference Interview," we consider the broader institutional context—library policies and training programs designed to help librarians improve information service through more effective reference interviews.

At the end of each chapter, we provide reference lists of sources cited in the chapter as well as annotations for references that can also be used as suggestions for further reading. This way, helpful sources appear at point of use for the reader, rather than in one long bibliography at the end. We know that some readers may want to read the book sequentially, while others may want to focus on specific applications, such as the reference interview with children or readers' advisory or new developments in chat environments. Therefore, we have written each section so that it is largely self-contained, with references, as necessary, to other places in the book where a particular skill or concept is further explained. You can dive into the book at any point and read backward or forward, following your specific interests.

Applications

We have written this book to provide a single accessible source that draws together the scattered findings of research and praxis and translates them into practical guidelines and exercises that can be used for training and for individual learning. Over the past two decades, research programs have filled in a lot of gaps in our understanding of the reference interview—what works and what doesn't, what can go wrong despite the best intentions of the librarian, and what explains puzzling user behavior (why *do* users ask for "everything on refrigeration" when they want to know how to repair a refrigerator?). Our goal here is to integrate the most valuable work done by ourselves and others on the reference transaction.

Materials presented here have been adapted and developed from numerous studies of human communication, especially sense-making and microtraining. *Sense-making* is an approach developed by Brenda Dervin at the University of Ohio that focuses our attention on how people use information to make sense of their lives. Instead of assuming that information is a commodity that is valuable in itself, sense-making directs us to ask, "How will this information help this particular individual deal with a particular situation in the context of his or her own life?" *Microtraining* was developed by Allen E. Ivey as an effective way to teach interview skills to counselors and is based on the idea that complex communication behaviors can be broken down into constituent parts that can be taught, one at a time. We have modified these innovative models to focus on the strategies and skills most useful for the reference interview.

The pages that follow combine our most useful training materials for the reference interview with a map to the most useful research—all set within a framework for thinking about information service. This book is based on the idea that people learn best when they are actively engaged. Each chapter therefore combines explanatory text with modeling, many examples drawn from actual reference interviews, exercises that provide opportunities for practice, and annotated references that provide recommendations for further reading. We have designed this extensively updated edition of *Conducting the Reference Interview* to be useful both to individual learners and to trainers and supervisors who want support materials for staff training on the reference interview.

Acknowledgments

This book could not have been written without the help and cooperation of all the people who participated in the many research studies in which we have been involved over the years. That research forms the bedrock of all we say here. First there were the librarians who participated in Patricia Dewdney's field study and in her Mental Models Study. Pat Dewdney, the co-author of the first edition, provided insights that remain a guiding spirit in the second edition. Next, we must thank the more than 400 graduate students from The University of Western Ontario and the University of Toronto who participated in the Library Visit Study, phases 1–3, over a period of fifteen years. They asked their questions in person and through e-mail and chat, and they provided the detailed accounts and incisive evaluations of their experiences from which we have freely quoted. A similar debt is owed to the more than 500 graduate students from The University of Western Ontario who participated in the RA Library Visit and wrote accounts of their experiences, good or bad, and to Jennifer Noon, who analyzed the RA Visit data reported in Chapter 7. Special thanks and gratitude to Lynne McKechnie who wrote the section on the reference interview with children and young adults.

For support in conducting the field research on chat reference, we thank OCLC Online Computer Library Center, Inc., and especially the Seeking Synchronicity Co-principal Investigator, Lynn Silipigni Connaway, PhD, and the rest of the grant team, including Patrick Confer, Timothy Dickey, PhD, and Erin Hood. Thanks also to the Rutgers University School of Communication, Information, and Library Studies' Seeking Synchronicity grant team, including Jocelyn DeAngelis Williams, Julie Strange, Susanna Sabolski-Boros, David Dragos, Vicki Kozo, Andrea Simzak, Jannica Heinstrom, PhD, and Jon Oliver. We acknowledge as well the contributions of all the anonymous VRS librarians, users, and non-users who participated in the Seeking Synchronicity focus group interviews, online surveys, and telephone interviews.

Particular acknowledgment is due to two leaders and researchers whose work has been so influential on our own thinking: Allen Ivey and Brenda Dervin from the fields of counseling and communication, respectively. Within the library field, we are greatly indebted to Mary Kay Chelton (Queen's), Joan Durrance (University of Michigan), Gillian Michell and Lorri Mon (Florida State University), Mike Oetting

(Hinsdale Public Library, IL), Rhea Joyce Rubin, and Duncan Smith (NoveList), and the Super-Readers interviewed by Catherine Ross: Cindy Orr, Nancy Pearl, Joyce Saricks, and Sharron Smith. We also thank the Internet Public Library.

The excellent staff at Neal-Schuman prompted us to write this book, supported us throughout its development, and badgered us to do a second edition. Finally we want to thank Gail Schlacter and the RASD selection committees who encouraged our research by awarding us the Reference Services Press Award for the following *RQ* and *RUSQ* articles: "Flying a Light Aircraft," "Oranges and Peaches," "Negative Closure," "So Has the Internet Changed Anything in Reference?" and "The Reference Interview: Why It Needs to be Used in Every (Well, Almost Every) Reference Transaction." We thank them all—and others too numerous to list here.

Why Bother with a Reference Interview?

1.1 What Is a (Reference) Interview?

An interview is a special kind of conversation directed intentionally to some purpose. There are, of course, many different types of interviews, and these vary widely along many dimensions including the power relations established between the participants, the degree of trust involved, the duration of the interview, the length of responses, the degree of structure in the questions, and the purpose of the interview. Consider the difference between two kinds of interviews. On the one hand is the police interrogation in which the interviewer is totally in charge and sets the agenda for the questioning. Trust is low in such interviews, while questions are structured and often closed ("Did you leave your house on the evening of the twentieth?"), and answers are often unforthcoming ("No"). The purposes of police interrogator and suspect are usually diametrically opposed. On the other hand is the oral history interview or research interview in which both parties are equal partners. Trust is relatively high in this case, with open-ended questions geared to the interests and priorities of the interviewee. Because answers are often very lengthy, these interviews may last an hour or more, and the purpose of the interview is mutually shared.

Clearly one of the most important factors in any interview is the extent to which the interviewer and interviewee share a common purpose. At one end of the scale, both parties share a common purpose and know that they do, while at the other end, each party has a separate and opposed purpose. Sometimes an interviewer makes an erroneous assumption about the interviewee's purpose, as in the case of a young user who asks for "a book about a classic novel" hoping to find a brief plot summary for a book report due today. He wants to do the minimum amount of work possible to get through the assignment and is not really interested in reading the book. The librarian, on the other hand, thinks that everyone should take advantage of educational opportunities to read classic works such as *War and Peace*. Such interactions are likely to go badly unless the interviewer takes the view that the goal of the reference interview is to find out what the user wants to do and then provide materials that will help him reach that goal (however different the librarian's own goal would be in a similar situation).

Despite obvious differences among different types of interviewing, all interviews share some common features. A growing body of literature has been developed to explain what some of these important features are. Although interviews seem to resemble ordinary conversations, they actually differ from normal dialogue in important ways. It is the job of the interviewer, not the interviewee, to keep in mind these differences between a well-conducted interview and a friendly conversation.

- Participants in conversations are expected to follow the rule of turn-taking where each person has a relatively equal share of talking and listening. In interviews, on the other hand, it is acceptable, in fact highly desirable, for the interviewer to do a lot more listening while encouraging the interviewee to talk. *See* Listening (2.4.5).

- Unlike typical conversations, interviews involve the asking and answering of questions, where one person normally asks the questions and the other answers. *See* Open and Closed Questions (3.2.1) and Sense-making Questions (3.2.3).

- Unlike typical conversations, interviews are directed toward a purpose. Any topic not relevant to the purpose of the interview can appropriately be excluded by a comment that brings discussion back to the purpose of the interview (e.g., "that's interesting about your holiday, but to get back to your question on submarines, what aspect of submarines interests you?") *See* Closure (3.2.5).

- Redundancy and repetition are drawbacks in conversation but desirable in interviews in which interviewers often ask the same question in different words in order to get a fuller picture. Interviewees often don't spill the beans right away because they are following the rules for conversationalists (don't be boringly repetitive or talk at length about yourself) rather than the rules for interviewees (provide as full an account as is useful about the topic of the interview). Effective interviewers use encouragers and probes to reassure the interviewee that they are not bored and to get the interviewee to expand on a statement (e.g., "What else can you tell me about your research project on bagpipes?"; "Uh huh, anything else?"; "That's interesting. Anything else?"; "Could you give me an example of that?"). *See* Minimal Encouragers (2.4.4).

- Unlike a participant in a typical conversation, a good interviewer uses a number of strategies to make sure that the interviewee has been fully understood and that the message has been accurately received. These strategies include paraphrasing and summarizing what has been heard (e.g., "Okay, so it sounds as if X is the case; you feel Y; you want Z to happen. Did I get that right?") as well as note-taking, and sometimes recording and transcribing when the interview is long and complex. *See* Reflecting Content (3.2.4).

- Unlike ordinary conversation, an interview has a structure that must reflect its purpose. The stages of an interview usually are:

  1. greeting user and establishing rapport;
  2. general information gathering or getting the big picture;
  3. specific information gathering;
  4. intervention, such as giving information, advice, or instructions; and
  5. ending, including feedback or summary.

These stages may be iterative, occurring in loops throughout the interview, such as when the interviewer needs to re-establish rapport or do some more general information gathering before the interview ends.

But what about the reference interview? The term *reference interview* suggests to most librarians a short face-to-face (FtF) interview conducted for the purpose of finding out what the user really wants to know so that the staff member can match the user's question to the library's store of information. Librarians generally agree that users' initial questions are often unclear or incomplete. The purpose of the interview is to elicit from the user sufficient information about the real need so that the librarian understands it enough to begin searching. The user's initial question often needs to be clarified, narrowed down, made more detailed, and contextualized. Nicholas Belkin's (1980) ASK Hypothesis suggests that users, who often don't understand their informational need totally or may be unable to articulate it, are in an "Anomalous State of Knowledge." Questioning during the reference interview may elicit information about what the user wants to know; how the user plans to use the information; what level of detail, technical specialization, or reading ability would be useful; and what format of information is preferred. Other restrictions may emerge such as how much work the user is willing to do to get the answer, whether there are time limits or deadlines, and how current the information must be.

The typical reference interview is shorter than most types of interviews described in the literature such as counseling interviews, ethnographic interviews, oral history interviews, and journalistic interviews. While reference interviews normally last three minutes or less, a reference interview with a client having complex research needs or a genealogist may last for twenty minutes or longer. Variations on the basic form often occur. In the readers' advisory interview (Chapter 7), librarians, before making recommendations, have directed conversations with users about their reading tastes, experiences with previous favorite books, and current preferences. Sometimes the librarian, unable to communicate directly with the user who wants the information, must work through a delegate who is asking the question on behalf of the user. Melissa Gross has called this situation "the imposed query" (5.3.1). A special case of the imposed query occurs when students need to get material to complete a school assignment about which they may have no personal interest (5.4.3). Nowadays interviews are often mediated electronically by telephone (5.2) or, increasingly, by live chat, instant messaging, or e-mail (Chapter 6). Often e-mail involves the user's filling out an electronic form in order to provide specific details concerning the informational need.

All reference interviews in their various guises can be defined simply as purposive conversations between librarians and users in which questions are asked to get a clearer and more complete picture of what users want to know and to link users to the system. In addition to these purposes of query negotiation, the reference interview may include related functions such as giving information, advice, or instruction, getting feedback, and following up to assess users' satisfaction with the help provided.

Although all reference interviews are unique, they have common structural features and go through similar stages: establishing contact with the user, finding out the user's need, and confirming that the answer provided is actually what was needed. There are a standard set of skills that staff members can learn, practice, and use to increase the likelihood that the interview will be productive. The interview can go wrong in predictable ways, and there are standard ways of recovering from "communication accidents." Whatever the purpose of the interview, interviewers should have a clear idea before the interview starts of why they are conducting it and what they hope to accomplish by the end.

Did You Know?
According to Solomon (1997), research on the physician/patient interview has found that doctors ask all the questions and patients provide the answers. When patients did ask questions, the question often was not heard.

1.2 Service Orientation of Libraries

Is a reference interview really needed? Reference as a core function in libraries has been around for scarcely more than a century, and for the first half of that period all attention was directed to learning about sources, not communicating with users. Patrick Wilson (1982), in his article "The Face Value Rule in Reference Work," points out that the literature seems to be divided on this issue. Some authorities say that a reference interview is almost always needed, while others say that a reference interview is needed only under certain circumstances, and definitely not for directional queries or for ready-reference questions. Wilson quotes one commentator who seems to be a spokesperson for bluff common sense speaking out against ivory tower concepts taught in library school: "the reference interview can't—and shouldn't—be applied as readily in public libraries as we were taught. Time and common sense won't permit it" (McCoy, 1985).

Two arguments, which we consider myths, have been advanced against worrying too much about reference interviewing skills. Both arguments, in our view, are wrong because, as a result of acting upon them, users don't get the service they need. This book is founded upon the principle that libraries must take a service orientation. We are convinced that the institutions that will survive in the twenty-first century are those that serve their clients and give them the help they need. If libraries don't provide helpful information services, users will turn to other service-providers who are more service-oriented. Online users are also turning to Web-based answering services such as "Yahoo Answers" (http://answers.yahoo.com) or the "ASK" (www.ask.com) search engines to meet their informational needs. Unlike these sites, however, librarians provide a professional "value added" knowledge component that is lacking in many commercial services. The RUSA (Reference and User Services Association, 2000) "Guidelines for Information Services" state, "Provision of information in the manner most useful to its clients is the ultimate test of all a library does."

Myth 1: Since users usually are pretty clear about their informational need, the reference interview is unnecessary.

According to this view, the user's question is straightforward, and the tricky part for the intermediary is knowing the range of tools that contain the answers. Writers such as Dennis Grogan (1991, 63) have maintained that "most of the library users who put questions to the librarian know exactly what they need and ask for it clearly." Robert Hauptman (1987) has called the reference interview a "myth," claiming that in a study he conducted only six cases out of 1,074 demanded an extensive interview. We do not advocate "extensive" interviewing in any case. Several properly focused questions are usually enough, but there's a big difference between the claim that *extensive* interviewing is not needed and that *no* interviewing is needed. The view that finding out the user's informational need is easy has changed as research increasingly has drawn attention to the complex nature of human interaction. While some users are able to ask initial questions that explain exactly what they are looking for, we know that about 40 percent of users do not, especially those who are unfamiliar with how libraries work. While the reference interview is a crucial tool for these novice users, it enhances the likelihood of receiving a helpful answer for *all* users. In short, you should give every user the chance to elaborate on the query; if it turns out to have been unnecessary, then no harm is done.

Myth 2: The onus is on the users to know what they want and express their needs clearly. Librarians should take users' questions at "face value."

One response to the fact that users' initial statements of their informational needs can be incomplete or misleading is Patrick Wilson's "face value" rule: "Assume that information requested is information wanted; interview only to clarify the initial formulation of the request" (1986, 469). When the user asks, "Where is your history section?" the face value rule would direct the librarian to take the user to the history shelves and say, "The history books are on these shelves here." If the user asks for the wrong thing (his actual question is, "How high is the Eiffel Tower?"), that's his look-out. The face value rule puts the onus on users to become more informed about libraries and the organization of information so that they can ask for exactly what they want. This rule makes the reference interview unnecessary in many cases. As a result, however, a lot of users won't get what they need. Patrick Wilson (1986) acknowledges that the face value rule "is plausible if the conception of

Did You Know?
Herbert White (1992) says that librarians need to emphasize their strengths. As computers increasingly take over clerical tasks that computers are good at, librarians should focus attention on aspects of service involving human communication that computers can't do well. Let computers get involved in document identification, document delivery, overdue notices, interlibrary loans and cataloging, White argues, and let librarians take a proactive role in information intermediation.

Is an Interview Needed?

Examine this interview, which lasted seventeen seconds, as tape-recorded in Dewdney's field study. The librarian followed the face value rule, asking a question only to clarify the initial formulation of the request:

Librarian: Hi. Can I help?

User: Where can I find the city directory?

Librarian: For [local city name]? (closed question)

User: Yes.

Librarian: Right here. You can take it to a table and just bring it back when you're finished.

(Dewdney, "City Directory")

For group discussion, consider the following:

- Do you think any further interviewing was needed here?
- Under what circumstances would further questioning be unnecessary?
- Under what circumstances might it be needed?
- How can the librarian distinguish in advance between these two sets of circumstances?
- What else could the librarian have said during this interview to enhance the likelihood that the user would not leave the library without finding what she was looking for?

Compare the seventeen-second interview quoted above with this one, conducted by the same librarian in the same library a short time later:

Librarian: Can I help?

User: I have a list of publications [reads from paper]. I don't know if those are magazines or journals or...

(Cont'd.)

Case 1: System Routines vs. User Needs

Librarian: Can I help you?

User: I don't know if it's published anymore, but did you get the *Million Dollar Directory*? The last one published? I want to see the third section.

Librarian: No, we don't. We didn't subscribe to it.

User: Pardon?

Librarian: We didn't subscribe to Volume 3.

User: You didn't get it?

Librarian: No. The reason is that the companies included were mostly smaller companies not in our area. So we didn't think we needed it. Did you find a reference to it? (*closed question*)

User: I thought it was here—the brown one.

Librarian: The brown one. (*acknowledgment*) No, that's a periodical directory. [She explains.] If you need Volume 3 of the *Million Dollar Directory*, the University still has a copy in the business library. (*referral*)

User: I can get it if I want it. Okay. Thank you.

(Adapted from Dewdney, "Million Dollar")

Comment: Does this user really need Volume 3 of the *Million Dollar Directory*? Maybe not. We'll never know. This one-minute-and-fifteen-second transaction focused almost exclusively on the library's subscription policy. No headway whatsoever was made into finding out what information the user hoped to locate in the *Million Dollar Directory* because the librarian chose not to conduct a reference interview. In some circumstances a user absolutely needs to see a specific reference tool and not a substitute (to write a review on it, for example, for a library school assignment). In the majority of cases, however, the requested reference tool is just a way station on the path to finding a specific piece of information. In this case the question was taken at face value and the user was directed to another distant library. But without conducting a reference interview, the librarian has no way of knowing that there are no other tools within her own library that could have answered the user's question. The user's question could possibly have been answered by another directory that the library did possess or by an online business directory.

library service that it reflects is acceptable." He continues, "The Face Value Rule seems to be a perfectly proper rule to follow if one conceives of the reference librarian as an intermediary, prepared to respond to requests for information, not professionally responsible (though sometimes personally interested) for the consequences of the use of the information" (474–475). A big drawback to accepting this conception of service and following the face value rule is that libraries with this limited orientation to service are less likely to be considered helpful institutions that are worth funding and preserving.

William Katz (2002: 130) put his considerable authority behind the view that "the original question . . . is rarely the *real* question," and "the purpose of the reference interview…is to clarify the question." According to research carried out since the late 1970s, however, in half of transactions in libraries the reference staff follows the face value rule and bypasses the reference interview. When researchers such as Mary Jo Lynch (1978) and Patricia Dewdney (1986) audio-taped actual reference transactions and began to look closely at exactly what the users and the staff members said and did, three things became very clear. Users don't express their informational needs clearly and completely in their initial question. In half of cases, staff members accept the initial question at face value and don't conduct a reference interview. Finally, when the initial question is taken at face value, users often wind up not getting the help they want.

In virtual settings, initial studies have found a somewhat higher level of accuracy for e-mail services than for chat services. Neil Kaske and Julie Arnold (2002) described an unobtrusive study in which twelve questions were posed both to chat services and e-mail services at a random sample of thirty-six libraries. In total, 180 e-mail questions were sent and 180 chat sessions attempted. The rate of correctly answered questions for e-mail services was 59.8 percent, while for chat services it was 54.8 percent. More recently, Arnold and Kaske (2005) investigated accuracy in live chat reference. They looked at 351 live chat transcripts at the University of Maryland and found a very high level of accuracy of 92 percent. Marilyn Domas White, Eileen Abels, and Neal Kaske (2003) evaluated the quality of live chat reference at both university and public libraries through unobtrusive methods, and found a similarly high level of accuracy. Live chat services have the advantage of producing a verbatim transcript of the reference encounter and allow researchers to perform accuracy assessments in an unobtrusive way.

Radford and Connaway (2007) examined a random sample of 581 live chat reference interactions from the international QuestionPoint service. These chat questions were answered by a mix of librarians from public, academic, and special libraries. They found that in 75 percent (434) of the transcripts, the librarians asked clarifying questions. In examining accuracy for the subset of ready-reference questions, they found that using a reference interview boosted accuracy considerably and was present in 84 percent of the 141 correct answers.

We strongly oppose the face value rule and advocate instead that a reference interview (the asking of one or more questions intended to discover the user's informational needs) must be conducted in *every* transaction. Users should be offered the invitation to expand or clarify. While some librarians object that they are too busy, we argue that some additional seconds spent in finding out the user's real informational need saves time in the long run. Less time is spent by library staff looking for the wrong thing; less time is spent within the library system processing book transfers, faxing documents, and seeking interlibrary loans for the wrong materials; and less time is spent by e-reference staff in typing out answers that direct users to the wrong electronic sources.

EXERCISE (Continued)

Librarian: They're all magazines [looking at paper]. [Reads names of magazines and gives directions on where to find them.] But before you look at magazines themselves, you'd want to know which particular articles you are looking for. (*open question*)

User: Do you have an index?

Librarian: Yeah. Are you looking at a particular topic? (*closed question that functions as an open question*)

User: Yes. I'm looking at wage restraint in the federal government.

Librarian: Okay. You might want to use the business index. [Explains index; shows index.] Have you used an index before?

User: No.

Librarian: [Explains and instructs. Together they find several headings related to wage restraint. Librarian gives directions on how to find the specific articles on wage restraint in the magazines themselves.]

User: Okay. Thank you.

(Dewdney, "Wage Restraint")

An important part of providing good service is the willingness to understand the user's perspective. A research study by Patricia Dewdney and Gillian Michell (1996) called "Mental Models of Information Systems: A Study of 'Ill-Formed' Queries Presented in Public Libraries" demonstrates how the users' initial questions are influenced by their "mental model" of how libraries work. Dewdney and Michell observed and recorded reference transactions in public libraries, conducted in-depth personal interviews with thirty-three adult public library users who had asked for help from a librarian, and later interviewed these same librarians. Among other questions, both the users and the librarians were asked how difficult they thought the question would be at the outset and how hard it actually turned out to be. Here are some of their findings:

1. **Users depend on librarians to help them find the information they need.** Even frequent library users do not have a very accurate or complete understanding of how library resources are organized and how to use them. Despite a general willingness to help themselves, they rely heavily on professional librarians to help them cope with this complexity, which is increasing with new information technology.

2. **Complex informational needs are presented in small libraries as well as large ones.** Even in small branch libraries, people ask difficult reference questions which require staff assistance. It is important for staff to be able to make effective referrals and be knowledgeable about resources in other locations.

3. **Users' questions appear to be easy to answer but are often difficult.** Apparently simple requests (e.g., "Can I look at the city directory?") often mask complex informational needs which require a range of resources and often a referral. Neither librarians nor users could initially predict how difficult a question might be to answer. Users in general thought their questions were easier than they actually turned out to be. Furthermore, users who thought questions had been easy to answer gave the presence of the librarian as the explanation; users thought their questions were easy for the librarians because of the librarians' skills, knowledge, helpfulness, understanding, technological abilities, etc.

4. **Nearly half of these questions could not have been answered without the librarian's help.** About 40 percent of these questions probably would not have been answered completely without the help of a professional librarian. One reason is that users often have unreasonable expectations of electronic information systems, e.g., that entering a company name into the public access catalog will result in information about that company. Even when users are knowledgeable about the library system, unexpected barriers may intervene, such as material that is missing or mis-shelved. If the user's own strategy does not work, the user may not be able to get an answer unless the librarian is available to suggest alternative strategies.

Did You Know?

In an unobtrusive study of reference service in Suffolk County public libraries on Long Island, Thomas Childers (1980) instructed surrogate users to pose "escalator" questions, starting initially with a broad request so that librarians would have to use probes to discover the specific questions the users really wanted answered. No matter how general the initial question was, in 67 percent of the cases library staff members asked no questions to clarify what information was required. The result was that these staff members got to the last step—the real question—only 20 percent of the time and hardly ever provided an accurate answer. By contrast, the third who did use probes to arrive at the specific question provided an accurate answer 62 percent of the time.

EXERCISE

Just Say No

Karen Hyman's "Rule of 1965" claims that anything a library did prior to 1965 is essential and everything else is extra, to be offered grudgingly—for decades. Check how well your library is following the Rule of 1965 by giving it one point for every "Yes" answer to the following:

1. You offer services that you don't publicize because too many people might want them.

2. The telephone reference staff won't fax answers to users even though the technology is now cheap and available because "that's not how it's ever been done in this department."

3. Your telephone voicemail says that you are too busy to answer and that the caller should phone back or come into the library in person.

4. On the Web page describing the virtual reference service (VRS), the very first thing users see is a disclaimer or a statement about the kinds of users or questions that are ineligible for service. Give an extra point if the VRS Web page advises users to come to the library in person for really good service.

5. The library restricts and rations Internet access through complicated sign-up procedures and/or extremely short amounts of computer time per library visit (less than thirty minutes) even during slow times.

6. Your policy disallows the use of the Internet for personal communication (e-mail, chat, MySpace or Facebook).

7. The link to your VRS is at least three clicks away from your main page.

8. The library's VRS tells users that they should use the service only for "ready-reference questions." Give an extra point if no examples or explanation are provided to help the user understand what libraries mean by a ready-reference questions.

If the score is 0 or 1, the library deserves congratulations. If the score is 2 to 4, more could be done to put a positive face on the library service. If the score is 5 or more, the library is in trouble and needs to review its policy on service and its communications with its users (if it still has any users).

(Adapted from Hyman, 1999. Used with permission.)

Did You Know?

Marilyn Domas White (1989) found that most librarians follow the face value rule in practice. She distinguishes between two models of the reference interview: the Question-Oriented Model, where the staff member tries to answer the user's *question* as asked; and the Needs-Oriented Model, where the staff member tries to find materials that address the user's informational need, or initiating *problem*. She analyzed seventy-six of Mary Jo Lynch's interview transcripts and determined that more than 80 percent of the reference interviews were question-oriented. Moreover, in six interviews where clients mentioned the problem in the initial query, the librarian did not follow up on their cues.

5. **Users depend heavily on librarians not only to find the information they need but also to find out how to use the system.** Users spoke of "learning one new thing each time I come to the library," usually through instruction by the librarian.

The data from this study repeatedly showed that *the librarian is the key to the information seeking process* for users. The solution to current stresses on library systems is not to reduce the human element but to make it stronger, more efficient, and more effective. The most important resource of a public or academic library is the staff which links people with collections, both virtual and print. These findings have implications for the concept of the do-it-yourself virtual library. How many questions go unanswered when users do not approach library staff for help? In this era of e-resources, the role of librarians as intermediaries between users and information has not diminished; it may actually be even more crucial.

1.3 Beyond 55 Percent

Unobtrusive studies have shown that when users ask reference questions in academic and public libraries, they get accurate answers from 50 to 60 percent of the time. So frequently has this result been found that it has been enshrined in the literature as the "55 percent rule," first articulated by Peter Hernon and Charles McClure (1986, 1987) in their analysis of unobtrusive studies of reference service. Unobtrusive observation was given impetus in social science research with the work of E. J. Webb et al. on unobtrusive measures in the 1960s. The advantage of unobtrusive measures is that they are unreactive. Subjects who are observed unobtrusively are less likely to change their behavior than are subjects who know they are being observed. Unobtrusive observation and testing got its start in the library field after Thomas Childers and Terrence Crowley published their two studies of reference service in 1971. In these two pioneering research reports and the many that replicated their methods, the researcher typically developed a list of questions with a known right answer. A research assistant or proxy asked the questions in a library and tabulated the percentage of correct answers provided. In these studies, accuracy of the answer given was the single measure used to evaluate the effectiveness of service. Answer accuracy is a recommended measure because, like precision and recall, it is a reliable variable that is not dependent on subjective judgments.

An answer might be accurate, however, and still fail on some other criterion of adequacy. It might be incomprehensible to the user, provided too late to be useful, or unacceptable because it was provided by a surly librarian. Moreover, accuracy is a useful criterion only for factual questions that have a single right or wrong answer, such as "How high is the Washington Monument?" or "What is the address of the Australian High Commissioner in Zimbabwe?" Most reference questions have a range of acceptable answers. Because users' questions typically take the form of "I want information on X," they might say, "I'm looking for information on prostate cancer," or "Do you have anything on carbon dating?" or "Where can I get information on the care of grapevines?" So even if we could agree that the correctness of answers is the best measure for factual questions, we might wonder about the validity of this measure for overall reference service.

Joan Durrance (1989) asks the rhetorical question, "Does the 55 percent rule tell the whole story?" and her answer is "No." She proposed and tested a new indicator: the user's willingness to return to the same staff member at a later time. In her study of 266 reference interviews in academic, special, and public libraries, Durrance (1989) found that a user's willingness (or unwillingness) to return was significantly related to eleven interpersonal and search skill variables. She observed that users were "far

EXERCISE

The 55 Percent Rule
Read "Unobtrusive Reference Testing: the 55 Percent Rule" by Peter Hernon and Charles R. McClure (1986). This article reviews many research studies that indicate that only about 55 percent of the answers provided by reference librarians are accurate. As a group discuss to what extent you think the accuracy rate could be increased by a more effective reference interview. Since the Hernon and McClure article was published in 1986, there have been many changes in libraries. Do you think that the Internet has made a difference to the reference success rate? In what way? See Chapter 6 to find out some ways to boost accuracy in virtual reference.

more forgiving when library staff members had weak interviewing skills or gave inaccurate answers than they were if the staff member made them feel uncomfortable, showed no interest, or appeared to be judgmental about the question" (1989: 35). In fact, in some cases where the answer was rated as largely inaccurate, over one-quarter of Durrance's users said they would return to that same librarian. Her study raised some interesting questions: Are users more impressed by the demeanor of the librarian than by the quality of the information provided? What factor or combination of factors influences the user's willingness to return?

In her book *The Reference Encounter*, Marie Radford (1999) examines factors that enter into the users' perceptions of reference success. Drawing on communication theory, she makes a key distinction between the content-oriented dimension and the relational dimension of interpersonal communication. Unobtrusive tests of accuracy measure only the content-oriented dimension. The relational dimension of the reference transaction encompasses the feelings of the participants and their attitudes toward one another and toward the reference encounter itself. Radford gathered the data for her study by observing reference transactions in three different academic library settings and then interviewing both parties to the transaction. She observed a total of twenty-seven reference encounters and tape-recorded and transcribed in-depth interviews with nine academic reference librarians and twenty-nine users. Her real interest was in perceptions of the reference transaction, and specifically whether the user's perception differed from that of the librarian involved in the same transaction. Not surprisingly, there were substantial differences.

According to Radford's book, users almost always attributed the success or failure of a reference transaction to relational factors. They said the librarian was "nice and helpful and pleasant," or "went out of her way," or, contrarily, was "not very patient," or was "really sour" (1999: 76, 80). In contrast, librarians, especially when discussing successful transactions, were apt to talk about issues of content such as the amount or quality of information available on particular topics. When discussing transactions considered unsuccessful, however, librarians focused on the relational factors of feelings or attitudes. Interestingly, librarians explained unsuccessful transactions in terms of the users' poor attitudes either toward the librarian or toward the task. Users were described as being closed-minded, angry, and interruptive (1999, 76–77).

Radford (2006) followed up on her research in the face-to-face (FtF) reference setting with a similar analysis of live chat reference. Unlike traditional FtF reference, live chat produces an artifact in the form of an exact transcript that can be analyzed by librarians willing to take on this rewarding but time-consuming job. Radford discussed results from two studies, the first of which was a pilot study that analyzed forty-four transcripts nominated for the Green Award given twice a year by Library Systems and Services, LLC (LSSI) in honor of Samuel S. Green, a pioneer in advocating excellent service to users. Second, Radford analyzed 245 transcripts from the Maryland AskUsNow! statewide chat reference service.

Identifying the interpersonal dynamics present in the VRS environment, Radford found that relational dimensions present in FtF encounters were also present in the chat environment, although in a somewhat different form because of the text-based nature of chat. For chat reference, she identified relational facilitators, interpersonal aspects that have a positive impact on perceptions of success, and relational barriers, those that have a negative effect. She also looked to see if there were any differences when comparing librarians' behaviors to those of the users. One difference Radford found, as might be expected, was that users displayed more deference to librarians by showing respect or agreeing to follow suggestions. Another difference was that interpersonal barriers created by users such as rudeness or impatience, were, for the most part, very different from those created by librarians such as negative closure (3.1.5). Radford's study emphasized the need for librarians in digital environments to develop strategies for cultivating excellent interpersonal relationships with users in FtF reference encounters.

With Lynn Silipigni Connaway, Radford built upon her earlier work, analyzing a larger sample of transcripts along with adding a large number of surveys and interviews with VRS users, non-users, and librarians in the Seeking Synchronicity project (2005–2008). They refined the list of relational facilitators and barriers Radford had found earlier in chat transcripts (see "Relational Facilitators and Barriers in Live Chat Reference"). They also developed a theoretical model, based on communication theory, that highlights the importance of both interpersonal communication (relational) and content (information) dimensions of the reference interview. For reference encounters to be described as successful by library users and librarians, both aspects are highly important.

This work on the relational dimension of the reference transaction adds to a growing body of research that acknowledges the insufficiency of answer accuracy as a sole indicator of reference success. Typically these studies emphasize the importance of other factors including the relational dimension, and use other indicators such as the user's willingness to return to the same librarian with another question. However, like the unobtrusive studies that use accuracy as the measure of success, these studies have also found a 50 to 60 percent success rate. In the Library Visit Study, which used willingness to return as a measure of reference success, Dewdney and Ross (1994) found that only about 60 percent of public and academic library users expressed a willingness to return. The troublesome fact remains that whether we examine public, academic, or special libraries, and whether we measure reference success by answer accuracy or by the users' willingness to return, the success rate for information service hovers in the 50 to 60 percent range unless there is a concerted effort to improve success. Fortunately training programs such as the Maryland Training Program described by Lillie Dyson (1992), the STAR program described by Laura Isenstein (1992), and Ohio Reference Excellence on the Web (Ohio Library Council, 2000) have been improving reference success and shown that we can get beyond a 55 percent success rate.

The good news is that progress is being made, as shown previously. VR live chat accuracy studies have suggested that accuracy may be higher in these environments, at least for factual, "ready-reference" queries and in the study of the University of Maryland's chat service. Progress was also found in the libraries observed in the Library Visit Study. When we compared the FtF reference transactions in phase one (1991–1993) and phase two (1998–2000) of the Library Visit Study, we found that overall success rates improved from 60 percent in the earlier period to 69 percent, measured by willingness of the user to return to the same librarian. Because the Library Visit Study does not measure answer accuracy, this improvement is entirely explained by improvement in the users' satisfaction with public library service.

The following data compare findings for FtF visits to public and academic libraries in phases 1 and 2, showing the percentage of those who said "Yes," they would return:

Phase 1: 1991–1993—100 library visits

In both public and academic libraries:	60%
In 71 public library visits:	53.5%
In 29 academic library visits:	76%

Phase 2: 1998–2000—161 library visits

In both public and academic libraries:	69%
In 111 public library visits:	66%
In 50 academic library visits:	74%

The third phase of the Library Visit Study made it possible to compare FtF with VR visits. Phase 3 involved seventy-four visits to VR services in public libraries and seventy-six to VR services in academic libraries, with 112 participants using e-mail services and thirty-eight using chat services. In all three phases of the research, participants were asked if they would be willing to return to the same FtF librarian or VR service again. The willingness-to-return findings for the phase 3 VR visits are broken down further to indicate both type of library and type of service:

Phase 3: 2003–2007—150 VR library visits

In both public and academic libraries	57.3%
In 74 public library visits	56.8%
In 76 academic library visits	57.9%
In 112 visits to e-mail services	52.7%
In 38 visits to chat services	71%

The success rate for chat services, measured as willingness to return, is much higher than for e-mail services. This difference is quite possibly caused by the relational barriers (see "Relational Facilitators and Barriers in Live Chat Reference") that are inherent in e-mail transactions. Unlike e-mail exchanges, chat transactions are synchronous and offer the same opportunity for an immediate back-and-forth exchange and clarification that is available in FtF reference transactions. Successful e-mail reference interviews occur only when libraries provide a well-designed form that users must fill in when submitting their questions. The form acts as a substitute for the reference interview (6.3.2).

Conducting the Reference Interview

RELATIONAL FACILITATORS AND BARRIERS IN LIVE CHAT REFERENCE

Radford (2006) and the Seeking Synchronicity project (Radford & Connaway, 2005-2008) identified Relational Facilitators and Relational Barriers by analyzing live chat transcripts.

Facilitators

Relational facilitators are defined as interpersonal aspects of the chat conversation that have a positive impact on the librarian/user interaction and that enhance communication. Found to be the most important facilitators, these should be included in chat reference interactions to improve success.

Greeting Ritual	A hello message, marking the beginning of an interpersonal interaction by exchanging "salutations" (Goffman, 1972, 76).
Rapport Building	Aspects of the interaction that "involve[s] conversation encouraging give and take, establishment of mutual understanding, and development of relationships" (Radford, 1999, 25). Rapport building includes use of humor, informal language, approval, reassurance, inclusion (e.g., "Let's look at this Web site"), self-disclosure, and praise.
Deference	Showing courtesy and respect for the other's experience, knowledge, and point of view. Regularly conveying one's appreciation and confirming the relationship between participants (Goffman, 1956). Deference includes polite expressions, apologies, offering thanks, and other expressions of respect.
Re-representation of Nonverbal Cues	The use of text characters or characteristics such as punctuation, emoticons, font, or abbreviations to compensate for nonverbal cues available in face-to-face communication. These include ellipses to indicate more is to come, emoticons, phrase abbreviations (e.g., LOL), and repeated punctuation for emphasis.
Closing Ritual	A goodbye message that signals the end of interpersonal encounters, "some form of farewell display performed during leave-taking" (Goffman, 1972, 79). The closing includes an invitation to return if necessary, making sure the user has no more questions, and explanations about the need to end abruptly. Sometimes the librarian offers to continue searching and e-mail the answer if time is short.

Barriers

Relational barriers were defined as "[i]nterpersonal aspects of the chat conversation that have a negative impact on the librarian-user interaction and that impede communication." These barriers are the ones that are most important to avoid in chat reference interactions in order to improve success.

Relational Disconnect/ Failure to Build Rapport	Failing to encourage give and take, establish mutual understanding, and engage in relationship development (Radford, 1999, 25). These include being condescending, disconfirming, failing to offer reassurance, ignoring humor, mirroring rude behavior, using jargon, etc.
Closing Problems	Ending the chat interaction without a closing ritual or exchange of farewell or goodbye (Goffman, 1972).
Negative Closure	Strategies "that library staff use to end the reference transaction, apart from providing a helpful answer" (Ross and Dewdney, 1998, 154). These include abrupt endings, disclaimer, failure to refer, ignoring cues that the user wants more help, and premature referral or attempted closing.

See Radford (2006) for examples of the previous facilitators and barriers.

Six Common Causes of Communication Accidents

The reference interview tends to go wrong in predictable ways that can be avoided or at least remedied through the use of basic microskills described in Chapters 2, 3, and 4. Avoiding these predictable communication accidents can go a long way toward increasing reference success, well beyond 55 percent. Here are six common problems together with suggestions for how to avoid them.

1. **Not acknowledging the user.** Establish immediate contact with users by acknowledging their presence through eye contact and other immediacy behaviors (2.4.2), and by restating the initial question (2.4.3).

2. **Not listening.** The inexperienced interviewer talks more than the experienced interviewer who does more listening. Librarians who are talking or thinking ahead about search strategies might be trying to help but they aren't listening (2.4.5), and they will probably miss important clues. Practice active listening; pause (2.4.2) or use an encourager (2.4.4) instead of responding at length to everything the user says. To show that you are listening, use appropriate body language and show that you have understood what was said by using the skills of reflecting content or summarizing (3.2.4).

3. **Playing twenty questions.** An open (3.2.1) or sense-making question (3.2.3) such as, "What would you like to know about X?" will get you further in less time than playing twenty questions and asking, "Is it this? Is it that?"

4. **Interrupting at inappropriate times.** If you are talking or cutting off a user who is telling you something that's relevant to the query, you're not listening (2.4.5). Use pauses or encouragers to signal to users that it's their turn to talk. When you need to redirect the conversation back to the purpose of the interview, wait until the user finishes and then employ closure (3.2.5).

5. **Making assumptions.** Some assumptions are necessary, such as assuming that a user would like some kind of help. But assumptions based on the user's appearance or on your own perception of the problem are usually inaccurate and may be offensive if you make them explicit. Instead of premature diagnosis (3.2.2), ask sense-making questions (3.2.3) such as, "Could you tell me a little bit about how you plan to use this information?"

6. **Not following up.** Recover from other communication accidents by following up (4.1.3). Ask a closed or open follow-up question such as, "Did that help you?" or "What other help would you like?" Even when you're busy, invite the user to ask for further help or give instructions ("If you don't find it, ask the person at the Information Desk"). (Ross and Dewdney, 1998)

Did You Know?

Accuracy is highly prized by librarians, but it is not the only, or even the most important, element that users look for. Users want information packaged in a certain format; they want it within a specified period of time; they want it in a certain amount; and above all they want it not to take more than a certain amount of effort to get it. Depending on their purpose, users may be quite satisfied with ballpark answers and won't require anything more exact. Part of conducting the reference interview successfully is to find out how finely-grained the helpful answer needs to be.

Matthew Saxton and John Richardson (2002) found that public library users were highly satisfied with the service despite lack of accuracy.

- Fifteen percent were highly satisfied even when they didn't find everything they needed.
- Three percent were highly satisfied even when the response they received was later judged to be inaccurate.
- Three percent were highly satisfied even when they didn't find anything useful.

These findings provide more evidence to suggest that accuracy is not the only indicator for satisfaction.

1.4 Why Didn't You Say So in the First Place?

If users were all experts in understanding how information is gathered, organized and retrieved, they would think about information differently—more like the way librarians do. They would also ask for information differently. Since they are *not* all experts, they often phrase their informational needs in terms that reference librarians find indirect, incomplete or misleading. The mirror image of this problem is that your extensive knowledge of the library system makes you unable to think about information the way that users do. Therefore it is important to examine how users actually do ask questions. The reference librarian's job is to be the human intermediary, linking users to the system, and this function involves understanding how users think about information and how they ask questions. In 1968, Robert Taylor wrote a seminal article about this phenomena and coined the term "question negotiation" to describe the reference interview process.

Consider the following reference requests, which are the initial questions of users who came to various public libraries for reference help. The questions look diverse but they all have something in common:

- I'm looking for information on ethnic arts and crafts, especially Mexico.
- What I'm looking for is information on stockbrokers—articles that have been written about stockbrokers.
- Where could I find information on a particular company—what they make?
- Do you have an industrial park listing?
- Is there a listing of companies and addresses?
- Can you tell me where I'd find a directory of museums?
- A friend of mine says that the government has a book out that lists all the different departments—their addresses and all that?
- Can you tell me where the newspapers are?
- Do you have any idea when the next *Vancouver Sun* will be coming out?

These questions were captured on tape as part of a field study conducted by Patricia Dewdney (1986) in which she recorded and transcribed reference transactions in public libraries. She recorded these transactions for a doctoral dissertation undertaken in the Library and Information Science program at The University of Western Ontario. We know more than usually is known about the context of these questions because follow-up interviews were conducted in which the users were asked, among other things, how they hoped the information requested would help them. The element linking these questions is that all were asked by people who needed help to prepare themselves for finding a job. The user asking the question about ethnic arts and crafts turned out to be

---

ANALYZE THIS REFERENCE TRANSACTION

Case 2: Job Search

User: I'm looking for information on ethnic arts and crafts, especially Mexico.

Librarian: Mhm. There's quite a lot in the section on arts and crafts—745.5. (*acknowledgment*) Then you would have to find crafts of Mexico. You probably just have to browse through the shelves and see what comes out of crafts of various countries. That's the sort of thing you want, isn't it? (*closed question for confirmation*)

User: Yes.

Librarian: [Checks catalog.] Okay, there's crafts of Japan, crafts of Mexico, crafts of New England, crafts of Papua, New Guinea. They should all be in the same area, but you may have to go further afield for some of them. I'll write these numbers down for you. *Crafts of the Indians*—you'd like that too?

User: Mmm.

Librarian: Right. That one is crafts of the world, so it should have different crafts in it. And then check these other ones. [Gives directions.]

(Dewdney, "Crafts")

Comment: This transaction is a good example of the so-called simple question that some people claim needs no reference interview. In fact, no reference interview took place here. The librarian accepted the initial question at face value and did not try to find out anything further about the user's informational need.

When the user was interviewed after this reference transaction as part of the research project, she explained that she was applying for a job where she would need to plan children's programs. She wanted to get some ideas for crafts that were "out of the ordinary" to impress a potential employer. What she really wanted, however, was to be put in touch with "someone who has done this before" so that she could talk to someone involved with arts and crafts programs for children. The user was only "somewhat satisfied" with the service she got and probably would not go back to the same librarian with a similar question. When the user tracked down the call numbers, many of the books were not on her topic. She said she felt that she had been left to sink or swim on her own, and had hoped to get more actual help.

For discussion:
1. How typical do you think this transaction is? What aspects are typical/ not typical?
2. Do you think it would have made any difference to the information that the user received if she had started out the interview by saying, "I'm preparing for a job interview." What difference, if any?
3. Was the user right to feel she had been given very little help? How do you account for the user's assessment of the service provided?

---

getting ready for a job interview involving programming for children. The question about stockbrokers was really a request for something describing what stockbrokers actually do in their day-to-day work; the user wanted to decide whether being a stockbroker was the sort of job he would enjoy. The questions about the listing of companies or industrial parks, the museum directory, and the listing of government departments

Conducting the Reference Interview

EXERCISE

Removing Communication Barriers

Consider the communication barriers suggested in the list "Why Can't They Just Ask Us for What They Want?" Which of these factors do you think might be barriers for the users of your library? For each factor that you think might be problematic, what solutions can you think of to address the problem? How many are solutions that would need system-wide administrative support? How many are within the control of the individual librarian?

WHY CAN'T THEY JUST ASK US FOR WHAT THEY WANT?

The library literature is full of guesses and attributions as librarians try to come up with explanations for why users don't think about information the way they themselves do. Here are some of these explanations:

- Users don't understand that it is the job of the reference librarian to help get them the right answer.
- Users think that a library is like a supermarket where they are expected to be self-reliant and find everything themselves and the most they can expect is to be pointed at the right aisle. Therefore they don't want to "bother" the librarian.
- Users think libraries are simple. Hence they could do everything for themselves, if only they had a tiny bit of direction or instruction.
- Users are inexperienced in asking for help because they do not really expect to get help. They haven't much confidence in the librarian's ability to find the information or even that there is any helpful information to be found on their topic or problem.
- Users don't think librarians have the subject expertise to be able to understand their specialized topic.
- Users sometimes avoid self-disclosure, especially with legal, medical or financial questions. Some want to protect their privacy because the particular topic is sensitive, while others are reserved and generally avoid talking about themselves to strangers, whether the topic is sensitive or not.
- Users are just beginning to explore a subject and don't really know what they want.
- Users know what they want but they can't articulate it in system terms. They don't know what information the librarian needs to know in order to find the information they need. Users will not volunteer information that they do not perceive as relevant. And they don't always understand the relevance because they don't know how the system works.
- Users ask for broader subjects than necessary because they know that libraries are organized by broad subjects.
- Users don't know the enormous extent of information available. When they ask for "everything on transportation," they are not envisioning thousands of items.
- Users don't know how information is organized and packaged, and lack the specialized vocabulary to distinguish accurately among different reference tools. They may think that all topics come in book-size packages, and so they ask for a book on topic X when actually the answer that they need is to be found in government statistics or in a directory or on a Web page.
- Users think they are being helpful by suggesting a source.
- Users are unaware of the ambiguity of subject requests (e.g., "I'd like information on fish"—what information? catching fish? cooking fish? caring for pet fish? starting up a salmon farming business? the diseases of fish? the symbolism of fish in Christian iconography?)
- The initial questions that users ask are just a way of starting the conversation.

(Adapted and summarized from Mount, 1966; Nahl, 1997; and Dewdney and Michell, 1996)

were all asked because job hunters needed names and addresses of potential employers to whom they could send résumés. The users asking for newspapers wanted to find classified job ads.

This juxtaposition of reference requests provides a striking illustration of the way that users typically formulate their questions. None of these users said, "I'm job hunting and I want..." Rather, the three users with questions about ethnic crafts, stockbrokers, and a particular company had a specific answer in mind but phrased their questions as requests for general information on a broad topic. The other users asked questions one step more remote from their original question. Starting with their job-hunting problem, they translated their specific need into a general topic and then *prescribed* the reference source that they thought most appropriate for their topic—an industrial park listing, a directory of museums, a book listing government departments, newspapers in general, and a particular city newspaper. Unfortunately, the further the presenting question gets from the actual information the user needs to know, the greater the chance of mistranslation, misunderstanding, and mistaken requests for inappropriate reference sources.

On the basis of these initial questions alone, it is unlikely that the librarian would understand what the users really wanted to know. Well, so what? Why be concerned, so long as the librarian provides the list or directory or newspaper that the user has asked for? Would knowing about the job-hunting context of the question change the kind of answer that the librarian would provide? Well, yes. Surely with at least some of these questions, it would make a difference to know the particular context of the question, but librarians should not ask why directly (3.2.3).

The rest of this chapter explores, from a variety of perspectives, the contrasts between the ways in which users and librarians think about information.

1.4.1 The Ill-formed Query

Librarians are familiar with the phenomenon of the "ill-formed" query—a term from linguistics given to a question that doesn't work because it leads to erroneous inferences. In fact one experienced librarian in the Mental Models Study said that she had come to expect incomplete or misleading initial questions: "He was quite specific in what he wanted. He knew exactly what he wanted and that's what he asked for. And it threw me. Because you're not used to people asking for what they want." Over the years, Dewdney and Ross have asked workshop participants for examples from their own experience of cases in which the real question has turned out to be different from the question as initially presented. Participants rarely have any difficulty in thinking of a recent situation. "Yes it happens all the time," they say, nodding. From the workshops and other sources, we have collected examples of ill-formed queries and now have a database of 945 examples of question pairs. The list in "What People Really Want to Know" gives some typical examples of question pairs of the initial question and the negotiated or "real" question.

A QUICK TIP

Go Beyond the User's Diagnosis of Source

In the Mental Models Study, an experienced librarian was asked if she had advice for a new librarian who was just learning about reference service. She advised, "If users suggest a source to you, such as, 'Is there such a thing as a [local city] business directory?' or 'Can I have the Almanac?' then you don't completely accept what they're saying." While showing them the source, go beyond their request and say, "What specifically are you looking for?"

Conducting the Reference Interview

WHAT PEOPLE REALLY WANT TO KNOW

Initial question	Negotiated question
1. Do you have anything on housing?	What are the rights of a tenant in a rental situation?
2. Do you have a copy of the Ocala, Florida, newspaper?	Does Ocala, Florida, have a car rental agency that I can contact?
3. Where are your books on alcohol?	I would like the times and places for meetings of local AA groups.
4. Where are your books on Canada?	I need a picture of an attacking grizzly bear for a book I am illustrating.
5. Does anyone on your staff speak German?	Will the library buy my collection of German books?
6. How extensive is your library?	I need a book on wedding etiquette that tells me what to do as best man at a wedding.
7. I would like a book on carving a duck. (assumed to mean carving a cooked duck)	I want books on wood carving with instruction on how to carve a duck decoy.
8. Do you have *Animal Graveyard*?	Do you have Stephen King's *Pet Sematary*?
9. Where is your ancient history section?	I need to read about the causes of World War I for a school assignment.

Did You Know?

In a posting to LIBREF, Pam Bidwell from New Zealand initiated a discussion "Humor: Oranges and Peaches" asking for examples of "communication accidents" of the sort discussed in the Dewdney and Michell (1996) article. Posters responded with about forty examples, including these: hustling/ hostelling; history of jeans/ history of genes; cheeses/ Jesus; gorilla art/ guerrilla art; rhapsodies/ rap CDs; European manners/ European manors; two-door architecture/ Tudor architecture. Bidwell noted, "The biggest confusions seem to occur when you've never heard of an alternative to what seems obvious, and so it seems so logical to go straight to the familiar." (Bidwell, August 11, 1997)

The reference interview is needed because people don't always express their informational needs clearly and completely. As we have seen, the user's initial question is often not the real question. These problematic initial questions, or "ill-formed queries," are questions that do not state the informational need clearly or completely enough for the librarian to effectively answer. The questions may be perfectly well-formed semantically and syntactically but in context they are somehow incomplete and even misleading. The key point is that the queries are "ill-formed" with respect to the information system; that is, they do not match the structure or "expectations" of the system.

While every question is different, an analysis of a large collection of ill-formed queries reveals some repeated patterns. Here are some typical problems (referencing examples from "What People Really Want to Know"):

1. **Users ask for something very broad and general** when they actually want a very specific piece of information within the broad category they have asked for. The example of "anything on housing" falls into this class. Other examples that recur frequently are initial questions that take the following form: "Where do you keep your medical books?," "Where is your law section?," or "What have you got on transportation?" The question, "Where is your law section?" can mask many different informational needs requiring different sources (e.g., finding out how to get out of a lease; doing background reading before seeing a lawyer about divorce; verifying a legal opinion on a problem with a neighbor; researching a project on copyright legislation for a college course.) If the initial questions are phrased as directional questions, users will probably not find the specific information they want. The user who asked about the location of medical books was worried about her daughter and wanted to find out more about anorexia, and its diagnosis, treatment, and long-term effects.

2. **Users ask for something specific but there is a mismatch** between the specific thing they ask for and what they actually need to answer their question. Often the mismatch happens because users ask for a specific source, thinking that the answer is either there or in that general vicinity, as in examples 2 and 3 (at left). Since most users aren't experts on sources, they are often wrong in their diagnosis of the best source. For example, a user who asked, "Where do you keep your encyclopedias?" actually wanted job listings in Australia. The users who asked for books on Canada and books about alcohol in examples 3 and 4 have diagnosed wrongly what the best source would be (the mismatch problem) and then added a second problem by asking for something too broad and general. A variation of the mismatch problem happens when the user is confused about library terms. Requests for bibliographies are often made in error when biographies are wanted, and vice versa.

3. **Users aren't exactly sure how the library system works** and ask a question based on a misunderstanding or to clarify their confusion. Examples 5 and 6 fall into this class. Sometimes questions about the library system ("I'm having trouble with this index" or "Excuse me, are the books arranged in any particular order?") are the users' way of saying they have run into a barrier and need help—not necessarily bibliographic instruction on how to use an index or understand classification schemes—but assistance with finding a helpful answer.

4. **Keywords in the user's question are ambiguous.** Ambiguity can be caused by either the user's mispronunciation or the staff member's faulty hearing. Homophones—words that sound the same but have different meanings as in example 7—are another source of ambiguity. Examples of the pronunciation problem include the Scottish user whose request for military badges sent the librarian off on a fruitless hunt for military budgies, or the question about venom that turned out to be about the Vietnam War. To clarify how confusion can arise, here are some other examples to consider: Tolkien books/talking books; bird control/birth control; hair pieces/ herpes; hairdressers in Saudi Arabia/addresses in Saudi Arabia; house plans/house plants; bamboo hearts/baboon hearts; silver service/civil service test; and the sick in California/the Sikhs in California. An example of ambiguity caused by homophones is the request for "something on whales," which may easily be heard as a request for "something on Wales," or, depending on the dialect, "something on wills." China, Greece, Turkey and Chile are also good candidates for confusion.

Workshop participants have provided us with many examples of ambiguous keywords, some of them humorous: eunuchs/UNIX; tofu/TOEFL; super vision/supervision; reproductive technology (interpreted as artificial insemination)/ reproductive technology (pertaining to photocopiers); make-up (cosmetic)/make-up (psychological). Then there's the old standby that we have heard so often we suspect it's an urban legend— youth in Asia/euthanasia. One of the best examples of a user's mishearing is the "Oranges and

---

A QUICK TIP

Questions about the System

Often questions about how to use an index or online catalog or some other library system mask an informational need. If a user says, "I'm having trouble with this index" or "Are the books arranged in any particular order?" it is often helpful to ask, "What are you trying to do?" or "What are you trying to find out." Here's a case where the librarian didn't follow this advice:

User: Have you got a book that writes down the Dewey Decimal System? Like in the 700s. I want to copy the divisions for the 700s.

Librarian: Do you? Sure. [Gives him the Dewey schedule.] There you go. Start there.

(Dewdney, "Dewey")

After the user spent a long time with the book, he came back and asked, "There's nothing in your filing system that gives series? Like a neighbor brought to my door a music book. This book had piano pieces with very simple arrangements by this man Tyndall. I thought the library might have some more of his arrangements."

A QUICK TIP

Translate Those Location Questions into Problem-centered Questions

Dewdney and Michell (1996, "Oranges and Peaches") point out that users typically present their informational needs as questions about locations and subjects as in "Do you have books or information or a section on X?" rather than as problem-centered statements. So users ask, "Where are your books on house plants?" and not, "I have whiteflies on my aspidistra." Unlike problem-centered statements, questions about locations and subjects provide no context and increase the chances that a request for X will be heard as a request for Y (e.g., "house plants" heard as "house plans"). Dewdney and Michell recommend that you don't immediately rush to provide directions on where information on Y is shelved but instead that you ask a question about Y: "What would like to know about house plans?" The user's answer almost always elicits the context from which you can distinguish between X and Y (e.g., between house plants and house plans).

Peaches" incident that provided the title for the Dewdney and Michell (1996) article on the ill-formed query. A user asks for a copy of *Oranges and Peaches*, but it turns out that he has misheard the teacher's instruction to find Darwin's *Origin of Species*.

A further complication that can occur with either of these two kinds of ambiguity is that the staff member may interpret the ambiguous words in the context of a particular mental set, predisposition, or expectation. For example, one librarian was busy weeding the sports books when he misheard a request for books on Socrates as "soccer tees" and began scanning the soccer books. Another librarian was engaged in bibliographic checking when she misheard a request for books on sea lamprey as a request for books on C. Lamprey, presumed to be an important person.

5. **The user's question involves a reconstruction** as the user tries to remember specific terms or details and reconstructs the meaning but not the form of a forgotten item. Sometimes the reconstruction involves substitutions of synonyms or near synonyms as in example 8. A user might ask, "Where is your gynecology section?" when the question is really about family trees. A request for information on Obama's closet might be made instead of Obama's cabinet. Users might ask for the book *Sex Before Dinner* when they want *The Naked Lunch* or *Shame on the Princess* instead of *Tales of a Shaman's Apprentice*. Additional examples to consider include sugar mommy/sugar daddy; IUD/*OED*; Rockin' Jim/*Rock and Gem*; the President of Utopia/the President of Ethiopia; the Kingdom of Phylla/an overview of biological classification; Malcolm the Tenth/Malcolm X; chow mein/Charlemagne. This type of problem is more apt to happen with what Melissa Gross has called the "imposed query" (5.3.1), in which the question is generated by someone else such as a teacher and the user has not completely understood the assignment.

6. **The user's question contains an error or misconception** not about the library system itself but about the outside world. In example 9, the student might regard anything before 1950 as ancient history, but this view, though understandable, is idiosyncratic and not consistent with accepted conventions of periodization. In this category of ill-formed questions, the error is embedded in the question as a taken-for-granted fact and is not easy to spot without asking a question such as "What are you looking for in 'ancient history'?"

1.4.2 Mental Models

We can explain the prevalence of ill-formed queries in terms of the users' mental models of how libraries work. The act of asking a librarian for help is a microcosm of information-seeking behavior governed by the participants' mental models of the system. A useful theory of mental models suggested by Donald Norman and Philip N. Johnson-Laird, experts in artificial intelligence and cognitive science, describes a mental model as a working model that individuals construct in their minds to facilitate interaction with the environment, other individuals, or technology. Such a mental model contrasts with the "real" model or "conceptual model" of the same object, which is, according to Norman, an appropriate representation of the target system "in the sense of being accurate, consistent and complete" (1983, 7).

An individual's mental model of any system is, by definition, inaccurate and incomplete in relation to the conceptual model. The degree of discrepancy between an individual's mental model of the system and the conceptual model is important. When users' mental models of the library system are at odds with the "real" or conceptual model of the library system, they are more likely to generate ill-formed questions. Librarians, on the other hand, have mental models of libraries that are much closer to the conceptual model. A crucial issue is whether the users' understanding of the library system—including the collection and its organization, the physical layout, the role of the librarian in the system, and the types of service that users can expect—differs in any important way from the librarian's understanding of that system. If there is an important difference, does either the librarian or the user discover it, and how does that discovery affect the outcome of the transaction? What can the librarian do to increase the likelihood of discovering such differences?

The mismatch between the user's mental model and the librarian's mental model can be used to explain communication accidents and misunderstandings that arise in the reference interview, with implications as described in the following.

Some Implications of Mental Models Research for Reference Staff

1. **Remember that users tend to phrase their initial questions in a way that they believe meets the requirements of the system.** However, users' models of the system tend to be over-simplified and incomplete and sometimes wrong, even in the case of frequent public library users. The problem of the inadequacy of the users' mental models becomes greater as computerized library systems become more complex in the options that they offer.

2. **Be aware of the likelihood of the discrepancy between the user's mental model of the library system and your own, and take steps to check for discrepancies.** The less experienced users are with the system, the more likely they are to have inaccurate mental models. Use the questioning skills described in Chapter 2 to find out what the user's mental model is. For example, when a user says, "Can you help me find some good historical books to read," a good readers' adviser checks by saying, "Can you tell me about an historical book that you have read recently and enjoyed?" or "What sort of historical books are you in the mood for?" The user may want Jean Plaidy or some other historical romance, not Winston Churchill on World War II. Fortunately, there are particular communication skills that librarians can learn or refresh to reduce the chances that the librarian never finds out what a user wants.

Did You Know?
Dewdney and Michell (1996, "Mental Models") decided to find out what the chances were of providing a helpful answer when the librarian took the initial question at face value. Their field study was based on observing thirty-three reference transactions and follow-up interviews of both the user and the librarian. In each case they asked, "What are the chances of the librarian being able to understand the real informational need from the initial question alone?" and rated the chances from 1 (not at all) to 5 (excellent—little or no question negotiation required). The following is a summary of the findings for the thirty-three cases:

Somewhat good (3), very good (4), or excellent (5):	60.6%
Not at all possible (1) or not very good (2):	39.4%

In 40 percent of cases, the librarian had practically no chance of discovering the real informational need without conducting a reference interview, or unless the user decided to volunteer more information. Words from these ill-formed initial questions could not be entered as keywords into an information retrieval system with any hope of finding something useful.

EXERCISE

Mental Models

Reread the case provided in "Mental Models of the Library System." We suggested the beliefs that may have been part of Mary's model of libraries when she asked, "Where's the science section?" in order to get pictures of wild orchids. What beliefs about libraries do you think were held by Arjun, Julia, and James that led each of them to ask their different initial question?

Did You Know?

In her study of academic library users, Virginia Massey-Burzio (1998) discovered that even those users who were at advanced levels in their fields had an inaccurate understanding of the library system and its complexity. Here are some of the misconceptions that she uncovered: They didn't understand the difference between a keyword and an assigned descriptor/subject term. They tried to look up the title of a journal article in the online catalog. They couldn't find fiction books in a Library of Congress-arranged collection because they expected to find them all alphabetically arranged in one sequence, not divided by country. They didn't understand that the reason they weren't finding anything was that the database or index that they were looking in did not cover their subject area. They felt overwhelmed by all the different databases and so they stuck to the one or two that they knew, irrespective of subject coverage.

MENTAL MODELS OF THE LIBRARY SYSTEM

Four different users are all looking for color photographs of wild orchids because they want to identify an unusual plant in their gardens. Mary says: "Where's the science section?" Arjun says: "Do you have *World Book*?" Julia says, "I want information on orchids." And James says, "I want to see the head librarian."

All four of these users have a goal, which is to find a color photo of a wild orchid to help identify the plant. All four have a plan to achieve that goal. Underlying the plan is a model that includes various beliefs about the world in general and about library systems in particular. Each person has developed his or her model on the basis of past experience, prior learning, and other factors. Mary's model of libraries may include some beliefs that can be stated as propositions:

1. Photos of orchids are often found in books.
2. Books can be found in large numbers in libraries.
3. Books in libraries are organized by general subjects.
4. The general subject for orchids is plants, but perhaps this is unduly narrow—so the subject is probably botany or even science. Based on past experience with libraries and their signage, science seems like a good bet.
5. If I can be pointed toward the science section, there will be a book there that contains a photo of a wild orchid. I'll be able to compare it with the plant in my garden.
6. I should be able to find what I need on my own with a minimum of help. Libraries are self-help places just like supermarkets.

These assumptions are not completely wrong. However, the librarian knows, because of her more accurate model of libraries that the more efficient procedure is not to start with a broad subject area since as the librarian believes:

1. Users don't always ask for what they want.
2. Not everything to do with science will be classified as science.
3. Science is a huge section. It is inefficient to search for "science books."
4. If I give directions to the science section, the user will probably not find what she needs.
5. My job is to help users find what they need. Once I find out what the user's goal is, I can substitute a more effective and efficient plan.
6. The appropriate step is to ask the user what she wants.
7. Photographs of wild orchids can be found easily in a specialized picture file or a gardening book.

When the librarian acts on these beliefs by conducting a reference interview and providing the desired wild orchid picture, she can modify the user's beliefs or model of the library in a way that will help the user better negotiate her way through the library next time she has a question. She can also show the user how to find pictures on the Web.

3. **Mental models change through an incremental learning process.**
    Each time users come to the library, they learn a bit more about what the librarian is doing and how to do it for themselves. This suggests that the users models of the library are fluid, changing, and in fact

may change quickly. A model may change even over the course of one interaction with the librarian. Librarians can help users develop more accurate mental models of the library system by explaining, not necessarily in great detail, what they are doing. This skill, called inclusion (4.1.1), is especially effective when you are working with users who value their own incremental learning.

In many cases, the most useful thing you can do to help users develop a more accurate mental model is to help them become more aware of the system's capacity. For example, users who think that all information comes in book-size packages could be informed that the library has a large range of sources available in different formats; that the sources on their topic may be scattered in different parts of the library; or that there are other formats available, including Web-based resources. Once users understand a bit more about the complexity of resources available, they are in a better position to choose whether to proceed on their own with some instruction or whether to ask you to draw on your knowledge of the system to help solve the problem.

4. **This does not mean, however, that you should insist on giving unwanted instruction.** You must assess—and not by guessing—what the users' level of knowledge or ability is and whether or not they want to learn more on that particular day. In their Mental Models Study, Dewdney and Michell occasionally observed librarians instructing users in the use of the library catalog. Some users told them later that they already knew how to use it while others said they were not at all interested in learning how to use it. Users don't necessarily need to be given a detailed picture of how libraries work. Your job as intermediary is to link users to the system in whatever way they find most helpful. One of the interesting questions for our field, especially in bibliographic instruction, is the point beyond which it is counterproductive for individuals to have a more complete understanding of the model. Some users want library use instruction; others are expected to want it—such as students; and still others just want the answer. This latter group of users is satisfied with their rudimentary mental model of how the library works even if librarians are reluctant to believe that some people are content to be uninformed about indexing systems. When users get helpful answers to their questions, their mental model of the library is at least likely to include certain understandings such as that the library is the right place to get help with information questions, and that librarians are willing and able to help.

1.5 The Helpful Answer: Two Ways of Thinking about Information

Everyone who works in libraries operates from a set of assumptions about what information is. Although these assumptions are often unac-knowledged and unexamined, they have a powerful influence nonetheless

---

A QUICK TIP

A Grain of Salt

When users ask for books, they are not necessarily intending to put a restriction on the format of the acceptable answer. An experienced librarian in the Mental Models Study reported that a user's question "Where are the books on coins?" was very typical. "The one before that asked, 'Where are the books on needlepoint?' It happens a lot. They say, 'Where are your books on back pain?' It's the way users phrase the question when they want information. They say, 'Where are the books on…?' Their assumption is that the information is in a book and that the books are all together in one place." In such cases, the user's mental model of the library may be inexact and the librarian knows of additional, or better, sources.

on what kind of service is provided to users. In this section we make the case for critically examining the way we think about information and for making explicit the metaphors we use to talk about information and its provision.

1.5.1 Information as a Commodity

In the profession of librarianship, several factors combine to make us think of information as a commodity. Most pervasive of all is the language we share, which provides us with a way of talking and thinking about information that is essentially metaphoric: we "store" information; we "retrieve" it; we "transfer" it, we feel "buried" in too much of it, and so on. These metaphors for information are part of a larger pattern that Michael Reddy (1993) has called the "conduit metaphor" for language. He has argued that the way we talk about language is structured by the following metaphors: ideas are *objects*; linguistic expressions are *containers*; communication is a process of putting idea-objects into linguistic containers and sending them along a *conduit* to a listener, who takes the idea-objects out of their word-containers.

Normally, of course, we are not aware of the metaphors we use. But once we start paying attention to them, we can see how strongly what we think of as ordinary reality is structured by metaphor. George Lakoff and Mark Johnson (1980), in their analysis of the entailments of the conduit metaphor, suggest that if we think of ideas as objects, then we think of meanings as existing independently of people and contexts. Moreover if words are thought of as containers for meanings, then we think of words and sentences as having meanings *in themselves*, independent of any context or speaker.

Likewise, if we think of information as a commodity, it too can be thought of as existing apart from people or contexts—an object to be transferred, retrieved, exchanged, stored, and stockpiled. This way of conceptualizing information makes it seem "natural" to think that a question can be posed and answered correctly with no reference to its context in the life of the asker. For example, no matter who asks, "When he was a senator from Illinois, how did Barack Obama vote on stem cell research?" and in no matter what context, the answer to the question remains the same: "He voted 'Yes' on the one bill that came forward while he was in the Senate."

Another reason why librarians tend to think of information as a commodity with no context is the way reference is often taught in library schools, and the way it is evaluated in the literature. Some library program instructors teach basic reference by giving students a list of questions to answer: How many goats are there in Bangladesh? What was the first short story that Alice Munro published and where was it published? What is a Fowler's octagon? What is the highest annual milk production for a dairy cow? What does a Manticore look like? Where does the expression "the whole nine yards" come from? The working assumption here is that there is one correct answer and the library student should be able to find the answer and verify it in a second source. In addition, as

Did You Know?

If you think that information is a commodity—and a precious commodity at that—then you will believe that the more information that the user is given the better. The reasoning here is that a big stockpile of information is always a good thing because information is a resource that is valuable in itself. However most people would much rather have a small amount of information exactly tailored to their needs. Library users, especially novices, feel overwhelmed when offered dozens of book titles, hundreds of articles, or thousands of Web pages. In fact, people commonly refer to "information overload" or "infoglut" and talk about feeling "swamped," "inundated," "overwhelmed," or "drowning in information." Sara Fine (1995, 17–20) has coined what she calls "the Saturation Principle" to cover this situation: "If the user is already saturated with information, additional information will not help in making a decision or aid in solving a problem."

discussed in section 1.3, reference service has often been evaluated by studies that use proxies posing as real users. These proxies ask pre-scripted questions and unobtrusively measure the accuracy of answers to queries like, "Where is the nearest airport to Warren, Pennsylvania?" Here again, it is understood that there *is* a correct answer. In fact, the way to develop such questions is to work backward from a known answer to a question that will elicit this answer. The students in a reference course or the librarians undergoing unobtrusive observation are being tested on whether or not they have succeeded in discovering this one pre-determined, correct answer. In these contrived cases, the questions truly do fit the paradigm of information as commodity. They are decontextualized and exist independently apart from any user—probably no real user has ever asked them.

1.5.2 Questions in Contexts

Now we come to a different situation—that of a real user asking a genuine question in a library setting. Whereas contrived questions have no context and no history, real questions are embedded in the context of users' day-to-day lives. Users ask questions out of the contexts of their immediate concerns. They don't take the trouble to go to the library, or to visit the library's virtual reference service, to ask a question for the fun of it; they ask their question as a means to an end important to them. They are trying to *do* something—apply for a job, make a decision, complete a school project, finish a grant proposal, remodel their kitchen, make a complaint, join a support group, understand an illness they have been told they have, give a speech at a wedding, contact a professional colleague, complete a literature search, draw an orchid, etc. They ask questions to fill in gaps in their understanding so that they can get on with these concerns. Therefore, a necessary part of understanding the question is knowing the situation out of which the question arises. The question is meaningful in its context, and its context is part of its meaning. We understand the question when we recover its framework.

The user may ask, "Do you know when the next *Vancouver Sun* is coming out?" and the librarian may choose to treat it as a decontextualized question requiring the answer, "The *Vancouver Sun* is still on strike and no one knows when it will be out." But a more appropriate way of thinking about information and information-seeking in this case would be to think of the question as having a context in the life of the person who asked it (see 1.4 on the job-hunting context). And a more helpful answer to this question, when it is asked because the user is job hunting, may be, "The *Vancouver Sun* is on strike just now, but we do have other sources for western news. What specifically were you looking for?" More generally, a helpful answer for job hunters is one that helps them, in their own terms, to get on with the business of job hunting. Users are helped to the extent that the answers they get in libraries help them to do something that they want to do. Distinguishing between the *"correct"* answer for the disembedded, contextless question and the *helpful* answer for a particular person in a particular situation is conceptually useful.

A QUICK TIP

Easy/Hard

You can't predict in advance how hard a question will be. In the Mental Models Study, Dewdney and Michell found that neither the user nor the librarian could predict difficulty in advance based on the initial question. Both users and librarians were asked independently the following questions:

1. Initially, how easy did you think it was going to be to find an answer to this question?

2. As it turned out, how easy was it to find an answer to the question?

They were asked to rate expected difficulty on a 5-point scale, 1 being extremely difficult and 5 being extremely easy.

The data indicate that, on average, both users and librarians overestimated the likely difficulty of answering. The questions, in other words, turned out to be easier to answer than they had initially appeared. Both before and after the transaction, users tended to think of their questions as easier to answer than librarians did. Although we might expect users to be unaware of the difficulty involved, a very interesting finding was the lack of significant correlation between the librarians' initial assessment of the questions and their final assessment. Librarians, apparently, do not seem to be able to predict in advance how easy a question is going to be.

The librarian who answers a question without knowing anything about the context in which the question became a question may provide an answer that is correct, but not helpful.

Now we come to the hard part. To be able to provide this helpful answer, the librarian needs to know the context. But, as we have seen, users normally don't present their initial question by volunteering the context. Users also have learned to think of information as a commodity that must be asked for in libraries in decontextualized terms. Rather than saying, "Next week I'm going on a trip to Perth, Australia, and I want to know what the temperature is likely to be, so I can pack appropriate clothes," a user may ask, "Where is your travel section?" They often try to translate their questions into what they think are library categories or classifications.

As the Mental Models research indicates, the problem here is that users are unlikely to understand the full complexity of how information is organized in libraries. A user who wanted names and prices of ski resorts in Colorado where his family might vacation said, "I'm interested in

---

EXERCISE

Providing the Helpful Answer

In the Mental Models Study, a user and an experienced librarian were each asked to talk about their experience with a reference transaction. The user said that she needed information on the city of Cambridge in England because she was getting ready to do a presentation for her book club. "I'm doing a book that takes place in Cambridge," she explained, "and I want to compare the reality with the fiction. It's my turn to do a report. Especially when I'm retired, it's something I look forward to." The user had done a keyword catalog search on the word Cambridge but had become discouraged when she got hundreds of irrelevant matches, including everything published by Cambridge University Press. The user's initial question was "I would like to find material on Cambridge." The librarian said that his first thought was, "Cambridge what? University? Travel? It could be a whole range of things." He said that if he had been downstairs in the education area where the college catalogs are kept, he could easily have assumed she wanted Cambridge University.

Evaluate each of the following possible responses that the librarian could have made to the user's initial question, "I would like to find material on Cambridge." Rank the responses in order of helpfulness from most to least, where helpfulness is defined as providing users with the information they need in order to advance their own goals. What are your reasons for your ranking? (You might want to skip ahead to sections 3.2.1 and 3.2.3 on questioning techniques for useful background for this exercise.)

1. Have you checked the online catalog?
2. The calendars for Cambridge are downstairs. You should ask the librarian at the downstairs desk for the Cambridge material.
3. What kind of information on Cambridge would help you most?
4. Do you want travel information?
5. Do you mean Cambridge, Massachusetts?

your ski section." We can assume that he had a rather nebulous view of what the "ski section" might include. He had probably not considered the differences among such aspects of skiing as ski resorts, learning how to ski, buying ski equipment, biographies of famous skiers, sports injuries connected with skiing, etc., or among such formats as vertical file materials, books, periodical articles, or Web sites. Despite the librarians' knowledge of resources, they can't use their professional expertise unless they have more to go on than just "ski section." The purpose of the reference interview is to find out, quickly and tactfully, the context for the user's question, including the user's goal.

1.6   Reference as an Art of Translation

A great deal has been written on the necessity of translating a reference question into a representation of the user's informational need that the system will accept. The system can be defined as the interacting components of an organization for providing information service, including not only the collection and its finding aids but also the library policy and the roles of the staff. An obvious example of translating the user's natural language request into the specialized language of the system is the need to transform keywords in the informational need statement into subject headings or controlled vocabulary. We should be aware, however, that translation is happening all along the line.

Users often try to do the translation themselves. They want pictures of wild orchids and so they try to translate that need into system terms, asking for "the science section." Since users are translating into an unfamiliar language—the language of the information system—it's not surprising that sometimes their translations are not helpful to the librarian. The proper person to do the translation into system terms is the librarian, not the user, just as the proper person to diagnose a drug prescription is the doctor and not the patient. When a patient comes into the doctor's office and says, "I need a prescription for prednisone," the doctor doesn't reach immediately for the prescription pad. He or she first asks some questions in order to understand the nature of the original problem and its symptoms. Similarly the purpose of the reference interview is to get back, as far as possible, to the original informational need. Until you do this, you don't really know what kind of question you are dealing with. One experienced librarian in the Mental Models Study reported, "The woman came in and said she wanted books about the Titanic. It turned out she had a great aunt who had survived the Titanic sinking and she wanted the passenger list to find this lady's name. So it was a genealogy question masquerading as information about the Titanic." The job of the savvy librarian is to strip off the masquerade.

Standard ways of categorizing reference transactions can be misleading. A common approach is to provide a classification scheme for different kinds of reference questions and suggest escalating levels of interviewing to deal with each. Directional questions require pointing

Did You Know?
Norman Hutcherson (2004) surveyed 297 first- and second-year college students and found that commonly used terms, including plagiarism, reference services, research, and copyright, have high levels of recognition, but library or computer terms, such as abstract, Boolean logic, bibliography, controlled vocabulary, truncation, precision, and descriptor, do not. Dina C. Cramer says that library staff and users speak different languages: Users "speak patron" while librarians use "library-speak." Consider her example of the young person who asked the reference librarian for a "journal on diabetes" to which the librarian questioned, "Are you sure you need a journal on diabetes?" He was sure, but it turned out he needed a journal article on diabetes. Notes Cramer (1998, 349), "It is tricky to know when the patron is using a word differently from us, but one clue is the frustration. If the interview doesn't work, consider that terminology might be the problem."

while ready-reference questions require a quick confirmation. Complex questions require an extensive interview, and intensive research questions may even require appointments. Here's what Ellen Sutton and Leslie Holt (1995, 36) suggest:

> In any library setting, various types of reference questions are asked. Some are straightforward and require only brief confirmation leading to short, factual answers; others require a fairly comprehensive search of literature on a complex or obscure subject. The latter type of inquiry often requires an extensive interview process in which the subject is increasingly better defined.

A variant of this approach is the adoption by some libraries of a "two-tiered" reference service in which nonprofessional or paraprofessional staff members handle the front lines and answer routine questions. Only the difficult reference questions get referred to librarians who stay behind the scenes. The fallacy here is the assumption that difficult questions are easily recognized as such and that users' informational needs can be sorted into straightforward or complex on the basis of the initial question. The reality is that you can't classify the reference question until *after* you have conducted a reference interview to discover what the real query is. There is a real danger that what these categories really capture is a decision on the part of the librarian about how much service to give to the user. Treat it as a simple, directional question, point, and hope that the user can do everything independently. Treat it as a complex question, find out what the person really wants to know, and then provide help in finding specific sources.

1.7 There Are No Bad Guy Users

Brenda Dervin has coined the term "bad guy user" to describe the person who won't use the system in system terms, refusing, for example, to read signs and follow instructions. This user asks for "books on transportation" when it should be obvious that there are thousands of such books. In *The Reference Encounter*, Marie Radford (1999) reports that when academic librarians were asked about barriers to good reference outcomes, they tended to think mostly of problems caused by bad guy users:

- The poor library user...is one that has not done the proper preparatory work, has not...read the assignment prior to the reference interview....

- They don't understand indexes at all.

- They don't know what they want, so no matter how much of a reference interview I did, I could never find it out.

- They really expect to be handed everything, and that's become far more prevalent in the last couple of years.

- [Poor users are] the ones who wait until two days before the assignment is due before they start thinking about it.

- The information that he was requesting was available in these particular sources, but he refused to even consider [using them].

- [T]hey're not interested in the options, they're not really interested in learning how to use the library, they just want the quickest way in and the quickest way out.... If they had come in earlier and were more willing to put more into it, maybe they would be better off.

- I don't know why they sometimes ask for something and then, you know, they practically throw it away as soon as you give it to them. (Radford, 1999: 60–62, 113, 122)

All of us, from time to time, are bad guy users in other people's systems, particularly when that system is unfamiliar. It's easy to label library users as bad guys who are ill-prepared, lazy, and procrastinating. However, to understand why users behave this way, it helps to think about ourselves trying to negotiate other people's unfamiliar systems. For example, we appear at the airline ticket counter with our ticket to Australia but somehow didn't realize a visa would also be needed and so the ticket agent has to get us one at the last minute. We call up the telephone company to report a problem and erroneously call the problematic service "call waiting" when it is really "call answer." We phone up a government agency to ask about nursing homes but it turns out we should have asked for retirement homes (or vice versa). When we order a "regular coffee," we are given coffee with cream and sugar added, but we really wanted caffeinated as opposed to decaffeinated coffee. We ask the driver, "Is this the bus to Albuquerque?" when the sign clearly says "Albuquerque." In short, people get things wrong because they don't know the specialized vocabulary of an unfamiliar system and are unable to make distinctions that are self-evident to system insiders. This is why library users may ask for a bibliography when they want a biography, or an encyclopedia when they need a directory. Library staff must conduct reference interviews, not just blame users.

We have found that in some cases users themselves take the blame for a less than successful encounter, in effect sharing the librarian's sense of them as bad guys. For example, one user in the Library Visit Study excused a staff member's manner by saying, "I have worked in retail and know it's not always easy to be pleasant when people ask dumb questions." Others apologized for asking a hard question, or blamed themselves for not formulating their initial question clearly enough ("I may have asked my initial question too fast or with an overly British accent"). "I was embarrassed that I had been so inept at formulating my question," said a user who asked about the location of the children's science section when his real need was for a diagram of the earth tilted on its axis to explain to his seven-year-old son the cycle of the seasons.

When staff members think of the users of library services as bad guys, this sometimes unconsciously held attitude can impair service and harm public relations. In the Library Visit Study, one user reported unhappily,

Did You Know?
Karen Hyman (1999) recommends that you treat every user as a unique individual: "When we categorize people—problem patron, angry mother, deadbeat borrower, greedy computer uses—we feel free to ignore their feelings and messages and transform ourselves into hall monitors or victims" (p. 58).

Did You Know?
In Marie Radford's (1999) study, one librarian said that the difficulty in understanding what users really wanted was the result of the users' lack of skill at "self-disclosure" or their unwillingness to trust the librarian. No mention was made of interviewing skills.

A QUICK TIP

Reassure the User
Users may worry that their questions might not seem important enough or that they might be made to feel foolish or a nuisance. In the Library Visit Study, users often said things like: "I worried about having the librarian scoff at my question." One user who was delighted with the reassuring treatment he received said, "I believe that one of the worst mistakes a librarian can make is to make a user feel they are wasting the librarian's time and that their question is not important. It is an intimidating feeling to approach a reference desk, and a good librarian can turn this experience into an enjoyable and fulfilling one." When this reassurance is given, it changes the users' mental model of the library from a self-service operation to a place where they can expect expert help.

"I distinctly overheard her remark that the reason there was so much need for shelving was because patrons always take out more books than they need and, what's worse, they don't even read them."

1.8 Annotated References

1.8.1 Principles of Interviewing

Benjamin, Alfred. 1981. *The Helping Interview*. 3rd ed. Boston: Houghton Mifflin. Written by a famous practicing counselor, this book contains many concrete examples to illustrate principles of how to conduct the helping interview.

Conroy, Barbara and Barbara Schindler-Jones. 1986. *Improving Communication in the Library*. Phoenix, AZ: Oryx Press.

Ivey, Allen E., and Mary Bradford Ivey. 2003. *Intentional Interviewing and Counseling: Facilitating Client Development in a Multicultural Society*. 5th ed. Pacific Grove, CA: Thomson/Brooks/Cole. Chapter 13, "Integrating Microskills with Theory" covers sequencing skills and interview stages.

Shipley, Kenneth G. and Julie McNulty Wood. 1996. *The Elements of Interviewing*. San Diego and London: Singular Publishing Group. A useful introduction to basic interviewing skills in various contexts.

Spradley, James P. *The Ethnographic Interview*. 1979. New York: Holt, Rinehart and Winston. Written for the student of ethnography, this book clarifies the difference between a conversation and an interview. and distinguishes between an interviewer style where the interviewer learns the language of the interviewee vs. the style where the interviewee has to learn interviewer language.

Stewart, Charles J., and William B. Cash. 2008. *Interviewing: Principles and Practices*. 12th ed. Boston: McGraw Hill. This classic guide to various kinds of interviewing is both practical and easy to read. Each chapter includes training exercises.

1.8.2 Bibliographic Guides to the Reference Interview

Dr. Matthew Saxton of the University of Washington and Dr. John V. Richardson of UCLA have developed a selected bibliography of one thousand citations on reference to supplement their book *Understanding Reference Transactions: Transforming an Art into a Science*, New York: Academic Press, 2002. The list is alphabetically arranged by the name of the first author and contains many items of interest on the reference interview.

Elaine Zaremba Jennerich and Edward J. Jennerich included a 300-item bibliography on the reference interview in their book *The Reference Interview as a Creative Art*, 2nd. ed. Englewood, CO: Libraries Unlimited, 1997.

"The Virtual Reference Bibliography," hosted by Marie L. Radford at Rutgers University, NJ, is a continually updated Web resource. It is built upon Bernie Sloan's bibliography on digital reference services that covered articles and Web sites on virtual reference up to 2004. The new Virtual Reference Bibliography includes items up to the present date and contains over 800 entries on all types of virtual reference (live chat, e-mail, IM, etc.) including approximately 400 items from Bernie Sloan's original site. Available: http://vrsbib.rutgers.edu (accessed November 15, 2008).

1.8.3 When Is a Reference Interview Necessary?

Grogan, Dennis. 1991. *Practical Reference Work*. London: Library Association.

Hauptman, Robert. 1987. "The Myth of the Reference Interview." In *Reference Services Today: From Interview to Burnout*, edited by Bill Katz and Ruth Fraley. Binghamton, NY: The Haworth Press. First published in *The Reference Librarian* 16 (1986): 47–52.

Hyman, Karen. 1999. "Customer Service and the 'Rule of 1965.'" *American Libraries* 30, no. 9 (October): 55–58.

Katz, William A. 2002. *Introduction to Reference Work*. Vol. 2: *Reference Services and Reference Processes*. 8th ed. Boston: McGraw Hill.

Lynch, Mary Jo. 1978. "Reference Interviews in Public Libraries." *Library Quarterly* 48, no. 2. (April): 119–142. A report of a pioneering and still valuable study of 751 reference transactions that occurred in four New Jersey public libraries that produced 366 reference interviews.

McCoy, Michael. 1985. "Why Didn't They Teach Us That? The Credibility Gap in Library Education." *The Reference Librarian* 12: 174.

Reference and User Services Association. "Guidelines for Information Services." 2000. Available: www.ala.org/ala/mgrps/divs/rusa/resources/guidelines/guidelinesinformation.cfm. (accessed November 4, 2008).

White, Herbert S. 1992. "The Reference Librarian as Information Intermediary." *The Reference Librarian* 37: 23–35

Wilson, Patrick. 1986. "The Face Value Rule in Reference Work." *RQ* 25, no. 4 (summer): 468–475.

1.8.4 Measures of Information Service Effectiveness

American Library Association, Reference and Adult Services Division (RASD), Evaluation of Reference and Adult Services Committee. 1995. *The Reference Assessment Manual*. Ann Arbor, MI: The Pierian Press. Contains summaries of instruments and includes a detailed 140-page annotated bibliography that covers a variety of aspects of evaluating reference, broadly defined.

Arnold, Julie, and Neal Kaske. 2005. "Evaluating the Quality of a Chat Service." *portal: Libraries and the Academy* 5, no. 2: 177–193.

Burton, Paul F. 1990. "Accuracy of Information Provision: The Need for Client-Centered Service." *Journal of Academic Librarianship* 22 (October): 201–215.

Childers, Thomas. 1980. "The Test of Reference." *Library Journal* 105 (April 15): 212–217. The first test of reference accuracy to use "escalator" questions that required probing by the reference staff.

Childers, Thomas. 1987 "The Quality of Reference: Still Moot after 20 Years." *Journal of Academic Librarianship* 13 (May): 73–74.

Crews, Kenneth D. 1988. "The Accuracy of Reference Service: Variables for Research and Implementation." *Library and Information Science Research* 10, no. 3 (July): 331–355. A meta-study that provides a useful table summarizing thirty-nine unobtrusive studies of reference accuracy in terms of percentage of correct answers reported, type of library, type of contact that proxy questioners made with the library being observed, etc.

Crowley, Terence, and Thomas Childers. 1971. *Information Service in Public Libraries: Two Studies*. Metuchen, NJ: Scarecrow Press. These two pioneering studies, "The Effectiveness of Information Service in Medium Size Public Libraries" by Crowley, and "Telephone Information Service in Public Libraries" by Childers, introduced the technique of unobtrusive observation into library research on reference evaluation.

Dewdney, Patricia, and Catherine Sheldrick Ross. 1994: "Flying a Light Aircraft: Reference Service Evaluation from a User's Viewpoint." *RQ* 34, no. 2 (winter): 217–230. The first report on the Library Visit Study, this article summarized the experiences of seventy-seven library users who asked a question that mattered to them personally. Users' detailed accounts of their library visits yielded contrasting lists of "most helpful" and "least helpful" features of the service received.

Douglas, Ian. 1988. "Reducing Failures in Reference Service." *RQ* 28, no. 1 (fall): 94–101. Argues that the uniformity of the 50 to 60 percent success rate is "as much an artifact of the methodology [of getting research confederates to ask a set of previously devised test question in libraries] as of the quality of reference services offered by libraries."

Durrance, Joan C. 1989. "Reference Success: Does the 55 Percent Rule Tell the Whole Story?" *Library Journal* 114 (April 15): 31–36. Questions the use of answer accuracy as the appropriate measure and suggests instead the more user-centered measure of "willingness to return" to the same staff member in future.

Durrance, Joan. 1995. "Factors that Influence Reference Success: What Makes Questioners Willing to Return?" *The Reference Librarian* 49/50: 243–265.

Dyson, Lillie Seward. 1992. "Improving Reference Services: A Maryland Training Program Brings Positive Results." *Public Libraries* 31 (Sept./Oct): 284–289.

Goffman, Erving. 1956. "The Nature of Deference and Demeanor." *American Anthropologist* 58, no. 3: 475–499.

Goffman, Erving. 1972. *Relations in Public: Microstudies of the Public Order.* New York: Basic Books.

Heritage, John, Jeffrey D. Robinson, Marc N. Elliott, Megan Becket, and Michael Wilkes. 2007. Reducing Patients' Unmet Concerns in Primary Care: the Difference One Word Can Make. *Journal of General Internal Medicine* 22, no. 10: 1429–1433.

Hernon, Peter, and Charles R. McClure. 1986. "Unobtrusive Reference Testing: the 55 Percent Rule," *Library Journal* 111, no. 7 (April 15): 37–41. A frequently cited study that coined the term "the 55 percent rule" for the repeated research finding that library users get the right answer slightly more than half the time. Reports results of unobtrusive testing in twenty-six U.S. libraries, specifically accuracy of answers, duration of the interview, search process, and use of referral.

Hernon, Peter, and Charles R. McClure. 1987. *Unobtrusive Testing and Library Reference Services.* Norwood, NJ: Ablex. Describes the role of unobtrusive testing in evaluating reference service, research design and methodology, as well as analysis of some actual study results.

Isenstein, Laura. 1992. "Get Your Reference Staff on the STAR Track." *Library Journal* 117 (April 15): 34–37.

Kaske, Neil, and Julie Arnold. 2002 "An Unobtrusive Evaluation of Online Real Time Library Reference Services." Paper presented at the Library Research Round Table, American Library Association, Annual Conference, Atlanta, Georgia, June 15, 2002. Available: www.lib.umd.edu/groups/digref/kaskearnoldunobtrusive.html (accessed November 14, 2008).

Katz, Bill, and Ruth A. Fraley, eds. 1984. *Evaluation of Reference Services.* Binghamton, NY: The Haworth Press. A theme issue with articles on various types of evaluation methods including unobtrusive testing, interviews with users, and output measures data analysis.

Larson, Carole A., and Laura K. Dickson. 1994. "Developing Behavioral Reference Desk Performance Standards." *RQ* 33, no. 3 (spring): 349–357. Reports the process used by the University of Nebraska Library system to develop a customized set of behaviorally- based reference standards.

Massey-Burzio, Virginia. 1998. "From the Other Side of the Reference Desk: A Focus Group Study." *The Journal of Academic Librarianship* 24, no. 3 (May): 208–215.

Ohio Library Council. 2000 (last updated 2008). *Ohio Reference Excellence on the Web.* Available: www.olc.org/ore (accessed November 4, 2008).

Radford, Marie L. 1999. *The Reference Encounter: Interpersonal Communication in the Academic Library.* Chicago: Association of College and Research Libraries. Chapter 1, "Literature on the Reference Interaction," reviews evaluative studies that report on percentages of correct answers, providing citations for a number of typical studies of this kind as well as criticism of research on the 55 percent phenomenon.

Radford, Marie L. 2006. "Encountering Virtual Users: A Qualitative Investigation of Interpersonal Communication in Chat Reference." *Journal of the American Society for Information Science and Technology* 57, no. 8: 1046–1059.

Radford, Marie L., and Lynn Silipigni Connaway. 2007. "Are We Getting Warmer? Query Clarification in Virtual Reference" Presented at the Library Research Round Table, American Library Association Conference, Washington. June 21–27, 2007. Available: www.oclc.org/research/projects/synchronicity/presentations.htm#upcoming (accessed October 31, 2008).

Ross, Catherine Sheldrick, and Patricia Dewdney. 1998. "Negative Closure: Strategies and Counter Strategies in the Reference Transaction." *RUSQ* 38, no. 2: 151–163.

Tyckoson, David. 1992. "Wrong Questions, Wrong Answers: Behavioral vs. Factual Evaluation of Reference Service." *The Reference Librarian* 38: 151–173. Argues that the unobtrusive testing of answer accuracy is too narrow because it neglects the process involved. Tyckoson recommends instead the obtrusive evaluation of reference by a supervisor who uses a behavioral checklist containing twenty-five indicators clustered into four groupings: availability, communication skills, search strategy skills, and individual attention given to patrons.

Watzlawick, Poul, Janet B. Beavin, and Don D. Jackson. 1967. *Pragmatics of Human Communication.* New York: Norton.

Westbrook, Lynn. 1989. *Qualitative Evaluation Methods for Reference Services: An Introductory Manual.* Washington, DC: Office of Management Services, Association of Research Libraries. An introduction for librarians to qualitative methods for evaluating reference service including observation, interviews, surveys and content analysis.

White, Marilyn Domas. 1989. "Different Approaches to the Reference Interview." *Reference Librarian* 25/26: 631–639.

White, Marilyn Domas, Eileen G. Abels, and Neal Kaske. 2003. "Evaluation of Chat Reference Service Quality." *D-Lib Magazine* 9, no. 2: 1–13.

1.8.5 The Ill-formed Query and Users' Mental Models

Belkin, Nicholas J. 1980. "Anomalous States of Knowledge as a Basis for Information Retrieval." *Canadian Journal of Information Science* 5: 133–143.

Cramer, Dina C. 1998. "How to Speak Patron." *Public Libraries* 37, no. 6 (November/December): 349.

Dewdney, Patricia, and Gillian Michell. 1996. "Oranges and Peaches: Understanding Communication Accidents in the Reference Interview." *RQ* 35, no. 4 (summer): 520–536. Classifies ill-formed queries into four main categories, and recommends specific interview techniques to avert communication accidents.

Dewdney, Patricia, and Gillian Michell. 1996. "Mental Models of Information Systems: Results of a Field Study of Ill-formed Queries in the Public Library Reference Interview." Unpublished conference paper presented at the ALA summer conference in August 1996.

Eichman, Thomas Lee. 1978. "The Complex Nature of Opening Reference Questions." *RQ* 17, no. 3 (spring): 212–222. Explains how the user's initial question functions more as a greeting than as a fully elaborated question.

Hutcherson, Norman B. 2004. "Library Jargon: Student Recognition of Terms and Concepts Commonly Used by Librarians in the Classroom." *College & Research Libraries* 65, no. 4 (July): 349–354.

Massey-Burzio, Virginia. 1998 "From the Other Side of the Reference Desk: A Focus Group Study." *The Journal of Academic Librarianship* 24, no. 3 (May): 208–215. A focus group study of users of the Johns Hopkins University library system focused on users' experiences in order to find out what kind of reference service would most help users.

Michell, Gillian, and Patricia Dewdney. 1998. "Mental Models Theory: Applications for Library and Information Science." *Journal of Education for Library and Information Science* 39, no. 4 (fall): 275–281.

Mount, Ellis. 1966. "Communication Barriers and the Reference Question." *Special Libraries* 57 (October): 575–578.

Nahl, Diane. 1997. "Re: Why don't they ask for what they want? Posted August 28, LIBREF. Available: http://listserv.kent.edu/cgi-bin/wa.exe?A2=ind 9708D&L=LIBREF-L&P=R3998&I=-3 (accessed November 15, 2008).

Ross, Catherine Sheldrick. 1986. "How to Find Out What People Really Want to Know." *The Reference Librarian* 16 (winter): 19–30. Discusses reasons why initial questions are often not complete and describes skills that librarians can use, including open questions and sense-making (neutral) questions.

Shultz, Suzanne M. 1996. "Medical Jargon: Ethnography of Language in a Hospital Library." *Medical Reference Service Quarterly* 15, no. 3 (fall): 41–47

Taylor, Robert S. 1968. "Question Negotiation and Information Seeking in Libraries." *College & Research Libraries* 29, no. 3: 178–194.

Wang, Peiling, William B. Hawk, and Carol Tenopir. 2000. "Users' Interaction with World Wide Web Resources: An Exploratory Study Using a Holistic Approach. *Information Processing and Management* 36, no. 2 (March): 229–251. In a study of twenty-four student searchers' attempts to answer two test questions using Internet sources, researchers concluded that users are likely to develop incomplete and fragmentary mental models of Web resources.

1.8.6 Useful Conceptual Frameworks for Thinking about Information, Mental Models, Etc.

Fine, Sara. 1995. "Reference and Resources: The Human Side," *The Journal of Academic Librarianship* 21, no. 1 (January): 17–20.

Johnson-Laird, Philip Nicholas. 1983. *Mental Models: Towards a Cognitive Science of Language, Inference and Consciousness.* Cambridge, MA: Harvard University Press.

Lakoff, George, and Mark Johnson. 1980. "Conceptual Metaphor in Everyday Language." *In Metaphors We Live By.* Chicago: University of Chicago Press.

Norman, Donald A. 1983. "Some Observations on Mental Models." In *Mental Models*, edited by Dedre Gentner and Albert L. Stevens (pp. 7–14). Hillsdale, NJ: Lawrence Erlbaum Associates.

Reddy, Michael J. 1993. "The Conduit Metaphor." In *Metaphor and Thought*, edited by Andrew Ortony (pp. 164–201). New York: Cambridge University Press.

Reilly, Ronan G., ed. 1987. *Communication Failure in Dialogue and Discourse: Detection and Repair Processes*. Amsterdam: Elsevier Science. Pages 99–120 provide a useful overview of research on communication accidents in ordinary conversation, as studied by researchers from various disciplines including linguistics, education, cognitive science, and artificial intelligence.

Solomon, Paul. 1997. "Conversation in Information-Seeking Contexts: A Test of an Analytical Framework." *Library and Information Science Research* 19, no. 3 (fall): 217–248. Provides an analytic framework that looks at linguistic features of interactions such as turn-taking, turn allocation, gaps, openings, closings, frames, repairs, etc. to examine how information-seeking conversations differ from ordinary conversation and conversations in other restricted domains such as physician-patient or teacher-student.

Sutton, Ellen D., and Leslie Edmonds Holt. 1995. "The Reference Interview." In *Reference and Information Services: An Introduction*, edited by Richard E. Bopp and Linda C. Smith. 2nd ed. Englewood, CO: Libraries Unlimited.

Setting the Stage for the Reference Interview: The First Thirty Seconds

2.1 Being Approachable

The reference interview begins when the user approaches a staff member and asks a question. Since users with informational needs are often hesitant to ask for help, many potential reference interviews never happen. Being approachable is the first step in giving good customer service. You have to be physically available, and you must appear willing to help. At the most basic level, you have to be located where users can see you—not behind a high desk or in an out-of-the-way location, and you have to look as though you genuinely want to serve users. Looking approachable involves using nonverbal skills such as a welcoming posture, smiling, and eye contact, wearing an identification tag, and being constantly on the alert for users who need help. Even if you have other work to do, it just takes an instant to lift your head to scan the area every few minutes so that you don't miss people who seem lost or confused, or who otherwise look as if they could use some help.

Taking a proactive stance in offering help is important because many users who need help hesitate to ask. Virginia Massey-Burzio (1998) conducted focus groups with users at the Johns Hopkins University library system to find out their experiences using the library and its services. At all levels from undergraduates to graduate students to faculty, focus group participants said they felt uncomfortable asking questions. Here are some comments: "I'm not a question asker. Maybe I'm just an idiot wasting time wandering around the library, but I'd rather do that" (undergraduate); "If I know what I'm doing [in my field], I should be able to find stuff" (graduate student); "There's a fear that someone is going to say—not that it ever happened—why didn't you come to our open house? We discussed that at length" (faculty).

These findings can be extended to younger people as well. Radford and Connaway (2007) held focus groups with teenagers and found that they had a preference for independent information seeking and frequently avoided reference librarians because the teens were afraid to ask questions. Similarly other researchers have found that teens may prefer to use

EXERCISE

Why Don't They Ask Questions?
An early study in academic libraries found that more than one quarter of users in the catalog, index and stacks area had a question that they would like to ask, but would not ask a librarian. They told the research interviewer that they would ask a friend or another student or even the interviewer, just not the librarian whose job it is to answer such questions. And why not? The most common reason was that they were unhappy with previous service (42 percent), while 29 percent feared their question was too simple for a librarian and another 29 percent said they didn't want to bother the librarian (Swope and Katzer, 1972). Similarly, Liu and Redfern (1997) found that minority students in an academic library avoided the reference desk because they lacked the knowledge of what a reference librarian does and because they were afraid that they might ask stupid questions or that their English might not be good enough to ask the question or understand the answer (5.5.2).

For this exercise, pick a particular library, possibly the library where you yourself work. Put on your user hat. Imagine that you are a user with a question, but you are unfamiliar with this library. What elements in the library environment would encourage you to approach reference staff with your question? What might discourage you from asking your question?

search engines such as Google, surf the Web, or ask their family or friends for help rather than approaching a reference desk (Agosto and Hughes-Hassell, 2005, 2006).

How can you tell if a library user of any age needs help? In the Mental Models Study, experienced librarians identified five signs that they used to identify those users who want help but don't ask:

- They're standing at the online catalog, maybe standing back from it, and not writing anything down or printing anything out.
- They walk aimlessly among the computers looking lost or confused.
- They look frustrated or even disgusted as they go through an index or other reference tool.
- They walk *slowly* past the reference desk and glance repeatedly in your direction.
- As they are looking at materials, they often stop and make eye contact with you, even though they don't come and ask.

The RUSA (Reference and User Services Association, 2004) "Guidelines for Behavioral Performance of Reference and Information Service Providers" suggest that the librarian who wishes to communicate approachability adopts the following behaviors:

- Establishes a "reference presence" wherever patrons look for it. This includes having Reference Services in a highly visible location and using proper signage (both in the library and on the library's Web site) to indicate the location, hours, and availability of in-person and remote help or assistance.
- Is poised and ready to engage approaching patrons. The librarian is aware of the need to stop all other activities when patrons approach and focus attention on the patrons' needs.
- Acknowledges others waiting for service.
- Establishes initial eye contact with patrons and acknowledges the presence of patrons through smiling and attentive, welcoming body language.
- Acknowledges patrons through the use of a friendly greeting to initiate conversation and by standing up, moving forward, or moving closer.
- Remains visible to patrons as much as possible.
- Roves through the reference area offering assistance whenever possible. Librarians should make themselves available to patrons by offering assistance at their point-of-need rather than waiting for patrons to come to the reference desk.
- When offering reference service remotely, provides prominent, jargon-free links to all forms of reference services from the home page of the library's Web site and throughout the site, wherever research assistance may be sought. The Web should be used to make reference services easy to find and convenient.

Some libraries have successfully experimented with a "roving librarian" whose job is to move around and approach users to see if they need help. Not every library can afford to have a position dedicated to a "rover," and sometimes it's too busy for librarians to leave the reference desk, but everyone can occasionally rove. In a bold and controversial move, Orange County Library System in Orlando, Florida stopped using a traditional reference desk in favor of roving librarians who greet each person as they enter the library and ask if they need help. Other librarians and staff members walk around the building and keep in constant contact to improve customer service.

Roving is particularly important in "the electronic arcade" or "information commons"—the area where library users access e-resources and the Web. In *Teaching the New Library*, LaGuardia (1996, 110) says that "one of the main attributes of a good rover is excellent interpersonal skills: you have to walk the line between offending or frightening some patrons, while gently sending others off on their own to fly after the first couple of hand-holding sessions. You need to be able to sense who invites approach and who will skitter away or refuse offers of assistance. If in doubt, approach." When offering help, a low-key, non-intrusive approach works best—not "You look like you need some help" or "That's not the right way to search" but rather something like "Excuse me, but are you finding what you're looking for?" (Thanks for this tip to Gary Klein, Willamette University, Salem, Oregon.)

ANALYZE THIS REFERENCE TRANSACTION

Case 3: "This person is really helping me."

In the Mental Models Study, both the user and the librarian were interviewed to get the perceptions of both parties to a reference transaction. Users were asked how often they visited or phoned a public library, how familiar they were with this particular branch, and something about their purpose for coming to the library on this visit. And then they were asked to recollect, step-by-step, what they said and did during the reference transaction, what the librarian said and did, and what they were thinking at each of these steps.

In this case the user was from out of town and had never been to this particular library before. He had come along with a friend. While he was in the library, he thought he might as well look up information on fish—specifically whether or not his big Oscar would eat baby ones if he were to buy some at the pet store. He was trying unsuccessfully to find information on the computer when the librarian asked if she could help:

User: She told us that the computer I was using was for this and that [he was using a computer dedicated to CD-ROMs], but that this other computer [with access to the online catalog] was the one I needed. So we walked over there and got that computer and then she showed me exactly where the books were. Next she took me over to the books, and she just asked me questions about what I would like to know about. Then she went to get my book for me.

Interviewer: What were you thinking?

(Cont'd.)

SOME QUICK TIPS

Go Where Users Are

RUSA (2004) "Guidelines for Behavioral Performance of Reference and Information Service Providers" recommends that librarians rove through the reference area offering help at the user's point of need. Here are RUSA tips for the roving librarian.

- Be mobile.
- Address the users before addressing their computer screen.
- Approach users and offer help along the lines of "Are you finding what you need?"
- Check back on the patron's progress after helping her start a search.
- Check the reference desk periodically to see if there is anyone waiting there for help.

Did You Know?

Approachability and interest are, for the most part, communicated nonverbally. Think of the importance of the "Trio of Tens" when at the service desk.

- 10 inches—the top of your head to the top of your shoulders. People look first at our faces to see if we are approachable. Eye contact and pleasant facial expressions will encourage users to engage.
- 10 words—what you say and how you say it. Think of the contrast between a cheerful "May I help you?" said with a smile and a clipped "Next!" or "Yes?" or "What?" said with a blank stare.
- 10 steps—the first ten steps you take. How you walk toward a person can demonstrate positive (confident, eager) or negative (despondent, reluctant) feelings.

User: That this person's really helping me. It's their job—they're librarians. [Laughs.] I was really being looked after. Like in my library at home, they just sit at the desk. Me, I'm not much of a book person and I have trouble reading too, and I can't find my way through the library. But this librarian actually took time and helped me look for what I needed. The book she gave me had a picture of an Oscar on the cover.

Interviewer: Thinking back to when you first spoke to the librarian, how easy did you think it would be to get an answer to your question?

User: I didn't think it would be that easy to find. If I had to do it myself, I would have been looking right now. But she made it real easy. She just typed in the thing on the computer and she knew exactly where to go and what to do. I think it was worth coming here. She actually took time to help me and figure out what I was doing.

When the librarian was interviewed, she said that the user seemed surprised when she took him to another computer: "people assume that all the computers are the same," she said, but in fact the computer that the user chose was set up for searching Books in Print on CD-ROM:

Librarian: Because of where he started, at the CD-ROM computer—I don't hesitate to approach people there. I don't assume that they know what they're doing when they sit down there, because they don't. People may spend ten or fifteen minutes there and find books on fish in *Books in Print*, but it will still be the wrong place to be. And the next thing you know, you're at the point where you have to interloan some book from another library. Users just see a computer [and assume they are interchangeable]. And we're probably lax that we don't label the computers so that users can tell which ones provide access to the catalog.

Comment: Unlike the librarians in the user's home library who "just sit at the desk," this librarian is a rover whose working principle is to offer help to anyone looking puzzled. Computers all look the same, and novice users in particular are likely to end up searching in the wrong place—they look for local library holdings in *Books in Print* or they look for a journal article in the library catalog.

In this case, the librarian provided such an apparently effortless mediation between the needs of the user and the complexity of the system that the user was unaware of all the steps involved. The user said that the librarian "knew exactly where to go and what to do," but the successful outcome of this transaction depended on a lot of background knowledge and activity that was invisible to the user including the reference interview. The user said, "she just asked me questions about what I would like to know about," but the librarian said she had to ask numerous questions to narrow the topic. "When he said, 'fish,' I asked him if he wanted aquarium fish or fishing for fish or fish cookbooks. Then I had to establish if it was salt-water or fresh-water fish.

For discussion: Brainstorm all the ways in which this librarian's intervention could have made a difference. Consider immediate effects and more distant effects, such as the user's mental model of the library, his likelihood of using libraries in the future, etc.

HOW DO USERS DECIDE WHICH LIBRARIAN TO APPROACH?

Radford (1998) studied nonverbal approachability at two academic libraries. She observed 155 library users interacting with thirty-four reference librarians. She also interviewed the users, asking them how they made their decision on whom to approach when given the choice between two librarians. In order of frequency, the five categories developed from users' responses as to their decision-making were as follows:

1. **Initiation.** Users believed that the librarian chose them instead of them choosing the librarian. They mentioned the librarian's eye contact or other welcoming approachability behaviors, including a verbal greeting, such as "May I help you?"
2. **Availability.** Users described their impression that the librarian was available to help them through their assessment of the librarian's nonverbal immediacy behaviors.
3. **Proximity.** Users said that they chose the librarian who was perceived to be physically closest although the librarian chosen was not always actually the closest.
4. **Familiarity.** Users said that they already knew the librarian through a previous reference encounter or library use instruction session.
5. **Gender.** Several users chose a female librarian over a male librarian.

2.2 The Library as a Physical Space

As we discovered in the Library Visit Study, the physical setting of the library has a large impact on what happens in the reference transaction. We asked beginning students in the early weeks of a basic reference course to go to a library of their choice and ask a question that mattered to them personally. They then wrote up an account of the library visit that included what happened step-by-step until the end of the transaction, and what they found helpful and unhelpful about the experience. They were also asked to rate the success of the transaction in terms of the helpfulness of the answer and their willingness to return to the same librarian with a similar question.

More than half the users in the Library Visit Study began their account with some comment about the library as a physical space. They praised well-marked reference areas and "large, well-placed easily identifiable signs," while singling out for criticism the lack of convenient parking, confusing floor plans, the lack of clear signage for reference desks and subject areas, and the lack of means of identifying the professional librarians. The reference desk itself could become a barrier to users who sometimes perceived library staff members as hunkering down with their terminals behind the garrison of their desk. One user said, "The high counters reminded me of a taxation office." When staff was occupied with other work, they sometimes seemed "too busy to be approached."

Since the environments we work in can become invisible to us, we need to cultivate what anthropologists call "anthropological strangeness"

(continued on p. 45)

A QUICK TIP

Recognizing the Experts

Joan Durrance (1989) has pointed out that libraries are different from all other professional settings in making it difficult for users to identify professional staff. Users have a better chance of recognizing the experts when the library uses well-designed signage and when staff members are identified by badges.

Conducting the Reference Interview

EXERCISE

How Approachable Are You?

Find out by taking this quiz. Circle the letter corresponding to the response that best describes your behavior. If you have never worked at a public service desk, pick the answer that describes your behavior in other contexts where you provide help. Though lighthearted, this exercise, adapted from Ellison (1983), has the serious message of raising awareness of approachability.

1. When at the service desk, your facial expression is best characterized as:
   - A. Patronizing
   - B. Pleasant
   - C. Ominous
   - D. Always smiling
   - E. Demonic

2. When at the service desk, which greeting do you use most often?
   - A. Yesss?
   - B. What do you want?
   - C. What can I do for you?
   - D. May I help you?
   - E. None, just a blank stare.

3. Do you look toward helping each potential library user as a(n) . . . ?
   - A. New adventure
   - B. Learning experience
   - C. Pain in the neck
   - D. Service that must be rendered
   - E. Adversary

4. When at the desk, how often do you make eye contact with library users?
   - A. Never
   - B. Rarely
   - C. Frequently
   - D. All the time
   - E. Don't know

5. How do you feel when helping each library user?
   - A. Uneasy
   - B. Natural
   - C. Like you are playing a role
   - D. Unsure
   - E. Terrified

6. What is the last thing you tell library users after providing assistance?
   - A. Good luck!
   - B. Keep looking.
   - C. "I am always available for assistance."
   - D. "Sorry . . ."
   - E. "Please return if you need additional help."

7. Typically, what is your reaction to negative comments or complaints?
   - A. Serious thought
   - B. To ignore them
   - C. To thank the person for bringing the problem to your attention
   - D. Thoughts of revenge
   - E. Self-defense

8. How do you respond when potential library users approach the desk?
   - A. Stop all other activity
   - B. Stand up if sitting
   - C. Greet the user
   - D. Continue working
   - E. Look at the user

9. When working at the service desk, in between users, do you . . . ?
   - A. Concentrate intensely on your work
   - B. Talk to co-workers
   - C. Use the computer
   - D. Use the phone
   - E. Glance up occasionally

(Cont'd.)

EXERCISE (Continued)

10. How often do you approach library users who are obviously having problems finding material?

   A. Never   D. Each time I notice such individuals

   B. Rarely   E. Why should I? If they want help,

   C. Frequently   they can come to me.

Your Score	Scoring				
1. _____	1. A–4	B–1	C–3	D–2	E–5
2. _____	2. A–3	B–4	C–2	D–1	E–5
3. _____	3. A–2	B–1	C–4	D–3	E–5
4. _____	4. A–5	B–3	C–1	D–2	E–4
5. _____	5. A–2	B–1	C–4	D–3	E–5
6. _____	6. A–2	B–4	C–1	D–5	E–0
7. _____	7. A–2	B–3	C–1	D–5	E–4
8. _____	8. A–2	B–1	C–1	D–5	E–1
9. _____	9. A–5	B–3	C–3	D–3	E–1
10. _____	10. A–4	B–3	C–2	D–1	E–5

Here's what your score indicates:

10–20   You are a very approachable person.

21–30   You seem more approachable than average.

31–40   This score indicates that you may have a problem in the area of approachability.

40+   You need to pay serious attention to your approachability.

---

to get past our habituated ways of seeing. We should make a deliberate attempt to look at the library's physical environment through the users' eyes. Having done that, we can take steps to remedy the problems identified. Sometimes the solutions can be quite simple. As one approving user commented, "Approximately three seconds after I entered the library, I noticed a sign that said, 'QUESTIONS? ASK ME.' I was very surprised and glad....I also thought that this sign was more effective and generally understandable than a sign indicating REFERENCE."

For library users in the Library Visit Study, the most important factors pertaining to the physical setting as a barrier were signage, the layout of the library including the positioning of desks, and the cues (or lack thereof) that allow users to identify reference staff. Here's a sampling of what these users said:

- The first thing I noticed was the absence of any specific orientation aid for patrons seeking help.

- Since there were no signs, it took me a couple of minutes to ferret out that the reference desk was behind a wall, making the desk invisible to anyone looking for information.

- None of the staff members wore name tags or any other identification clarifying their professional function. *(continued)*

- The librarians were working behind their big desks and I didn't want to disturb them.

- The placement of the computer screen is such that the client cannot see what is going on and it obscures the reference librarian. I had the feeling that in this particular situation the catalog was being used as a shield.

- I noticed in this reference area that the librarians were shut in. They couldn't get out. I suppose there were doors, but my impression was that they stayed in that little pen all day. My idea of a librarian is that they go to the shelves with you—not always, but that they would browse around and look for you and interact with books too. But they just sat there with this machine [the computer]. That was their job.

A common problem for library users was that they did not know where to go to ask their question. Users often go to the first likely-looking desk they see which may be the circulation counter or the desk of the security guard. This is what happened in the following case in which a student user was interviewed about her reference experience by another classmate:

User: As I went into the public library, right in front of me was a desk, so I approached that and asked my question. She directed me to the reference desk.

Interviewer: Did you know if she was a reference librarian?

User: No, I didn't know who they were. I just saw this woman as I walked in. I realized afterwards that it was the circulation desk.

Interviewer: And then what did you do?

User: I went up to the reference desk. The woman said, "Yes?" Didn't smile.

Interviewer: Did you ask her if she was a reference librarian?

User: No. She was sitting behind the reference desk, but my impression was that she was a library assistant. One of the things I've always felt is that it's very hard to find out who's the librarian. I think they should wear name tags.

In addition to the physical layout of the library and the desk, users rely on other physical cues such as the appearance of the staff. One reason to adopt a professional appearance is that it helps library users identify you as an employee. From an unobtrusive study conducted in various types of libraries, Durrance (1989) concluded:

> Appearance of the staff member (including age and dress) plays an important role in helping observers make decisions, especially when the environment fails to send a clear message; 56% used environmental clues to decide if they had been working with a librarian. Well-dressed, older individuals were assumed to be librarians while casually dressed younger people were thought to be students.

In this study, one of Durrance's participant observers approached a young man seated behind the reference desk, who said that he was not the

EXERCISE

Approachability

If you don't normally wear an identification tag, make one and wear it for an hour while you stand near your online catalog. Do you find that more people tend to ask you questions? If people still do not ask you for help, try asking them if they found what they wanted. The results may be surprising.

librarian, but a friend of the librarian. When "the librarian emerged from the stacks, the observer concluded from her age, her casual clothing, and her bright pink hair that she was not a librarian either" (Durrance, 1989, 9, 33).

These examples raise the much debated issue of whether or not library staff who serve the public should wear identification tags. Some research indicates that library users feel that they have been better served if they know the name of the staff member who is helping them, in much the same way as they like to know the name of the doctor who treats them in an emergency ward. However, for those employees who are concerned about privacy and security, the purpose is served by tags that indicate their function or position. Some libraries give employees the option of using an "alias" on tags. The key consideration in the name tag debate, and indeed in the entire issue of appearance, is really accessibility: can people identify you as someone who is able to help them, and do they feel comfortable in approaching you?

2.3 Establishing Contact

As seen in section 1.4, reference interviews often start out in one of two possible ways: the user asks a very general question ("What information do you have on health?") or the user asks a very specific question ("I'd like to see the University of Wisconsin's academic calendar"). When these questions are answered literally ("Thousands of books, articles, clippings, and Web pages" or "Here's the academic calendar for the University of Wisconsin"), the answers may not help the user. Suppose, for example, the users in these examples wanted to locate research that compares St. John's wort and Prozac as treatments for depression, or needed the first name of a scientist thought to be on the faculty at Wisconsin.

But why would a person wanting articles on specific drugs ask for general information on health? Why don't people ask for what they want in the first place? On off days, a librarian may be tempted to think that users do this to be difficult. It may help, however, to think of the user's initial question not as a fully articulated query, but as a way of making contact and of opening the channel of communication. Remember that the user may have gone to the wrong place and have already asked someone else—the clerk at the circulation desk or the person at the security desk—before bringing the question to you.

Linguists have an explanation for what sometimes seems to be the perverse way in which people phrase their initial requests for help. This explanation is based on the fact that language can have a number of different functions, among them exchanging information and establishing contact. During a reference encounter, two strangers meet in a public place. According to Thomas Eichman (1978), the librarian expects an exchange of information from the user in the form of a clear statement expressing the informational need. The user, on the other hand, feels the need to establish contact. He has unspoken questions in mind that need

---

A QUICK TIP

"Hello, can you help me?"

Think of the user's initial question not as a fully formed request but as a kind of greeting. In this greeting, the user is asking for some reassurance that you are listening and are the right person to help. Thomas Eichman (1978) uses John Searle's speech act theory to make the case that the initial question has the illocutionary force of performing a greeting. To the librarian, the initial question may seem to have the linguistic function primarily of exchanging information. To the user on the other hand, the initial question often has the linguistic function of establishing contact and asking, "I wonder if you might help me."

A QUICK TIP

HALT

An acronym to help us achieve excellent service at the reference desk is HALT. We are more likely to be cranky and to have negative interactions with library users when we are:

- Hungry
- Late
- Angry
- Tired

These conditions are likely to make us more stressed and less able to deal with the rigors of service encounters. So prepare yourself for reference desk time by making sure you are none of the above.

answering before he will be willing to invest time telling the whole problem: Am I in the right place? Are you available and listening to me? Are you the person who's going to help me? Can you help me with a problem that falls into this general area?

You need to respond in a way that answers these unspoken questions. PACT is an acronym for remembering what the user wants to know first.

P **P**lace is right
A **A**vailable and listening
C **C**ontact made
T **T**opic (in general) understood

Communicate these responses ("Yes, you've come to the right place," "I'm the person to help you," etc.) through nonverbal skills such as eye contact, smiling, and standing up (2.4.2) and through verbal skills such as acknowledgment (2.4.3) and encouragers (2.4.4). When the user asks for health information, look up, perhaps stand up, smile, and acknowledge the user immediately by saying, for example, "Health information, uh-huh." By using PACT, you establish the contact that will encourage the user to tell you more. It also is very useful in cross-cultural transactions or in cases where the user's first language is not English.

2.4 Skills for the First Thirty Seconds

You can use a cluster of skills known as attending skills to establish contact and set the stage for the rest of the interview. In the first thirty seconds, you won't have a chance to say much, but you still are conveying strong messages to the user of one kind or another. When you use attending skills, many of which are nonverbal, you show an interest in others by paying attention to the other person. The use of attending skills in interviewing has been explained best by Allen E. Ivey, who has developed a framework called microtraining for teaching interview skills to counselors. In her doctoral dissertation, "Microcounseling in Library Education," Elaine Jennerich (1974) was the first to recognize the value of Ivey's microtraining approach in relation to the reference interview.

2.4.1 The Microtraining Approach

In the early 1960s at Stanford University, Allen E. Ivey developed the microskills approach as a way of teaching new counselors to use the basic communications skills necessary in any interview. He identified the smallest components of effective interviews as "microskills," beginning with the basic listening sequence that includes attending behavior such as eye contact, body language, and verbal tracking skills like acknowledgment. These formed the basis of his hierarchy of microskills, from the basic listening sequence through asking questions and culminating in skill integration. Attending skills are the foundation of Ivey's microskills hierarchy, because they establish a good communication climate for further conversation. Attending behavior, including acknowledgment (or restatement) and minimal encouragers, is the most basic skill that we must learn before moving on to other skills such as questioning or summarizing.

Microtraining is based on the idea that complex communication behavior can be broken down into its constituent parts or small (micro) skills, and that these skills can be taught, one at a time, in a systematic way that involves the following steps:

1. Defining the skill and identifying its function
2. Observing the skill modeled
3. Reading about the skill and the concepts behind it
4. Practicing the skill in a context that provides feedback (e.g., audiotaping or videotaping; getting a peer coach to provide observations on your use of the skills)
5. Using the skill in a real world context and observing what happens
6. Teaching the skill to others

A key principle of microtraining is that you learn a skill one at a time and practice it. For each skill, you first learn to identify or recognize the skill by observing others' behavior or by picking out the skill in a transcript, videotape, or some other exercise. Throughout this book, we have provided many examples of the skills as they were used in real reference interviews so that you can identify them and see how they work. Reading about the skill and how it works, and being able to define and recognize it, though necessary, is not enough. You won't really understand the skill and its function until you practice it yourself. So the next level in learning a skill is basic mastery in which you practice the skill in a sheltered environment such as a role-played situation. After that comes the level of active mastery in which you demonstrate the appropriate use of the skill in a real life setting such as the reference desk. In the final level, which is teaching mastery, you are ready to pass on the skill by teaching it to others.

For Ivey, perhaps the most important concept in microtraining is "intentionality." Intentionality has to do with choice: once you have learned the skill and how it works, you need to be able to judge when the skill is appropriate and what effect it is likely to have. From a range of responses that you could make in a particular situation, you are choosing the response that is potentially the most helpful. In short, you are choosing to use a particular skill *intentionally* in order to accomplish some particular goal in the interview. You need to understand the function of each skill so that you can use it intentionally as a choice among a range of options, and not by rote. Intentionality means flexibility—the ability to use a range of skills and to improvise.

A corollary of the principle of intentionality is that every rule can be broken—*if* there is a good reason. However, before breaking the rule, it is important to know what the rule is and how it is supposed to work.

A QUICK TIP

Learn a Microskill

Focus on learning and practicing just one skill at a time. Eventually, you will integrate all the microskills into one seamless interview. But when you are first learning a skill, you should focus your attention on just one skill. Schedule a specific time when you are on the reference desk to practice a new skill. Promise yourself that, for this time period, you will use one skill, say acknowledgment (2.4.3), in every interview.

2.4.2 Nonverbal Attending Skills

Inappropriate body language can keep a reference interview from ever getting started. Looking down at work on the desk rather than up to catch the user's eye says, in effect, that the librarian is too busy to be approached. On the other hand, putting aside the materials you are working on, looking up, smiling, and using eye contact communicate a readiness to help. Nonverbal messages are conveyed by "behavior" such as eye contact, tone of voice, facial expression, posture, gestures, positioning of arms and legs, style of dress, or your distance from another person. Researchers have distinguished various dimensions of nonverbal behavior:

- **The way we use our bodies**—head, arms, and legs, as well as facial expression, posture and movement

- **The way we use interpersonal space**—the distance we stand from another person; body orientation such as leaning forward or turning aside

- **How we say something**—the pitch, rate, loudness, and inflection of our speech

- **The way we time our verbal exchanges**—the way we manage turn taking; duration of turns and duration of pauses

- **The way we look**—the formality or casualness of clothing styles; the use of accessories and cosmetics

While these nonverbal cues are missing from virtual reference interviews that are simply exchanges of typed text, in face-to-face (FtF) communication, people rely very much on nonverbal cues to convey emotion. Moreover, they are experts at detecting any discrepancy between spoken words and nonverbal cues. Your words may intend to signal interest when you say, "How may I help you?" but if you frown and speak in a flat, bored tone, users will not experience you as interested in helping.

You should think of the nonverbal attending skills as the foundation for the rest of the interview. In the Library Visit Study, users emphasized the importance of body language in establishing contact and encouraging them to ask their question in the first place. "He looked up from his work right away and smiled," said one satisfied user. On the other hand, the absence of appropriate eye contact was often mentioned as a discouraging factor that could persist throughout the reference transaction: "She did not look me in the eye but looked at the ceiling, as if the information was there." It is important to be aware, however, that body language is culture-specific. Eye contact, for example, is usually understood in western cultures as a sign of attentive listening, but in some eastern cultures it may be taken as a sign of disrespect.

When library staff members didn't smile and use appropriate eye contact, users interpreted this failure as a lack of interest in them and/or in their question. One user commented, "She didn't seem interested in medical questions and acted as if I were wasting her time." In more extreme cases of unwelcoming body language, users felt the library staff members considered their question an annoying nuisance like the librarian who "looked puzzled and pursed her lips and rolled her eyes. From her expression, she seemed to be saying, 'Why did I get stuck with this question?'" When another librarian was asked for materials on contemporary music, she "started to grimace or wince and let out an 'ooooow.' I was not sure if her reaction reflected a dislike of the topic, her recognition that materials on that topic would be scarce, or a combination of both factors and perhaps others." Tone of voice can be more important than what is actually said. In one case, the staff member eventually looked up from her computer screen and said, "Can I help you with something?" The user noted, "Her tone implied I was taking her away from something very important, although a quick survey of the library indicated I was the only one in there."

If your goal is to cut down on service and reduce the number of questions asked, here's how to do it: avoid eye contact, look very busy with the work on your desk, turn away from the user and become very absorbed with the computer screen. This can be readily interpreted by users to mean "Do Not Disturb," especially if you lean on your hand as if shielding your eyes. These behaviors confirm the users' common concern of being a bother to the librarian. If the user musters the courage to ask the question anyway, additional discouragements can be added, as happened in the case of a user of a large central public library who asked, "I'm looking for some information on polling companies." According to the user's account, the librarian "turned away, narrowed her eyes, and, after wincing for five seconds, proclaimed, 'I don't think we have anything.' I think she hoped I would be satisfied and leave." These librarians whose body language was interpreted as unwelcoming may indeed have been thinking hard about the user's question and doing their very best to help. They may have thought they were looking both serious and professional. Whatever their intention, however, their body language conveyed a message that discouraged users from expecting help.

Eye Contact

Eye contact is an attending skill that people learn in childhood. Culturally appropriate use of eye contact is one of the most powerful cues for opening and maintaining communication. Middle class white Anglo-Americans communicate that they are listening by looking at other people. Without eye contact, they may feel that no communication is occurring. Children who are resistant to parental messages communicate this by looking pointedly away, hence the adult reprimand, "Look at me when I'm speaking to you." In the reference context, making eye contact is the most important way that you can signal to the user that you are approachable and available to help.

We can powerfully influence how much another person talks by our use of eye contact. Looking at the person who is talking to you usually indicates warmth, interest, and a desire to communicate. Frequent breaks

Did You Know?
Body language in the interview situation often expresses perceptions of status and power. In an interview between people of different cultures, it's important to pay attention to body language. For a discussion of communication between black students and white librarians, see Errol L. Lam (1988).

Did You Know?
According to Helen M. Newman (1990, 271), silence is perceived positively if it occurs appropriately during any conversation. If, on the other hand, there is no apparent and appropriate reason for the silence in a conversation, it will be anxiety-producing. She notes that "silence takes its meaning partly from the context in which it is embedded." So in reference interactions, natural silences are fine, but when they happen unexpectedly or at unusual moments in the conversation they can be interpreted negatively.

A QUICK TIP

Showing an Interest
Librarians who show interest in users generate higher levels of user satisfaction. Librarians demonstrate interest when using the following nonverbal behaviors: facing the user when speaking or listening; maintaining or re-establishing eye contact throughout the transaction; establishing a physical distance that appears to be comfortable to the user based on the user's verbal and nonverbal responses; signaling an understanding of the user's needs by head nodding; appearing unhurried; focusing attention on the user.
(Adapted from RUSA, 2004, "Guidelines for Behavioral Performance")

Conducting the Reference Interview

A QUICK TIP

Look Up and Smile

When Marie Radford (1996) asked users, "How did you decide which staff member to approach?" they said they chose the staff member who used welcoming body language including eyebrow flash, eye contact, smiling, and nodding. Eye contact was found to be the most important behavior for signaling availability even if the librarian was otherwise busy. Negative nonverbal indicators included lack of immediate acknowledgment of user, no change in body stance as user approached, covering the eye with the hand, reading, tapping fingers, twitching mouth, or pacing.

Did You Know?

Librarians who show interest in users generate higher levels of user satisfaction. Librarians demonstrate interest when using the following nonverbal behaviors: facing the user when speaking or listening; maintaining or re-establishing eye contact throughout the transaction; establishing a physical distance that appears to be comfortable to the user based on the user's verbal and nonverbal responses; signaling an understanding of the user's needs by head nodding; appearing unhurried; focusing attention on the user.

(Adapted from RUSA, 2004, "Guidelines for Behavioral Performance")

EXERCISE

Approachability Factors

According to a review of research on nonverbal approachability, users are put off when librarians read, talk to others, or use the computer at the reference desk (Radford, 2005). The good news is that looking up occasionally to make eye contact can be a powerful antidote, allowing us to continue to be approachable, even when working at the service desk. We should make eye contact, preferably at eye level, immediately acknowledge the user by leaning or moving forward, nod, and use mirroring gestures and minimal encouragers such as "Mmm hmm." We should have a pleasant demeanor, including a welcoming facial expression, as well as an open posture with relaxed body and arms. Finally we should remain mobile, accompanying the user to resources, if possible. Factors that decrease approachability are, contrarily, avoidance of eye contact, failure to acknowledge the user, staying seated, and leaning away. Check this out by unobtrusively watching some reference transactions. How many positive and negative factors did you observe?

in eye contact are usually interpreted as inattention, lack of interest, embarrassment, or even dislike. Therefore, looking down at the floor, up at the ceiling, or over at a file will get the other person to stop talking. Maintaining appropriate eye contact indicates interest and encourages the other person to continue talking.

But what is appropriate eye contact? Too much can be as bad as too little. An unwavering stare can seem hostile, rude, or intrusive while prolonged eye contact can seem threatening. Appropriate eye contact involves neither staring nor avoiding. The time spent looking directly into the other person's eyes, however, is actually very brief. Your eyes will move from eyes to chin, hairline, mouth, and back to the eyes. Listeners and speakers tend to adopt an alternate pattern of looking and then looking away. Moreover, the looking times of speaker and listener are not symmetrical: in mainstream North American culture, listeners spend twice as much time looking as do speakers.

Smiling and Nodding

Looking impassively at the other person with a "still face" discourages communication. Smile and nod occasionally to reassure the other person that you are friendly, interested, and listening. In conversation, smiling and nodding function as minimal encouragers (2.4.4). Although in most cultures, smiling is understood as a sign of warmth, sometimes—in Japan, for example—smiling may indicate discomfort or even hostility. In France, where smiling is considered inappropriate unless there is something to smile about, smiling at dogs or other pets is always acceptable, but smiling when you are buying a newspaper or sandwich is considered strange. When in doubt about cultural norms, "mirror" the body language of others, imitating their nonverbal behaviors. Be careful not to overdo it. At the reference desk, a pleasant

---

EXERCISE

What's Wrong?

Harold Garfinkel is a social scientist who encourages his students to investigate taken-for-granted social norms by sending them out on assignments where they deliberately break these norms (e.g., standing in an elevator so that they face the inside wall instead of the door). Use a version of the Garfinkel technique to investigate the power of the nod during a social interaction. For this exercise, pick someone whom you can trust not to be permanently offended. While this person is telling you a story about something completely uncontroversial, shake your head from side to side in a tiny but perceptible movement. Keep this up. Watch the effect that it has on the other person's ability to continue with the story.

---

expression on your face is important, but a continuous smile would seem strange. And when someone is revealing personal information, such as an illness of a family member, a concerned expression is more appropriate than a smile.

Nodding the head up and down is also a positive signal, although in some cultures the side-to-side nod means agreement and the vertical nod means disagreement. If you usually listen impassively, try nodding occasionally. Again, don't overdo it. While an occasional single nod of the head encourages people to say more, successive nods get them to stop because they think you want to interrupt.

Try to be aware of how you might look to others who are deciding whether to approach you. An inadvertent grimace or frown, perhaps at an irksome e-mail request, might be misinterpreted by the user while looking up occasionally and smiling at people whose eye you catch may encourage them to step forward with a question.

Pausing

Pausing is really a kind of nonverbal behavior, although it is often combined with speaking and listening skills. A pause can take the place of a conversational turn. Pausing is defined as intentional silence in place of a statement or question. For example, when it is your turn to speak, you wait, saying nothing until the other person speaks again.

The effect of pausing varies according to culture. In some cultures, lengthy and frequent pauses are taken as a sign of inattention and boredom. In other cultures, such as some Native American cultures, pauses are a sign of respect, an indication that the listener is taking the speaker's last statement seriously and considering a worthy answer. It is important to know what effect your pauses may have in different situations. In mainstream North American culture, effective pausing enhances an interviewer's listening skills and conveys attentiveness to the interviewee. A pause may function as an encourager or a probe. It says to the interviewee, "I'm listening," and "Go on." Because the interviewer relinquishes her turn at the conversation, the interviewee is likely to expand on what he has previously said. For example:

Did You Know?
Nonverbal communication is extremely powerful. We make instant judgments about people on the basis of quick impressions. But we must take care when interpreting the nonverbal behaviors of library users, especially those from other cultures. The meaning of nonverbal behavior varies among different cultural groups. Don't assume that nonverbal behavior in one culture means the same thing as it would in your own culture. For example, in a branch library in New York City a librarian made the "thumbs-up" gesture at the end of a difficult reference encounter to celebrate success at finding the answer. The library user, an Iranian, was deeply offended—this gesture is considered obscene in Iran (and in other Middle Eastern countries).

Did You Know?
According to experiments on behavior in the online search interview, effective pausing is more difficult to learn than one might think. Pauses longer than ten seconds may confuse the user who becomes unsure whether the interviewer is still listening. Very short pauses tend to be unnoticeable. It seems that some librarians habitually pause while considering what the user has said or deciding what to do next. But pausing too often or too long is awkward (Auster and Lawton, 1984).

Wait before Interrupting

Radford (1999) found that librarians frequently interrupt library users before they have finished asking a reference question. Usually librarians interrupt to ask a question or to make a suggestion. Become conscious of this urge to interrupt and discipline yourself to wait for users to finish their statements. If you do, you often can avoid misunderstanding, thereby saving time in the long run.

Did You Know?

In some North American Indian nations, people deliberately leave a silence between a statement or question and the response as a sign that they are considering the answer very carefully. Many Euro-Americans feel uneasy with this prolonged pause and tend to react by repeating or talking louder.

EXERCISE

Silence Is Golden

A common problem in the reference interview is asking a perfectly good open question and then spoiling it by rushing in with the answer instead of waiting for the user to reply. For example: "What kind of legal information do you want? Is it criminal law?" Try this experiment. For a period of, say, half-an-hour on the reference desk, make a conscious effort to use pauses. Ask a question and then wait. One or two seconds of blank air time may seem endless to you, but you are not on the radio. So just wait. Some people need more time than others to think about what they want to say. Note what happens after the pauses. How, if at all, do these interviews differ from ones where you are not making a conscious effort to wait for the user's answer?

Librarian: Tell me about your research.

User: Well, my field is geography.

Librarian: (*pause, combined with encouraging body language such as smiling and nodding*)

User: The project I'm working on right now is a stratigraphy of a particular area on the shoreline of Lake Superior.

Librarian: (*pause, plus nodding*)

User: And you see, what I'm really looking for is [explains].

Pause after you ask your question and wait for the answer. When librarians are first practicing the skill of effective question-asking (3.2.1), a common problem is remembering to pause long enough to give the interviewee time to formulate an answer. Hence they may ask an open question, "What sort of thing are you looking for?" and then answer it themselves, "A reference book?" Used correctly, pausing is a skill that helps reduce the common mistakes of talking too much, cutting the user off, interrupting, and answering one's own question. The skills that supplement pausing are restatement, encouragers, and nonverbal skills that show attentiveness.

ANALYZE THIS REFERENCE TRANSACTION

Case 4: Wait for the answer.

User: Hi.

Librarian: Hi.

User: I'm doing a project on social problems in undeveloped regions. And I've looked under the different social problems—like divorce and suicide and robbery and all I could find is case studies.

Librarian: Okay. (*minimal encourager*)

User: And I have to relate this topic to native—native people.

Librarian: Native people. (*acknowledgment*) Okay, what have you done so far? Where have you looked? Just in the catalog? (*two open questions followed by a closed question*)

User: Mhm.

Librarian: This topic is going to be more in magazines, as opposed to books, okay? [Shows the user how the periodical index works.]

(Dewdney, "Native People")

Comment: The librarian asked an excellent question, "What have you done so far?" and then got panicky and started answering the question herself instead of pausing and waiting for the answer. Some users are put off by this catalog question as it implies that they should have done something before asking for help. A better way to phrase this might be "Have you had a chance to get started yet?" Notice that narrowing the question down to a closed question which asked if the user had looked "[j]ust in the catalog" ended up producing no useful information (see section 3.2.1).

Posture

Your posture, or the way you hold your body, signals your mood and attitude. Slumping is read as a sign of fatigue, discouragement, or boredom. Rigidity suggests nervousness or disagreement. Closed postures, such as crossing your arms or orienting yourself away from the other person, tend to convey detachment or disagreement, regardless of your actual words. On the other hand, a symmetrical mirroring of the other person's posture or orientation conveys approval or agreement. When you send mixed messages, people believe your nonverbal cues more than what you say.

Whenever possible, it is a good idea to be at eye level with the user. This may mean standing up and moving toward a user. Or it may mean inviting a user to sit down beside you at the computer as you demonstrate how to use an e-resource or find something in the online catalog.

2.4.3 Acknowledgment

Verbal acknowledgment is a skill that involves restating or "playing back" the content of what the other person has just said. You restate a key part of the previous statement using either the same words or a paraphrase. This restatement encourages the other person to confirm, correct, or explain further. Thus you might respond to the request, "Do you have anything on lupus?" by repeating "lupus, uh-huh" or "You want material on the illness lupus." This gives the user the chance to make a correction if you misheard, "No, lupines, the flower."

EXAMPLES

User: I need some information on transportation.

Librarian: We have quite a bit of information on transportation [or simply "Transportation, uh-huh"].

User: I need some information on Vitamin D.

Librarian: Vitamin E, uh-huh.

User: No, actually Vitamin D. I'm doing a project on additives to milk and its role in reducing rickets.

User: Have you anything on shingles?

Librarian: Shingles for roofing? (*paraphrasing to ensure a shared understanding and to give the user a chance to correct*) [The skill of acknowledgment will help you distinguish among homonyms that sound the same such as Wales/whales or Tolkien book/talking book.]

User: No, viral shingles; it's a disease.

User: I'm doing a study on transcription factors related to adipocyte differentiation. I'm especially interested in any recent research on the role of Wnt.

Librarian: Uh-huh. You're doing research on transcription factors related to—what was that again?" [With complicated statements, the librarian may catch only part of what's been said. That's okay.

A QUICK TIP

Trunk Lean

To convey relaxed attentiveness during a conversation, stand or sit so that you are leaning slightly toward the other person. This is called "trunk lean."

Did You Know?

Radford (1998) applied the earlier work of Albert Mehrabian (1971) to library reference encounters in academic settings. Mehrabian developed the "Immediacy Principle," asserting that people move toward others who exhibit nonverbal immediacy behaviors such as eye contact, movement towards, forward lean, and turning the body towards the other. These movements may be very subtle, but are easily read by others. Radford found that users were much more likely to approach librarians who were showing these immediacy behaviors than those who were not.

EXERCISE

Acknowledgment

Remember that acknowledgment involves repeating, or sometimes paraphrasing, the keyword(s) of the user's question to make sure that you have heard and understood. What could you say to acknowledge a user who asks one of the following questions:

1. Where are your travel books?
2. Where is the *Globe*? [a newspaper]
3. I'm looking for something on China. [Check your own mastery of the skill of acknowledgment. Was your response useful in clarifying what kind of china is wanted? If not, what could you say instead? Look again at the shingles example.]
4. Do you have recent information on viruses? [Are you sure you know what kind of viruses are meant?]

The procedure is to repeat what you can and ask for repetition on what you missed. In really complex statements, it may take two or three attempts before you have the whole statement. You may also need to ask for the spelling of unfamiliar terms such as Wnt.]

Most people already use acknowledgment in certain situations, such as repeating a phone number that they have been told. So it is not a question of learning an entirely new skill but of using consciously a skill

---

ANALYZE THIS REFERENCE TRANSACTION

Case 5: Acknowledgment

User 1: They say you're an expert on symbols.

Librarian: They must have been lying. [Laughs.] What exactly would you like? (*open question*)

User: Are you familiar with the Roman symbol for authority—the battle-axes and staves, bound into a bundle?

Librarian: You said it was a Roman symbol. (*acknowledgment*) Mythological? (*closed question*)

User: No. The real thing.

Librarian: And it's a battle symbol, is it? (*acknowledgment*)

User: No, it's a symbol of authority that they displayed in the Senate of Rome. They carried it in front of official parades. It's the symbol of authority in ancient Rome.

(Dewdney, "Roman Symbols")

User 2: I want recordings of church bells.

Librarian: Actual church bells playing? (*acknowledgment*)

User: Yes.

Librarian: Do you have something specific in mind? [The librarian might have hoped that the user would understand this as an open question, "What do you have in mind?" but the user interprets it literally, as a *closed question*.]

User: No.

Librarian: Just the sound of church bells playing? (*acknowledgment*)

User: Yes, anything to do with bells, actually, would be okay.

Librarian: Anything to do with bells. (acknowledgment) Okay. Let me just check the call number. Oh . . . handbell music. Chimes at dusk. Wedding Chimes.

User: All right!

(Dewdney, "Church Bells")

Comment: In both interviews, the librarian repeats the skill of acknowledgment through several turns. In the first case, acknowledgment allows the librarian to correct the erroneous deduction that the user wanted a battle symbol. Although he has not recognized the user's description of the Roman *fasces*, he now has a very good description in the user's last statement and the new clue, "symbol of authority." In the second case, the librarian repeats the initial restatement "just the sound of church bells playing" and is rewarded by an expanded definition of bells. Acknowledgment is especially effective at the beginning of an interview.

already employed in other communication contexts. Use the skill of acknowledgment routinely, especially at the beginning of the reference interview as your response to the user's initial question. Restatement is an excellent quick way to indicate that you have been listening (see section 2.4.5) and helps to establish a good climate of communication. In acknowledging, follow these guidelines:

- Be brief. A phrase or even just one word is often enough. You don't want to parrot back everything that's been said.
- Use a matter-of-fact, accepting tone. Responding with an upward intonation ("Vitamin E?") may convey amazement or even disapproval about what has just been said.
- If there is any ambiguity in what is being asked for (e.g., Turkey, Chile, *Grease*), then provide a paraphrase to clarify between different meanings, such as "Turkey, the country?" or "Chili, the sauce" or "*Grease*, the musical?" In these cases, it is not enough simply to repeat Turkey or *Grease*.

2.4.4 Minimal Encouragers

In conversations, there is a tacit rule that people should take turns speaking, but a very brief remark will count as a turn. When you are conducting an interview, your turn can be very short. You do not need to respond at length to every statement made. Examples of useful minimal encouragers are short phrases such as these:

- Uh-huh.
- I see.
- Go on.
- That's interesting.
- Tell me more.
- Anything else?
- Can you give me an example?

These phrases, which encourage the other person to say more, are nonjudgmental and free of content. Let the other person describe the problem, and use encouragers, along with appropriate body language, to indicate that you are interested and are listening.

EXAMPLE

User: I'm trying to find some books for my neighbor.

Librarian: Yes, uh-huh [in an interested tone].

User: You see, she's just broken her ankle and can't get out, but she needs some mysteries to read while she's stuck at home.

Librarian: Mysteries, I see. [Here the librarian uses *acknowledgment* followed by an *encourager*.]

User: Yes, she especially likes mysteries written by women.

Librarian: Right. [Here the librarian *nods*, along with using a *minimal encourager*.]

User: And of course Patricia Cornwell is a favorite, but she's read all of Cornwell. I know she doesn't like those cozy English mysteries. She finds them too tame.

EXERCISE

Attending Skills

Find a partner with whom you can role-play a conversation. Ask your partner to talk about a topic in which he or she is personally interested. Your role is to listen and to encourage your partner to say more by sticking as much as possible just to the attending skills of eye contact, smiling, nodding, and using minimal encouragers. Which of these skills do you feel comfortable doing? Which ones need more practice? Change roles. How does your partner's use of attending skills affect your role as speaker?

ANALYZE THIS REFERENCE TRANSACTION

Case 6: With minimal encouragers, a little goes a long way.

User: I'm looking up Noranda Mines.

Librarian: Mhm. (*encourager*)

User: And trying to find an address for it.

Librarian: Okay, anything else? (*encourager*)

User: I'm looking for pulp and paper companies. There's two companies—but the second one is missing [from this directory]. There's another pulp and paper mill missing.

Librarian: Mhm. (*encourager*)

User: I don't know the name of the second one. Maybe it's not here. And they just recently changed the name.

Librarian: Oh. Okay. (*encourager*)

User: So I'm not sure. I think it's called the James Bay Project. This mill was going under, so the company bought them out and changed the name to the James Bay Project.

Librarian: Where was it located? (*open question*)

User: Near Marathon.

Librarian: Near Marathon. Okay. (*acknowledgment*) [Librarian finds contact information for Noranda Mines and also for a second pulp and paper mill just outside Marathon.]

Comment: The user wants to know contact information to apply for a job in these two pulp and paper mills. This librarian got a lot of mileage from using minimal encouragers and letting the user talk. She needed to use only one open question, "Where was it located?" to fill in a gap. All the rest of the information was volunteered by the user.

(Dewdney, "Noranda")

2.4.5 Listening

Good listening is the foundation of all oral communication. A good listener is always engaged in selecting, interpreting, remembering, making guesses and trying to confirm them, coming to conclusions, and checking out the conclusions by playing them back to the speaker. Naturally listening is crucial throughout the interview, but it is especially important in the first thirty seconds when you are setting the foundation for the rest of the interview.

Effective listening involves a variety of things that are interconnected:

1. You have to be actually listening, not just pretending to listen. Listening is not the same thing as not talking. Instead of really listening, people who are not talking might be: daydreaming; waiting for their turn to talk; or thinking about something else, such as sources or search tactics, or, for that matter, what they are planning to cook for dinner.

2. You have to let the other person know that you are listening. This is where nonverbal attending skills come in, such as eye contact, nodding, acknowledging, and using minimal encouragers.

3. Allow time for the user to answer your question. Don't be afraid of silence (2.4.2).

4. Listen for what is important to the user. When a user describes a complex information need, you may feel overwhelmed by the amount of detail that you get. Skilled interviewers use active listening techniques to focus on the elements of the situation that the user considers most important.

5. Check out that you have heard and understood by restatement, followed by a checkout (3.2.4). For example you could say, "So what you really need is a table showing the breakdown of domestic wine production by year, is that right?"

6. Don't interrupt or try to speed things up by finishing the user's sentence. You may think that you have heard the question before and that you know what is wanted, but you may be wrong. Interrupting is a way of exercising power, especially over people considered of lower status, and is not a good way of showing respect.

Active listening is an effective technique for defusing angry or upset people in many situations including the reference desk (Rothwell, 2000). It requires giving full attention to the person speaking—listening and using attending skills. Here are some examples of situations that require active listening—listening, so to speak, between the lines to understand the emotions behind the words.

Example 1: A user wants you to find information on a journal database. A line of other users is also waiting for your help.

User's feeling: Scared, frustrated, anxious, bewildered, or lacking in confidence.

Typical response: "Try this and then let me know if you still need help."

Active listening response: "I know that computers can be really frustrating. Here, let me show you how to get started. I need to help the others who are waiting, but I can stop back in a few minutes and see how you are doing."

Example 2: A user gets upset when referred to another department or service desk.

User's feeling: Frustrated, worried, and disappointed.

Typical response: "The information you need is only found in the Periodicals Department."

Active listening response: "Sounds like you are worried about getting the runaround again. Let me call the Periodicals Department to let them know you are coming and to make sure that they can help."

EXERCISE

Don't Listen

With a partner, role-play a conversation in which your partner is describing an event that happened recently and you play the role of the worst listener that you can possibly be. Recruit a third person as an observer who records all the ways in which you showed poor listening behavior. Here are some possibilities: interrupting, changing the subject, fidgeting, looking away, drumming your fingers, yawning, looking at your watch, remaining impassive, and making no response to what was said. After three minutes, stop and ask the observer to report all the poor listening behaviors recorded. Ask your partner how these behaviors made him or her feel. Trade roles, so that all three people have a turn with each role.

> ### WHAT USERS SAID ABOUT NOT LISTENING
>
> - She assumed I wanted a child's book on turtles because my twelve-year-old son was with me.
> - Even when I asked her questions, she was more preoccupied with searching than with paying any attention to what I was saying.... What was not helpful was her indifference to any comments I made.
> - I felt she had not listened to what I had said.... I was usually interrupted before I could actually complete most of my sentences.
> - When I asked for books on paper-making, she asked, "Are you interested in recycling?" I said, "No, I want to make paper." She said, "We don't have too much on paper-making. I think you'll find more in recycling books. I'll give you two call numbers."...Under call number 696 (Pulp and paper technology) were books on making anything but paper. Under call number 363.7282 were books on toxic waste and pollution.
>
> (Library Visit Study)

Example 3: The user blames the reference librarian when a new item, listed in the online catalog, is not yet ready for use.

> User's feeling: Disappointed, frustrated.
>
> Typical response: "It's not my fault; I can't do anything until the Cataloguing Department releases the item."
>
> Active listening response: "I know it is frustrating. It frustrates me too because I like to give users what they need. In the meantime, perhaps there is something else that will work for you?"

2.5 Approachability in Virtual Spaces

The text-based environment of virtual reference (VR)—whether e-mail, live chat, or instant messaging—requires the adaptation of most of the nonverbal cues that we have just discussed in the context of the face-to-face (FtF) reference interview. Approachability in VR environments is still important, but it is conveyed differently. Locating the button for virtual reference service in a prominent place on your library's Web site, for example, is one way of conveying approachability online (6.1.1)

Projecting an approachable presence in e-mail is more difficult than in live chat where the more interactive back-and-forth conversation in real time mimics the FtF reference encounter. In both e-mail and live chat it is a good idea to use a personal greeting as well as a personal farewell. In chat, there is likely to be an automatic scripted welcome such as, "Welcome to our virtual reference service. A librarian will be with you very soon." But the virtual librarian should also add a personal greeting such as, "Hello, Jamal, you have a very interesting question for me!" Whether or not you can see the user's name depends on the live chat interface that your VR service uses. But if you can address the VR user by name, it is a personal touch, especially appreciated by younger users.

MAKING YOUR VR SERVICE APPROACHABLE

Library Visit Study participants who evaluated e-mail and chat services offered many suggestions for increasing the approachability of VR service. Here are some ideas to consider:

Prominence or visibility

- Give the service a name such as "Ask a Librarian" and use it consistently.
- Don't call your service different names in different places on your Web site.
- Provide a single button that is clearly a link and use the same button throughout your Web site. It should be obvious and accessible from the home page as well as from every other page of your Web site.
- Differentiate the link from others on the page.
- All links to the service should lead to the same place.
- Make sure your users can come across the service serendipitously. Not all users know the service exists, and so will not look for it if it's buried deep in drop-down menus.

Ease of use of the service

- Distance from the library's home page link to the service should be no more than two clicks. The first click can lead to a single page that provides a brief description of the services and contains links to supporting information. The second click should lead directly to the question form for e-mail reference or to the chat service.
- Users should be able to bypass the explanatory page if they wish.

Supporting information

Explanatory information (which can be on a FAQ page) should describe the services offered and note the response times, service specifications, and limits to service, if any. It should indicate the types of questions answered (don't just name the types—how can users know if a question is "ready-reference" or not—but provide sample questions). Also provide an archive of previously asked questions with responses (with identifying information removed).

Radford (2006) and Radford and Connaway (2005–2008) have identified a range of text-based strategies used in live chat transcripts to replace, and in some cases go beyond, the nonverbal cues available in face-to-face communication. Radford (2006) defined "Re-representation of Nonverbal Cues" as the use of text characters or characteristics such as punctuation, emoticons, font, or abbreviations to represent nonverbal cues available in the face-to-face interaction. Here are the categories of text-based strategies that were found with definitions and examples from live chat transcripts:

- All Caps: UPPERCASE, can be a FLAME or used just for emphasis (e.g., use EXACTLY these terms).
- Alpha-numeric Shortcuts: Abbreviating phrases by using a combination of letters and numbers (e.g., L8r [later], G2G [got to go], ne1 [anyone]). *(continued)*

Did You Know?

Although many nonverbal cues are missing in VR, Joseph B. Walther (2006) says that chronemics (i.e., use of time) is one element of nonverbal communication that does exist in e-mail, live chat, and instant messaging modes. Users don't know how long it will take for someone to return an e-mail, but they do pay close attention to the amount of time they have to wait. The importance of answering live chat VR quickly is underscored by the frequency of abrupt endings when users sign off before the librarian has had a chance to respond. Encouragingly Radford and Connaway (2005–2008) have found that the large majority of live chat VR queries were picked up in ninety seconds or less. Chat transcripts also provide evidence that the users expect instant responses to their queries and may become impatient if they do not "hear back" from the librarian in a timely fashion. Users may type a question like "r u there?" or "hello?" if they think that too much time has gone by in chat. Chat savvy librarians use the ellipsis to let users know they are working on the query by typing "...more" or "...still searching." This technique of "word contact" instead of eye contact is highly recommended.

- Asterisk or Symbol for Emphasis: Demarcating a word for emphasis or to make a spelling repair through use of asterisk, (e.g., those who *are* affiliated or sarry *sorry).

- Phrase Abbreviations: Using letters for phrase abbreviations (e.g., LOL [laughing out loud], BRB [be right back]).

- Spelling Out Nonverbal Behaviors: Spelling out words for facial expressions or nonverbal behaviors (e.g., Grin, wink wink, ha ha).

- Ellipsis: Using ellipsis to indicate "word contact" (e.g., "More..." or "still searching...").

- Emoticons (aka smileys): Using text characters to represent facial expressions (e.g., ;-) for a wink).

- Punctuation or Repeated Punctuation for Emphasis: Generally involves the exclamation point (e.g., Wow! Thank you VERY MUCH!!!!!).

ANALYZE THESE REFERENCE TRANSACTIONS

Case 7: Can users find your VR service?

Participants in the Library Visit Study who asked questions of chat or e-mail services were frequently surprised at how difficult it was to find these services. Here are some of their comments:

- XX Public Library does a dismal job of advertising and promoting the service. In fact nowhere on the site is it even mentioned that it provides virtual reference to users, let alone a brief description of virtual reference or a set of instruction of how to access or use the service.

- I was looking on the XX University Library home page for the "Ask a Librarian" button, but there was none. Then I realized right in front of me, on the home page it said in huge letters, "got questions, get answers!" But it wasn't obvious this was a button/link—it looked instead like decoration. When I clicked on it, it brought me to a page entitled, "Academic Librarians by Department." I thought I'd come to the wrong page. This looked like a contact page, not an "Ask a Librarian" page. I went back to the home page. I saw there was a little box with pictures of librarians entitled, "Meet your Librarian." I thought maybe this was it. I clicked on it, and it brought me to the same contact page again. I went back to the home page and looked through all the top menu items, with their drop-down menus. I found under Services a link to "Ask a Librarian," and clicked on this thinking it would bring me to an e-mail form, but once again I was on the same "Academic Libraries by Department" page. I then realized this was the only way to ask a question virtually. From this point I wasn't sure who to e-mail. My question related to poetry, so I thought I could either e-mail the English subject librarian or e-mail it as general inquiry.

- Because of the seemingly endless number of pages it took to get to the actual question form, this was not a simple process for the first-time user.

- [I] was able to locate [the link to the VR service] buried in the middle of the "Quick Search" navigation bar on the left hand side of the page in incredibly small font between the e-journal and single search link.

(Cont'd.)

ANALYZE THESE REFERENCE TRANSACTIONS *(Continued)*

- [I] received this message, "The Ask A Librarian Chat Reference Service is now closed. Please refer to the posted hours to the left. Alternately you may choose to send us an e-mail query using the button provided." [No button was provided. The XX University Library's chat service advises users only that "the service is not available during the weekend and late in the evening."] The reference desk is open on the weekend, and simply providing a phone number would help students outside the library access reference services during these times.

Comment: This last example illustrates that users must be offered flexibility because a phone call might solve an immediate problem. In this and other examples, too little information was provided, but sometimes too much information is given—e.g., the "seemingly endless" pages of explanatory pages that users had to click through every time they used the service. Users often found themselves playing hide-and-seek as they tried to imagine under what drop-down menu the link to the VR reference service was put. As one frustrated participant said about finally locating the service in the "Ask Us" subcategory of the Help menu, "While this may seem logical to some, it was surprisingly difficult to find."

For discussion: Brainstorm all the various causes of problems for users in accessing VR reference service in these examples. What, specifically, could be done to fix each problem you have identified? How many of these problems are also present in your own library's virtual service? How widespread do you think these problems are?

2.6 Annotated References

2.6.1 General

Agosto, Denise E., and Sandra Hughes-Hassell. 2005. "People, Places, and Questions: An Investigation of the Everyday Life Information-Seeking Behaviors of Urban Young Adults." *Library and Information Science Research* 27, no. 2: 141–163. Research focusing on urban teens reports that they have a heavy preference for people as information sources (including friends and family), but hold unfavorable views of libraries and librarians. Includes questions for librarians to consider when designing services for urban teens.

Agosto, Denise E., and Sandra Hughes-Hassell. 2006. "Toward a Model of the Everyday Life Information Needs of Urban Teenagers, part 1: Theoretical Model." *Journal of the American Society for Information Science and Technology* 57, no. 10: 1394–1403. Presents a theoretical model, built on a research base, that describes the information needs of urban teens.

Durrance, Joan, C. 1989. "Reference Success: Does the 55% Rule Tell the Whole Story?" *Library Journal* 114, no. 7 (April 15): 31–36.

Durrance, Joan. 1995. "Factors that Influence Reference Success: What Makes Questioners Willing to Return?" *The Reference Librarian* 49/50: 243–265.

LaGuardia, Cheryl. 1996. *Teaching the New Library: A How-To-Do-It Manual for Planning and Designing Instructional Programs.* New York: Neal-Schuman. For a discussion of helping users in the electronic arcade, see pages 109–134.

Liu, Mengxiong, and Bernice Redfern. 1997. "Information-Seeking Behavior of Multicultural Students: A Case Study at San Jose State University." *College & Research Libraries* 58, no. 4: 348–354. Reports on an important study of cultural differences at the reference desk.

Manusov, Valerie, and Marie L. Radford. 1993. *The User-Friendly Service Desk: Improving Staff's Nonverbal Behavior*. Rutgers University, NJ, April 8, 1993. Handout on types of nonverbal communication developed for this workshop.

Massey-Burzio, Virginia. 1998. "From the Other Side of the Reference Desk: A Focus Group Study." *The Journal of Academic Librarianship* 24, no. 3: 208–215.

Orange County Library System. Orlando, Florida. Available: www.ocls.info (accessed December 1, 2008).

Radford, Marie L. 1996. "Communication Theory Applied to the Reference Encounter." *The Library Quarterly* 66, no. 2 (April): 123–137.

Radford, Marie L., and Lynn Silipigni Connaway. 2007. "'Screenagers' and Live Chat Reference: Living Up to the Promise." *Scan* 26, no. 1: 31–39. Details focus groups with teens that reveals their information behaviors and communication preferences and their use of libraries and opinions of FtF and VR.

Reference and User Services Association. 2004. "Guidelines for Behavioral Performance of Reference and Information Service Professionals." Available: www.ala.org/ala/mgrps/divs/rusa/resources/guidelines/guidelinesbehavioral .cfm (accessed December 6, 2008). Includes techniques for showing approachability and interest, listening/inquiring, searching and providing follow-up.

Swope, Mary Jane, and Jeffrey Katzer. 1972. "Silent Majority: Why Don't They Ask Questions?" *RQ* 12: 161–166. Classic, often-cited study that examines why students at academic libraries didn't ask their reference questions at the reference desk.

2.6.2 Microtraining

Ivey, Allen E., and Mary Bradford Ivey. 2003. *Intentional Interviewing and Counseling: Facilitating Client Development in a Multicultural Society*. 5th ed. Pacific Grove, CA: Thomson/Brooks/Cole. This classic textbook on microcounseling provides a structured approach for learning the hierarchy of microskills.

Jennerich, Elaine Z. 1974. "Microcounseling in Library Education." Unpublished doctoral dissertation. Pittsburgh, PA: University of Pittsburgh Graduate School of Library and Information Sciences.

2.6.3 Nonverbal Behavior: General

Adler, Ronald B., and Jeanne Marquardt Elmhorst. 2008. *Communicating at Work: Principles and Practices for Business and the Professions*. 9th ed. New York: McGraw-Hill. Includes an expanded consideration of culture and gender. Chapter 2, "Communication, Culture and Work," provides an excellent overview of diversity in the workplace, broadly interpreted. Chapter 3 focuses on "Listening" skills. Chapter 4, "Verbal and Nonverbal Messages" deals with personal space and distance, appearance and the physical environment as well as body language.

Birdwhistell, Raymond L. 1970. *Kinesics and Context: Essays on Body Motion Communication*. Philadelphia: University of Pennsylvania Press. A classic work on body language originally published in 1940.

Burgoon, Judee K., David B. Buller, and W. Gill Woodall. 1989. *Nonverbal Communication: The Unspoken Dialogue*. New York: Harper & Row. Excellent review of all aspects of nonverbal communication from a scholarly perspective. Extensive bibliography.

Burgoon, Judee K., and Laura K. Guerrero. 1994. "Nonverbal Communication." In *Human Communication*, 3rd ed. (122–171), edited by Michael Burgoon, Frank G. Hunsaker, and Edwin J. Dawson. Thousand Oaks, CA: Sage Publications. A scholarly review.

Burgoon, Judee K., and Gregory D. Hoobler. 2002. "Nonverbal Signals." In *Handbook of Interpersonal Communication*, 3rd ed. (240–299), edited by Mark L. Knapp and John A. Daly. Thousand Oaks, CA: Sage Publications. An overview of scholarly research, with an extensive bibliography.

Carter, Kimberley A. 2003. "Type Me How You Feel: Quasi-nonverbal Cues in Computer-mediated Communication." *Etc.* 60, no. 1: 29–39. Analysis of how emotions are communicated in the instant messaging environment.

DeVito, Joseph A., and Michael L. Hecht, eds. 1990. *The Nonverbal Communication Reader*. Prospect Heights, IL: Waveland Press. Accessible overview of nonverbal communication with individual chapters written by experts.

Giles, Howard, and Richard L. Street Jr. 1994. "Communication Characteristics and Behavior." In *Handbook of Interpersonal Communication*, 2nd ed. (103–161), edited by Mark L. Knapp and Gerald Miller. Thousand Oaks, CA: Sage Publications. A scholarly review of research on individual differences (e.g., gender, culture, socioeconomic status and psychological variables) and communication behavior.

Hall, Edward T. 1973, c1959. *The Silent Language*. Garden City, NY: Doubleday. A classic book on cross-cultural differences in the way cultures experience time and space.

Hunt, Gary T. 1985. *Effective Communication*. Englewood Cliffs, NJ: Prentice-Hall. Chapter 5 on nonverbal communication includes exercises and questions for discussion.

Ivey, Allen E., and Mary Bradford Ivey. 2003. *Intentional Interviewing and Counseling: Facilitating Client Development in a Multicultural Society*, 5th ed. Pacific Grove, CA: Thomson/Brooks/Cole. This latest edition is particularly good on how culture and gender affect nonverbal behavior.

Knapp, Mark L., and Judith A. Hall. 2005. *Nonverbal Communication in Human Interaction*, 6th ed. Belmont, CA: Wadsworth. An edited compendium of readings on nonverbal communication with chapters written by noted scholars.

Manusov, Valerie, and Miles L. Patterson, eds. 2006. *The Sage Handbook of Nonverbal Communication*. Thousand Oaks, CA: Sage Publications. Compendium of recent research in nonverbal communication from preeminent scholars from a variety of disciplines. Includes lengthy and comprehensive bibliographies.

Mehrabian, Albert. 1971. *Silent Messages*. Belmont, CA: Wadsworth. A seminal book on all aspects of nonverbal communication. Includes detail on the immediacy principle and immediacy behaviors that add to approachability.

Newman, Helen M. 1990. "The Sounds of Silence in Communicative Encounters." In *The Nonverbal Communication Reader* (266–275), edited by Joseph A. DeVito and Michael L. Hecht. Prospect Heights, IL: Waveland Press. Chapter on how silence communicates in an edited book on all aspects of nonverbal behavior.

Tannen, Deborah. 2001. *You Just Don't Understand: Women and Men in Conversation*. New York: Quill. A popular, easy-to-read book by an expert on gender differences in communication.

Tannen, Deborah. 2001. *Talking from 9 to 5: How Women's and Men's Conversational Styles Affect Who Gets Heard, Who Gets Credit, and What Gets Done at Work*. New York: Quill. Popular follow-up to You Just Don't Understand.

Walther, Joseph B. 2006. "Nonverbal Dynamics in Computer-Mediated Communication, or :(and the net :('s with you, :) and you :) Alone." In *The Sage Handbook of Nonverbal Communication* (461–479), edited by Valerie Manusov and Miles L. Patterson. Thousand Oaks, CA: Sage Publications. Chapter that traces the use of nonverbal communication in virtual environments. Includes review of current research and lengthy bibliography.

2.6.4 Listening

Jaffe, Clella Iles. 1995. *Public Speaking: A Cultural Perspective*. Belmont, CA: Wadsworth. Chapter 6, "Listening" (119–135), includes a section on active listening and also explains cultural differences in expectations about listening.

Jaffe, Clella Iles. 2007. *Public Speaking: Concepts and Skills for a Diverse Society*, 6th ed. Belmont, CA: Wadsworth. Chapter 4 is on "Effective Listening."

Rogers, Carl, and Richard Farson. 1973. "Active Listening." In *Readings in Interpersonal and Organizational Communication*, 2nd ed. (541–557), edited by Richard Huseman, Cal M. Logue, Dwight L. Freshley. Boston: Holbrook Press. This article introduced the term "active listening."

Rothwell, J. Dan. 2000. *In the Company of Others: An Introduction to Communication*. Mountain View, CA: Mayfield Publishing Co. Further applies active listening techniques with examples.

Smith, Nathan M., and Stephen D. Fitt. 1982. "Active Listening at the Reference Desk." *RQ* 21, no. 3 (spring): 247–249. Brief but still useful introduction to this important skill.

Wolvin, Andrew, and Carolyn Gwynn Coakley. 1996. *Listening*, 5th ed. Dubuque, IA: William. C. Brown. A basic textbook.

2.6.5 Initial Contacts and Nonverbal Behavior in the Library Context

Auster, Ethel, and Stephen B. Lawton. 1984. "Search Interview Techniques and Information Gain as Antecedents of User Satisfaction with Online Bibliographic Retrieval." *Journal of the American Society for Information Science* 35, no. 2: 90–103.

Devlin, Mary, and C. D. Green. 2000. "One Hundred Percent Communication." *Serials Librarian* 38, no. 1/2: 130–142. Provides insights on nonverbal communication in the library environment.

Eichman, Thomas Lee. 1978. "The Complex Nature of Opening Reference Questions." *RQ* 17, no. 3 (spring): 212–222.

Ellison, J. W. 1983. "How Approachable Are You as a Public Service Librarian?" *Unabashed Librarian* 46: 4–6. Lighthearted self-assessment quiz with a serious message on being approachable.

Fagan, Jody Condit, and Christina M. Desai. 2002/2003. "Communication Strategies for Instant Messaging and Chat Reference Services." *Reference Librarian* 79/80: 121–156. Provides practical advice on how to improve communication in VR.

Jennerich, Elaine Z., and Edward J. Jennerich. 1997. *The Reference Interview as a Creative Art*, 2nd ed. Littleton, CO: Libraries Unlimited. Includes a brief discussion of nonverbal skills.

Kazlauskas, Ed. 1976. "An Exploratory Study: A Kinesic Analysis of Academic Library Public Service Points." *Journal of Academic Librarianship* 2, no. 3 (May): 130–134. An early study of nonverbal behavior in libraries.

Lam, R. Errol. 1988. "The Reference Interview: Some Intercultural Considerations." *RQ* 27, no. 3 (spring): 390–393.

Page, Daniel. 2004. "The Importance of Nonverbal Communication in Information Services." *Library Mosaics* 15, no. 6: 11. Practical guide to understanding nonverbal communication in reference encounters.

Radford, Marie L. 1989. "Interpersonal Communication Theory in the Library Context: A Review of Current Perspectives." In *Library and Information Science Annual* (3–10), edited by Bohdan S. Wynar. Englewood, CO: Libraries Unlimited.

Radford, M. L. 1998. "Approach or Avoidance? The Role of Nonverbal Communication in the Academic Library User's Decision to Initiate a Reference Encounter." *Library Trends* 46, no. 4: 699–717. Research at academic reference desks involving interviews and observation of library users to discover how they make a decision as to which of two librarians to approach with a reference question when given the choice. Provides list of approachability behaviors, of which eye contact was the most frequently mentioned.

Radford, Marie L. 2005. "'She Looked at Me Like I was from Mars': Nonverbal Communication at the Service Desk." New Jersey State Library Staff Day, Trenton, NJ, April 29, 2005. Handout developed as part of this workshop.

Radford, Marie L. 2006. "Encountering Virtual Users: A Qualitative Investigation of Interpersonal Communication in Chat Reference." *Journal of the American Society for Information Science and Technology* 57, no. 8: 1046–1059. Research focusing on transcript analysis to reveal interpersonal dimensions present in live chat reference.

Radford, Marie L., and Lynn Silipigni Connaway. 2005–2008. "Seeking Synchronicity: Evaluating Virtual Reference Services from User, Non-User, and Librarian Perspectives." Funded by the Institute for Museum and Library Services, Rutgers, the State University of New Jersey, and OCLC, Online Computer Library Center. Grant Web site available: www.oclc.org/research/projects/synchronicity (accessed October 4, 2008).

Reference and User Services Association. 2004. "Guidelines for Behavioral Performance of Reference and Information Service Professionals." Available: www.ala.org/ala/mgrps/divs/rusa/resources/guidelines/guidelinesbehavioral.cfm (accessed December 6, 2008).

Warnement, Mary. 2003. "Size Matters: The Debate Over Reference Desk Height." *Libraries and the Academy* 3, no. 1: 79–87. An interesting examination of the controversy regarding whether reference desks act as barriers to users.

Westbrook, Lynn. 1984. "Catalog Failure and Reference Service: A Preliminary Study." *RQ* 24, no. 1: 82–90.

Finding Out What They Really Want to Know

3.1 Some Common Problems

After you have established contact, you still have to find out what the person wants to know. Whether the format is face-to-face, by telephone, or by live chat or e-mail, the next stage in the reference interview involves the use and integration of specific skills that will be considered in this chapter: open and closed questions, avoiding premature diagnosis, sense-making questions; paraphrasing and summarizing, and closure. A good reference librarian uses these skills intentionally and combines them in order to advance the purpose of the interview.

The use of the skills discussed in this chapter provides a solution to most of the commonly recurring problems identified in the reference interview. A small number of recurrent problems account for a large proportion of failed reference transactions. Elimination of these commonly occurring problems will go a long way toward getting beyond the notorious 55 percent success rate. The following example from the Library Visit Study illustrates many of these common problems. In this transaction, the user wanted information on jet lag. Here is her account of what happened as she reported it to a student-interviewer from the same reference class:

> **User:** I was trying to look normal—to take a normal user's approach to the library. . . So I said that I was looking for some books on flying. She [the staff member] just turned around and started punching on her terminal. . . . After a few minutes, I realized she wasn't going to ask me anything more, and I knew I'd get sent to the wrong section. So I said, "Well, actually, I'm looking for jet lag, but I don't know if it's in 'flying' or not." She just kept punching, but I intuited that she was getting another subject heading. And then she said that there's nothing on jet lag. Then she wrote down a number and tore it off the paper and gave it to me. . . . The specific number she gave me was a book on how to fly a light aircraft.

A QUICK TIP

Get to the Bottom Line

In the Mental Models Study, an experienced librarian described a transaction in which the user's initial question was: "Do you have any information about Canadian universities?" The librarian reported that when she heard this initial question her first thought was "That's not the bottom line. I had no idea what the real question was at that point." The rest of the interview went like this:

Librarian: Can you be more specific?

User: I'm looking for information on Middle East graduate studies.

Librarian: What kind of information on Middle East graduate studies do you need?

User: Scholarship information. The two programs I'm interested in are at Toronto and McGill.

When asked how she would explain or describe this type of reference situation to a new librarian who was just learning about reference service, the experienced librarian said, "Keep sitting in your chair until you figure out the bottom line of the question. I could have spent a lot of time looking for Middle East programs. This type of [initial] question is the next level down from, 'Where are your science books?' but is still too broad."

Interviewer: Did you ask again?

User: No, I didn't feel like going to her again. I was too upset.

Interviewer: Did you tell her anything?

User: No.

Interviewer: How did you feel?

User: I felt like dropping out [of library school]. . . . I thought, if that is the experience that the general public gets, they can't be getting the books they want, because I didn't get anywhere near my subject.

This case highlights five common problems with the staff member's role in the transaction:

1. **Failure to establish contact** by using appropriate attending skills (2.4.2). In this case, the terminal was a physical barrier. The staff member didn't speak to the user but spent her energy "punching on her terminal." The user's impression was that "her job was to punch on the machine . . . just somebody typing. It was just like getting an airline ticket—just like saying, 'I want to go to London,' and they start punching at the desk. . . . There was me and the machine, and she was the thing that punched in."

2. **Bypassing the reference interview** and accepting the initial question at face value (1.2)

3. **An unmonitored referral**, which occurs when the staff member refers the user to a source, either inside or outside the library, without taking any steps to check whether or not the user eventually gets a helpful answer. In this case, the user later reported, "We had to go back—my little girl had lost her toy—we went past her desk several times, but she didn't even ask if we'd found a book. I don't think she'd recognize me" (3.1.4).

4. **Failure to pay attention** to cues from the user that the transaction was going off-track. In this case, when the user realized that she was going to be packed off to the wrong section, she volunteered further clues about the information she wanted in order to get the staff member to search a different subject: "Well, actually, I'm looking for jet lag, but I don't know if it's in 'flying' or not." However the librarian was too busy punching to hear.

5. **Lack of knowledge of appropriate sources**. Searching the library online catalog for a keyword from the user's question should not be the default search strategy for every question. In this case, it would not have been difficult for the staff member to use an e-journal index to find a couple of articles written at various levels of specialization. (Reported in Dewdney and Ross, 1994, "Flying a Light Aircraft")

This reported reference transaction was the epitome of almost every possible deficiency. The staff member didn't smile or use appropriate eye contact, didn't conduct a reference interview (in fact spoke only one sentence in total), didn't listen, and didn't use a follow-up question to invite the user to return if the source provided wasn't satisfactory. In the following sections, we will look in more detail at some of these common problems.

3.1.1 "Without Speaking She Began to Type"

In about one-quarter of the Library Visit Study transactions, users reported that as soon as they asked their initial question, the staff member silently started to perform some mysterious activity, without asking any questions or providing any explanations. Most often, the silent activity was typing keywords from the user's initial question into a catalog search statement. After encountering so many observations in the Library Visit Study accounts along the lines of, "She didn't speak to me after I asked my question but just started punching the keys," or "He turned to the computer without explaining to me what he was doing," we began to think of this response as the "Without-speaking-she-began-to-type" maneuver as described in Dewdney and Ross (1994). Quite possibly the staff member was being very efficient in executing a search strategy, but the user doesn't know that, and isn't learning anything about the search process. Meanwhile, the staff member has started searching before doing anything to clarify the real question.

Especially in public libraries, the following scenario was a common occurrence as reported by users in the Library Visit Study. The user asked an initial question requesting, for example, information about the best scuba diving spots/information on optical character recognition, books about how to choose the right breed of dog/books on Richard Wagner, or instructions on how to plant a pine tree. Then, without asking any questions or providing any explanation, the staff member searched the catalog by typing the keywords of the user's initial statement: scuba diving/optical character recognition, dogs/Richard Wagner, or pine trees. By fixating on the catalog, the staff member in effect translated the user's request for "information" on a topic into a request for a book on that topic. A frequent automatic response, whatever the initial question, was to use the keywords from the user's initial question as a catalog search statement. Unfortunately this response prevents the staff member from thinking of other sources, often more appropriate, such as encyclopedia entries, periodical or e-journal articles, vertical file materials, or Web pages.

In the Library Visit Study, the user sometimes did end up with an acceptable answer when the librarian bypassed the reference interview, typed some keywords into the catalog search statement, and provided an unmonitored referral (3.1.4). This strategy might be successful if the requested information is addressed by a whole book on the topic and not just a section within a book on a broader topic, if the keywords in the user's initial statement happen to match the title of a book in the catalog, and if the book is on the shelf. For example, the person wanting to buy a dog was given a call number which got her within browsing distance of *The Puppy Report: How to Select a Healthy, Happy Dog*. In

Did You Know?
"Without speaking, she began to type…" is a common complaint of library users. Librarians need to acknowledge the users' questions, explaining, before they begin typing, that they are going to check the online catalog. Otherwise, users feel that the librarian may not have heard their question, because they don't know what the librarian is doing. For more examples from the user's point of view, see Dewdney and Ross (1994).

contrast, the staff member who was asked for information on optical character recognition was unsuccessful at finding anything in the online catalog through a keyword search and blamed the topic itself for being too technical. The user provided this account: "I stood there for several minutes while she searched. I could not see the screen and she did not ask me any questions. The silence grew a little awkward as I watched her mutter and purse her lips as her searches seemed to render negative results. Finally she said, 'This may be too technical.'"

In the case of optical character recognition and a number of other topics, the online catalog did not produce a match between the keywords of the user's request and the title of a book, and the user was told either that the information didn't exist at all, or that it didn't exist in this library and the user would have to go elsewhere—to another type of library, to another city, or to another type of institution altogether (Ross and Nilsen, 2000). A very frequent occurrence in public libraries, especially branch libraries, was that a match would be found between a keyword in the user's question and a book in the catalog, but it would turn out that the book in question was not available within the particular library either because it was at another branch or it was checked out. At this point the staff member would offer to recall the book or to have the book sent from another branch to be picked up later.

This way of handling the transaction got rid of the user for the time being but created additional work for the library system to handle the recall or transfer, and additional work for the user to return to the library to pick up a book that still may not answer the question. Remember that the librarian in these cases has chosen not to conduct a reference interview, and therefore has no way of knowing what kind of material is really needed to provide the help that the user needs. Conducting a proper reference interview is especially crucial when the user has to make a special return trip to pick up the requested material transferred from another location. The equivalent maneuver is evident in VR transactions. Copies of Library Visit Study e-mail and chat transactions show that librarians often respond very quickly to users' questions without conducting interviews. They send along a cheerful message, "Here are some sites that might help!" and a list of URLs. More often than not, the URLs are not identified by name or source. If the link doesn't work, the user probably won't be able to find the site (Nilsen, 2004, 2006).

3.1.2 Bypassing the Reference Interview

Reference interviews are conducted only half the time in face-to-face service encounters, a figure that has scarcely varied over twenty-five years of reported research. Only 50 percent of the FtF users in the Library Visit Study (Ross and Nilsen, 2000) reported that they were asked one or more questions intended to elicit further information about their informational need. The reference interview is even scarcer in virtual reference. In phase 3 (2003–2007) of the Library Visit Study, 150 users asked questions using e-mail and chat services at public and

ANALYZE THIS REFERENCE TRANSACTION

Case 8: What's wrong with this picture?

The following account described what happened when one of the users in the Library Visit Study visited a branch of a public library:

> At the desk, I asked, "I was wondering if you could help me find some information about degenerative muscle diseases." The librarian reacted to my question by grimacing somewhat. She was not responding in a negative way, but rather in a way that indicated that this question would be tricky. She did not comment at all however, which I found rather awkward. She began typing at her monitor and continued to type quite a long time without saying a word.... I felt so silly standing there silent that I finally spoke when she stopped typing for a moment. I said, "Are you searching for the subject, 'Degenerative Muscle Diseases?'" She said, "Yes, but I'm not finding anything with those terms."... Then she said that the only thing she could suggest I do would be to go to the stacks and try looking at the medical books. She told me the medical books were assigned the number 610.
>
> In the stacks I did manage to locate a dictionary of medical terms. The entry for Lou Gehrig's Disease indicated that it is Amyotrophic Lateral Sclerosis (ALS). I took this book to the desk and informed her that I had located a possibly useful search term. She told me that it really wouldn't be helpful to search using a term of such technical specificity.... Then she said nothing and seemed to be indicating that our search was at a dead end. I told her that none of the books in the stacks looked helpful for my particular interest. I asked if there might be books anywhere else that I could look at now that I knew the name of the disease. Her response was to say, "The only other place that you might find something would be the reference section over there. You can look up the same number, 610." (Ross and Dewdney, 1998)

Comment: Despite the fact that the user rated the answer that she obtained as a seven ("very helpful") on a seven-point scale, the user reported that she was "not sure" whether she would return to the same staff member with another question. A clue to the user's dissatisfaction is that she revised the question on the questionnaire, "How helpful was the answer given in terms of your own needs?" She deleted "answer *given*" and wrote in "answer *obtained*." Assuming that the user's report is accurate, how justified was she in finding the librarian unhelpful since, after all, she did find the information she wanted? What specific problems can you identify in the librarian's handling of this transaction? What could she have done instead?

Did You Know?

The 50 percent frequency of the reference interview in FtF settings has been a remarkably robust finding. According to Mary Jo Lynch's study (1978), the library staff member chose to conduct a reference interview in only about 50 percent of cases. Patricia Dewdney (1986) observed 851 transactions, of which she categorized 222 as *directional* questions. In the 629 remaining transactions classified as *reference transactions*, reference interviews took place in 332 cases, or 57 percent of the time. In the Library Visit Study, Ross and Nilsen (2000) reported 129 reference interviews in 261 FtF transactions—again almost exactly half.

In live chat reference, the results have been better, but still leave room for improvement. Only 50 percent (nineteen of thirty-eight) Library Visit Study chat transactions involved a reference interview. However, in the Seeking Synchronicity Project of 581 live chat transcripts, Radford and Connaway (2007a) found a higher percentage—75 percent (434) of the VR librarians asked clarifying questions. This result challenges the application of the 55 percent rule to live chat in which there are transcripts that can be systematically reviewed. Perhaps the possibility of review of one's transcripts by others (including by reference service administrators) is a factor in the better result. As they say, "More research is needed..."

academic libraries. Analysis of e-mails and chat transcripts revealed that reference interviews occurred in only twenty-five (16.7 percent) of these transactions. Of 112 e-mail transactions only six (5.4 percent) included a reference interview. Of the thirty-eight chat transactions, nineteen (50 percent) included a reference interview. This low percentage of chat interviews compares unfavorably with the 75 percent rate of chat interviews found in Radford and Connaway's study (2007a), and may be an artifact of the small number of chat transactions analyzed in the Library Visit Study.

Whenever the reference interview is bypassed, the staff member usually proceeds to latch on to a keyword in the user's initial query and uses it

WHAT USERS SAID ABOUT TAKING THE QUESTION AT FACE VALUE

Here are some observations by participants in the Library Visit Study.

- What was least helpful about the service I received was the few questions they asked me when I first approached them. If they had clarified what it was that I wanted, the search might not have taken as long.

- On hearing only part of my question, he dashed off into the stacks.

- He didn't ask me any questions about what I was looking for, and his manner was quite severe. I felt that he was rebuking me for asking for help rather than looking for the information myself.

- I asked the librarian for materials on the stock market. She entered "stock market" into the subject search of the library computer catalog. When the result came up, she swung her screen around and showed me what results she had found. . . . I found the books listed on the computer, but I did not feel I understood the stock market. I did not have all the information I wanted but I did not know what additional questions to ask. I did not want to seem like a pest. However I did not think that the librarian had done that much for me. She looked up the information on the computer, but I could have done as much on my own. I remember thinking that there was little point in having librarians if they did not do anything for the users that they could not do for themselves.

- The response [to my e-mail question] made me feel that the librarian did not even truly read my question. I asked for sources on these topics; the librarian told me how to use the terms I gave her in the online catalog.

as a search term (as seen in 3.1.1). Far from saving time, this practice often wastes time. In the Library Visit Study, a user who had asked for books about Richard Wagner returned to say that none of the books on Wagner contained the desired information. At that point, the librarian discovered belatedly that the user needed plot summaries for all of Wagner's operas, and then recommended an opera guide. The librarian admonished, "You could have saved a lot of time if you had just asked for that initially"—a good example of blaming the bad guy user (1.7).

In addition to wasting time, the failure to ask any questions to pinpoint the user's real interest can end up leaving the user irritated and dissatisfied. In the Library Visit Study, one public library user who asked for "anything on the subject of the paranormal" observed that "unfortunately... I was presented with a multitude of information, some of it pertinent and some of it peripheral to my question. The broad range of information I received would have taken me weeks to wade through." Another remarked, "I was irritated that the librarian did not try to ascertain what I was asking her. She didn't understand me and didn't try to—she just fit my question into her frame of reference, without consulting me, and tried to answer me that way."

3.1.3 Taking a System-based Perspective

Even when the library staff member does conduct an interview, a common problem is that too many of the librarian's questions relate to the library system, not to the context of the user's informational need. In the Dewdney transcripts, librarians asked a lot of questions such as, "Did you check the catalog?"; "Have you used this index before?"; "What were the indexing elements?"; "Did you come up with some call numbers?"; "Have you checked the 282s?"; and "I suppose you've checked our circulating collection?" Sometimes these system-based questions were *all* that they asked.

Why is it a bad idea to take a system perspective? Library professionals obviously feel comfortable talking about the system which is their home ground where they are the experts. *They* are the ones who know all the acronyms, understand the difference between a bibliography and biography, or a keyword and an assigned subject heading, and are very fluent in the specialized vocabulary of information systems. However, you should remember that, for many users, entering a library is like going into a foreign country where a foreign language is spoken. So rather than asking users to use *your* language and fit their questions into your systems, you should ask them questions that allow them to describe their informational needs in *their* own terms and in their native language.

ANALYZE THIS REFERENCE TRANSACTION

Case 9: A system question or a user-centered question?

User: I checked the catalog but couldn't find what I was looking for.

Librarian: Not on the shelf? (*acknowledgment*)

User: No.

Librarian: What is it that you wanted? (*open question*)

User: The books.

Librarian: Yes, but what type of information? (*open question*)

User: It's on body work.

Librarian: Okay. (*encourager*)

User: I'm helping a friend.

(Dewdney, "Auto body")

Comment: Users are so accustomed to being asked system-based questions in libraries that sometimes they misinterpret a user-centered question as a system question. In this case, the librarian had to rephrase her question "What is it that you wanted?" which produced a system-based answer, "the books." By persisting and asking, "Yes, but what type of information?" she ended up uncovering the user's situation. An even better question would have been, "Books, okay. But what were you hoping to find out?" We recommend that you avoid the term "information" when possible because it has now become a system word.

A QUICK TIP

Avoid the Catalog Question

You might worry that if you don't ask users if they have searched the catalog, they will expect you to do all their work for them. But how much work you do versus how much the user is expected to do independently is a policy question. You are still free to follow your library's policy if, instead of asking the question about catalog use (which many users dislike), you ask, "Have you had a chance to get started yet?" or "What have you done with this question so far?" If the user says, "Well, actually, nothing really," you can still say, "The best place to start with this question is with the online catalog. Are you familiar with how our catalog works?" However the user might tell you something quite useful that will guide your handling of the question, as, for example, "Well, first I asked the staff member on the other side of the library, and he asked if I had checked the catalog. And then I looked in the catalog and I got these numbers. But then, when I went to the shelves, none of the books I found contained what I want." Now you can ask, "What specifically did you want the books to include?"

EXERCISE

302.2 WIN

Consider this example from the Library Visit Study. The user asked for information on the impact of technology on literacy. The librarian did a search, found two promising titles, and wrote the call numbers on a slip of paper. The user commented, "At this point I wondered why the librarian did not give me any directions to find the shelves. I guess maybe she thought I was familiar with the physical layout of the library. I thought that was a lot to assume, and making assumptions like this might be a hindrance to a shy patron using the facility for the first time. . . . People who are versed at using the library system might take the organization of information for granted in the library but for the novice it could be a devastating experience. I was thinking that if I had not known the meaning of the call number 302.2 WIN that I would be embarrassed to ask for an explanation. The librarian assumed that the symbols she had written on the paper were meaningful and helpful to all."

In this instance, the librarian took for granted a number of things about the user's familiarity with the library's layout and the classification system. What could the librarian have done to take a more user-centered approach?

Brenda Dervin was one of the first to turn away from the system perspective in favor of a user-based perspective. Her colleague Douglas Zweizig (1976) provided a succinct summary of this perspective in an article called "With Our Eye on the User." The main point is that taking a user's perspective requires a transformation in the way in which we think about library services. Instead of looking at the user in the life of the system, Zweizig argued that we should be looking at how our services fit into the life of the user. Once we shift the focus of our attention from the system to the user of the system, the types of questions we ask in the interview change and become more user-centered.

Instead of asking a system question	Ask a user-centered question
Have you looked in the catalog/looked at the author field in the MARC record/checked the shelves/checked the databases for your subject?	What have you done so far?
Do you know the subject heading/search terms? keywords	What would you like the book/article/Web site to cover?/What would you like your map to show?
Do you want a directory?/encyclopedia/biographical dictionary?	How do you plan to use the information?
Do you want books or articles?	What format would help you most?
That particular book is out right now. Do you want us to put a hold on it?	Perhaps we have another book available that will cover the same topic. What specifically were you hoping that book would include?

3.1.4 The Unmonitored Referral

One surprising finding in the Library Visit Study was how often users reported unmonitored referrals. An unmonitored referral occurs when the reference librarian refers the user to a library source but does not follow up to make sure that the source is not only found but also answers the question adequately. The unmonitored referral routine too often follows immediately after the "Without-speaking-she-began-to-type" maneuver described earlier.

The unmonitored referral follows a standard pattern. The user starts the reference encounter by asking for information on some topic. Often without conducting a reference interview, the staff member does a catalog search using terms from the user's initial question, gives the user a call

WHAT USERS SAID ABOUT THE UNMONITORED REFERRAL

- Without saying anything, she handed me the piece of paper with the books listed on it and automatically assumed that I knew where to locate them. I asked her, "Where do I search for these books?" feeling that I better ask, since she was not going to tell me. She said, "Oh, right over there."

- She took for granted that I would be able to figure out for myself how to use the *Book Review Index*, as she offered me absolutely no guidance.

- The reference staff member wrote two call numbers down and handed them to me. . . . It bothered me that she did not take the time to point me in the right direction. As it was, the two books were found, but they were of no use to my topic.

- The librarian handed me a yellow piece of paper [listing call numbers]. I looked down at the numbers and asked, "Where do I find these books?" She replied, "They're over there in that direction, pointing to some place past the reference desk. . . . [The user found nine of the eleven books listed.] None of them mentioned [the topic the user had asked about]."

- In her e-mail response, she said, "Yes we have quite a few books [on the topic]. Here are some." There was no indication given in regards to her selection [of the fourteen titles listed].

- Based on my experience with the three suggested databases, I suspect that the reference staff did a very superficial analysis of the issue, rather than examining the question or the resources.

- She did not explain to me what she was doing. She handed me a slip of paper with numbers scrawled on it and pointed me towards the stacks along the far wall. . . . I went to the stacks and found the call number for the book she had recommended. She had not written down the author or the title of the book on the slip of paper and, since the subject of the book was not evident by its title, I was not sure if this was the book I was searching for. I glanced through the book and it seemed inadequate. I headed back towards the reference desk to ask about medical journals, but she was gone. I suppose it was her coffee break. (Library Visit Study)

Did You Know?
In a study of academic reference services, Murfin and Bunge (1984) reported that, when the librarian was busy and made unmonitored referrals, the average success rate dropped from sixty-nine percent to twenty-five percent in the five libraries studied. They concluded that the practice, policy, or necessity of directing the user rather than of accompanying the user on the search was a factor that caused these libraries to perform far below their potential. Nonprofessional staff members were affected to an even greater extent by this adverse factor.

number, points to some shelves, and recommends browsing, saying something like, "I suggest you just browse the shelf around the call numbers I have given you." Sometimes the librarian points the user in the right direction but not always. For example, one user asked for information on cellulitis, which is a skin infection, and was given a call number for a book on unwanted fat. The user said, "I found the book (not quite in its right place). It was called *Cellulite: Defeat It through Diet and Exercise*." In another case, a public library user who wanted information on endangered species was told, "Well, they seem to run from 591 to 599" and was given a slip of paper with 591–599. An academic library user who wanted the names of five US corporations that had closed their corporate libraries was advised to "try Lexis/Nexis." When the user asked in what she called her "ignorant undergraduate" tone, "Lexis/Nexis?" the staff member said, "That's one of the databases" and departed. The implication is that a list of call numbers or a URL or

Conducting the Reference Interview

Did You Know?

According to Marie Radford, librarians often experience a particular reference transaction very differently from the way in which the user experiences it. She gives the example of a student who asked for help finding journal articles on psychology. The librarian directed her to a computer terminal and briefly showed her how to use *PsychLit* on CD-ROM. When asked about the transaction, the student said, "I felt like she couldn't help me on my subject. [It] isn't that she didn't know the answer, but I felt that she didn't want to [help]... she looked like she did not know what I was talking about, a blank stare and also almost like irritated." On the other hand, the librarian reported the same transaction this way: "I think it went all right from my viewpoint because I didn't have to really interact too much. She seemed capable; she seemed to know what she was doing. I felt she had found what she wanted because she said she had what she needed. She seemed to be capable of handling it on her own" (1999, 4).

WHAT TEENS SAID ABOUT THE UNMONITORED REFERRAL

Radford and Connaway (2007b) reported the following discussion from a focus group with urban teenagers (whose names have been changed for anonymity). They commented on the unmonitored referral:

Lisa: Yeah, like if they're [adult librarians] not helpful, they'll point me in the direction and say "Oh... [over there].

Joe: Yeah. Sometimes, sometimes I've asked them like where's a certain book and they'll be like, they'll just point at a random shelf.... And then, and then I look and there's like three shelves next to each other and I'm like "Which one is it?" So, it's like you have to go and look at every book to see if the book is there.

Sarah: And you get embarrassed; you don't want to ask them again once you've already asked them...

Joe: It's like they close their eyes and they're like "That one right there." (*laughs*)

Multiple Participants: (*laughter*)

Sarah: And then cause you've already asked them, you don't want to feel like you're pestering them too much so you don't go and ask them again. It's like, it's like, you don't want to go "So which shelf are you pointing at?" Because, I mean, once they do their famous point, it's just like... (*laughs*)

Multiple Participants: (*laughter*)

Sarah: You don't want to go near them again. That's it. So, you'd rather try your luck in searching it out yourself or going on the computer.

Ed: I have actually, uh, left the library and came back another day for the book. Because they would do the point and then....

It is especially poignant that Ed "actually, uh, left the library and came back another day for the book" rather than interact with the librarian a second time to clarify directions" (33). One of the teens, Sarah refers to "their famous point," evoking one of the components of the unmonitored referral—pointing instead of walking the user over to the stacks or at least indicating the location on a floor plan map.

the name of a database is all the help to be expected, and that users are on their own to sink or swim after that. Instead of providing an answer, the librarian provides a slip of paper and some call numbers. Usually no authors' names or titles are provided, which makes finding the actual book tricky for novices.

In "Reducing Failures in Reference Service," Douglas (1988) has classified six types of reference failure identified in studies that support the 55 percent rule. One of these is "Referral to a source within the library (e.g., another service point) or referral to a printed source but not actually locating the answer for the patron." Although Douglas stated that this type of failure was not often mentioned in the studies he reviewed, we have found it to be a frequent occurrence. The unmonitored referral was reported in somewhat more than one-third of the Library Visit Study accounts—in 96 out of 261 accounts (Ross and Nilsen,

2000). When we examined these accounts to see what happens after an unmonitored referral, we observed that some users were able to succeed on their own. But too often they do not and are left feeling dissatisfied. The user who was given a range of call numbers when she wanted information on endangered species remarked, "The librarian seemed to feel her job was done, but I felt quite unsatisfied with her assistance."

Another user who asked for information on fibromyalgia was told, "The best place to look would be Medline, which you can access from our computers here in the library." The staff member gave the user a piece of paper with the URL for Medline and said, "When you type this in, it'll bring up Medline. Then all you do is type in 'myofascial-fibro' or whatever, and it will bring up the citations." In reflecting on this experience, the user said, "I felt that if he had helped me to use the database, I might have found some useful information. But as it was, I only tinkered with the database for a little while and then left empty-handed." There seems to be a high rate of search failure when users are not interviewed, given minimal instructions, and left on their own.

This doesn't mean that all the users who were given an unmonitored referral and who then found little of use left the library empty-handed. Some of them returned to the same librarian for help or pursued other strategies, including starting over again with a second librarian. In some cases, the user took a proactive approach by explicitly asking for help in using the database and was more likely to get useful information. For example, a user who said she wanted to know how to find "information on a certain person" was immediately told, "The best bet is to use Biobase." The user commented, "I think he expected me to know what that meant and to get going on my way. So I explained that I was new to this library and didn't know *what*, let alone *where*, Biobase was." While this user ended up getting excellent help, other novice users who were less assertive were on their own, and often missed out finding information because unassisted they were unable to navigate through the library resources (Ross and Nilsen, 2000).

3.1.5 Negative Closure: How to Make Users Go Away

In busy libraries and in heavily used VR services, staff members face the practical problem of processing an endless stream of questions and sending users out of the system. Of course, the best way to do this is to provide an answer that is helpful. Highly-rated librarians in the Library Visit Study faced with a challenging question showed no inclination to give up, but instead said things like, "Okay, let's not get discouraged. There are other places we can check," or "Here are some more things that you can try. Make sure you come back if you don't find what you need." In live chat environments, savvy librarians will offer to keep looking and e-mail a more complete answer to the user when there are time constraints. But less highly-rated librarians in the Library Visit Study too often gave the impression that their goal was to get rid of users. Users made comments such as, "I think she hoped I would be satisfied and leave," or "I felt she

Did You Know?
In the Library Visit Study, 39.3 percent of the 150 VR transactions involved unmonitored referrals; which is about the same as the 37 percent of unmonitored referrals recorded for FtF transactions. Academic librarians were more likely than public librarians to make unmonitored referrals (49 vs. 29 percent, respectively). E-mail transactions were more likely to include unmonitored referrals than were chat transactions (41 vs. 33 percent, respectively). However the figures for unmonitored referrals in VR do need to be taken with a grain of salt. When a URL is provided in an e-mail or chat response, the transaction is identified as monitored unless the user reported being unable to locate the needed information on the site provided. Otherwise it is impossible to know if the staff member actually checked the site or not. Thus the 60.7 percent figure for the total number of VR transactions that included monitored referrals may be inflated.

	NEGATIVE CLOSURE IN VIRTUAL REFERENCE
	Radford and Connaway (2005–2008) have found that librarians providing live chat reference sometimes use many of the same negative closure strategies as Ross and Dewdney (1998) reported.

	Description and Examples from Seeking Synchronicity (Radford & Connaway, 2005–2008)
Abrupt Ending	Person disappears in the middle of the encounter or at the end with no closing ritual or closing script.
Disclaimer	Librarian states that information is not available, or they can't help. Librarian (L): "I am not an attorney," "I don't think I will find that," "This is all I can find."
Failure to Refer	Librarian is unable to help user but does not make an appropriate referral. Turns user away empty-handed or with only a partial answer to a query.
Ignoring Cues That User Wants More Help	Librarian ignores request for additional help. L: "This is all I can find," "For more please go to your public library." User: "You did not help much."
Premature or Attempted Closing	L: "Why don't you call some of your classmates to see what they are doing about this," "I have to go now."
Premature Referral	Sending to another service, or physical library without clarifying the question.
Sends to Google	L: "Go back to Google and in the search box type in 'segregation in education in the 1930's."

Did You Know?

In about one-third of Library Visit Study cases, users decided to cut their losses and start all over again with another staff member within the same library or in another library. From a system point of view, there are obvious inefficiencies when the job has to be done twice. From the user's point of view, this lack of quality control is experienced as poor service. Clearly it would be preferable for the first librarian to conduct a proper reference interview and find an acceptable answer. Radford and Connaway (2005–2008) reported that in chat reference, some users will even ask for another staff member during the session: "Can I have another librarian?" or "Do you know ne1 [anyone] else who can help?"

would be glad if I went and found the materials for myself," or "He made it clear that he didn't want to be bothered with me when I came back to say that the first suggestion hadn't worked."

The ten following strategies (apart from providing a helpful answer) are sometimes used by librarians to get rid of a user, a phenomenon called *negative closure* (Ross and Dewdney, 1998):

1. **The librarian provides an unmonitored referral.** In the unmonitored referral the staff member gives the user a call number or refers the user to a source without taking any steps to make sure that the source is found and answers the question (3.1.4). Making a referral is sometimes helpful, and staff members should probably be doing *more* referral both inside and outside the library. The key here is to build into the referral process some way of checking that the source being suggested is both available and appropriate. Referral is a strategy of negative closure only when the librarian doesn't know enough about the real question to have any reasonable confidence that a user who follows the advice will find an acceptable answer.

2. **The librarian immediately refers the user somewhere else, preferably far away**—to another floor within the library itself or to another agency altogether. When asked for information on

the relationship between homicide rates and capital punishment, the librarian immediately said, "That would be on the third floor." The librarian on the third floor said, "Have you tried the criminology library at University X [in another city]?" When this strategy of referral elsewhere is used *before* the library staff member has conducted a proper reference interview, often the distant information provider is *not* in fact the appropriate place to answer the user's question, and the user is referred elsewhere yet again.

3. **The librarian implies that the user should have done something else first before asking for reference help.** When a user asked for information about good mystery writers, the librarian said in a manner that was "quite severe: 'Well, of course you've already checked in our catalog under authors' names to see if there is any information there.' . . . I felt he was rebuking me for asking for help rather than looking for the information myself." Questions such as "Have you checked the catalog?" feed into users' anxiety about asking for help.

4. **The librarian tries to get the user to accept more easily found information** instead of the information actually asked for. When a user refused to accept the answer that there are no fiction writers in Newfoundland (see strategy 9), the librarian "pointed out all kinds of information that she *could* find . . . reference books for French Canadian literature, the literature of Canadian women, Western Canadian writers, etc." Whether the suggestion to switch to a more readily answered question is negative closure or an offer of genuine help in finding an acceptable answer depends on the context and what else the librarian knows about the user's informational needs. In VR transactions, staff members may search Google and send some URLs that happen to appear in the first ten hits.

5. **The librarian warns the user to expect defeat** because the topic is too hard, obscure, large, elusive, or otherwise unpromising. Asked for information on how carnival glass is made, one staff member typed in "carnival" and got sixty entries dealing with carnivals and fairs. She typed in "glass," found glass manufacturing, and said defeatedly, "This is quite large." Another user commented, "She seemed to imply that this was going to be a long drawn out process and that probably nothing would be found." "Your question is rather elusive," warned another librarian. This strategy blames the anticipated failure to get an answer on the supposedly intractable nature of the question itself rather than on ineffective search skills.

6. **The librarian encourages the user to abort the transaction voluntarily.** When a user asked for the educational background of Camille Paglia, the librarian "rolled her eyes and said 'Oh, her.' and then said, 'Is it really necessary to find out her major(s)?

Why do you want to know?'" This strategy is often preceded by strategy 5, since users are more likely to say that the search is not worth pursuing if they expect that a search will end in failure. See section 3.2.3 for a discussion of why staff members should not ask "Why?" directly.

7. **The librarian signals nonverbally that the transaction is over** by tone of voice, turning away, or starting another activity. One user observed, "I knew from the tone of her voice that this was her final offering," while another said, "She was obviously finished with me at this point because she turned away and began shuffling through some papers." VR transactions often end abruptly when the librarian says, "Hope that helps!" or "Good luck!" followed by the farewell script: "Thank you for using our chat service! etc."

8. **The librarian states explicitly that the search has reached a dead end.** Examples include "I'm not sure what other information we might have on that," or "I am sorry. This is everything we have in our catalog under 'New York City in art.'" An international student who wanted to understand health insurance coverage was told that, apart from an out-of-date pamphlet, "I'm not sure what other material we might have available that would be of use." When a user wanting literary criticism of Margaret Atwood's novels returned after an unsuccessful unmonitored referral to ask for help finding material on the Internet, the staff member said, "Well, we're very busy right now, but if you come back later, someone will be available." In this case, the user noted that there was no one else in line and there was another librarian behind the desk reading a newspaper.

9. **The librarian claims that the information is not in the library or else doesn't exist** at all. When a user requested some information on archaeology, the immediate response was that there was "not much material available at the library on this subject." In another case, when the user asked for help in finding the names of some fiction writers from Newfoundland, the librarian "registered that this was a very difficult question," and then, without consulting anything, said "that she didn't think there were any."

10. **The librarian tells the user he's going away to track down a document but then never returns.** One user reported that after the librarian said, "I'll go and see what I can find," she waited for forty-five minutes but "never saw the man again, neither at the desk nor with the promised document." Another said, "I waited at the shelf for a while, but she did not come back." In a variant of this tactic, another staff member advised the user to go home and wait for a call with the requested information, but no one ever called back. Joan Durrance (1995) has described this phenomenon as the "disappearing librarian." (Reported in Ross and Dewdney, 1998, "Negative Closure")

Did You Know?

Sometimes the answer that there is *no* published material on a particular topic is a helpful response. For example, a student doing a literature review for a proposed area of thesis research finds it useful to be told that a thorough search of the relevant databases has found little or nothing of relevance on the topic. The negative search result differs from negative closure Strategy 9 because it comes after a thorough search rather than being a strategy to avoid doing a search, which, had it been done, may have found numerous sources.

ANALYZE THESE REFERENCE TRANSACTIONS

Case 10: How different can e-mail services be?

One Library Visit Study participant (we'll call her Jane) sent the following question to two different public libraries in cities where she did not live: "Hello, I am interested in tribes in the Amazon. A couple of years ago I read about two children who were discovered who were believed to be the only survivors of a particular tribe. Could you please send me some information about this tribe and these children?" Here are the two responses:

Library A: This library in a medium-sized city in central Canada provided a prompt response: "We do not have specialized information on your topic. Please contact the public library in your own city for assistance. Thank you." The staff member who responded did not address the user personally nor was his or her name provided.

Library B: This library in a smaller city in a more remote area of Canada responded to the question, sent on a Friday afternoon, with two e-mails, as follows:

> Monday 9:16 a.m: "Hi [Jane]—just got your e-mail sorry about not getting back till now—I had the weekend off...I'll take a quick look inside our news/magazine database and have a look on the internet and get back to your shortly. More to come!" [Signed by first name of staff member]

> Monday 11:16 a.m: Two URLs are provided, though the sites are not named. The staff member added this comment following one of them: "THIS TRIBE IS CALLED THE PANARA—LOTS ABOUT THIS TRIBE" Then the message continues, "[Jane] a few links for you to look over! I was able to find some information about the names of Amazon tribes and it seems the one with the fewest numbers is one called the Isanahua with only between 20–40 people in the entire tribe. I'll attach that document [attached]. It doesn't tell the story about two found boys so I'll keep looking and get back to you right after lunch. I'll do a better search then— busy morning! [name of staff member] (No further e-mails were received by the time the report of the transaction was due to the course instructor).

Comment: Regarding Library A, the user wrote, "I got the impression that they did not want to be bothered." Regarding Library B's responses, the user wrote, "The overall tone was friendly and I appreciated being addressed by name.... I felt as though my request was valued. I appreciated the apology very much as well. It made the librarian appear much more approachable and welcoming." Concerning the second e-mail from Library B, Jane wrote: "The information was not quite what I was looking for but was very interesting," and the promise of more information to come was encouraging." Jane reported, "I e-mailed the librarian immediately to let her know I thought the information was fascinating. However up to 10 p.m. on Tuesday evening there was no further response. I felt like I had been left hanging since the librarian did not fulfill her assurances."

For discussion: There was no reference interview in either response—what questions might have been asked? Has the user asked for "specialized" information as Library A suggests? Should it matter that the user was from another city? What might be the reasons for Library A's failure to provide an acceptable answer? What specific elements in the staff member's communication made the response from Library B seem friendly? What do these two examples suggest about staff training for e-mail reference? What does the Library B example suggest about what happens when you promise to send information and do not follow up?

UNHELPFUL BEHAVIORS IDENTIFIED IN THE LIBRARY VISIT STUDY

- The staff member didn't smile/nod/look at me when I approached the desk during the reference encounter.
- Seemed to be using the desk or the terminal as a barrier.
- Didn't listen. Cut me off when I tried to explain.
- Made assumptions about what I wanted or why I wanted it (e.g., for a school project).
- Treated my question as unimportant or bothersome. Made me feel that I was inconveniencing the library staff and wasting their time.
- Took a judgmental stance toward the content of the material I was looking for.
- Didn't ask me anything about my question. Didn't find out why I needed the information and so gave me information that was too general.
- Didn't try to understand my question but just fitted my question into his/her frame of reference.
- Without speaking, she/he just began typing at the computer.
- Looked up something in the computer, wrote down a call number, and said, "Try this," but didn't give me a title or author's name.
- Was unwilling to move out from behind the desk to help me find material.
- Made me feel that I shouldn't expect to get an answer to a question like that/that the question was too technical/that there probably were no reliable answers.
- Made me feel it was not the librarian's job to answer questions about anything but the resources that were in the immediate library.
- Made me feel stupid.
- Said, "I suppose you've done the obvious and tried X?"
- Didn't let me see the screen/the index/as she/he was doing the search, so I couldn't tell how to do it myself next time.
- Didn't explain what she/he was doing and left me wondering if I should follow her or wait.
- Didn't explain how to use the catalog/indexes/microfilm reader/library interface.
- Made me feel left out of the search.
- Just said, "No, we don't have it" and made no effort to suggest anything further to do.
- Seemed impatient or vexed by my question and anxious have me leave. Seemed to be trying to get rid of me.
- Made no effort to follow up or verify that I had found what I was looking for.
- Seemed more interested in time management than in helping me find an answer. (Dewdney and Ross, 1994)

3.2 Skills for Negotiating the Question

When most people think of interviewing, they think of question asking. In this section we consider various kinds of questions and how they work. And we also consider some related skills that need to be used in conjunction with questioning skills including summarizing, avoiding premature diagnosis, and closure or the skill of keeping the conversation on track. The eventual goal, of course, is to integrate all these skills into one seamless interview that moves smoothly from acknowledgment to an open question or two to a summary to a concluding statement that includes a follow-up question and an invitation to return. However, when first learning a new skill, you should focus on one skill at a time to start with. After you feel comfortable using the single skill, then you can think about the integration of skills (discussed in section 4.2).

ANALYZE THIS REFERENCE TRANSACTION

Case 11: It just depends on what you need.

Librarian: Hi.

User: Is there a listing of companies and addresses and stuff like that?

Librarian: We have different manufacturers' directories. (*acknowledgment*) Is that what you're after? (*closed question to confirm*)

User: Yes.

Librarian: Companies? (*acknowledgment*) Okay. Now are you looking for any specific area in— Is it American companies you're looking for? (*closed question*)

User: Yes. American.

Librarian: Are you looking for a special area, like a city? (*closed question that functions as a polite version of the open question*, "What specific geographic area are you looking for, if any?")

User: No, no. Definitely not a specific area, but maybe like engineering and stuff. Manufacturing.

Librarian: Okay. Okay. Now these [pointing to some print sources] are industrial directories. For manufacturers. The companies actually have to produce a product. It's not going to be like ABC Insurance Company. (*library use instruction*)

User: Right.

Librarian: Okay. What we have here is a *Trade Index*, okay? [She explains how it works and shows him other sources. She describes how some directories have more information of different kinds.] It just depends on what you need.

User: See, what it is, is that I'm going to be sending out resumes and job applications. I just need the company names and what they do—and addresses—that's all.

(Cont'd.)

Did You Know?
Open questioning has received growing endorsement within the library literature. Geraldine B. King (1972) was one of the first to point out the value of open questioning in her often-cited article, "The Reference Interview: Open and Closed Questions." By the 1990s, the value of asking open questions had been firmly established to the point that the RUSA guidelines for appropriate behavioral performance of reference and information services providers specify that the effective librarian "uses open-ended questioning techniques to encourage patrons to expand on the request or present additional information." Some examples of such questions include: "Please tell me more about your topic"; "What additional information can you give me?"; "How much information do you need?" (RUSA, 2004, reference guidelines 3.7 and 3.8)

ANALYZE THIS REFERENCE TRANSACTION *(Continued)*

Librarian: Yeah. You know what's good, though, is to have a name of a person, rather than just sending it to the company. Some of these do include personnel. [She explains.]

User: Okay, thanks a lot.

(Dewdney, "Manufacturing Job Search")

Comment: In the interview that the researcher conducted with the user just before he left the library, this user said that he was very satisfied with the results of his conversation with this librarian and would definitely be willing to return to this same staff member for help.

For discussion:

1. How successful do you think this interview was overall? Which questions seemed to work best? Which not so well?
2. How might this transaction have turned out had the librarian treated this as a directional question and said, "Our company directories are over there"?
3. Is there anything that the librarian could have done to get sooner to the user's real informational need?
4. Look closely at the two questions in which the staff member asks about "specific area." What happens in terms of the way the staff member phrases the question? In terms of how the user responds? Did the staff member get the answer hoped for?
5. Take a second look at that statement, "It just depends on what you need." It's not formally a question. How does it function in this exchange?

A QUICK TIP

When to Use Open Questions

Use open questions when you want:

- to hear in the other person's own words the nature of a problem or situation;
- to encourage the other person to talk;
- to avoid guessing or making assumptions.

3.2.1 Open and Closed Questions

The different ways in which you can ask a question determine the sort of answer you are likely to get. Research involving tape-recording reference transactions in real settings has found that, without training, library staff tend to ask certain types of question. For example, if a user asks, "Do you have anything on computers?" the librarian might respond with any of the following questions:

- Have you checked the catalog?
- Is this for a class project?
- Would you rather have books or articles?
- Are you interested in hardware or software?
- Do you want to buy a computer?

These are all *closed questions*—questions that require a yes/no, this/that response. A closed question requires the other person to choose from the options provided and works best in circumstances where there exists only a small set of options known in advance. For example, at the coffee bar, the clerk might ask, "Small, medium or large?"

In situations where there may be many options that can't be known in advance—the usual case at the reference desk—open questions are

ANALYSIS OF LIVE CHAT INTERACTIONS

Clarifications Requested; Clarifications Provided

Radford and Connaway (2007a) analyzed 434 live chat reference interactions. They found that VR librarians tried to get additional information on the following, in descending order of frequency. The examples provided are verbatim from the transcripts.

- **Topic** information ("Is there a specific animal that you're researching?") sought by 45 percent (195).
- **Background** information ("When is your paper due?" "Are you in the NYC area?") sought by 31 percent (133).
- **Verification** of their understanding ("So you are looking for the reasons why the Japanese attacked Pearl Harbor?") sought by 20 percent (87).
- **Search history** information ("Okay, and have you checked their Web sites yet?") sought by 19 percent (83).
- **Type of resource** information ("Are you looking for books, articles, or online information?") sought by 11 percent (49).
- **Extent or depth** needed ("Were you looking for in-depth history? Or a summary?") sought by 11 percent (48).
- **Referral** question ("Do you want me to refer your question to your library?") sought by 4 percent (16).

How about the Users?

In the 434 live chat interactions, 130 VR users provided clarifying information of the following types, in descending order of frequency. Topic and background information are important to VR librarians and users alike. On the other hand, users give more relative weight to the extent or depth of informational needed.

- **Topic** information ("I am doing marketing reseach on marylands restaurant industry") was provided by 45 percent (58) of the 130 users who clarified.
- **Background** information ("I am in 7th grade GT Science and I am Doing a 2 year research project...") was provided by 24 percent (32).
- **Extent or depth** needed ("the thing is i need it to be simple and not to wordy") was provided by 20 percent (26).
- **Correction** of the librarian's misunderstanding ("No. The form says I need the correct name for the position.") was provided by 16 percent (21).
- **Verification** of their own understanding ("So the best thing is to find it on the online catalog... is that correct?") was sought by 14 percent (18).
- **Search history** information ("I looked in the card catalog and didn't see it there...") was provided by 14 percent (18).
- **Type of resource** information ("...And [not] a book, online though"; "Yes, but I'm looking for more historical and architectural resources") was provided by 9 percent (12).
- **Referral** information ("Can you contact me with anyone from the [...] Library") was requested by 4 percent (5).

A QUICK TIP

Imagine the Title

Here's an open question that often works when all else fails in the reference interview. Ask the user to imagine the title of the perfect source: "If you could have the perfect article (book, solution, help etc.), what would it be called?" Be sure to give the user a few minutes to think about this. Often the imaginary title contains most of the keywords or concepts that you need to do the search. (Thanks for this suggestion to one of the trainees at our Reference Interview Workshop in Fredericton, New Brunswick)

Did You Know?

In her posting to LIBREF (August 28, 1997) on the topic of "Why don't they ask for what they want?" Dr. Diane Nahl emphasized the need for practice: "My students always have trouble learning to use open questions. [Asking open questions] is unnatural, somehow, and must be focused on and practiced explicitly... . For ten years I have taught reference interviewing in a professional library school and I have always emphasized finding out what the person really wants through role plays, analysis of real interviews, and through fieldwork at real reference desks in which students analyze their live interviews."

(Used with permission)

A QUICK TIP

Sometimes It's Better to Be Indirect

In some cultures, direct questions (either open or closed) may be interpreted as *too* direct or even impolite. Instead of asking, "What do you want to know about X?" you may want to rephrase your question as a statement such as the following:

- I may be able to help you better if you could tell me more about X.
- We have a lot of different materials on X in various parts of the library. I may be able to help you better if you could tell me more about X.
- Perhaps if you tell me a bit about how you plan to use this information, I could help you locate some relevant articles.

These statements work because they let the user know why the librarian needs more details from them but at the same the librarian is being respectful by not demanding an answer.

Did You Know?

Some questions that look like closed questions are really open in function. For example, "Can you tell me...?" and "Would you mind telling me...?" seem as if they invite a limited answer such as "Yes" or "No." But in English, prefaces such as "Can you..." or "Will you..." are politeness strategies, or softeners, that can be interpreted as meaning, "If you are able, please tell me..." or "If you are willing, please tell me..." (Thanks to Gillian Michell for this analysis)

ANALYZE THIS REFERENCE TRANSACTION

Case 12: Closed system-based questions

User: Excuse me, but I'm looking for some poems.

Librarian: Some poems. What poems are you looking for? (*acknowledgment followed by an open question*)

User: Love poems.

Librarian: Love poems. (*acknowledgment*) Okay, is there anything in particular? By anybody—American, Canadian, British—does it matter? (*a question that is open in its function—"anybody in particular"—gets turned immediately into a closed question.*)

User: No, just a project on love poems.

Librarian: Okay, do you know how to use the catalog here?

User: No.

Librarian: Okay. [Explains the catalog] Did you want books that you can take home or is it all right to work here? (*closed question*)

User: Mhm. No.

Librarian: Do you know how to work the index? (*closed question*)

User: No. [Librarian explains the index.]

(Dewdney, "Love Poems")

Comment: After a good start with the open question, "What poems are you looking for?" the librarian switched to closed question related to the library system and its organization and retrieval tools: authors classified by nationality because that's the way the library classification system organizes them; books divided into circulating or reference because that's how the library works; the user's familiarity with the library's catalog and indexes because the user is expected to use these tools. Since these questions focused on library-related areas that the user didn't know anything about, rather than on areas related to the user's own interests and purposes, the information produced was minimal.

What else could the librarian have done here? After the response, "just a project on love poems," more useful information would probably have been elicited by an open question such as: "What kind of project are you doing on love poems?" or "What are the requirements of your project?" or even "What did your teacher tell you about this project?"

more useful, especially at the beginning of the interview. *Open questions* differ from closed questions in both function and effect. Unlike a closed question, an open question allows people to respond in their own terms. A handy way of recognizing whether a question is open or not is to look at the way it begins. If it begins with Who, What, Why, Where, When, or How, the question is probably open. "What format do you want for the information?" or "How did you hear about this particular computer virus?" are examples of open questions. The less restrictive structure of open questions invites elaboration and longer answers. When you ask open questions, you give up some control over what gets talked about. Instead of specifying the aspect of the topic to be discussed ("Do you want

SOME USEFUL OPEN QUESTIONS

To find out what a person wants in order to supply the need:

- What sort of thing are you looking for?
- What information would you like on this?
- What sort of material do you have in mind?
- What requirements do you have (for the project, design etc.)?

To get a description of a problem or event:

- What have you done about this question so far?
- Where did you hear about this?
- What did your teacher/ boss/ tell you about this topic [for the "imposed question"]?

To encourage the person to elaborate:

- What aspect of X concerns you?
- What else can you tell me about X?
- Perhaps if you tell me more about this problem [project], I could make some suggestions.

To get clarification:

- What do you mean by X?
- What would be an example of that? Can you give me an example? Please give me an example.
- Can you help me to understand X?

(Adapted from Brenda Dervin)

A QUICK TIP

Wait for the Answer

After you have asked your question ("What would you like to know about endangered species?"), wait for the answer. Don't succumb to the common temptation to turn your open question into a closed question by guessing, "Do you need statistics?"

Did You Know?

Radford and Connaway (2007a) wanted to find out the type of questions asked by librarians in live chat VR sessions. They found that out of 838 questions asked by the librarians in 434 chat reference interactions, 66 percent were closed questions and 34 percent were open questions. Surprisingly, there were two different patterns of clarification. While librarians usually asked for clarification at the beginning of the interaction (in 51 percent of 434 transcripts), users actually provided clarification in the middle of the interaction (in 18 percent of 132 transcripts). When librarians bypassed the reference interview and failed to ask any clarifying questions, sometimes users would jump in and clarify without prompting. A reference transaction, however, shouldn't depend on the rescue work of the user, but rather on the professional skill of the librarian in doing the job right.

hardware?"), you ask users what aspect of the topic concerns them ("What did you want to know about computers?"). The user might possibly say hardware. But chances are he will mention something altogether different that you would never have been able to guess, such as listings of local continuing education courses on designing Web pages. Guessing "Is it this?" or "Is it that?" can be risky and sometimes offensive because this involves making assumptions. Open questions make no assumptions.

To summarize, closed questions restrict the user's response and furthermore restrict it to aspects of the topic that concern the librarian but not necessarily the user. Many commonly asked closed questions are attempts to relate the user's request to the library system and its methods of organizing, retrieving, and providing information (see 3.1.3). A staff member in an academic library may ask, "Are you a student here?" because access to licensed databases require passwords available only to students and faculty of that institution. Usually closed questions elicit very short answers. Since sometimes short answers are wanted, there is a place for closed questions in the reference interview.

Closed questions are effective in focusing wandering conversations and can also be useful, especially at the end of the interview, to verify that the librarian understands what really is needed (e.g., "So all you want to know is the name of the archaeologist who discovered the

A QUICK TIP

You Don't Have to Know Everything

As a library professional, you are supposed to be an expert on how to find sources of information; you are not expected to know everything on every subject. If the user asks about a person, place, or thing that you are unfamiliar with, don't try to fake it. The user will usually see through this ruse, and you may be embarrassed. Ask the user to tell you what he or she knows about it.

In the Mental Models Study, a user asked for "information on Sheridan." (She was doing a college project on the eighteenth century British playwright Richard Sheridan and wanted to find criticism on *School for Scandal*.) The librarian reported that when he heard this initial question he thought: "It's a name, but I don't know who this is. My immediate reaction was that it must be the Civil War general. I was stalling until I could figure it out—it didn't ring any bells with me. So I showed her how to walk through the catalog search. I got her to type in the name Sheridan. She was very quiet, so I didn't want to ask her too many questions. I was hoping to pick up some cues from off the screen about whether Sheridan was an author or politician or whatever."

Instead of hoping for cues to appear magically on the screen, why not say at the outset, "I'm not sure I know which Sheridan you mean. What can you tell me about him or her?" or "I'm not familiar with Sheridan. If you could tell me a bit about this topic, I would do a better job of searching." If it turned out that the user wanted calendar information for Sheridan College available on the Web, then the catalog would not have been the best place to search.

ANALYZE THESE REFERENCE TRANSACTIONS

Case 13: Closed questions that are intended to function as open questions

User: Do you have a section on true-to-life murders that have been committed?

Librarian: Yes we do. Is there—are you just interested in general reading? There isn't a particular murder that you heard...?

User: Yes. No.

(Dewdney, "Murders")

User: I have a list of publications [reads from paper]. I don't know if those are magazines or journals or...

Librarian: [Looks at list] They're all magazines.... Are you looking at a particular topic?

User: Yes. I'm looking at wage restraint in the federal government.

(Dewdney, "Wage Restraint")

User: Where would I find the US phone books?

Librarian: They're over here. We've just got the major cities. You can also get them on the Internet. Were you looking for one in particular?

User: No, two: Cleveland and San Mateo, California.

(Dewdney, "San Mateo Clinic")

User: Where would you have books on credit cards?

Librarian: Books on credit cards? (*acknowledgment*)

User: Yes.

Librarian: Okay. How to manage credit cards? The history of credit cards? Or...?

User: I'm doing an essay on credit cards.

(Dewdney, "Credit Cards")

Comment: In each case the librarian asked a question that is technically a closed question—it can be answered by a yes or no. However the librarian intended the question to function as an open question. Sometimes the user understands what is intended. Sometimes the user misunderstands, as in the first case where the user takes the questions literally. In the second case, the user interpreted the closed question, as intended, to mean, "What topic are you looking at?" The third user initially answered, "Were you looking for one in particular?" as if it were a closed question, responding, "No, two." But then, he continued on as if the question had been, "Which one(s) in particular were you looking for?" In the final case, the librarian used two closed questions that were intended to say in effect, "We have a lot of material on credit cards from managing them to the history of them. It all depends on what you need." Note that two closed questions followed by "or?" to suggest an open-ended menu of possibilities work differently than a single closed question, "Do you need something on how to manage credit cards better?" The user responded as intended by explaining the context for the question. However closed questions can be tricky to use because they involve assumptions and sometimes the assumptions can be offensive. (The user might think indignantly, I can manage my credit cards just fine right now, thank you very much.)

Crystal Skull?"). But at the beginning, it is usually preferable to get users talking, and this can be done best by asking open questions ("What do you want to know about the Crystal Skull?" or "How did you hear about the Crystal Skull?" or "I'm not familiar with the Crystal Skull. What can you tell me about it?). Asking open questions encourages users to say in their own words what is wanted. Compare these two sets of questions:

CLOSED QUESTIONS

User: Do you have any information on bipolar disorder?

Staff: Is this for a school project?

Do you want books or articles?

Have you checked the catalog?

Do you want information about drug treatments?

Do you want recent research articles on this disorder?

Do you want first-hand accounts of living with bipolar disorder?

Do you want the contact number for a support group?

OPEN QUESTIONS

User: Do you have any information on bipolar disorder?

Staff: What would you like to know about bipolar disorder?

What aspect of bipolar disorder are you most interested in?

We have material on bipolar disorder in different areas of the library. Perhaps if you could tell me what aspect interests you, I could help narrow things down. [Not strictly speaking a question but this statement functions as a question, inviting the user to say more.]

So if open questions are so good, why does it seem to be second nature to ask closed questions? Mary Jo Lynch reported that an analysis of the 366 reference transactions recorded in four public libraries in New Jersey in the late 1970s showed that 10 percent of all questions asked were either open questions or functioned as open questions and 90 percent were closed such as, "Do you need pictures of frogs or material about them?" (1978, 131). In Dewdney's study, before providing training in specific skills, she recorded and transcribed 166 reference interviews to establish a baseline of interview behaviors. She found that in about 80 percent of transactions either no open questions were asked or the open question was immediately converted to a closed question, as in, "What would you like to know about antique dolls? The prices?" (1986, 109). Often, as we have seen, closed questions are system-based. Although system-based questions are logical to the library staff member, they often put the user on the spot by asking for information the user doesn't know, as in this example:

Staff: You're looking for a song, "The Lamplighter's Serenade." Do you know if it was written recently? (*closed question*)

Evaluating Questions

This exercise can be done on your own or in a group discussion with either small break-out groups or a large group.

1. Look closely at the list of closed questions provided in the bipolar disorder case. Closed questions usually involve assumptions. For each closed question, specify what the assumption is. How confident should the librarian be that this assumption is right?

2. To ask a closed question, you need background knowledge. One kind of background knowledge concerns the library system, how information is collected, organized, retrieved, stored. The other kind is subject knowledge about the user's topic. For each closed question, specify the kind of background knowledge needed to generate the question.

3. Now look at the list of open questions. How do they differ in terms of assumptions made and knowledge needed about the topic?

4. Suppose another user asks, "Do you have any information on fish?" How many of the listed open and closed questions could you use again with this new user by replacing references to bipolar disorder with references to fish? (e.g., "Do you want recent research articles on fish?"; "Do you want the contact number for a fishing organization?") What conclusions can you draw from this exercise about the flexibility of open and closed questions? If you could ask only *one* question and had to use it in every reference interview, which one of these open and closed questions would you pick?

Conducting the Reference Interview

User: No, I'm afraid I don't.

Staff: Was it written by an American?" (*closed question*)

User: Sorry, I don't know.

Staff: Is it a popular song? (*closed question*)

User: I think so. No, I'm not sure. I shouldn't really bother you about this. I can come back later.

As this example illustrates, staff members often ask closed questions that are related to the way that information is organized in reference tools (by time period, geographical region of origin, type of song such as popular song, German *lieder* etc.). But unfortunately, when users don't know the answers to these closed questions, the interview can seem like a game of twenty questions. Worse, users may be left with the impression that they should have researched the topic far more thoroughly before bothering the librarian. Instead of asking a series of closed questions that the user can't answer, the staff member could have asked, "What can you tell me about this song?" Although it is sometimes argued that busy staff don't have time to listen to long stories elicited by open questions, the fact is that open questions save search time.

A question that is frequently asked by prospective and practicing librarians and reference workshop participants is: "Won't it take too long to ask open questions and use all these other skills?" Well, no. You can conduct short interviews by taking the user's initial question at face value and answering it literally ("Sorry, all our copies are out"), but is that real service? Our answer is that asking open questions may take a little longer (although often it won't). But extra time spent at the beginning to clarify what the user really wants saves time in the long run—time that would otherwise be wasted searching for the wrong thing or transferring the wrong book from another branch. For example, one librarian reported going to the cookery section with a user who had asked for a book on carving game birds. It turned out that he didn't want to carve cooked fowl for the dining table; he wanted to do wood sculpture. An open question such as, "What would you like to know about carving game birds?" would have saved the librarian time and embarrassment. In contrast, another librarian reported her success using open questions with a young user who had asked, "Do you have cookbooks from different lands?" An open question elicited the further information, "I have a grade seven project on special Christmas recipes and I'm supposed to do *buche de Noel*." The librarian summarized the transaction, "We had two books for her in one minute." Open questions usually save time because they give users the chance to focus immediately on whatever is important to *them*.

In virtual environments, the reference interview takes a very small amount of time in comparison with the searching process, but it is time well spent. As in FtF encounters, asking an open question can save valuable effort by making sure that the searching process is directed to answering what the user really wants to know.

3.2.2 Avoiding Premature Diagnosis

Premature diagnosis is another term for jumping to conclusions. For example, a young adult, who is wearing running shoes, jeans and a tee shirt, asks for some material on eating disorders. The librarian asks, "Is this for a school project?"A woman in her thirties asks for pictures of Scandinavian costumes. The librarian asks, "Is this for a costume to make for your child?"An elderly man asks for books on entomology. The librarian asks, "Are you trying to get rid of ants?"

In each of these cases, the librarian assumed something about the user's situation and asked a closed question that made the assumption explicit to the user. Sometimes the librarian is right (the elderly man *did* want to get rid of carpenter ants), but that's just good luck. When the librarian is wrong, the user may find the explicit assumptions offensive (the woman who was asked if the Scandinavian costume was for her child thrust out her ringless left hand indignantly, and said, "Does this look like I have a child?").

Premature diagnosis, one of the commonest causes of communication accidents in libraries, should be avoided. You can't help making assumptions, but you can avoid making these assumptions explicit to the user. Instead of guessing and asking a closed question based on your guess, ask an open question that makes no assumptions.

Compare the following ways of handling the same question:

User: Do you have an elementary math book?

Librarian: Is this book for a child?

User: No, I want it for myself.

Librarian: You must be teaching in the adult basic education program then.

User: No, I'm not a teacher.

Librarian: Oh, I thought you were. A lot of teachers come in asking for basic books for their courses.

User: Is that so?

User: Do you have an elementary math book?

Librarian: We have books of that sort in both the children's and the adult's sections. How do you plan to use this book?

User: It's for myself. To brush up.

Librarian: What areas do you want to brush up in?

User: Pie charts. You see, I have to write a report for my work and need to be able to use pie charts and graphs but I can't figure out how to make them on the computer.

Asking closed questions at the beginning of the reference interview almost always involves the librarian in making assumptions. Often the assumption involved is of the following order: this aspect of topic X is most important to *me* and therefore it must be the most important thing for the user too. Such assumptions, when they are mistaken (as so often

---

ANALYZE THIS REFERENCE TRANSACTION

Case 14: Jumping to conclusions

Librarian: Can I help you?

User: Do you have a sports section?

Librarian: Yes, we do have a sports section. (*acknowledgment*) What specifically were you looking for? (*open question*)

User: Something on golf.

Librarian: Golf? (*acknowledgment*)

User: I want to learn to play golf.

Librarian: [Walks with user to the shelves and shows him the books on learning to play golf] You're not introducing golf to your wife, are you? (*closed question that makes an assumption*)

User: I am single.

Librarian: [Laughs.]

User: I'd have to find a wife first.

(Dewdney, "Golf")

Comment: In Anne Tyler's novel *Accidental Tourist*, the central character Muriel is a dog-care provider who is interested in starting a relationship with another character Macon. She angles to find out about his marital status by asking, "Can't you leave [your dog Edward] home with your wife?" so that she won't waste her time on an unlikely prospect. Unlike Muriel, the librarian in this interview transaction may just have been making small talk, but the question about a wife did seem to startle the user and sidetrack the interview. In general, closed questions that make assumptions about the user should be avoided.

---

they are), lead to questions that are not salient for the user and hence not readily answered. More problematic are personal questions such as "Is this something for your child?" which run the danger of offending the user.

3.2.3 Sense-making Questions

Open questions are effective at getting people to talk. But what we said earlier about the contextualized nature of people's questions (see section 1.4) implies that librarians have to do more than just get users talking. They have to get them to talk about the context of the question. Sometimes asking an open question is all that is needed to encourage the user to talk about contexts, but often users need more guidance. They need to be told what information the staff member needs to know in order to do her job. A good way of guiding the reference interview into useful channels is to ask a special form of open question that we used to call a "neutral question." We now call them "sense-making questions" because this type of questioning technique is derived from Brenda Dervin's sense-making theory. Sense-making questions provide more structure than open questions, but are less likely to lead to premature diagnosis than closed questions.

EXERCISE

Asking Open Questions

This exercise provides practice in distinguishing between open and closed questions. It can be done individually or as a group exercise. For a group exercise, divide participants into small groups of three to five people.

Library user: I have to give a speech on Saturday and I'm looking for some books I can use.

1. Write down three possible **closed** questions that you could ask.
2. Write down three possible **open** questions that you could ask.
3. Examine your open and closed questions to determine whether your closed questions are really closed and your open questions are really open. (Remember: A closed question limits the response to a "yes/no/I don't know" or a "this/that" answer). Which of your six questions do you think would work best and why?

If you want the small groups to share their experiences afterward with the larger group, you can assign a different user's question to each group. Think up your own user questions that are typical of ones asked in your setting. Some possibilities:

- Do you have information on high technology?
- I'm looking for something on children's reading.
- Where do you keep your travel books?
- I would like to find recent research on allergies.
- I'm looking for your pet section.
- I'd like a book on racing.
- Can you help me find some information on milk products?
- Could you direct me to your map section?
- Where are your materials on breast cancer?
- Do you have any books on witchcraft?
- I'm looking for information on plants.

EXERCISE

A Costly Misunderstanding

The user of a branch library asked for "a book on bats."

"Bats as in the animal? not baseball bats?" asked the librarian, using acknowledgment to solve the homophone problem (1.4.1).

"Bats that fly, yes," confirmed the user.

So the librarian ordered the book from the central library and within a week was pleased to present the user with a new natural history book with a hundred color plates and everything you could possibly want to know about bats. But not quite everything; the user was very disappointed.

"I wanted to know how to get rid of them," he said.

1. What could the librarian have asked the user to avoid this misunderstanding?
2. What could be the economic consequences of this misunderstanding? Might there be other consequences? How serious are they from the viewpoint of the user, from the viewpoint of the branch librarian, and from the viewpoint of headquarters?
3. If you were the headquarters librarian and had received this request for a book on bats, what would you have done? What training or procedures would help to avoid this problem in future?
4. What are the policy implications of this example?

The strategy of sense-making grew out of three decades of Dervin's research on how people seek and use information. Dervin uses the term sense-making to refer to her model of information seeking which really deals with how people "make sense" of the world. According to this model, informational needs grow out of specific situations in a person's life. Individuals go through their everyday lives, trying to make sense out of what is happening, seeking certain outcomes, and trying to avoid others. Sometimes, people can't achieve particular goals by themselves and turn to other people for help. For example, if they have to fill out their income tax forms but don't understand the difference between an expense and a capital cost, they go to an accountant. If they are looking for a job and need tips on how to write a résumé, they go to the public library for a book on the topic.

In general, people often have some gap in understanding that must be filled in before they can achieve a goal. If it is your job to provide help,

Conducting the Reference Interview

Closed Questions Are Not Faster

This next exercise can be done with a group. Get a thirty-sided die of the sort used in games like Dungeons and Dragons. Throw the die, note the number, and ask group members to find out from you what the number was by asking you *closed* questions (e.g., "Is it thirty? Is it less than fifteen? Is it an even number"). Ask one member of the group to keep track of how many questions it takes before the correct number is guessed. Then throw the die again and ask the group to find out from you what the number was this time by asking you *open* questions (e.g., "What is the number?"). The point of this exercise is that guessing is not faster.

Playing Twenty Questions

This role-playing exercise can be done as a group exercise with two volunteers playing the parts of the user and librarian and the rest of the group as observers. Before the exercise begins, cards must be prepared in advance for the users' roles. Each user card includes a single initial question that the user asks plus a scenario that gives some background information about the question. Some examples are given here. Think up scenarios of your own for additional cards.

Scenarios:

- Initial question: "Where is your agriculture section?" The user wants to know what makes Mexican jumping beans jump.
- Initial question: "I'm interested in information on Disney." The user is taking a leisure studies course, and has to write a short assignment on Disney theme parks. Specifically the user needs to know about the Disney theme park in France, how long it has been open, how many people on average visit it, and any special features about it.
- Initial question: "Where is your literature section?" The user is a member of a book group and wants to bring a list of local authors who write adult fiction to the next meeting. The user is interested in both literary fiction and popular fiction in any genre.
- Initial question: "Do you have information on snow conditions?" The user wants to know what the skiing is like in Colorado in February.
- Initial question: "Where can I find information on allergies?" The user has a family member with allergies, and wants recipes for bread that do not contain gluten. The user would also be interested in the name of a local support group for people with gluten allergies.
- Initial question: "I need information on popular music." The user has just heard of a group called My Chemical Romance and wants the names of their best songs and CDs and some recent information about the group itself.
- Initial question: "I was looking for something by Barbara Kingsolver, but I can't find it on the shelf." The user has read all of Barbara Kingsolver's fiction and would like to read *High Tide in Tucson*, a collection of essays.

Roles:

- User role: The user presents the initial question and thereafter answers only closed questions, responding "yes," "no," "this," or "that." The user must be careful not to volunteer any information and not to answer if, by mistake, the librarian asks an open question before the three minute time limit is up.
- Librarian role: The librarian is instructed to find out as quickly as possible what this user wants to know, using only *closed* questions.
- Observer role: Observers watch to make sure that all questions are closed, to count the number of closed questions asked, and to call time if the librarian does not discover the true query in three minutes. If the query is not fully negotiated in three minutes, the librarian may at this point ask open questions and the user improvises answers according to the scenario on the card.

Discussion:

After each role-play, the group leader may ask the observers to analyze what happened in the interview. Which questions worked, which didn't, and what was the difference between asking open questions and closed question?

you need to know the *situation* the person is in, the *gaps* in his or her understanding, and the *uses* or helps—what the person would like to do as a result of bridging this gap. In order fully to understand the question, the librarian needs to know all three of these elements. To find out these three things, ask sense-making questions. A *sense-making question* is a special kind of open question that asks specifically about situations, or gaps, or uses.

To clarify the differences among closed, open, and sense-making questions, consider the following three responses to the same request for information on travel.

EXAMPLE

User: Excuse me, but can you tell me where to find information on travel?

Librarian: Would you like a book on travel—a travel guide? (*closed question* that makes an assumption)

User: Yes, I guess so. Thanks.

Librarian: Our travel guides are over there (points to shelves).

In this case, the librarian does not discover anything about either the situation or the gap or the uses.

User: Excuse me, but can you tell me where to find information on travel?

Librarian: What sort of travel information do you have in mind? (*open question that encourages the user to say more*)

User: Information on New York City. I'm traveling there next month.

Librarian: We have several good travel guides to New York City. Here's the *Fodor Guide*...

In this case, the librarian finds out the situation (making a trip to New York City) but does not discover the gap or the uses.

User: Excuse me but can you tell me where to find information on travel?

Librarian: We have quite a lot of travel information in different parts of the library. If you could tell me how you would be using this information, I could help you find something. (*sense-making question focusing on uses*)

User: I need New York City information. I'd like to read up on plays that will be on in New York next month so that I can order some tickets in advance.

Librarian: Okay, you want to learn about what's playing in New York so that you can order tickets. (*acknowledgment*) You'll need really current information for that, and so the Internet would be a good place to look.

In this case, the librarian finds out all three: the situation (the user is making a trip to New York City); the gap (what plays will be on in New

Practice and Persist

Any new skill must be practiced before it can be used with confidence. As a way of getting started using this skill, pick two questions from the list "Some Sense-making Questions" and use them until you feel comfortable asking them. Observe what happens when you ask these questions. This experience in real situations will help you understand the function of sense-making questions.

Be prepared to ask more than one question. If the first sense-making question you ask doesn't produce enough information for you to recognize whether a source would be helpful, follow it up with a different one.

SOME SENSE-MAKNG QUESTIONS

Here are some examples of good sense-making questions to ask when you want to help someone but must first determine the precise nature of what would help:

To encourage the person to describe the situation:
- What are you working on?
- How did this question arise?
- What happened that you need to know this?

To find out how the person sees the situation:
- What problem are you having in this situation?
- Where would you like to begin?
- Where do you see yourself going with this?

To assess the gaps:
- What kind of help would you like?
- What are you trying to understand?
- What would you like to know about X?
- Where did you get stuck with this project?

To identify the kind of help wanted (uses):
- What would help you?
- How do you plan to use this information?
- What would you like to see happen in this situation?
- What are you trying to do in this situation?
- If you could have exactly the help you want, what would it be?

York during the visit); and the use (the user wants to be able to order theater tickets in advance).

To consider another example, suppose a user asks, "Do you have anything about crime?" The librarian could ask *closed* questions that involve making assumptions and invite short answers: "Do you want criminal law? Do you want a crime story? Do you want statistics?" The librarian could ask an *open* question that encourages the user to talk: "What are you interested in?" or "What more can you tell me about your question?" Or the librarian could ask a *sense-making* question focused on the situation, gap, or use such as "What are you working on?" "What would you like to know about crime?" or "How would you like the information to help you?"

Answering these sense-making questions, the user might respond, "I've been looking in this index under crime, but I can't find anything on the James Bulger case," or "I want the address of the Crime Writers of America," or "I need statistics of the crime rate in Florida for a school project." Following up with a second neutral question in a process that Dervin calls "help-chaining," the staff member could ask, "If we could find X, how would *that* help you?" This will usually elicit more details about the context of the question: "I'm compiling information on a list

EXERCISE

Sense-making Questions

Try this exercise in pairs. Before starting, copy this page and paste each scenario on a separate card. Make up more scenarios of your own. For the exercise, one person plays the role of the user and is given one of the scenarios below. The other person is a librarian who asks sense-making questions to find out what the user really wants to know. The librarian should have close at hand the list "Some Sense-making Questions." The librarian should keep asking sense-making questions until the user is satisfied that the question is really understood.

Scenario 1: User is a student who has to write an English essay that provides "a close analysis of the text" of an American colonial poem. He doesn't have a fixed topic in mind, and his first problem is that he doesn't know what is meant by "a close analysis of the text." He asks, "Where is the section on American poetry?"

Scenario 2: User is planning to take the Police College entrance exam and wants to prepare himself as much as possible in advance. He has heard that there is often a question about proverbs. He says, "I'm having trouble with this catalog."

Scenario 3: User has a neighbor who is building an addition to his house right up to the property line. The user wants to find out whether there are any building codes that would prevent this building from going up. She asks, "Where is your law section?"

Scenario 4: User wants to write a letter to a local author, saying how much she enjoyed the author's most recent book. She thinks that current information about where the author lives may be on the book jacket. She says, "I'm looking for [recent title] by [fairly well-known author] but it's not on the shelf. [In this scenario, the person taking the user's role should use the name of an author who comes from the local region.]

Scenario 5: User thinks that ingesting caffeine could be causing ringing in his ears. Therefore he wants to be able to identify foods containing caffeine so as to avoid them. He already knows that coffee, tea, chocolate, and certain soda drinks contain caffeine, but he wants to know if there are any other foods that he should avoid. He asks, "Where is your section on drugs?"

Scenario 6: User is worried about a change in her daughter Laura's behavior that has happened recently. Laura used to be a straight A student in her high school, but recently her grades have dropped. She has stopped seeing her previous friends and is hanging out with a group of kids that are not doing well in school. She has become uncommunicative and rebellious. The mother has heard that drugs can cause behavior changes. She asks, "Where is your section on drugs?"

A QUICK TIP

Here's What I Want to Do

Using the sense-making framework is useful in everyday contexts as well. Jane Houston posted this tip to LIBREF (August 26, 1997): "I finally have learned to tell the hardware store clerk, 'Well, I'm not sure what I want, but let me tell you what I'm planning to do and perhaps you can help me.' Needless to say, it works like a charm." (Thanks to Jane Houston, Reference coordinator in the Government Information Center in the Idaho State Library, Boise, Idaho.)

of cases involving very young children who have committed homicide," or "I've written a detective story that's sure to be a bestseller if only I can find the right publisher," or "I need to get ready for a debate on the efficacy of capital punishment."

We know from extensive research on people's information-seeking behavior that the kind of answer that is most helpful depends on the use they plan for the information—what it will help them do. Someone

Conducting the Reference Interview

writing a short essay on the symptoms of Alzheimer's disease, for example, requires a different reference source than will a person who is trying find out about the best care for a relative suffering from the disease. Until you know how the user hopes the information will help, you will not be able to make effective use of your knowledge of reference sources. In a Norwegian study that observed and audiotaped the interactions between users and librarians during reference transactions, Ragnar Nordlie (2000) noted that only 6 percent of the questions that librarians asked users were concerned with the users' purpose or plan for using the information. In contrast, purpose was the second most frequent theme of users' own voluntary contributions occurring in 30 percent of cases. When librarians discovered that they needed to change the direction of their search, the most frequent cause for modifying the search was the discovery of the user's purpose.

When we teach the skill of sense-making questions in workshops, we find that participants sometimes report reservations about asking for the context of a question when the situation might turn out to be personal or embarrassing. Potentially embarrassing situations include, unfortunately, most of the human situations in which people desperately need help—situations of bereavement, serious illness, and approaching death; situations of family problems, sexual dysfunction, divorce; situations of job loss and economic hardship. Something worth asking parenthetically is this: Whose embarrassment are we as library professionals really concerned about—the user's embarrassment in revealing something personal about himself, or our own in hearing it? If it is our own embarrassment, then we will be more comfortable *not* asking sense-making questions, and simply saying to the user, "We have some materials on crime/ health/ small businesses over there and if you just look through those you might find something." The downside to this hands-off approach is that it deprives the user of your professional help in finding the appropriate source.

But if it is the user's embarrassment that solely concerns us, it may be reassuring to remember that sense-making questions leave the user in control. In response to a sense-making question, the user can say as much or as little as he chooses. He can say, "My niece has just been diagnosed with non-Hodgkin's lymphoma and I want to read about treatment and survival rates." But he doesn't have to. He could say, "Oh, I'd like to just browse in the medical books, thanks." He need not say any more about his situation than he feels comfortable revealing. You could respond with, "Here are the medical books along these shelves. But if you don't find what you're looking for, let me know because we have additional information in other places, including in electronic sources." This way, the user can return later if he has not been able to find the information on his own.

While librarians do not normally ask sense-making questions as a matter of course, they can learn to use this skill intentionally, as Dewdney (1986) demonstrated in her doctoral thesis "The Effects of Training Reference Librarians in Interview Skills." Twenty-four practicing librarians in three relatively large public libraries volunteered to participate in a

WHY NOT ASK "WHY?" DIRECTLY?

Library professionals have long recognized that they can be most helpful if they understand the users' intended purposes. Moreover, most users are quite willing to explain how they plan to use the information if you ask the question appropriately. There are four guidelines for asking this question:

1. Never ask "Why" directly. "Why do you want to know that?" sounds abrupt and possibly judgmental. It runs the risk of the user's responding, "What's it to you why I want to know?" or even "None of your business." Moreover, "why" questions aren't necessarily efficient at eliciting answers about situations or uses because users may not understand why you are asking why. They may say "Because this library is closest," "Because the teacher told me to ask," or "Because I can't find what I want." If pushed into a corner by a direct "why?" question, some users may deliberately conceal their personal interest, and answer, perhaps, "It's for a friend." (5.3.1)

2. Make it clear that you are asking about intended uses because it *is* your business. You are not just prying. You are an information professional who can do the job better and provide more helpful sources if you know how the information will be used. If the user says, "Where do you keep your Alzheimer's information?" you could say, "We have a lot of material on Alzheimer's—it all depends on what you're looking for. Can you tell me a bit about how you plan to use this information?" or "I could help you better if I knew what you are trying to do."

3. Avoid assumptions. A user who looks like a student may be asking the question for personal reasons, while an older harried-looking person may be trying to get a few statistics for an assignment due tomorrow for a continuing education course. Let users tell you themselves what they are trying to do. Don't guess. Don't ask, "Is this for a school project?" Younger users are especially put off by the question: "Is this a homework question?" The implication here is that it is inappropriate for the user to ask for homework help.

4. Leave the user in control. When you ask a sense-making question like, "How do you plan to use this information?" users can say as much or as little they want. They may tell you the whole context, which will help you suggest the most appropriate material. But they might also say, "Oh, I'm just interested," a response that lets you know they don't want to say anything further just now.

Did You Know?
Dewdney and Michell (1997) draw on speech act theory to explain that "why" questions are often misinterpreted because the user doesn't understand their relevance. The problem is that the librarian's "why?" question does not fit into the user's mental model of a reference interview. The librarian can avoid misunderstandings by prefacing questions about intended uses with an explanation such as, "I could help you better if I knew something more about how you plan to use this information."

field experiment. One-third received no training, one-third were trained in microskills, and one-third were trained in the use of neutral or sense-making questions. Before and after the training period, tape recordings were made of 332 interviews between each librarian and the adult users who presented an informational need. In addition, 236 of these users were interviewed afterward by a research assistant who asked what kind of help they wanted and how helpful was the answer provided. Users received significantly more helpful answers from librarians trained in sense-making questioning, in comparison with librarians trained in microskills and with untrained librarians.

In our workshops on the reference interview, a frequently asked question is, "When someone asks for something specific, do I still need to conduct a reference interview?" As is well-known, people often ask for a particular title or reference tool such as Charles Dickens's *A Christmas Carol* or the *Encyclopaedia Britannica*. A reference interview might seem redundant because the user obviously knows what's wanted. But are you sure? If the requested item is easy to provide, give it to the user along with the follow-up "If this doesn't have everything you need, make sure you come back" (see section 4.1.3). However, if the specific source or person asked for is unavailable or hard to access, a good rule of thumb is *not* to say, "Would you like us to recall that book?" or "Come back in three weeks when our German specialist has returned from her holiday." The user, not familiar with the whole range of sources available, may have asked by name for the one source he happens to know about, but the library may have additional or better sources.

When you find yourself about to suggest an interlibrary loan or refer the user to another library or agency, first ask, "Perhaps there's something else that would help you. What sort of information are you looking for?" In the case of *A Christmas Carol*, for example, it turned out that all copies were out. But the librarian was able to determine that the user wanted to put on a play with her grade seven class and was thinking of making a play out of Dickens's Christmas story. The librarian was then able to provide a collected edition of Christmas plays for children that included a dramatic version of *A Christmas Carol*. In another case, a user was disappointed that all the Harry Potter books were checked out and had many people ahead of her on the reserves list. When the librarian noticed that the spoken word version of one of the books was available and offered this as an alternative, the user was delighted. A successful reference transaction occurs whenever users are helped to achieve the goals that brought them to the library.

3.2.4 Reflecting Content: Paraphrasing and Summarizing

After asking some open or sense-making questions, summarize what you have understood just to make sure that you have a complete and accurate picture. Reflecting content is a way of demonstrating that you have been attentively listening. Moreover, like acknowledgment, this skill gives you a chance to check that your understanding is correct. When you reflect content, you are not supplying any new information of your own. You are mirroring back to the user what you have understood. If you have gotten something wrong or left something out, the user has a chance to provide a correction. The two major ways to reflect content are *paraphrasing* and *summarizing*.

PARAPHRASING

Paraphrasing feeds back what has just been said in the previous comment. In the reference interview, paraphrasing is prefaced by an introductory clause such as: "So you're looking for...," "What you need is...,"

ANALYZE THIS REFERENCE TRANSACTION

Case 15: "I'm not sure what you are asking about."

This verbatim excerpt of a chat reference transaction is from the Seeking Synchronicity Project, Radford and Connaway (2005–2008). In this early part of a lengthy interaction, a law librarian is trying to understand the user's complex question about the legality of a municipal vote on a business improvement issue. After a good open question ("What is it you are looking to find?") and some closed questions ("Was this a state election? Or a county one?"), the librarian uses a series of summary statements as a way of confirming a shared understanding of the question. Examine the effectiveness of these summary statements in helping to clarify the real question.

1. Librarian: [Hello, this is the law librarian. I'm reading your question...]
2. Librarian: What is it you are looking to find? (*open question*)
3. User: Yes thank you. In tohousand there was a business improvemnet vote 6 property owners were not counteed what ae guidelines
4. User: city attorney says election
5. Librarian: I am not sure what you are asking about. Was this a state election? Or a county one? (*closed questions*)
6. User: is legal, however those six property owners were not counted which give the against the majority. I need to know where to get legal guideline on procedure
7. Librarian: So there was some kind of vote in your county back in 2000? Is that correct?
8. User: No vote in 2000,this is first
9. User: time,in [city]
10. User: mayor asked if any more ballots were to be turned in I said yes and then clerk didn't count them 60 ballots to be exact.
11. Librarian: So there is a vote of some kind in [city, state] and you saying that you need to know if the vote was legal?
12. User: the vote acording to clerk wa so close for won by 2%
13. User: YET IF 6 Property owners were counted against would have won by 1.5%
14. Librarian: Okay, so it sounds like you want to protest the election results. Is that correct?
15. User: Yes and why 6 property owners were excluded as well as 60 ballots

Comment: Starting at line 7, the librarian begins a series of paraphrasing and summarizing statements with the purpose of confirming an understanding of the real question ("You are saying..."; "It sounds like..."). Note the repeated use of the checkout statement, "Is that correct?"

A QUICK TIP

Don't Be a Parrot

Like every microskill, paraphrasing and summarizing needs to be done intentionally and for a purpose. Use this skill only when it is important to have a shared understanding of what another person means. Used in everyday small talk, the conversation may go like this:

User: Looks like we're in for some rain.
Librarian: You think it looks like rain.
User: Yes, that's what I just said.

"You mean...," or, "As I understand you...," followed by a concise summary giving the essence of what you think was meant.

For example, a user says, "All the leaves are falling off my poinsettia and I need some help." The librarian paraphrases by saying, "So you're looking for plant care information for your poinsettia? Is that it?"

Tips for paraphrasing:

- Be concise. Usually a short pithy sentence is enough.
- Feed back the essence by restating what you understand to be the main idea of what was just said.
- Try not to add to or change the meaning of what you have heard.
- You may want to use a checkout such as, "Is that what you wanted?" or "Was that it?"

SUMMARIZING

Summarizing is like paraphrasing except that it covers a larger span of conversation and requires you to distill the essence of what was said over the course of a longer series of questions and answers. It may be used as a good conclusion to an interview before you start looking for sources.

> So you are doing a project on the tobacco industry for your media studies course. And you would like to find some analyses of recent class action lawsuits against tobacco companies. You also want to know if there has been any recent legislation that is relevant to tobacco advertising. You need it soon because your project is due on Friday. Have I got that right?

Tips for summarizing:

- Synthesize the gist of what was said in the course of a number of previous statements.
- Condense.
- Go for the big picture.

3.2.5 Closure

Closure is the art of the tactful ending. It really consists of a cluster of skills that are used to signal leave-taking. We are all familiar with some of the ritualistic nonverbal skills that signal the end of any conversation—changes in body orientation such as moving away from the other person, or changes in eye contact such as looking toward an exit or a clock. Sometimes, however, these nonverbal cues give the other person a feeling of being suddenly cut off. To return the topic of discussion back to the purpose of the interview or to wrap up a conversation smoothly, you may want to use the verbal skills of closure. Some functions of closure are to indicate that the discussion of a topic has been completed, at least for the moment, to focus the participant's attention on what has been achieved in the discussion, and to establish a good communication climate so that the other person looks forward to the next encounter (Hargie, Saunders, and Dickson, 1994, 162–163).

In the reference interview, you should use closure when the conversation is wandering in order to bring the talk back to the purpose of the interview. Don't make the mistake of cutting the other person off

---

A QUICK TIP

Closure That Helps

Closure can also be used when you realize you're going to have to refer the user to someone else. For example: "This sounds like a pretty technical topic, so what I'd like to do is find our science and technology librarian." The difference between this use of closure and the negative closure strategy of the unmonitored referral (3.1.5), is that here you are monitoring the referral by making sure that the science and technology librarian is available, and is, in fact, the right person to help.

mid-sentence or of changing the subject abruptly. Not only will you be perceived as impolite, but the other person may, despite appearances, have been telling you something that is important to your understanding of the problem. However, when it is apparent that the conversation is clearly off-track, you can get back to the point tactfully by acknowledging what the other person is saying and then moving quickly back (not pausing) to the main purpose of the conversation. You might say, "Yes, it sounds like your daughter's graduation dress will be very suitable. Now about your genealogy project—what information are you interested in today?" Knowing the effect of the questions you ask enables you to choose an appropriate questioning style—using open questions to encourage reticent users to talk about what concerns them but practicing closure to focus digressers.

The second way to use closure is to signal the end of an interaction. If the conversation has been brief, perhaps all that is necessary is a one-phrase summary or a comment to suggest future steps, such as, "So now you know how to request an interlibrary loan," or "Next time you'll know that we have other material that's not in the catalog." In almost all reference transactions, it's a good idea to use a follow-up question (4.1.3) which will provide you with a chance to confirm that the user has got what she or he wanted, as well as to close the conversation. You could say, for example, "If you find that you can't get logged on, please be sure to come back and ask again."

The skill of closure is a way to be helpful and keep the interview on track. This skill should not be confused with negative closure, which is a way to get rid of the user without providing a helpful answer (3.1.5).

3.3 Annotated References

3.3.1 Problems in the Reference Interview

Bunge, Charles A. 1985. "Factors Related to Reference Question Answering Success: The Development of a Data-Gathering Form." *RQ* 24, no. 4 (summer): 482–486. Identifies factors that lead to success and failure.

Dewdney, Patricia, and Catherine Sheldrick Ross. 1994. "Flying a Light Aircraft: Reference Evaluation from a User's Viewpoint." *RQ* 34, no. 2 (winter): 217–230. Describes user reactions toward librarians' use of acknowledgment, questioning skills, giving instructions, and making referrals.

Douglas, Ian. 1988. "Reducing Failures in Reference Service." *RQ* 28, no. 1 (fall): 94–101.

Durrance, Joan. 1995. "Factors That Influence Reference Success." *The Reference Librarian* 49/50: 243–265.

Lynch, Mary Jo. 1978. "Reference Interviews in Public Libraries. *Library Quarterly* 48, no. 2 (April): 119–142. Reports the author's research done for her doctoral degree at Rutgers in which she tape-recorded reference transactions in public libraries.

Murfin, Marjorie, and Charles Bunge. 1984. "Evaluating Reference Service from the Patron Point of View: Some Interim National Survey Results." *The Reference Librarian* 11: 175–182.

Ross, Catherine Sheldrick, and Patricia Dewdney. 1994. "Best Practices: An Analysis of the Best (and Worst) in Fifty-two Public Library Reference Transactions." *Public Libraries* 33, no. 5 (September/October): 261–266. Contrasts the best and worst and provides some practical suggestions for improving service.

Ross, Catherine Sheldrick, and Patricia Dewdney. 1998. "Negative Closure: Strategies and Counter-strategies in the Reference Interview." *Reference and User Services Quarterly* 38, no. 2 (winter): 151–164. Examines ways that librarians get rid of the user, apart from providing a helpful answer.

Ross, Catherine Sheldrick, and Kirsti Nilsen. 2000. "Has the Internet Changed Anything in Reference? The Library Visit Study, Phase 2." *Reference & User Services Quarterly* 40, no. 2 (winter): 147–155.

Zweizig, Douglas L. 1976. "With Our Eye on the User." *Drexel Library Quarterly* 12, no. 1/2 (January/April): 48–58.

3.3.2 Works of Relevance to the Reference Interview in General

Berinstein, Paula. 1994. *Communication with Library Users: A Self-Study Program.* Washington, DC: Special Libraries Association. This workbook provides exercises to practice questioning, avoiding premature diagnosis, and other skills.

Hargie, Owen, Christine Saunders, and David Dickson. 1994. *Social Skills in Interpersonal Communication*, 3rd ed. London: Routledge. The authors use a skills-based model to describe basic interpersonal strategies.

Hutcherson, Norman B. 2004. "Library Jargon: Student Recognition of Terms and Concepts Commonly Used by Librarians in the Classroom." *College & Research Libraries* 65, no.4 (July): 349–354. Reports result of study that found that many terms librarians commonly use in reference interviews are not understood by academic library users (e.g., bibliography, index).

Ivey, Allen E., and Mary Bradford Ivey. 2007. *Intentional Interviewing and Counseling: Facilitating Client Development in a Multicultural Society*, 6th ed. Pacific Grove, CA: Brooks/Cole. The latest edition of this classic work focuses on solution-centered and person- centered interviewing, and relates these to microskills. An online instructor's guide is available separately.

Jennerich, Elaine Z., and Edward J. Jennerich. 1997. *The Reference Interview as a Creative Art*, 2nd ed. Littleton, CO: Libraries Unlimited. Using the metaphor of a reference interview as a dramatic production, this book discusses verbal and nonverbal skills for the reference interview in a chapter called "The Actor's Tools." This book builds on the pioneering work done by Elaine Jennerich in her doctoral dissertation, "Microcounseling in Library Education" (University of Pittsburgh, 1974).

Lesikar, Raymond V., and Marie E. Flatley. 2005. *Basic Business Communication: Skills for Empowering the Internet Generation*, 10th ed. New York: McGraw–Hill Irwin. Part 5 provides a useful section on speaking skills.

Malbin, Susan L. 1997. "The Reference Interview in Archival Literature." *College & Research Libraries* 58, no. 1 (January): 69–80. A review essay on the writing about reference from within the archival field. Malbin concludes that the reference interview and communication skills for successful query negotiation have not been studied or taught within the archival setting which has led to detrimental service.

Nilsen, Kirsti. 2004. "The Library Visit Study: User Experiences at the Virtual Reference Desk." *Information Research* 9, no. 2." Available: http://

informationr.net/ir/9-2/paper171.html (accessed December 22, 2008). This is the first report covering VR transactions done for the Library Visit Study.

Nilsen, Kirsti. 2006. "Comparing Users' Perspectives on In-Person and Virtual Reference." *New Library World* 107, no. 1222/1223: 91–104. Compares findings from 261 FtF and 85 VR Library Visit Study transactions. The second edition of *Conducting the Reference Interview* includes previously unpublished data from the Library Visit Study, covering a total of 150 VR transactions (see index under "Library Visit Study").

Nolan, Christopher W. 1992. "Closing the Reference Interview: Implications for Policy and Practice." *RQ* 31, no. 4 (summer): 513–523.

Ohio Library Council. 2000 (last updated 2008). *Ohio Reference Excellence on the Web*. Available: www.olc.org/ore (accessed November 4, 2008). The Ohio Library Council has produced a very useful Web-based training program on the reference interview which it calls "the key to the reference process." Skills covered in the ORE program include paraphrasing, asking open questions, clarifying, verifying, following up, and ending the interview.

Radford, Marie L. 1996. "Communication Theory Applied to the Reference Encounter: An Analysis of Critical Incidents." *The Library Quarterly* 66, no. 2 (April): 123–137. In-depth study of the factors that are critical to users' and librarians' perceptions of successful and unsuccessful face-to-face reference encounters in academic libraries.

Radford, Marie L. 1999. *The Reference Encounter: Interpersonal Communication in the Academic Library*. Chicago: Association of College and Research Libraries. Finds that users and librarians have different perceptions of what is happening in the reference transaction.

Radford, Marie L. 2006. "Encountering Virtual Users: A Qualitative Investigation of Interpersonal Communication in Chat Reference." *Journal of the American Society for Information Science and Technology* 57, no. 8 (June): 1046–1059. This analysis of live chat transcripts highlights interpersonal facilitators and barriers in a statewide virtual reference service, and includes examples and coding scheme.

Radford, Marie L., and Lynn Silipigni Connaway. 2007a. "Are We Getting Warmer? Query Clarification in Virtual Reference." Presented at the Library Research Round Table, American Library Association Conference, Washington, June 21–27, 2007. Available: www.oclc.org/research/projects/synchronicity/presentations.htm#recent (accessed December 15, 2008). Reports findings from an analysis of 434 live chat reference transcripts; reveals that 75 percent of librarians asked clarifying questions and that these questions boosted accuracy of information.

Radford, Marie L., and Lynn Silipigni Connaway. 2007b. "'Screenagers' and Live Chat Reference: Living Up to the Promise." *Scan* 26, no. 1: 31–39. Report of a series of three focus groups with teens that reveals their perceptions of librarians and virtual reference.

Radford, Marie L., and Lynn Silipigni Connaway. 2005-2008. "Seeking Synchronicity: Evaluating Virtual Reference Services from User, Non-User, and Librarian Perspectives." Funded by the Institute for Museum and Library Services, Rutgers, the State University of New Jersey, and OCLC, Online Computer Library Center. Grant Web site available at: www.oclc.org/research/projects/synchronicity (accessed December 15, 2008). Findings and presentations from a multi-year study of live chat reference. Includes guidelines for practice.

Reference and User Services Association. 2004. "Guidelines for Behavioral Performance of Reference and Information Service Professionals." Available:

www.ala.org/ala/mgrps/divs/rusa/resources/guidelines/guidelinesbehavioral .cfm (accessed December 6, 2008). Includes techniques for showing approach-ability and interest, listening/inquiring, searching and providing follow-up.

Ross, Catherine Sheldrick. 2003. "The Reference Interview: Why It Needs to Be Used in Every (Well, Almost Every) Reference Transaction," *RUSQ* 43, no. 1: 38–42.

White, Marilyn Dolmas. 1998. "Questions in Reference Interviews." *Journal of Documentation* 54, no. 4 (September): 443–465. Categorizes the types of questions asked in a pre-search interview before online searching, and finds that about half the questions were verification questions such as "Have you looked at Psych Abs yet?"

White, Marilyn Domas. 1989. "Different Approaches to the Reference Interview." *Reference Librarian* 25/26: 631–646. Distinguishes between two models of reference interview behavior: the needs-oriented model and the question-oriented model.

Whitlatch, Jo Bell. 1995. "Question Classification." In *The Reference Assessment Manual* (42–46). Ann Arbor, MI: Pierian Press.

3.3.3 Questioning Skills

Dervin, Brenda, and Patricia Dewdney. 1986. "Neutral Questioning: A New Approach to the Reference Interview." *RQ* 25, no. 4 (summer): 506–513. Explains the theory and practice of sense-making questions. Readers who want to find out more about Brenda Dervin's sense-making methodology can find articles, papers, and commentaries on sense-making at: http://communication .sbs.ohio-state.edu/sense-making/ (accessed December 17, 2008).

Dewdney, Patricia H. "The Effects of Training Reference Librarians in Interview Skills: A Field Experiment." Doctoral dissertation. London, Canada: The University of Western Ontario, 1986. [Microform edition, Ottawa: National Library of Canada, 1987]. Reports a field experiment in which twenty-four experienced reference librarians from three Ontario public libraries were observed both before and after training in specific listening and questioning skills.

Dewdney, Patricia, and Gillian Michell. 1997. "Asking 'Why' Questions in the Reference Interview: A Theoretical Justification." *Library Quarterly* 67, no. 1 (January): 50–71. Explains the linguistic reasons that "why" questions are often misinterpreted, and suggests other strategies for finding out "why." This article is a good starting point for references on research regarding question-asking from the literature of linguistics as well as from the library literature.

Dyson, Lillie Seward. 1992. "Improving Reference Services: A Maryland Training Program Brings Positive Results." *Public Libraries* 31, no. 5 (September/ October): 284–89.

Gers, Ralph, and Lillie J. Seward. 1985. "Improving Reference Performance: Results of a State-wide Study." *Library Journal* 110, no. 8 (November 1): 32–35.

Gothberg, Helen M. 1995. "Communication and the Reference Interface." In *The Reference Assessment Manual* (76–81). Ann Arbor, MI: Pierian Press.

Isenstein, Laura. 1992. "Get Your Reference Staff on the STAR Track." *Library Journal* 117, no. 7 (April 15): 34–37. Describes a program for training reference staff to use open questions, paraphrasing, and follow-up.

Jordan, Peter. 1985. "Training in Handling Library Users." In *Handbook of Library Training Practice*, edited by Ray Prytherch. Aldershot, Hants, England; Brookfield, VT: Gower.

King, Geraldine B. 1972. "The Reference Interview: Open and Closed Questions." *RQ,* 12, no. 2 (winter): 157–160.

Lynch, Mary Jo. 1978. "Reference Interviews in Public Libraries." *Library Quarterly* 48, no. 2 (April): 119–142. Analyzes 309 reference interviews recorded in public libraries in order to find out how often a reference interview occurs, and what proportion of the questions asked by the staff member are open or closed.

Nordlie, Ragnar. 2000. "Conversing with the Catalogue: How the Reference Interview Can Inform Online Catalogue Searching." *Scandinavian Public Library Quarterly* 33, no. 2: 22–7. This study used two sets of data gather in Norwegian public libraries—transaction logs of end-user searches, as well as audiotaped and transcribed reference transactions—to see what online catalog designers could learn from reference interactions.

Ross, Catherine Sheldrick. 1986. "How to Find Out What People Really Want to Know." *The Reference Librarian* 16 (winter): 19–30. Theory and practice of open and sense-making (neutral) questions.

Ross, Catherine Sheldrick, and Patricia Dewdney. 1986. "Reference Interviewing Skills: Twelve Common Questions." *Public Libraries* 25, no. 1 (spring): 7–9.

3.3.4 Reflecting Content and Feeling

Dickson, David A. 1997. "Reflecting." In *The Handbook of Communication Skills,* 2nd ed. (159–182), edited by Owen D.W. Hargie. London and New York: Routledge. This scholarly overview of verbal and nonverbal reflecting behavior may be useful to trainers.

Evans, David R., Margaret Hearn, Max Uhlemann, and Allen Ivey. 2008. *Essential Interviewing: A Programmed Approach to Effective Communication,* 7th ed. Monterey, CA: Brooks/Cole. Chapter 2 in this workbook deals with attending behavior, Chapter 3 with effective questioning, and Chapters 4 and 5 cover reflecting content and feeling.

Beyond Negative Closure

4.1 Skills for Working Together

In *Information Ecologies*, Bonnie Nardi and Vicki O'Day (1999) describe librarians as a "keystone species"—one of the species in an ecology whose loss leads to the extinction of other species in the ecosystem. They say, "We believe that the diverse services available in the library are still important and useful, and we believe that the increase in online information presents more opportunities to leverage the skills of professional librarians than ever before. Through our fieldwork in libraries, we have identified librarians as a keystone species." They argue that the work of librarians is not well understood (or appreciated) because so much of it is invisible work. One of the most valuable and unrecognized services that they identified is "to help clients understand their own needs—a kind of information therapy" (85).

What Nardi and O'Day are writing about, of course, is the reference interview, a creative problem-solving process which is collaborative. Few library users, even experienced ones, have ever heard of the reference interview or know that they are being interviewed. But through the questions they answer during a well-conducted reference interview, they are able to clarify in their own minds what their question really is. This narrowing and clarifying process is most evident in situations such as school assignments where the user often has no idea of how much is available in a particular area. The librarian's questions help the user narrow a topic like plant adaptations to a manageable topic for a science project, such as the carnivorous diet of the pitcher plant as an adaptation to life in an acidic bog. At the end of the process, the library professional and the user, by working together, have achieved a new understanding that neither could have arrived at individually.

A good reference interview is a collaboration. User and staff member are equal partners in the search with different areas of expertise. The user is the expert in the question itself, knowing how the question arose, what necessary information is missing from a complete understanding of the topic, and how the information will be used. The staff member is the expert on the library system and the organization and retrieval of information. Both need to work together. The staff member can't find the most appropriate sources without the user's active collaboration and vice versa. By asking questions to identify the real informational need and working with the user in checking what is available, staff members can help users clarify in their own minds what information is wanted, but users need to be kept engaged in the process.

It is important to emphasize the user as active agent because in so much of the published literature on reference service, the user's question is considered largely as an "input" into the system. As one user in the Library Visit Study lamented, "I felt that once I had handed over my question, the question developed a life of its own apart from me, and I was no longer of interest to the librarians. Only the question was of interest. Neither of them asked me any questions concerning my question." In this construction of the user role as passive bystander, the user gets the ball rolling by asking the initiating question, but then the librarian takes charge, asks the questions during the reference interview, finds the sources, evaluates the sources, gives directions and advice, and so on. The user is there mainly to tag along, answer the librarian's questions during the reference interview, and receive the answer at the end.

In contrast, our research on users has led us to construct a picture of an active user energetically pursuing goals. In successful transactions, the staff members help the users achieve their goals while in unsuccessful transactions, staff members are obstacles and stumbling blocks that users have to work around. In the latter cases, when users experience negative closure, they often adopt strategies of their own to elicit more help from library staff and keep staff from giving up too soon. Users in general want to be accepted as active partners in the search and are most satisfied with their experience when library staff members take steps to involve them. Three skills for getting beyond negative closure by making the user an active partner are inclusion, library use instruction (bibliographic instruction), and the follow-up.

4.1.1 Inclusion: Telling People What You Are Doing

You can prevent many communication accidents from happening simply by telling the user what you are doing. Inclusion, or telling people what you are doing, is especially important when users can't see you (e.g., in a telephone interview) or when users can't tell what you are doing from observation alone. Inclusion is an attending skill: it maintains the communication process between two people when one person must perform a task that does not, in itself, require interpersonal communication, or when one person must do something that might otherwise signal an interruption or termination of the conversation. This skill works because it helps to answer such unspoken questions as, "Are you still there?"; "Are you still working on my problem?"; and "Why are you doing something that doesn't seem related to my problem?" In the Library Visit Study, users often reported feeling confused and left in the dark when staff members didn't explain what they were doing or what they expected users to do. Users said things like, "He left me standing there and didn't tell me where he was going or how long he would be," "I wasn't sure whether I should be following her or whether I should wait at the desk for her to return," or "I couldn't tell if he heard me."

Inclusion reassures the user and is an easy solution to the "without-speaking-she-began-to-type" problem described in section 3.1.1. If you have to focus your attention on the computer screen to search for information on the user's topic, you should explain what you are doing, whether it be checking a special database, looking for other subject headings, or whatever. Instead of silently abandoning the user, explain, "I'm going to check the shelves for you and will return in a minute." Inclusion makes the user a partner in the search and not a bystander. Users like to be treated this way. "I did wish," said one user, "that she explained what she was doing and included me more." Since it doesn't take any longer to explain things to the user as you are doing them, this is something that librarians should consider standard practice.

In addition, inclusion often serves an instructive function. Describing and explaining your behavior helps the observer learn how to replicate that behavior. So the librarian could say, "Often a good place to start with this sort of question is with the catalog. I am going to search for books on your subject by using the term, 'Technological innovations—Social aspects.'" And when the librarian says, "What I am doing now is looking for other headings we could use," the user learns that an index provides synonymous or alternate terms.

Inclusion is a skill that is particularly useful in the following situations:

- When the other person cannot see what you are doing. On the telephone or in a chat exchange, always describe behavior that interrupts normal conversation. For example, "I'm going to put you on hold for a minute while I check an index for you," or "I'm writing this down as you speak," or "I'm looking in our directory of community services." It is especially important to use inclusion with blind people, saying, for example, "I'm going over to the other desk for a minute to ask Margaret if she knows the name of the organization you were asking about. She is our in-house expert on business questions."

- When the relationship between your behavior and the problem is not immediately apparent to a layperson. For example, a library user may expect you to answer his question off the top of your head, but you need to check a reference source to be sure. Say, "I want to be sure so I'm verifying this in the current directory."

- When you want to instruct the user and the user is agreeable to being instructed. Explaining precisely what you are doing helps the user learn the procedure. "I'm going to look in a medical database called Medline. Here it is ... and I'm looking under the heading Anorexia Nervosa ... I see ten items ... one called, 'Researchers study causes' ..."

Did You Know?
In a controlled experiment conducted by Michell and Harris (1987), librarians who demonstrated the skill of inclusion in the reference interview were judged to be more effective information providers under certain conditions. This study suggests that males and females may perceive the use of inclusion differently.

Conducting the Reference Interview

Include the User

In general, users in the Library Visit Study reported far greater satisfaction with the process when they were able to see the screen and follow what was going on. This principle of letting the user see what you are doing applies not just to the computer screen but also to book-based resources. For example, one user said approvingly, "She did the search while tilting the book towards me, so that I could see what steps she was taking." An additional advantage with letting the user see is that the user sometimes notices that the search process is going off track and can volunteer a correction or supplementary information. For example, one user who wanted biographical information on the naturalist F. W. Kortright noticed that the librarian was searching under C and intervened to say, "Kortright is spelled with a K not a C." Obviously this opportunity for user feedback and correction can occur only when the user has some way of following what the librarian is doing.

- When you ask a question or make a request that may seem unrelated or inappropriate to a library user. Users sometimes do not understand that it is necessary for you to determine the scope of their query and may think you are prying. For example, instead of asking "Why do you need this information?" you can use inclusion to introduce your question, saying instead, "The library has a great deal of material on this topic. We'll have a better chance of finding the best sources if you can tell me a little bit about how you plan to use the information" (3.2.3).

- When the other person will have to wait because the task takes a few minutes, you need to concentrate on the task without talking or without typing in chat, or you are going to be out of sight. People usually do not mind waiting so long as they know what to expect. If there's a line of people waiting for help at the reference desk, people become less impatient when you acknowledge them even if you can't immediately help them. For example, say, "I'm going to help this man, and I have a telephone call waiting, and then I will be right with you," or "I'm going to my office and will be back in about three minutes," or "This will take me some time to check because I have to call the university library. Would you like to wait while I do that, or would you rather do some other work and come back in five minutes?" or "Would you like me to e-mail you the information when I find it?"

- When you are instructing large groups in the use of a particular information resource during a library use instruction session, since not everyone can see exactly what you are doing.

Inclusion involves four basic steps:

1. **Acknowledge.** Restate the problem or otherwise indicate that you are listening so that your next action will be seen to be related. For example: "So your parrot's feathers are falling out and you want a book on what to do about it."

2. **Describe briefly what you are doing, have done, or are about to do.** For example: "I'm looking under 'Parrots—diseases' in our catalog to see what books we have on this subject." If you want to instruct the user about the difference between subject headings and keyword searching, you can provide more detail.

3. **Explain briefly why you are doing it.** State the reason for your behavior, or summarize the advantages. For example: "This could be in the biology section or it could be in the pet books. The catalog will tell us all the places we should look and it might also tell us what else to look under."

4. **Indicate how much time the task will take if appropriate.** Be specific, saying, for instance, "I should be able to call you back this afternoon" rather than "I won't be able to call back right away," or "This may take a while."

ANALYZE THIS REFERENCE TRANSACTION

Case 16: Clueing in the remote user.

In live chat reference, you can use inclusion in much the same way as you would in a face-to-face transaction. It's even more important because the user otherwise doesn't know what you are doing or why. Consider the verbatim excerpt from a transcript from the Seeking Synchronicity Project (Radford and Connaway, 2005–2008). In this case, the academic librarian uses multiple instances of inclusion. How many examples can you find?

1	Librarian:	[Hello. I'm a reference librarian at University X. How may I help you?]
2	User:	Where can I find the leading companies in boston doing diabetes treatment/prevention R&D?
3	Librarian:	[Please hold on while I check a few sources.]
4	Librarian:	I can probably give you a few sources to get started, but I may wind up referring you to a business and/or medial librarian specialist. Let's start witht [univ] library web page...
5	User:	ok great thanks
6	Librarian:	Are you a studnets or faculty member at [univ]?
7	User:	student
8	Librarian:	OK. I'm going to try the "co-browse" option—that might let us see the same information at once... (if it's working!)
9	User:	wonderful
10	Librarian:	since what you want to find are drug companies, I'll try to get you into a busienss database...
11	User:	perfect
12	User:	thank you
13	Librarian:	[Page sent - subjectlist]
14	Librarian:	I clicked on article datbases
15	User:	alright
16	Librarian:	by the way, wht's your email address in case I need to send you a transcript?
17	User:	[email address]
18	Librarian:	Business and Company ASAP and Business Source Premier both look good. I'll try business and company asap.
19	Librarian:	[Page sent]
20	Librarian:	hmmm. I treid the keywords "diabetes and boston and research" and tht came up with some possibilities...
21	Librarian:	[Page sent]
22	User:	uh huh, more specifically im looking for maybe some kind of list of who is doing what, for respective drug companies

1. For each instance of inclusion that you found, consider the function of the skill within the context of the interview. How, if at all, do these uses of inclusion help the user?
2. Compare line six and line sixteen in terms of using the skill of inclusion. Which form of questioning would you prefer, if you were the user?
3. At line twenty-two, the user provides new information. What, if anything, could the librarian have done to get this information earlier?

4.1.2 Library Use Instruction

Most of the library literature on library use instruction, or bibliographic instruction, concentrates on the formalized instruction that happens in the classroom, lab, or workshop, or on a library tour when instruction is the main purpose. Another form of library use instruction is the incidental instruction that happens one-on-one at the point of use when the main purpose of the interaction is finding information. In the broadest sense, a library user learns something about the library in every reference transaction, and every interaction produces a change in the user's mental model of what a library is and does. When users get help in libraries, they learn at a minimum that the library is the right place to come for help with information problems, and that they are more likely to be successful if they ask a staff member for help (1.4.2). In addition, if library staff uses inclusion to describe or explain a procedure as it is carried out, the user develops a more sophisticated understanding of how the catalog, indexes, or particular bibliographic tools work. In the instruction situation as elsewhere, the basic attending skills of nonverbal behaviors, acknowledgment, minimal encouragers, and listening (2.4.2–2.4.5) are the foundations that help establish a good communication climate.

In the context of the reference interview, library use instruction often involves working step-by-step with the user who is using an information source for the first time. When the reference desk is so busy that the staff

---

QUESTIONS FOR ONE-TO-ONE INSTRUCTION

To assess the need:

- What are you working on? (not "Is this for a term paper," or "Is this a science project?")
- What have you done so far? Where have you looked? (not "Have you looked in the catalog?")
- What happened? What got you stopped? (not "Are you having trouble with the headings?")

To assess the gap:

- What do you want to find out? (not "Do you want a review article?")
- What do you already know about this index? (not "Do you know how this index is arranged?")
- What don't you understand about it? (not "Do you know how to limit by date?")

To assess the help required:

- What do you want this index (or database or search engine) to do for you? (not "Do you want abstracts?")
- What would help you most?
- What other help do you need to do this? (not "Do you need to know how to operate the machine?")

member has to send the user off on his own, library use instruction consists of giving the user some specific advice on how to get started plus an invitation to return for more help if he gets stuck. In the Library Visit Study accounts it was clear that, even in academic libraries, staff members overestimate the users' expertise and underestimate the difficulty of navigating the informational resources. For example, a user who wanted to know how many times the work of a particular author had been cited in the research literature was given a piece of paper on which the librarian had written "Web of Science," and was told to click on the Web of Science icon in the library gateway. When the user accessed the Web of Science as directed, he discovered to his confusion that he "was confronted with many choices, as it appears *Web of Science* is actually a collection of various databases." The user commented, "It would have been very useful if the librarian had specifically directed me to search the *Science Citation Index* once I had accessed the *Web of Science*." A generalization that can be drawn from these examples is that nothing should be taken for granted about the user's level of information literacy and search skills. You should *never* assume that a user knows how to use a particular resource unless you are explicitly told this.

Quick Tips for Providing Library Use Instruction in the Context of the Reference Interview

- **Conduct a proper reference interview** so that you are sure that the tool you are providing instruction about is actually going to help the user find a satisfying answer. The user might initially ask, "Where are your encyclopedias?" Before launching into an explanation about online encyclopedias and specialized subject encyclopedias, find out what the user wants to know. Maybe he really needs a directory to find an address in which case instruction in encyclopedias is wasted. Library use instruction is effective only when the user comes to understand that the tool has actually saved him time.

- **Get at eye level with the user**, if possible. If you are showing a user how to use an e-resource, it works best if the two are you are sitting side by side so that you can see the screen as well as each other. However, be careful not to take the mouse or the keyboard from the user without asking permission, as this may be off-putting.

- **Guide users through the process** while letting the user do the work. Said one user, "What I found most helpful was that the librarian let me perform each step myself." Users who have been guided through the steps in this fashion are more likely to be able to do it on their own the next time. It also becomes immediately clear where the user is running into trouble.

- **Don't set a pace that is too fast.** None of the Library Visit Study accounts indicated that the library instruction was performed

(continued)

A QUICK TIP

Beware

In the Mental Models Study, an experienced librarian described what happened when a user came to the desk and asked, "Is music listed in the computer?" It turned out that, for a fiftieth wedding anniversary party the next day, he wanted to borrow a recording of a popular song with the word "dream" in the title. When asked how she would explain or describe this type of reference situation to a new librarian who was just learning about reference service, the experienced librarian said, "I would tell the new staff person to beware. Often you can tell users the whole way music is set up, when all they want is a particular song. I stopped doing that [launching into system descriptions]. I was taught years ago to say, 'What exactly are you looking for?'"

Did You Know?

Users need help sorting out reliable sources of medical information from the not so credible. Jana Allcock (2000) recommends that librarians take library use instruction beyond showing users how to use health databases such as EBSCO's *Health Source Plus*. She says that the explosion of health information on the Internet has created a new need to help users distinguish between trustworthy and questionable Internet sites.

Easy for Leonardo

Don't assume. When a user in the Library Visit Study asked for information on Saudi Arabian women, the librarian directed her to a database, saying, "Well, the system is quite straightforward." However, systems that seem straightforward to experts are often far from straightforward to novices. The user reported, "I found the *Women's Resources International* database very useful but not as 'straightforward' as the librarian said it would be."

I Already Know That

Find out how interested the user is in receiving instruction before launching in on a one-to-one library instruction session. In the Mental Models Study, some users observed that the librarian's need to instruct considerably exceeded their own need to be instructed. One user said, "He sat me down in front of the microfiche reader and showed me how to use it. I already knew about the index and how to use it, but he wanted to show me anyway."

Case 17: Putting the user in the driver's seat.

A user in an academic library wanted information on the physiological effects of silicone in human blood. The librarian took the user to a computer terminal and provided instruction in logging on. Then she said she would be back in two minutes to help with Medline, after she had finished with another person she was helping. When she returned, she began to explain the features of Medline. Here's how the user described what happened next:

> Although she suggested I type in "silicone," she also insisted that I be the one doing the typing and clicking, since, she said "that would be the only way" I would learn. I really appreciated this gesture, as I have encountered librarians who have taken over the search project and zipped through the reference sources, leaving me unsure of how the results were actually obtained.
>
> She then took the seat beside me because it became available. I felt more comfortable that she was sitting beside me rather than standing behind me as before, because it enabled us to make eye contact so that we could see if we understood each other.... Above all, she did not just climb into the driver's seat. She allowed me to interact with the database. [The librarian next provided instruction on how to limit the search.] At this point, she said she would leave me alone and let me complete the search. I appreciated the fact that she respected my autonomy. She also sincerely invited me to come and ask her more questions "if [I was] not finding what [I was] looking for."
>
> (Library Visit Study)

Comment: In this transaction, the user was very happy with the help she got. Make a list of all the specific behaviors that this librarian performed that contributed to making this bibliographic instruction so positive for the user. How many of these things are within the control of the individual librarian? How many of these things could be done in your own library setting?

too slowly. On the other hand, there were frequent comments about the process being too quick to follow. One way to slow down when showing e-resources is to let the user take the mouse or keyboard while you walk them through the process in the FtF setting.

- **Provide instruction in stages** as needed. The first step might be instruction to help a user begin using an electronic index. Later the librarian might be involved in providing help with narrowing down a search or evaluating the sources found.

- **Leave the user in control** of how much or how little instruction is received. Some users just want the answers rather than to know about the different algorithms that various search engines use to retrieve Web pages—they just want the Web page for, say, the White House. Other users treasure their independence and prefer to work on their own, at least initially. Use your attending skills of listening and reading body language to determine how much instruction a particular user wants. If in doubt, ask.

ANALYZE THIS REFERENCE TRANSACTION

Case 18: "If it's an R."

User: Can you tell me where to start? I have things to look up in—like—the files?

Librarian: Yes. (*encourager*)

User: Where do you start if you want to look up...?

Librarian: Are you looking for a particular book? Or...? (*closed question that functions as an open question*)

User: Yes. A book on mortgages.

Librarian: On mortgages, okay. (*acknowledgment*) So what you're looking for then is a subject.

User: Right. Yes.

Librarian: Right? You use the subject listing. If you were looking for a particular title, you'd very obviously use the title listing and ditto authors. [Explains more how the catalog works.] This will tell you what books we have under that subject [mortgages] and it will tell you where to find them on the shelf and what departments and branches have copies...and whether or not it's a reference or a circulating book.

User: Oh. Okay.

Librarian: Now when there's no letter-number combination after it, that means it's a circulating book. When it says CE SC, that means it's Special Collections and it means that it's non-circulating. Or if it's an R, same thing.

User: What I wanted was the chart for amortization tables, which shows various interest rates.

Librarian: Okay, now when you see *that* number, it means the book is just at the [branch] library reference, okay?

User: Oh.

Librarian: But it's unlikely that the branch would have something where there's not something similar here. Most of these items seem to be in the same general area.

User: Okay, 332, yeah.

Librarian: They're all going to be basically in two areas. You should look in the 330s, which is economics, just the first two aisles over there. And then there is 511, which is mathematics, right down there, okay.

User: Thanks very much for your help.

(Dewdney, "Mortgages")

Comment: Evaluate the library use instruction provided in the context of the "Quick Tips for Providing Library Use Instruction." Consider:

1. How well do you think the librarian understood what the user really wanted?

2. What proportion of this interview is devoted to finding out the user's needs as opposed to explaining the library's system for assigning letters and numbers?

3. Where did this reference interview start to go wrong? What could the librarian have done instead?

A QUICK TIP

Focus on Users' Goals, Not the System

An experienced librarian from the Mental Models Study never says that he's going to explain how the computer works, instead focusing on the user's end goal of finding information. He explains, "I find that if you start telling people you're going to explain the computer to them, it turns them off. Once you say, 'how the machine works,' they get intimidated. I just say, 'Well, this is how you can find it.'"

Did You Know?
Taddeo and Hackenberg (2006) described a survey to evaluate instruction in the hybrid reference service of the University of New York at Buffalo. They used AOL Instant Messenger (IM) in addition to FtF and e-mail. They found that IM was well suited to promote self-directed learning and the use of active learning techniques to answer a range of questions from simple to complex.

A QUICK TIP

Electronic Follow-up

Many e-mail and chat services have auto-formatted invitations to return if the user has another question. Do not count on the canned message as a substitute for a personalized follow-up—this generic message does not work to invite the user to ask for more help on the current question. It's best to write a follow-up question that's directed at the individual user and relevant to the question. For example, "If this Web site/ book/ article doesn't meet your specific need for information on XX, let me know and we can try again." Alternatively, you can try adding this follow-up question to your signature line when you answer reference questions by e-mail or as a closing script in live chat environments: "If this answer doesn't help you, please send us another message and we'll try again."

4.1.3 Follow-up Questions

Research has shown that asking follow-up questions is one of the most important skills you can use in the reference interview. Make the follow-up question a standard part of every (well, almost every) interview. It is especially useful at the end of a reference interview. Staff members who routinely ask, "Did you find what you needed?" or "If you don't find what you are looking for in that section, make sure you come back." In many cases, a follow-up question can make the difference between a satisfactory experience for the user and a frustrating series of events. The follow-up question is so useful because it allows you to discover and repair communication accidents before the user leaves the library. Gers and Seward (1985, 34) have said that the follow-up question "may be the single most important behavior because it has the potential for allowing one to remedy lapses in other desirable behaviors." Lillie Seward Dyson's (1992) influential article, "Improving Reference Services," provides statistically significant evidence that asking follow-up questions enhances your chances of giving a correct answer. There are two kinds of follow-up questions: those that invite the user to ask for additional help if needed, and those that allow users to tell you whether they got the kind of help they were really hoping to get.

Users in the Library Visit Study commonly expressed their appreciation of follow-up questions when they were used. For example, a user wanting articles on Toni Morrison and motherhood said that the librarian ended the transaction "by welcoming me back if I had more questions, saying 'If you have any other questions, come on back.' I felt very relieved to hear this and felt like it would be okay to come back if I got stuck in my search." The follow-up statement helps the user feel good about the transaction, even in cases where a satisfactory answer is not immediately available (Nilsen, 2006).

A word of warning, however—users may have good reasons for not answering a follow-up question regarding whether they found what they were looking for. They may fear "losing face" were they to acknowledge

---

SOME FOLLOW-UP QUESTIONS

To invite the user to ask for additional help:
- If you don't find what you are looking for, please come back and ask again.
- Is there anything else I can help you with today?
- [In an e-mail response] If this information isn't helpful, please let me know and I can look further for you.

To discover if the need has been met:
- Does this completely answer your question?
- Is that the kind of help (information, material, direction) you were hoping to get?
- Will this help you?
- Are you finding what you are looking for?

ANALYZE THIS REFERENCE TRANSACTION

Case 19: Hot Peppers

This reference transaction, conducted by e-mail, demonstrates how easy it is to include a follow-up question and how much it is appreciated by users. Here is the transaction between a Library Visit Study participant "John K." and a public librarian "Barbara."

User: I would like to find out what type of pepper(s) are used to prepare the hottest sauces that are used in foods like Chicken Wings etc. I though jalopenos would be most likely, but I was unable to substantiate this opinion. I was curious because of the adverse reaction I had from a bottle of hot sauce a friend sent me. It was reputed to be 450 times hotter than tobasco sauce. I would like to learn of what type of pepper could possibly make a sauce so hot. I m worried that such heat is generated artificially rather than by a mere pepper. Any information that I could receive on this front would be greatly appreciate since I was unable to find out what type of pepper could generate such heat. Thank you. John K.

Librarian: [One hour later] Hello John! I have a few links for you to look at. I thought to first look up the word pepper in the encyclopedia and see if it gives me any ideas. This link is a good start: [Wikipedia link]. This link talks about the fruit of Capsicum plants commonly called "chilli pepper: red pepper, bell pepper. This link to types of peppers is interesting: [URL listed]. [This "types of peppers" site provides an overview types of peppers, their pungency ratings and their uses as well as health value.]

John—this was just a quick search so please let me know if I'm way off or if you like this information I'll find more detail for you! (:Barbara

(Library Visit Study)

Comment: The user said this response was "amongst the most courteous and earnest that I have ever received through e-mail, not just through a reference transaction, but through an e-mail in general. The information proved completely accurate and beyond my expectations. The personalized e-mail response and the encouragement to e-mail back if I needed more information filled me with confidence and a brighter view regarding the work of reference librarians."

For discussion: Look closely at the wording of the follow-up question. What specifically made it so effective?

A QUICK TIP

A Second Chance to Help

Most people will only ask their question once, unless they are invited to return for further help. Therefore, follow-up questions are especially useful when you are too busy to do a complete reference interview or to provide further help right away. See Case 19: Hot Peppers, as an example of follow-up by a busy librarian.

Did You Know?

The RUSA (Reference and User Services Association, 2004) guidelines for reference behaviors advise that the "librarian is responsible for determining if the patrons are satisfied with the results of the search, and is also responsible for referring the patrons to other sources, even when those sources are not available in the local library" (section 5). For a successful follow-up, the guidelines recommend that the librarian ask patrons if their questions have been completely answered, and encourage patrons to return with such invitations as "If you don't find what you are looking for, please come back and we'll try something else."

that they couldn't use a particular tool or find something in an online database. Moreover, in some cultures, it is considered a lack of respect to say that the service provided was not helpful, particularly as a response to a person presumed to be an authority such as a teacher or a librarian (see section 5.5.1). So when you ask some international students if the material you provided was helpful, they may say "Yes" out of politeness, even if it was not at all helpful, to help *you* save face. To interpret the response, first watch for nonverbal signs of hesitancy or dissatisfaction, and then try another way of finding out what is needed, perhaps avoiding direct questioning. For example you could say, "If that is not exactly what you are looking for, I would be glad to look for some more material."

The good news is that follow-up questions are easy to ask. Here are some questions asked by librarians in Dewdney's study in which she tape-recorded real reference questions in public libraries. The specific words used are different, but all of these statements have the same function, which is to reassure the user that it is okay to ask again:

- If that doesn't work, come back and I'll see what else.
- If you need further help, let me know.
- Double-check the shelf with those numbers, and if the books aren't there come back to the desk.
- If you find that's not enough, there's another alternative. You can come back and use the encyclopedia.
- If you need more, come looking for me and I'll pursue it further if necessary. [Gives name.]
- Start with this. If you're not happy with what you find, come back to the desk.
- Take a look through those books. If they don't help you, come back and we'll try again.

4.2 Integrating Reference Interview Skills

When librarians first attempt to apply new interviewing skills in an intentional, integrated way, they often wonder about the appropriateness of some skills, about the effect of the skill on the user, or whether they will ever be able to use the skill without awkwardness. It may be that the first time you use a skill that you *will* sound awkward—but more awkward to yourself than to the user. If possible, try out the skill in a role-played situation in which you practice a single skill with another staff member or trainee. You will find that the skill becomes more natural with practice. Eventually you will feel comfortable making the skill work for you in a variety of situations and the skill will become part of your normal behavior.

Skills must be learned individually, but together they form a repertoire from which the helper can draw spontaneously, selecting one skill in a certain situation, adapting another skill to supplement, trying yet another skill if the first one doesn't work. Intentionality means flexibility—the ability to use a range of skills and to improvise. It means not depending on one skill or always using the same skill in similar situations. As mastery of skills increases, so does intentionality. Intentionality is not limited to verbal skills. The intentional helper also becomes adept at using nonverbal skills as the need dictates.

We recommend that initially you focus on these separate skills one at a time. But it is a simplification to think of these skills as separate—a fiction used to make the initial learning easier. Eventually when used in a real library setting, the skills are combined, each one supporting the rest in a smooth and seamless integration in the service of a larger purpose, which is to help the user. As you develop mastery, you will see how one

BEHAVIORS THAT HELPED

When student participant observers in the Library Visit Study were asked to reflect on librarians' behaviors that had helped them, it turned out the same factors emerge repeatedly in accounts of successful reference transactions. Fortunately all these factors are communication behaviors that are within the control of the individual staff member and not dependent on external changes in the system. Here are some "best practices."

Staff members:

- Smiled/nodded/moved out from the desk/used eye contact.
- Were friendly/warm.
- Took the initiative by approaching me and offering help.
- Appeared interested.
- Accepted my question as important.
- Responded to my initial question by saying, "What do you want to know about X?"
- Asked questions that helped me clarify in my own mind what information I wanted.
- Included me as a partner in the search and seemed interested in my suggestions.
- Didn't just point or give directions, but took me to the shelves/indexes/reference tools and made sure that the answer was there.

- Pulled out several books for me to look at while they checked something else.
- Explained what she/he was doing/where she/he was going/what she/he expected me to do.
- Left me with some leads and didn't close off the search.
- Was very knowledgeable about the sources of information. Introduced me to some helpful starting points for my search.
- Didn't get discouraged easily but was willing to investigate further.
- Didn't overwhelm me with too much information.
- Invited me to come back if I didn't find the answer.
- Came over and asked, "Did you find the information you were looking for?"

(Dewdney and Ross, 1994)

In virtual reference, Library Visit Study participants singled out elements of best practice that are most relevant to the virtual environment.

VR staff members:

- Addressed me personally, thus acknowledging me as well as my question.
- Wrote in the first person and gave me her name.
- Used a friendly and enthusiastic tone.
- Asked me a little more about my question so that the information she sent was relevant.
- Didn't rush; she took time to explain what she was doing and when she pushed pages, she left them up long enough for me to understand them.
- Didn't assume that I could come in to the library to use the materials there.

- Didn't just send me a list of URLs but gave me the names and authority of each of them.
- Verified that the resources she sent were appropriate and on track; told me where to look on each site that she referred me to.
- Used a professional writing style that was casual in tone yet had no spelling mistakes or grammatical errors.
- Asked me to get in touch with him if the information he sent was not helpful or if I needed more information on the topic.
- Ended with a cheerful Good bye/Good luck! and gave his name and e-mail address.

(Adapted from Nilsen and Ross, 2006, and from Library Visit Study accounts)

skill can be substituted for another and how several skills can be integrated to achieve specific purposes in the process of communication.

Sometimes when library staff members are introduced to new communication skills, they might react by saying that they're being taught to manipulate their own behavior in order to manipulate others. Some trainees say that they feel deceptive when they try to make the transition from practicing a skill in a training setting to using the skill in a real-life setting. They may feel that it is not natural to use encouragers or ask open questions to get people to talk. After learning these skills and using them, users open up and answer questions. Is there something deceptive and manipulative about this? Well, there might be, depending on your motive. Any skill can be abused. But in the service of shared goals these skills facilitate communication and allow you to be more helpful.

4.2.1 Tips for Practicing

There's no substitute for real practice. Changing your communication behavior is hard work—it's not easy to break old patterns of response. But unless you practice your new skills, you'll lose them. When you are first practicing new skills, most users will understand that you're trying hard to help and will appreciate your efforts. Here are ten tips to help you through the learning process.

1. **Make a commitment.** Promise yourself that for a specified period of time—the next hour or on Thursday afternoons—you will consciously use one of your new skills.

2. **Start immediately.** Begin practicing the skill right away. Remind yourself by taping a photocopy of "Some Sense-making Questions" (see 3.2.3) to your desk. At first, you may feel awkward, but practice anyway. Most library users respond positively when they see that you are trying hard to help.

3. **Practice one skill at a time.** Best results come from practicing one skill over and over. Don't try to use all the skills at once. A good skill to start with is acknowledgment or restatement. An easy sense-making question to use is, "What kind of help would you like?"

4. **Use support groups.** Practice with a co-worker who has made the same commitment. Give each other feedback and share experiences. Or set aside time at regular staff meetings to discuss your progress. Sharing live chat or e-mail transcripts with colleagues can be extremely helpful.

5. **Learn from missed opportunities.** Each time you do *not* use one of these skills, think about the situation afterwards. Would acknowledgment have helped prevent a misunderstanding of what the user meant by "books on Wales"? How could you have used a follow-up question to find out sooner that the information provided was not useful?

6. **Develop your own style.** There is no magic list of open questions and no perfect sequence in which to use your skills. Adapt your behavior in a way that is comfortable for you in the situation at hand. Use words that function in the same way as the examples, even if the exact words differ.

7. **Learn from communication accidents.** When you are first learning these skills, you may find that they do not always work. If the user seems puzzled, you may have had a communication accident. Recover by explaining to the user what you are trying to do. For example: "I asked you that question because I can help you more if I know a little bit about what you plan to do with the information," or "I want to make sure I understand what you're looking for." Users hardly ever become angry in such situations, but, if they do, recover simply by saying, "I'm sorry" and explaining.

8. **Practice off the job.** Microskills work in any situation where your help is being sought—by family, friends, even strangers asking directions. Practice these skills in your daily life—you may be surprised at how much everyday communication improves.

9. **Observe others.** Notice how others use microskills—the salesperson who restates your request, the talk show host who asks open questions, the physician who encourages you to describe your problem, the consultant who is trying to find out what features the new system software needs to include. Pay particular attention to those people you like dealing with—chances are they are using microskills.

10. **Teach someone else.** After you have learned a skill and practiced it, pass it on to someone else. Teach a co-worker one skill that you have found to be particularly effective. Your ability to teach someone else demonstrates that you have really mastered the skill.

4.3 Annotated References

Allcock, Jana C. 2000. "Helping Public Library Patrons Find Medical Information—the Reference Interview," *Public Library Quarterly* 18, no. 3/4: 21–27.

Avery, Susan. 2008. "When Opportunity Knocks: Opening the Door through Teachable Moments." *The Reference Librarian* 49, no. 2: 109–118. Discusses how to find teachable moments in the different reference contexts.

Dewdney, Patricia, and Catherine Sheldrick Ross. 1994. "Flying a Light Aircraft: Reference Evaluation from a User's Viewpoint." *RQ* 34, no. 2 (winter): 217–230.

Dyson, Lillie Seward. 1992 "Improving Reference Services: A Maryland Training Program Brings Positive Results." *Public Libraries* 31, no. 5 (September/October): 284–289. Persuasively makes the case that the follow–up question is one of the most important skills for the reference interview.

Gers, Ralph, and Lillie J. Seward. 1985. "Improving Reference Performance: Results of a Statewide Study." *Library Journal* 110, no. 8 (November 1): 32–35.

Michell, Gillian, and Roma M. Harris. 1987. "Evaluating the Reference Interview: Some Factors Influencing Patrons and Professionals." *RQ* 27, no. 1 (fall): 95–105. Reports an experiment in which the level of inclusion was varied in videotaped reference interviews that were evaluated by both public library users and by librarians.

Nardi, Bonnie A., and Vicki L. O'Day. 1996. "Intelligent Agents: What We Learned at the Library." *Libri* 46, no. 2: 59–88.

Nardi, Bonnie A., and Vicki L. O'Day. 1999. *Information Ecologies: Using Technology with Heart.* Cambridge, MA: The MIT Press. With the combined skills from the domains of anthropology, computer science, and special librarianship, the authors examine what they call "information ecologies" which they define as a system of people, practices, values, and technologies in a particular local environment.

Nilsen, Kirsti. 2006. "Comparing Users' Perspectives of In-Person and Virtual Reference." *New Library World* 107, no. 1222/1223: 91–104. Identifies staff behaviors that lead to user satisfaction in both FtF and VR transactions.

Nilsen, Kirsti, and Catherine Sheldrick Ross. 2006. "Evaluating Virtual Reference from the Users' Perspective." *The Reference Librarian* no. 95/96: 53–79.

Radford, Marie L., and Lynn Silipigni Connaway. 2005-2008. Seeking Synchronicity: Evaluating Virtual Reference Services from User, Non-User, and Librarian Perspectives. Funded by the Institute for Museum and Library Services, Rutgers, the State University of New Jersey, and OCLC, Online Computer Library Center. Grant Web site available: www.oclc.org/research/projects/synchronicity (accessed December 22, 2008).

Radford, Marie L., and Lynn Silipigni Connaway. 2007. "Are We Getting Warmer? Query Clarification in Virtual Reference." Presented at the Library Research Round Table, American Library Association Conference, Washington, DC, June 21–27, 2007. PowerPoint and handouts available: www.oclc.org/research/projects/synchronicity/presentations.htm#recent (accessed December 21, 2008).

Reference and User Services Association. 2004. "Guidelines for Behavioral Performance of Reference and Information Service Professionals." Available: www.ala.org/ala/mgrps/divs/rusa/resources/guidelines/guidelinesbehavioral.cfm (accessed December 22, 2008).

Ross, Catherine Sheldrick, and Kirsti Nilsen. 2000. "Has the Internet Changed Anything in Reference? The Library Visit Study, Phase 2." *Reference & User Services Quarterly* 40, no. 2 (winter): 147–155.

Taddeo, Laura, and Jill M. Hackenberg. 2006. "The Nuts, Bolts, and Teaching Opportunities of Real-Time Reference. *College and Undergraduate Libraries* 13, no. 3: 63–85. Discusses findings from a survey of University of New York at Buffalo reference service that includes FtF, e–mail, and AOL Instant Messenger. Describes their use of active learning techniques in IM. Contains literature review of real–time reference.

White, Marilyn Domas. 1981. "The Dimensions of the Reference Interview." *RQ* 20, no. 4 (summer): 373–381. Describes how the librarian can increase the coherence of the reference interview by explaining to the user what is happening.

Special Contexts for the Reference Interview

5.1 Introduction to Special Contexts

In this chapter, we consider the reference interview with a difference. In the special reference contexts considered here, you still need the same attending skills, questioning skills, and summarizing skills discussed in Chapters 2 and 3. But in addition, extra considerations result because of the communications medium used, such as in the case of the telephone interview, or the particular client group served, such as users who ask questions on behalf of someone else, children, adults with special language-related needs, or people with special needs. Special purposes (e.g., questions dealing with legal or medical issues), and the implication of consortial reference across different modes of delivery and for all kinds of interviews also demand special consideration. In the sections that follow, we focus on what makes these contexts special and how to adapt the reference interview for these special circumstances.

5.2 The Telephone Reference Interview

Users who called the reference desk by telephone were the original remote, interactive real-time users (Kern, 2004). Some remote users choose virtual reference, as discussed in Chapter 6, over telephone reference, but others still prefer to communicate by talking rather than by typing, especially with the convenience of cell phones that can connect from any location. Users without easy access to computers or the Internet will continue to call, as will those who are uncomfortable with computers. Even when the question is presented originally using e-mail or chat, participants sometimes find it easier to switch to the telephone to complete the negotiation of a complex question or to communicate detailed explanations. (The reverse may also happen—an interaction that starts as a phone call may end with an e-mail that delivers information, a URL for a Web resource, or a full-text article in PDF.) But just as other older technologies such as radio and film have found their own niche,

Did You Know?

Cell phones offer another way for users to contact the reference service, but they also have introduced new challenges. What to do when you are in the middle of an FtF reference interaction, the user's phone rings, is answered, and a prolonged conversation ensues? This situation is especially troublesome when a line of users is waiting. Some libraries have taken to posting signs, asking users to turn off their cell phones when approaching the reference desk. Others try to regulate cell phones in public areas where loud talking disturbs other users who are reading or studying. Lever and Katz (2006) report results from eighty-seven academic libraries surveyed to find out what policies the libraries had instituted regarding cell phones, which were seen as an "invasive mobile technology." They found that many libraries have established policies to curtail disruptive use of phones. Policies may prohibit cell phone use in designated quiet areas or restrict it to selected areas such as cybercafés, lounges, stairwells, or group study areas. Policies that prohibit cell phone use altogether are impossible to enforce. It is much better to designate areas for cell phone use and to have signs that say, "Please use your cell phone in the lobby" rather than "No cell phones allowed."

PROMOTING PHONE REFERENCE IN INSTRUCTION SESSIONS

Why not take advantage of the fact that almost everyone carries a cell phone to market phone reference, an underused service in many libraries. You can promote phone reference in library use instruction, orientation sessions, or programs.

Here's a script that could be used by anyone doing an orientation session in an academic library instruction setting:

> Greetings students! I am now about to ask you to do something that **none** of your other teachers/librarians have ever asked you to do . . . [Pause, wait for it . . .]
>
> **Take out your cell phones and turn them on.** [There may be gasps and nervous laughter from startled students, but they will do it eagerly.]
>
> Now, enter this library reference desk number into your phone buddy list right now. [Give reference desk number.]
>
> Next, here are the library hours when you can call this number for reference help. [Now the students have a reason to pay attention to the times when the library is open.]
>
> And during the other hours we are available by . . . [chat, IM, e-mail, whatever services your library offers—give particulars.]

Thus, you are marketing chat, e-mail, etc., services along with the phone services. This script can be easily adopted for public library use as well in adult programs and training sessions.

and have not been replaced by television and video, we predict that telephone service will remain a valued service that will complement the evolving new forms of remote reference, and may even grow in importance in this time of ubiquitous cell phones. Some users continue to prefer the simplicity of talking to a real person in real time using the familiar technology of the telephone.

The rationale for telephone reference is to offer a service that provides an alternative to face-to-face reference that saves the user time. Many libraries and community information centers have developed telephone reference service into a specialty, marketing it under names such as Night Owl, Maryland's late night reference service that stresses short answers and convenience (Duke, 1994). Traditionally telephone reference has focused on ready-reference questions with answers that don't take long to read over the phone. In an article from the 1930s regarding telephone reference, Emily Gannett (1936) explained that most libraries declined to provide information over the telephone on the following topics: "genealogy, identification of insects, plants, paintings, coins, etc., long lists of names and addresses, patent information, definitions of words unsuitable for relay over the telephone. Most libraries will not read long articles or poems."

Today, librarians working at Enoch Pratt's telephone reference service in Baltimore, Maryland, answer a variety of questions "from the mundane to the bizarre," and do read short items to callers on occasion. They spend about five minutes on a question and if they can't find an answer among their reference tools, will transfer it to the appropriate subject specialists (Glaze, 2007). Students or faculty calling the academic reference desk can also be given ready-reference type of answers, correct citations, and item availability information, or guided to appropriate e-resources by phone. Fax machines have extended the options beyond the limits of data that the voice can convey in a few minutes. A faxed page may contain a map, a graphic symbol, a table of numbers, a mathematical formula, or a highly technical textual passage.

The special constraints of the telephone reference interview are byproducts of the technology used: you can't see users or rely on visual cues; you can't use the physical setting as a prop for the interaction or work through problems by showing users a book or resource and getting their feedback; you can't very easily provide bibliographic instruction. But, on the other hand, a plus for the user is that you can't just say, "Have you checked the catalog?" which might be off-putting, as it suggests that the user should have done something before asking a question.

5.2.1 Interview Skills for the Telephone

The telephone reference interview heightens the need for good interviewing skills and attentive listening. You lose all visual cues when you conduct a telephone reference interview; you can't see that look of annoyance, the shrug, the unsure or worried expression, or the look of doubt in the eyes. And you can't see the look of pleasure and appreciation when a user gets exactly the answer needed. Users also are at a disadvantage because they don't see your welcoming smile and they can't know what you are doing unless you tell them. On the plus side, neither you nor the user is quite so likely to leap to conclusions based on age, physical appearance, or clothing (3.2.2). Unlike the e-mail or chat interview, you *can* get nonverbal cues that can be conveyed vocally. You can hear the enthusiasm, interest, affirmation, annoyance, or insecurity expressed through the voice. Moreover, in the interactive real-time environment, you have the chance to ask clarifying questions immediately while the caller is on the phone.

In this section we focus on the skills you need to conduct an interview over the telephone and take the appropriate action. Sometimes the staff member who picks up the phone does not answer the question but must make a referral. At other times, when the question cannot be answered over the phone, the user can be advised to come in person to the library. But before you can make appropriate referrals or recommendations, you must still find out what the user really wants to know. Users with telephone questions are as likely as FtF users to ask questions that are too broad or too specific, or may be even more likely to ask obvious questions (e.g., after the staff member answers the phone with "Riverbridge University Reference Department," the user asks, "Is this the reference department?"). Because they can't see you there at the reference desk, they need to be reassured that their phone call has reached the right place and that you won't be transferring the call elsewhere. Use PACT

Did You Know?
Since Enoch Pratt Free Library's Telephone Reference Service in Baltimore started in 1967, staff have answered six million requests for information. Along with search engines and online resources, the librarians work "The Wheel," a five-platter lazy Susan turntable of reference books. And, of course, they also keep lists of frequently asked questions, such as the "big seven" misspelled words: camaraderie, copacetic, eleemosynary, ornery, pejorative, prerogative, and triathlon (Glaze, 2007).

Conducting the Reference Interview

ANALYZE THIS REFERENCE TRANSACTION

Case 20: Telephone reference

User: Is this the reference department?

Librarian: Yes, it is. How can I help?

User: I'm trying to track down information on a book by an author, Beerhohm.

Librarian: Beerbohm. Hmmm. The name I've seen; I just can't connect it with anything.

User: I think he's English.

Librarian: Uh huh.

User: The title I'm looking for is *Zuleika Dobson*.

Librarian: When . . . approximately what time period?

User: I'm not sure exactly. Maybe the 1930s?

Librarian: What field is Beerbohm associated with?

User: He writes novels.

Librarian: Oh, okay. Hold on a minute then. Let me just check something right now.

User: Okay, thanks.

Librarian: [Returns.] I thought I might be able to tie it down. I thought of a couple of things that listed works, but it didn't list that particular one. Let me take your name and number and we'll call you back.

(Adapted from Mary Jo Lynch and used with permission)

Comment: This telephone transaction has been adapted from an interview recorded by Mary Jo Lynch as part of her pioneering dissertation research on reference transactions in public libraries. Which skills do you think this librarian used successfully? Which additional ones could have been used? Next consider each one of the librarian's conversational turns. Consider each turn separately. What is the librarian trying to do in each case? Categorize each turn according to its primary function by assigning one or more of the following codes:

Code	Intended function
1	Establishing rapport (opening communication, reassuring, demonstrating availability and listening)
2	Gathering information from the user (questioning, clarifying, confirming)
3	Giving information (explaining sources, policy, procedures; explaining what is being done)
4	Giving instructions or directions (e.g., how to use an index, e-resource, or database)
5	Giving opinions (e.g., assessing the likelihood of finding an answer, evaluating the problem)
6	Other (specify)

You can use these same codes to analyze other reference transactions presented in this book. Which functions would you expect to find more often in a telephone interview than in an FtF interview? Which functions would you expect to find less often?

(2.3) to establish contact and reassure the user that you are indeed the right person to be answering the question.

Be sure to acknowledge the user's question promptly by restating or rephrasing it. Since users cannot see you, it is often a good idea to explain what you are doing. Rather than leaving them to wonder if you have forgotten them, use inclusion (4.1.1) to explain that you are working on the question, that you are just checking the online catalog, or that you are going away for a moment to get a city directory. As with the FtF interview, open questions (3.2.1) and sense-making questions (3.2.3) work well. Some librarians feel that the users' anonymity over the phone makes it easier to ask how the information is expected to help, but the guidelines for asking about intended uses remain the same as they are for an in-library user. Explain that you are asking this question so that you can be more helpful, and don't make any assumptions. Since your caller cannot see that you are nodding and smiling over the telephone, you should pay special attention to vocal qualities and verbal skills.

For the caller at the other end, your voice represents the whole library. You are literally on the front line. The following are some suggestions for developing your telephone interview skills.

1. Develop a pleasant speaking voice. Monitor how you sound over the phone. Is your tone interested and courteous? Do you speak slowly and clearly enough to be easily understood? Do you sound as if you welcome the caller's question? Or does your tone imply that you experience the call as a nuisance or an interruption of other more important work?

2. Talk to the caller. Don't pick up the receiver to stop the ringing while continuing a conversation with someone else.

3. Identify yourself. When you answer the phone, your greeting should clearly identify your library and your role or name but most important it should indicate your willingness to provide service. Instead of simply saying, "Yes," or "Hello," try something like "Reference Department. Ahmed Hassan speaking," or "The Legal Information Center. This is the librarian, Mimi Holland. How may I help you?"

4. Volunteer your help. Don't force the caller to pry help out of you. If the caller asks, "Is Mrs. Lopez there?" don't just say "No"; say, "Mrs. Lopez will be back at one o'clock. If you'd like to leave a message, I'll make sure she gets it when she returns," or "Mrs. Lopez is not here right now. Can someone else help you?"

5. Acknowledge (2.4.3). Be sure to acknowledge the caller's question promptly by restating at least part of it. If you didn't quite catch the question, repeat what you did understand and let the caller fill you in on the rest. Consider the following examples:

- Yes, I'd be happy to check that for you in WorldCat.

- Tom Jonsson. And that's spelled J-O-H-N-S-O-N? . . . Okay, so it's J-O-N-S-S . . .

- Uh-huh, so it's the *Cairo Trilogy*. What was that first title again? . . . Okay, *The Palace Walk*. . . . And you just wanted to know if the book was in?

A QUICK TIP

Tone of Voice

The actual words of your opening greeting might be fine, but the pace might be too fast or you might sound grumpy. Rochelle Yates (1986) gives the following example:

Librarian: [Fast and grumpy] Good morning, Middletown Public Library, May I help you?

Caller: Is this the library?

Librarian: Yes [in a tone of voice that implies, "You dummy"].

Walters (1994) recommends that you smile when you're on the phone, even though the user can't see you. Smiling conveys warmth in your voice.

Conducting the Reference Interview

- So you want the phone number for a support group for parents of children with autism?
- Your professor has required that you use APA for your assignment and you want to know if there is an online version?
- Okay, so your question is how to log on to the library's Web site to find full-text scholarly articles for a research paper?

6. Use minimal encouragers (2.4.4). Minimal encouragers like "Uh-huh," "Go on," "That's interesting," and "Anything else?" are especially important over the phone as cues that you are listening. Without these encouragers, the caller is apt to wonder if you are still there.

7. Listen. Listening skills (2.4.5) are even more important than in an FtF interview because you have no visual clues that could let you know that things are going off track. After your initial greeting, give the caller a chance to explain what is wanted. Don't interrupt. Initially, don't do much talking yourself except for minimal encouragers.

8. Clarify the question or request. Use open questions (3.2.1) or sense-making questions (3.2.3) to find out what kind of help the caller wants. For example:

- How may I help you?
- What information would you like on that?
- What aspect of X are you interested in?
- What kind of help would you like?
- How would you like this information to help you?
- How would you be using that information?

As in the FtF interview, it might take several questions before you think you understand the question well enough to begin to look for an answer. You can say, "I'm not familiar with X. What more can you tell me about it?" or "Is there anything more you can tell me about your requirements?"

9. Verify. After users respond to your clarifying questions by telling you what they want, repeat and verify the key facts before you rush off to find the answer or before the phone connection with the caller is ended (3.2.4).

10. Write it down. Write down the question while the caller is still on the phone. Check spellings, dates, and other particulars with the caller. As you are writing it down, you may realize that you don't quite understand what the caller really wants to know about migration patterns in Wales (or was it whales?). You can ask another question to clarify before you start to look for sources—a step that can avert the need to call back to get more of the context of the question.

11. Explain. Remember that the caller cannot see you. If you are going to ask people to wait, don't just say, "Hang on," or "Okay, I'll look," and then go away. The caller won't know what you are doing or how long to expect to wait. Studies show that people can cope better with frustrating experiences if they are told ahead of time what to expect. Therefore explain what you are doing. Say, "I'll check that for you in the *Academic Search Premier* journal index. It will take about two minutes.

ANALYZE THIS REFERENCE TRANSACTION

Case 21: "I didn't have a pencil handy."

User: I'm looking for information on caffeine.

Librarian: Uh huh. On the effects of caffeine? (*acknowledgment*)

User: Yes. Caffeine.

Librarian: Did you call us earlier this week? (*closed question*)

User: Pardon?

Librarian: Did you call us earlier this week?

User: I did. Yes.

Librarian: You did. (*acknowledgment*) And what did the gentleman tell you? (*open question*) Because I remember he was working on it.

User: I didn't have a pencil handy and I didn't write it down, and with me it's gone. I should have said "Excuse me" while I got something.

Librarian: Yes. You don't remember what he told you? Because he spent some time on it.

User: Something about a digest or something. Something like that. You see, I want to avoid things with caffeine in them.

Librarian: Mhm. (*encourager*)

User: Because it was making me deaf—I'm getting noises in my ears.

Librarian: So you want to know which foods contain caffeine? (*acknowledgment* to restate the librarian's understanding of the question)

User: No, I want to know the deleterious effects of caffeine.

(Dewdney, "Caffeine")

Comment: Users sometimes ask their question more than once, with the result that several people within the library system have worked on the same question. If the answer provided by the first librarian has not fully answered the question, the user may start over, as happened here. Users may be tentative if calling back and may need reassurance that it is okay for them to do so. The earlier transaction with the male librarian was hampered by several features of the telephone as a communication medium. Unlike in FtF transactions where users can be shown materials or be given photocopied pages, in the telephone transaction everything depends on the ear and on clear explanations by the librarian. And since users are never sure when the staff member may call back, they may not be prepared to record the answer. To fend off this problem, the librarian could ask, "Do you have paper and pencil handy?" and then could spell out words or names that are likely to misheard or misspelled.

For discussion: How could different tones of voice change the user's perception of this exchange? For example, how might "You don't remember what he told you?" be spoken in different manners that suggest incredulity or impatience or demean the user? How might it be spoken in a sympathetic or understanding manner? How might different voice tones for "Because he spent some time on it" make the user feel?

Did You Know?
Agosto and Anderton (2007) found that out of 125 telephone reference transactions, 93.6 percent of the answers provided were correct (which they attributed to the simple nature of the ready-reference questions asked). On the other hand, using harder questions based on current issues and emerging trends identified in news stories, Dilevko and Dolan (1999) found a correct answer rate of only 34.2 percent of 231 telephone reference transactions. They argued that librarians need to keep current in order to answer questions correctly. While Agosto and Anderton reflected on the importance of some aspects of the reference interview, Dilevko and Dolan did not indicate whether interviews occurred. They did note, however, that "accuracy has a way of increasing patron loyalty and generating a positive reputation in the community" (1999, 77).

Would you like to wait, or should I call you back?" If the problem turns out to be unexpectedly difficult, return immediately to the phone to give your waiting caller a progress report. Say, "I haven't forgotten you.

I'm checking that information and will have it for you in a minute." If they are impatient, or if you think it may take a while to find the information, you can offer to e-mail it, making sure you get an e-mail address. Tell them when they should expect an answer. Say, "If you give me your e-mail address, I will send that information to you this afternoon."

12. Refer. If you can't answer the question yourself, don't say, "No, I don't know anything about that program," or "That's not our department." Instead you could say something like this:

- If you would leave your number, I'll find out about that program and call you back within a half hour.

- Let me transfer you to our reference librarian who specializes in legal materials.

- Our business reference librarian is away from her desk. Would you like me to put you into her voicemail so she can call you back?

- We have a term paper clinic on campus. Here is the phone number. It is open from nine to five, Monday through Friday. Would you like me to transfer you?

But don't make an unmonitored referral (3.1.4). Invite the user to call back if the referral is not successful and provide your name again so that the caller can ask for you.

13. Call back. Don't leave people on hold. If finding an answer will take longer than a minute or so, offer to take the number and call back, e-mail, or fax the answer. Often things take longer than expected or other interruptions occur. Rather than stranding your user on the phone and tying up your phone line, it is often better to offer to call back. Ask what would be a good time to call. But make sure that you *do* call back within the agreed upon time, even if you have not been able to find the answer. Don't be what Joan Durrance (1995) called the "Disappearing Librarian." And if you are about to end your shift and someone else will make the call back, be sure to tell the user what to expect. If your library has a policy that you are not permitted to make a call back, ask the user to call back at a specific time and be sure to leave the information for the next librarian.

14. Identify the caller accurately. If you are going to call back or send an e-mail response, restate names and telephone or fax numbers as you write them down (2.4.3). This will give the caller a chance to correct errors. Standard message forms are helpful and save time. Even if you are going to send the answer by e-mail, it's a good idea to ask for the phone number as well in case your message bounces back. With telephone interviews, you can request the user's name, asking, "Who should I ask for when I call back?"

15. Follow up. After you have provided the answer, don't forget to follow up (4.1.3). Say, "Did this completely answer your question?" or "Is there anything more you would like to know?" If you have referred the user to an outside source such as a Web page, agency, or another library, be sure to monitor the referral. Say, "If this source doesn't completely answer your question, make sure you call back and we can try something else."

EXERCISE

Telephone Reference Guidelines

Telephone reference policies commonly indicate the length of time to take on any one question, the number of questions from a single caller at any one time, and any limits on types of questions to be answered. Because the service users receive should not vary depending on who picks up the phone, many libraries prepare guidelines designed to encourage staff consistency and shared understanding of expectations. Does your library's reference policy include staff guidelines for telephone reference service and the telephone reference interview? Your guidelines should provide specific procedures on answering the phone, putting people on hold, transferring calls, clarifying the user's question, time periods for calling back, etc. Consider the following Austin (Texas) Public Library telephone reference guidelines:

- Providing information by telephone is an integral part of library service. Austin Public Library's Telephone Reference service gives customers the opportunity to ask questions without coming to the Library. Telephone staff can briefly answer questions on any subject, search the catalog for holdings, assist with the Library's electronic databases, and provide customer account information.

- The Telephone Reference staff can answer three short fact questions or search for five minutes, whichever comes first. When a telephone reference request requires more than five minutes of staff time, a callback will be arranged. Librarians will spend up to 20 minutes searching for an answer to a clear specific question. The response time is 24 hours for callbacks. Users requiring more answers or extended searching will be encouraged to come to the library. In all instances, the source and date of information will be cited.

- Telephone reference is open Monday–Thursday from 10 a.m. to 9 p.m., Friday & Saturday 10 a.m. to 6 p.m, and Sunday 12 noon to 6 p.m. Customers may request searches for items held at the Faulk Central Library.

- Restrictions due to limited staffing:

    1. No more than three items may be requested by phone per day. Titles can be held at the Faulk Library or transferred to a branch.

    2. No more than three Interlibrary Loan requests will be taken per call.

    3. No telephone renewals of checked out items. Same day shelf searches made after 5 p.m., or on weekends, will be performed on the next weekday.

Compare this telephone reference policy with your own library's policy. What do you consider to be strengths of this policy? How might it be improved? Do you see ways in which your own library's policy could be improved?

---

16. Indicate the source of the answer. Don't just provide the correct answer—think of yourself as an educator and take the opportunity to teach users about information sources. Since you can't show the source to the user, explain which source you used. If you used an e-resource, provide the name or other information about the source. Provide the URL, if the user wants it. If you used a printed source, give the user the

Did You Know?
Agosto and Anderton (2007) found a "disappointingly low" frequency of source citing, with complete citations provided only seven times (5.6 percent) and partial citations provided an additional thirty-one times (24.8 percent). For almost 69 percent of the questions, no source was mentioned whatsoever. Moreover, in only six (4.8 percent) of the 125 transactions, did a respondent offer to locate additional information if necessary. Thus most failed to follow up. Agosto and Anderton commented that respondents seemed to take little interest in the questions, and their first reaction "was to type something immediately into a computer, even when the information requested likely could have been found more quickly and more easily in a print format." Sounds to us like another version of the "without-speaking-she-began-to-type" maneuver (3.1.1; Dewdney and Ross, 1994).

author, title, date, and page number. See Denise Agosto and Holly Anderton's (2007) study on telephone reference for their findings on source citing.

17. Keep a record. Especially if the question is likely to require a follow-up by someone else later, keep a record of the question and the sources found, so that a second staff member doesn't have to start over from scratch. These should be kept in a prominent place at the reference desk. Some libraries have a "phone log" or a "pending call back" file at the desk to track return calls. Notes written on small sticky paper can fall off or easily be overlooked.

5.2.2 Voicemail

If you can't answer the telephone within three or four rings, the caller should automatically be routed to your voicemail system. The library's voicemail system is the first point of contact between users and the library. Be sure that the initial automated response is pleasant, welcoming, and not too complicated. Voicemail systems can be as simple as the recorded message that invites the callers to leave their names and numbers or as complicated as a multi-level menu of choices that connect the caller with the right department. Well-designed voicemail systems offer convenience and efficiency to callers, allowing them to leave a message at any time, twenty-four hours a day, seven days a week. It should be immediately evident to callers which menu choice they need to make if they have a reference question—and they shouldn't have to wait through descriptions of irrelevant services before they can choose the reference option.

In attempting to contact telephone reference service in the twenty-five largest public library systems in the United States and Canada, Agosto and Anderton (2007) experienced great frustration with the telephone labyrinth. They noted:

> Some of the telephone navigation systems necessitated making long series of selections, totaling five minutes or more on the telephone just to reach an actual person. And often, instead of a person at the end of this frustrating process came a recorded message saying that all staff were busy and the call should be tried again later—thereby requiring the waste of still more time later having to navigate the same system.

Increasingly, people are put off by automated message answering, especially when faced by an instructional menu that is too long or complicated. For some users, voicemail can be such an obstacle that they simply won't try to get through to a librarian. Some voicemail systems with multi-level menus seem to have been designed as a trial to weed out callers, just like the tests of piling logs in fairy tales that weed out unworthy suitors. Make sure that the voicemail in your library system helps users and is not just another obstacle to service.

Here are some tips for creating an effective automated greeting or menu:

A QUICK TIP

What's Your Number?

Your library's telephone number should be listed prominently on its Web page, preferably at the top left-hand corner—"the golden triangle"—of the home page. Alternatively the phone number should be accessible in one click near the top of the "Contact Us" drop down menu. If there is a direct line to your telephone reference service, be sure it is readily accessible as well, along with times of service and types of question limitation if any. Promoting phone reference with tent cards on library tables may encourage users who will not leave their lap-top computers to ask a question at the reference desk or those who won't get up for fear of losing their place at a library computer. These users could call the reference desk on their cell phones if they knew this was possible. In the Seeking Synchronicity Project research, focus groups with teenagers revealed that they often did not know the library had a phone. 74 percent of teens and adults responding through online surveys had never used phone reference services (Radford and Connaway, 2005–2008).

- Keep routine announcements short and simple. Avoid non-essential statements such as "Thank you for calling. The reference desk is not staffed in the evening..." and get to the point: "You've reached the reference desk. Please leave a message or call back. Our hours are..."

- Reduce the time callers have to spend listening to menu options by putting the most frequently used options first and by explaining how to skip the items that are not relevant.

- Simplify actions required of the caller. Break down instructions into manageable steps. Avoid complicated, confusing, or unnecessary direction, e.g., "Enter the first three letters of your last name, press the number sign and then choose one to hear our hours of opening, two to place a reserve, or three to be connected with our circulation desk. Press four if you want to talk to someone in Spanish. Press five if you want to hear an automated message about our new Home Library service. Press six if you want to talk to our reference staff."

- Where possible, give callers the option, early in the message, to transfer to a real person if that is their preference.

Answering your messages promptly is an important part of effective voicemail. You should have a policy that calls are returned within a certain period of time, e.g., within three working hours.

5.2.3 Who Gets Priority?

Do callers almost always get a message saying, "The reference staff is busy right now. Please call back or leave a message?" Alternatively, do in-house users get interrupted while you respond to a phone call? Trying to serve two different kinds of users can turn into a juggling act where no one is satisfied. In many library policies, the in-house user is given precedence over the telephone caller on the grounds that a user should be rewarded for taking the time and effort to make the trip to the library. On the other hand, it does seem odd to set up a service the whole point of which is to provide convenient access to remote users, but then regard these users as second class—and quite possibly lazy.

The best solution, if staffing levels allow, is to avoid the problem altogether by separating the two services: one staff member gives top priority to an in-house user while another gives top priority to a telephone caller. This way both types of users get the undivided attention of the reference staff. Some libraries combine the telephone reference function with the virtual reference function, both of which can be handled in a quiet office away from the busy reference desk. A separate telephone reference service with its own name, phone line, and dedicated staff can be advertised and promoted as a service without the concern that callers will swamp regular FtF reference service.

EXERCISE

Evaluate Your Voicemail Service

Using the criteria listed at left for a good voicemail system, prepare an evaluation checklist that could be used to evaluate your service. First, check the library's Web page to ensure that the library's telephone number is readily available. Then call that number yourself from home. Evaluate the voicemail service of the library as a whole, and of the reference department in particular. Then ask three friends who are not connected in any way with the library to do the same. Compare the evaluations. Are there differences in the results? What do the results tell you about your library's voicemail service? How might it be improved?

5.3   The Secondhand Reference Interview

In some situations you cannot communicate directly or immediately with the user who has the question. You receive the reference query at secondhand, mediated through a written message or through a second party, who might not know the context for the question. For example, you might be expected to do a search from a written request or search form. You could receive an interlibrary loan (ILL) request by mail or by telephone through an intermediary or be forwarded a question through a consortial arrangement (5.8). You might have just a secondhand account of the information needed. A colleague might say to you, "Jen, I'm leaving now. Would you get some stuff on rock paintings for Mr. Martin? He'll pick it up at six." Or "Jen, I'm leaving for the day. Dr. Ramirez is having her graduate class come over tonight—could you pull some materials on U.S. economics for her?"

If you feel you don't have a complete picture of what the user wants, try to contact the person who spoke to the user ("Hold it, Santos, tell me more about what Mr. Martin said he needed. What kind of rock paintings?" or "Santos, before you leave, do you have a phone extension for Dr. Ramirez—I might need to call to find out more about what her students need?") If the intermediary didn't do an adequate reference interview, you should contact the user directly before you put in much searching time, request an interlibrary loan, or e-mail or fax a lot of material. When there's no way of contacting the user, the best you can do is to find one or two examples of what you think may be wanted (as a gesture of good intentions), and invite feedback through a note asking the user to e-mail, call back, or write again if this material doesn't help (a written version of the follow-up question).

A better way to solve this problem is to prevent it. Make sure that everyone who is in a position to receive requests knows the importance of the reference interview, and knows how to ask at least one or two basic questions such as, "What would you like to find out about X?" or "If we can't find X for you, what else might help you?" Then ask everyone who might receive a request to write down everything the user says while the conversation is happening—this reduces the chance of premature diagnosis or incorrect interpretation. You can also avoid some communication accidents and save a lot of time by routinely asking the user, "If we have any trouble finding this, do you mind if we call you to get more information?" and take down a phone number. These should be routine procedures for accepting requests, no matter how clear the requests seem to be. You might supplement (but not replace) these procedures with a brief form that is filled out by the user or with the user present.

5.3.1   The Imposed Query

For reference librarians, the following scenario may sound familiar—a lost-looking user approaches the desk in an academic library and asks, "Does Eric work here?" After some conversation about staff members

How Many Imposed Queries Cross Your Desk?

Are 25 percent of your users asking imposed queries? You can find out how many you are dealing with in your library with this quick survey of users of your adult reference desk. For one week, give each person who asks a reference question a short questionnaire that asks, "Who is this information for?" and lists six predetermined answers: *myself*, *spouse*, *child*, *boss*, *instructor*, or *other* with space for a write-in response. Do not ask any other questions. Try to catch every reference desk user during the entire time that your library is open for the period of the survey. This survey replicates the method described by Gross and Saxton (2001). By tabulating the responses you will be able to compare your findings with theirs. You can do this exercise in any kind of library, adding categories of imposers appropriate to your particular setting (e.g., *social or volunteer group*, *co-worker*). Knowing the prevalence of imposed questions will heighten staff awareness of the need to treat these questions with special attention.

Follow Up

With imposed queries, it is more difficult to get useful answers to follow-up questions such as, "Does this completely answer your question?" The agent may not know if the question has been answered adequately or not. Gross (1999, 59) cautions, "Even agents who feel confident won't know for sure until the answer is evaluated by the imposer." However, you can teach the intermediary to ask a follow-up question when giving the information to the person who will be using it. Suggest that the agent say, "If this book/ video/ map isn't exactly what you need, the librarian says that additional materials can be found. It would help if you could explain what aspect of topic X you are looking for and say a bit about how you plan to use the information."

that goes nowhere, the librarian finally finds out what the user is trying to do. It turns out that the user is a student in Professor X's class, and this professor has said to the class, "To get background on your topic, you should go to the education library and ask for ERIC." This scenario is an example of what Melissa Gross (1999, 2001) has called "the imposed query," a situation in which the question asked at the reference desk was generated by someone else. When questions are imposed and not self-generated, they are very apt to be presented to reference staff as an "ill-formed query" (1.4.1) because the person asking the question may not fully understand it. The phenomenon of the imposed query is more common than was once supposed. In a survey of public libraries in southern California, Gross discovered that 25 percent of questions asked at the reference desk were "imposed queries." Imposed queries are asked at someone else's request: e.g., a wife asks a question on behalf of her husband; a student asks a question that is generated by a school assignment; an employee asks a question to get information for a boss.

Gross (1999), whose pioneering work on the imposed query has established the terminology generally used, calls the person who generates the question "the imposer" and the person who asks the question "the agent." The interview concerning an imposed query provides special challenges for the interviewer. Often the agent doesn't know the real context for the question, how it arose, or to what use the information will be put. Gross has pointed out that when the person asking the question is not the person who generated the question, "many [of the recommended] question-negotiation techniques lose their effectiveness" (54). This problem arises because recommended interview skills function by tracking the question back to its origins in the life of the user, a process that is hampered when the user at the desk, on the phone, on e-mail, or chat is not the person who generated the question. However the agent will know *something* about the context. The whole trick to conducting an interview with an agent who has an imposed query is to get him to talk about what

---

ANALYZE THIS REFERENCE TRANSACTION

Case 22: "I was just given this topic."

User: I need to find out something about this subject here. It's Generic Behavior Management Training for Parents.

Librarian: Where did you hear about this? (*sense-making question*)

User: I have this topic for a service proposal for school. It's an MRC course.

Librarian: What's MRC? (*open question/acknowledgment*)

User: Mental retardation.

Librarian: Okay. And what is Generic Behavior Management Training . . . ? (*open question*)

User: I don't really know . . .

Librarian: You don't know any . . . ?

User: No. I was just given this topic.

Librarian: You don't know if it's a certain kind of training that . . . ?

User: Supposedly. I guess so.

Librarian: I've never heard of it, but it *sounds* like some kind of a special program. We would have it listed in the catalog, if we have anything about it.

User: I checked the catalog under "Generic Behavior Management," but it's not there.

Librarian: Hmmm. Is that all you know—just the name of it? You don't know what it deals with, or anything? (*closed question that functions like the open question* "What else do you know about it?")

User: I have to do a service proposal on it.

Librarian: What school is this for? (*open question*)

User: [Local community college].

Librarian: Is there *anything* else you can tell me about it? (*closed question that functions as an open question*)

User: No. Well, our service proposals are supposed to go to COMSOC, which is Community and Social Services or whatever.

Librarian: All I can suggest is that you give them a call and maybe they can give you some suggestions as to what to look for. Because if it's not in our catalog, I don't know where we could really start. If we had anything it should be listed.

User: Oh, okay. Thank you.

(Dewdney, "Generic Behavior Management")

> **Comment:** In this interview, the question, "Where did you hear about this?" worked well because it makes no assumptions while at the same time it encourages the user to talk about context. Examine the other questions that the librarian used. Which ones worked well/ which ones worked less well?
>
> **For discussion:**
> 1. How successful overall was this interview in finding out about the context of this imposed query?
> 2. Given the documented studies of users' failures in using the catalog, what do you think of the librarian's statement that, since the user couldn't find "Generic Behavior Management" in the catalog, that there would be nothing on the topic in the library?
> 3. How would you rate the helpfulness of the suggestion that the user give COMSOC a call?

he *does* know, not what he doesn't. A series of closed questions is even less efficient with an imposed query than it is with a self-generated question. Gross advises that the first step in conducting a successful reference interview is to identify the kind of question you are dealing with—is it self-generated or is it an imposed query? This advice doesn't mean that it's a good idea to ask a closed question such as, "Do you need this information on X for a school assignment?" But that it is better to ask something like, "Can you tell me a bit about how this information will be used?"

The following are some common situations that give rise to imposed queries together with some useful open questions that you can ask to get users to tell you what they know about the context of their question.

1. **A student with a school assignment.** Students at all levels frequently come to libraries with imposed queries (5.4.3). In school libraries, Gross (2001) found that younger children tend to ask self-generated questions, but that up to 50 percent of the reference transactions with older children are imposed queries. While school librarians often get advance notice from teachers about impending assignments, public librarians are flying blind when it comes to school assignments. However, students with school assignments may not know very much about the topic (e.g., the Globe Theatre in the time of Shakespeare), but there are many things they do know that provide a useful context to the question. They know, for example, the subject or course for which they are writing the essay (e.g., English literature), the grade level they are in, when the essay is due, how long the essay is supposed to be, what their teacher told them about the expectations for the assignment, and so on. In fact the real context of this question—the situation, gaps, and uses—have to do with the student's needing to find materials to use in completing an assignment in order to pass a course. As Flowers (2008) noted with respect to teens, they "often do not know or are not interested in the content of what they are asking, but only know that they have to have it, usually at once." To get at this context, you can ask these questions:

- What did your teacher tell you about this assignment?

- If you have the assignment sheet handy that your teacher gave you, it might help if I took a look at it.

- What requirements does your teacher have for this assignment?

And here's an added challenge. In a study of public library users at adult reference desks, Gross and Saxton (2001) found that 35 percent of all imposed queries were made by adults on behalf of children. To help a child with a school assignment on, say, "Major exports of a country in South America," a parent might ask for "everything you have on Argentina." These questions are what Gross calls a "double imposed query," because there are two consecutive imposers, first the teacher and then the child—with twice the chance for confusion and misunderstanding. In the case of the double imposed query, a good question is: "what did the teacher tell your child about the assignment?"

2. **Someone asking a question on behalf of a neighbor, friend, or family member.** In this case, the agent is asking on behalf of someone

---

Did You Know?

When they analyzed 581 live chat reference queries, Radford and Connaway (2007) were able to determine that 24 percent (140) were imposed queries related to school assignments, 1 percent (9) were imposed queries related to work, and 28 percent (165) were self-generated queries. It was impossible to determine the origin of the remaining 46 percent (267) from looking at the transcripts. Here is an example from the chat transcripts of an imposed query related to a school assignment: "For a history project, I must do a poster diagram of the evolution of pyramids from masatbas to step pyramids to straight-sided pyramids."

ANALYZE THIS REFERENCE TRANSACTION

Case 23: Why can't a kid be more like a businessman?

In her doctoral thesis, Mary K. Chelton (1997) focused on the adult-adolescent service encounter and identified a number of barriers to providing good service to this user group. She quotes a reference librarian's posting on a listserv to illustrate how attitudes to specific user groups, specifically adolescents, can be a barrier to service:

> I'll be happy to tell you why I find this age group "problematic." So many come to the reference desk with no idea of why they are there. They shove a sheet of paper in my face and say, "This is my homework. Where can I find this?" When I ask them what the assignment is, they appear to be looking at it for the very first time. Or they simply mumble, "I don't know." It's a total lack of concern and the assumption that I'll figure it all out for them and go fetch the materials that irritates me.
>
> We have OPACS, and many of these patrons won't even go near them. When I ask them if they've checked the catalog, they reply they don't know how to use it.... They don't come to the library for any other purpose than to socialize and bother patrons who have legitimate business in the library.... Having homework assignments and reading lists shoved in my face by healthy, intelligent, able-bodied young people who have no interest in their own homework just plain bugs me. (193–194)

Comment: Sounds like another case of bad guy users (1.7). Chelton notes that this librarian has a tacit "theory of practice" which she uses to identify "legitimate" users and distinguish them from deadbeat users. Legitimate users are the ones who come prepared, are interested in their homework assignments, already know how to use the catalog, and expect to do most of the work themselves. Unfortunately there is a mismatch between her perception of what is appropriate behavior and the actual behavior of most adolescents.

For discussion:

1. What difference might it make to the librarian's attitude if she reframed this situation by identifying it as a case of an imposed query? How prepared/ interested/ knowledgeable/ and keen on work is a person likely to be when the question is generated by someone else?

2. How widespread in libraries do you think this attitude is toward adolescents? How problematic do you think such attitudes are when they do occur?

else but doesn't necessarily indicate who the requested information is really for. Often certain individuals in a family or community act as information gatekeepers, bringing information into a social network for others to use. In immigrant families, for example, children may function as cultural mediators for parents and grandparents who are less proficient with English. In these situations, ask, "Can you give me some idea of how your friend/ husband/ daughter/ father will be using this information?" or "Can you tell me a little bit about the situation your friend is in where he will be using this information?"

When a user says that material is needed "for a friend," sometimes this formulation is a defensive strategy to avoid self-disclosure about a sensitive topic. The person is saying in effect, "It's not really me who wants to know about pancreatic cancer or abortion or divorce proceedings or herpes; it's someone else who has this problem." In such cases, since the question is in fact self-generated, the user is in a good position to describe what the "friend" is looking for. To ease awkwardness you can work the conversation toward "people in general." Say, "People who do X sometimes find this useful," or "Some people with X just want a list of symptoms, but others want to read about treatments," and then wait for the response.

3. An employee asking a question for a boss or supervisor. In their study of imposed queries in public libraries, Gross and Saxton (2001) found that 12 percent of the agents identified the imposers as their boss. This is often the trickiest situation of all. Often the only thing the user knows is that the boss has said, "Go to the library and get everything they have on illiteracy," possibly adding that it is needed for a report. All you can do in such cases is to give the agent something to take back to the boss—your best guess as to what is really wanted—and then use a follow-up with a special twist. Essentially you are teaching the agent how to ask the right question of the supervisor in order to be a better go-between. You may also need to teach the intermediary how to ask an appropriate follow-up question. In this context, the follow-up question works the same way that it does in regular reference interviews to repair mistakes and offer a second chance to get it right. Say to the agent, "When you give this material to your supervisor, you could ask if it completely answers the question. If not, we can find other materials if your boss can tell you what specifically is missing in the materials provided."

The ubiquitous cell phone may come to the rescue in these situations. Ask users if they can get the boss on the phone, in which case you will be able to conduct the reference interview with the imposer rather than the agent. It may surprise you how often this is possible, now that many business people are carrying Blackberries and other handheld devices.

> **Did You Know?**
> In their research on imposed queries, Gross and Saxton (2001) identified fourteen categories of imposers, but four of these (employer, instructor, spouse, and children) together accounted for 79 percent of the imposed queries at the adult reference desks of public libraries.

5.4 The Reference Interview with Children and Young Adults

This section was written by Lynne (E. F.) McKechnie, Professor, Faculty of Information and Media Studies, The University of Western Ontario.

Conducting reference interviews with children and young adults presents special challenges for the reference librarian. Not only is this group of users developmentally different from adults, but they have less experience with libraries and information sources. Life contexts associated with their age have an important bearing on the reference interview, such as attendance at school, the need to develop information literacy skills, and their strong relationships with parents or other adult caregivers. In this section we focus on the skills needed to address the special needs of children and young adults in the context of the reference interview.

5.4.1 "Got Any Books on Fleas?"

Here's a scenario that has been reconstructed from an actual reference question received at the reference desk of a public library. Jeremy, who was about six years old, approached the information desk.

Jeremy: Got any books on fleas?

Librarian: So you want some books on fleas.

Jeremy: Yup. Fleas.

Librarian: Well, I think we do. Come on over here with me where the insect books are.

Jeremy: [As he and the librarian walk to the children's nonfiction section] Like with pictures.

Librarian: Pictures?

Jeremy: Yup. Pictures. And names. Like word names.

Librarian: Pictures and word names? Do you want pictures of different kinds of fleas? Or maybe a picture book about fleas.

Jeremy: Not a picture book! Them kinds of stories is for little kids. I need a book with real stuff, a book with facts.

Librarian: Oh, a book with facts. A nonfiction book.

Jeremy: Yup. A nonfiction book. With fleas. And words for names. Especially names of cats.

Librarian: Cats!

Jeremy: Especially cats.

Librarian: Jeremy, I think it would really help if you could tell me what you want this nonfiction book for.

Jeremy: We're going to get a cat. My Mom says I can pick the kind of cat. So, I need to know all, ALL the kinds of cats. To make sure we get the best kind.

Librarian: I see. You need some information about cats. The different kinds of cats so that you can pick a breed, a type of cat, that you like.

Jeremy: Yup. That's it. Breeds of cats. With pictures. And maybe Yoyos.

Librarian: Yoyos? . . .

Ten minutes later the librarian helps Jeremy check out two books about cats. The next summer Jeremy brings his Persian cat named Yoyo to the library's pet show.

This scenario demonstrates some of the special considerations that arise in interviews with children as a result of their state of cognitive development as well as their more limited experience with information sources and libraries. Jeremy's vocabulary is not yet large enough to include specific words like "breed." While it is clear that Jeremy understands what a picture book is, he did not understand the term "nonfiction" until the librarian explained the meaning of the concept.

Although limited and inaccurate, Jeremy's request for a book on "fleas," a concept related to what he really wants, shows awareness of the library as an organized body of information. Jeremy's response to the offer of a picture book points to the need for age-appropriate materials, including items that are not only accessible in terms of reading level and other cognitive abilities, but also materials that are not considered by young library user themselves to be beneath or beyond their ability. Finally, this reference interview, like many with children and teens, took longer than it might have done had Jeremy's mother or another adult had asked the question. As a result of asking this question himself and getting it satisfactorily answered, Jeremy's mental model (1.4.2) of the public library has expanded; he now knows that the library is a good place to come to get books on "real stuff" and "facts" and that it's a good idea to ask the librarian for help.

Quick Tips for Meeting the Special Needs of Children and Young Adults

- Be respectful and nonjudgmental when interacting with children and young adults at the reference desk. Treat all of their questions as seriously as you would those from adults.

- Although children and young adults may have less experience with and knowledge of information sources and libraries, they are actively making sense of the world and are often eager to learn how things work. Involve them in the reference process. Ask what they know about the topic. Give them opportunities to browse shelves, search the library catalog, or find an article in an encyclopedia. Seek their feedback about the quality and suitability of resources found. This will increase their understanding, their self confidence, and their sense of being a partner in the reference interaction.

- Many children and some young adults may have never asked for help at a library. They might feel shy, awkward, and reluctant to approach the reference desk. Be proactive. Approach children and teens in the library. Smile and make eye contact so that you appear open and welcoming. In the case of small children, try kneeling or bending over so that you are at their level, or at least closer to it.

- Remember that children and young adults are still developing language skills. They have more limited vocabularies than adults, may more frequently mispronounce words, and are still learning how to frame questions.

- Never assume that children and young adults understand library jargon. Unless they have been to library school, many adults do not know what a monograph or a periodical is. Children and young adults may never have encountered even more basic terms such as fiction, nonfiction, table of contents, index, or bibliography. Even adults often confuse biographies and bibliographies. Either avoid using this professional jargon or identify and explain it. For example, you could say, "To find the name of an organization to

Did You Know?
According to Behrmann and Vogliano (1991, 52), children are "quick to discern a lack of respect for their needs or an unfairly small amount of time allocated to them." Patrick Jones (Jones, Gorman, and Suellentrop, 2004) states that many young people feel adults assume that all teenagers are trouble makers. While equitable access to all services is a basic premise of providing library services for children and young adults, a study by Judith Dixon (1996) called "Are We Childproofing Our Public Libraries?" identified many barriers to library use by young people. It is neither correct nor fair to assume that children's and young adults' reference questions are simpler or less important than those asked by adults.

contact for your project on milk, we can look in this directory. A directory is like a specialized telephone book with addresses and contact information."

- Accompany both children and young adults to the shelves. They may not be able to retrieve items using call numbers. The time it takes to walk to and browse through the shelves can be used for further clarification of the user really wants to know.

- Attempt to match information materials to the reading level and conceptual abilities of the child or young adult user. A quick way to assess reading level is to ask a child to read a few lines; if errors are made or the child struggles with the text, look for a document that is written at an easier level. You can also suggest materials at a variety of levels of difficulty, giving children or young adults the opportunity to decide for themselves what would be best.

- As recall memory does not fully develop until midway through childhood and emerges later than recognition memory (Gross, 2000), children tend not to remember book titles and author names. A study conducted in Denmark (Wanting, 1986) indicated that when children want specific titles, they often mention characters (both people and animals), the subject, and visual or auditory elements such as the cover illustration or a rhyme. Try to elicit clues like these during the reference interview.

- Children are multi-sensory learners. Give them opportunities to explore materials through their eyes (have them look at illustrations and other parts of documents like a table of contents or list of references), ears (have them read a portion of a source aloud or read selected bits to them), and hands (have them run their fingers along an index as they search for a specific entry).

- According to Patrick Jones (Jones, Gorman and Suellentrop, 2004), young adults are proud of their growing independence and will therefore often not ask for help. Again, be proactive and approach teens in the library. But instead of asking if they "Need help?" try something like "Are you finding what you need?"

- Remember that reference interviews with children and young adults may take longer.

5.4.2 Information Literacy

Most librarians believe that it is important for children and young adults to learn how to find information and use libraries, but a few carry this to the extreme of insisting that they do all this learning without any help. This tends to happen when a school assignment is involved because library staff may assume that the teacher has imbedded an information search in the requirements. When it comes to child and teen users, there is often a debate about whether librarians should provide reference services or whether they should provide only instruction in information literacy.

ANALYZE THIS REFERENCE TRANSACTION

Case 24: Self-help

Librarian: Do you need some help?

User: Yes. I need to find a picture of a baby.

Librarian: Okay. (*encourager*) What kind of baby? (*open question*)

User: Just like a young baby.

Librarian: Okay. Um, let's go up and look in the baby section.

User: Okay.

Librarian: Let me take a quick look here for the call number. [Interruption by an interaction with another student.] Okay, I got the number. You still here? 649. Here's some baby books.

User: I'd like a full-body picture.

Librarian: A full-body and a photograph picture. (*acknowledgment*)

User: Mm-hmmm.

Librarian: Okay. Let's go down and look in *Parents' Magazine*. They have lots of pictures of babies. [Goes with the user. Some further discussion.]

User: Actually, I'm doing—I'm drawing a baby.

Librarian: Here's all the *Parents' Magazines*, and they often have pictures of babies in them.

User: Okay.

Librarian: So you can [find] lots of babies. So you can just sit here and grab a stack of them and thumb through here and find the perfect baby.

(Reported in Chelton, 1999, and used with permission.)

Comment: In analyzing this reference transaction that she audio and videotaped in a school library media center, Mary K. Chelton (1999) points out that the librarian does not define her role as providing information but rather as helping people find information on their own. The staff member points the user in the direction of some likely materials, but it's the user's job to evaluate and choose information on his own. "There is an embedded presumption of real or potential user competence here."

For discussion: Do you think that the model of information provision identified by Chelton is typical of school library media centers in general? How appropriate is this model for the school library media center? How appropriate would it be for a public libraryor for a special library? What other model could be used instead?

Did You Know?
According to Mary K. Chelton's 1997 Rutgers thesis, "Adult-Adolescent Service Encounters: The Library Context," school library media specialists are faced with special demands and challenges that are not acknowledged in such canonical statements as the RUSA "Guidelines for Behavioral Performance of Reference and Information Services Professionals" (Reference and User Services Association, 2004). In her study, summarized in a 1999 *RUSQ* article, Chelton argues that information work is not the predominant activity in the school library media center. Reference work has to compete with routines of discipline and the enforcement of rules. The mental model of service held by both staff and students is that the school media center is a place where users can help themselves after the staff gets them started.

A QUICK TIP

Scaffolding for Learning

Be a role model for the skills of finding information in libraries. Provide a running commentary as you go through the information search process with a child or teenager. For example, to indicate to a teen that more than one tool may be needed to find resources on a topic, you could say, "We'll need to check the library catalog. It lists what books the library has on endangered species. We'll also have to check the periodical index to find out if there are any magazine articles." As you do the catalog search, describe aloud each step—a form of inclusion (4.1.1). The young adult might choose not to pay attention to what you are saying, but you will have provided an opportunity for learning.

This issue seldom arises in connection with other categories of library users. When an adult asks for the address of a particular company, the librarian provides the address and a citation for the source, possibly explaining how to use business directories in the course of finding the address. Child and adolescent library users deserve the same level of service. It is dangerous to assume that children and young adults have the skills needed to work independently. Some might, but it's important to check at the outset and use a follow-up question to invite young users to return if they aren't finding what they need. At the same time, librarians are also uniquely positioned to help young people acquire the information literacy skills essential for successful participation in the new knowledge society. A recommended compromise for the reference versus instruction dilemma is to incorporate instruction into the process of helping the user find the information needed. That is, you provide unobtrusive opportunities for young users to learn information literacy skills during the reference transaction.

5.4.3 The School Assignment

Except for the very young, children and young adults spend a good deal of time at school or doing school-related work. Not surprisingly, many of the reference questions from this category of user also relate to school work. For some children, especially those from social and cultural backgrounds without a strong tradition of library service, the first school project might be the stimulus for visiting a public library for the first time. Librarians should welcome this opportunity for helping the child develop a mental model of the library as a helpful and pleasurable place to visit.

Reference questions arising from school assignments differ from others in several ways. Almost all are secondhand queries that have been imposed by a teacher (Gross, 2000). The same assignment may have been given to every student in the class. As a result, a librarian may encounter, all in a short period of time, a number of questions from different students that are all generated by the same assignment. Patrick Jones (1998) talks about the "garbled assignment" problem, where it soon becomes clear that the student really doesn't understand what is required. As we have seen in section 5.3.1 on the imposed query, this kind of problem is very common when the question has not been self-generated.

Some students ask questions that are more concerned with how to do the project than with its information content—questions like, "How do I do an outline/ table of contents/ bibliography?" or "How do I find a topic for a science project?" Some librarians find this kind of request frustrating and interpret it a request "to do their homework for them." However, it isn't doing their homework for them to provide students with the help that they need to move through all the steps necessary to complete the assignment. This is why it's important, even if you think you have seen the question before, to conduct a reference interview with the student at the desk. Even when two students are working on the same assignment assigned by the same teacher, what each student needs to know may not be the same. One student might need help narrowing down the topic, another may need help with the proper format for doing a bibliography. Don't assume that the same information that suited the last student will help the next one. Some sense-making questions (3.2.3) that work well with children are, "How did you get the idea for this?" "What are you going to do with this?" and "What would you like to know about frogs/global warming/ tree rings?"

ANALYZE THIS REFERENCE TRANSACTION

Case 25: "My project is due tomorrow."

User: I have to write something for a seminar on the Mennonite family—or maybe Amish. I'm not sure if they are really the same thing or not.

Librarian: On Mennonites? (*acknowledgment*)

User: Yes, a seminar.

Librarian: What are you trying to write? The Mennonite family? Is that what you said? (*acknowledgment* to confirm that the topic was heard)

User: Yes. Like the children—how they grow up.

Librarian: Okay, did you check some of our circulating books yet? Have you been over to our 282s? [They go to shelf.] You've already been to this section then? The Mennonites. Did you try this book?

User: Yes. It's too old. There wasn't anything about the family. [User has taken another copy of this book home.] There's nothing in there.

Librarian: You're sure. If this has education . . . ? You did see that there are some things in this book though? I just want to make sure before we give up on the book that you tried it, okay?

User: No . . . There's nothing about the family itself.

Librarian: Okay. [She recommends that the user read particular pages.] Did you try the reference books? [Shows the user in turn entries on Mennonites in four different encyclopedias, but each time the user says the articles aren't what he wants. The librarian recommends a periodical search and suggests an index, but the user thinks it may take too long.]

User: You don't have videos that I could watch?

Librarian: [Librarian explains how to find videos in the catalog.] This project is due tomorrow? [And so on . . .]

(Dewdney, "Mennonites")

Comment: This is a classic example of the frustrations that librarians often face in trying to answer questions generated by school assignments. The user's purpose here is to find materials—preferably ones that won't take too much time to access and process—so that he can achieve his real goal, which is to hand in a passing assignment by the next day. In this transcript (edited here for brevity because it goes on for five pages), the librarian, despite trying very hard, is never able to provide any information that the user is willing to accept. In the course of the interview, she asks one open question ("What are you trying to write?") and twenty-three closed questions. The problem seems to be that the user has a very specific understanding of what he means by Mennonite family life. Therefore the book that the librarian thought had lots of good material on the Mennonite family was rejected: "There wasn't anything about the family." That should have been a red warning flag to the librarian. At this point, instead of asking twelve more closed questions, she could have asked a sense-making question like, "If we could find the perfect book or article for you today, what specific information would it include?" or even, "What is missing from this book *The Mennonites* that you absolutely need to have?" Before she spends more time recommending sources and giving bibliographic instruction in their use, she needs a better idea of what she should be looking for (3.2.2).

Conducting the Reference Interview

Quick Tips for the School Assignment

- Never assume that all reference questions are related to school assignments. The child who asks for information on diabetes may not be doing a science fair project on the topic. Maybe a friend or family member has just been diagnosed with the disease. To find out what is really needed, use open questions (3.2.1) such as, "It would be helpful if you could tell me what you plan to do with this information."

- Try to find out as much as you can about an assignment. Ask if the student has a copy of the teacher's written instructions that you can look at. Try to find out the due date, the length of the assignment, whether or not a specific number or types of resources are needed, if students are also required to report where and how they got the information, and if there are any other special requirements. This will help you determine exactly what type and amount of information is needed by the student to complete the assignment.

- If there is time, try to speak directly with the teacher who has given the assignment. As with all imposed queries, it is best to negotiate the question with the individual who originally asked it. Students may have misunderstood or completely missed the teacher's instructions.

- Don't expect all children and young adults to be interested in the questions they ask. Remember that many school-related topics have been assigned rather than freely chosen.

- While it is hard for library staff to stay enthusiastic about a reference question that they have already been asked thirty-seven times from

---

ANALYZE THIS REFERENCE TRANSACTION

Case 27: "Do u know what she means by that?"

In this verbatim excerpt from a live chat transcript from the Seeking Synchronicity Project (Radford and Connaway, 2005–2008), a young user is struggling to understand what the teacher means by an assignment apparently on ancient Greek vocabulary.

1	User:	hi, my name is [Patron Name] and i am learning abot the ancient greeks.our homework was to dothe vocab wors and i did ,but now she tells me that i need a 2nd fact .do u know what she means by that?
2	Librarian:	Hello, this is the reference librarian. I'm reading your question . . . and plese dont close this chat session
3	Librarian:	By a "second fact" do you think your teacher means some additional piece of information about each of the words? Or about the Greeks?
4	User:	by the way we have to take notes
5	User:	and i think its about the words
6	User:	am i right or wrong?
7	Librarian:	OK, so any additional information about each word?
8	User:	yes
9	User:	like one of our words are monotheism
10	User:	r u still there
11	Librarian:	And you are to see what this word meant for the Greeks?
12	User:	yes we r sopose to do that and a dfinition
13	Librarian:	OK, I understand now . . .
14	Librarian:	There are many dictionaries on the web - though you can also use Google by typing define:monotheism
15	User:	i already found all of the definitions
16	Librarian:	OK, good - then what we can do is use Google to search for: monotheism Greeks
17	User:	i only need the second fact but i still dont understand what she means by that
18	User:	And so on . . .
22	Librarian:	The Wikipedia says: Monotheism (in Greek monon = single and Theos = God
23	User:	what do u mean by and so on
24	Librarian:	You can use the same type of search for your other words. Or it may be the list of words all have Greek origins?
25	User:	so is that kinda like the 2nd definition

Comment: And so on. The first challenge for this user is to understand not what the ancient Greeks meant by certain words but what the teacher means in the assignment. A number of exchanges try to puzzle out what the teacher means by expressions such as "a second fact" and "and so on." This is a good example of the mismatch that Carol Kuhlthau describes between anxious confusion of a student user ("What do you mean by and so on?") and the orderly desire of the librarian to get on with a proper search ("What we can do is use Google").

For discussion

1. In lines 3 and following, the librarian recognizes that this is an imposed query and focuses on what the teacher said and may have meant. What else, if anything, could the librarian have done in this situation to get a better sense of the real question?

2. Line 10 suggests that the user has had to wait for the librarian's response. How could the librarian have let the user know that he/she has not "disappeared" but was still present?

grade five children all doing the same project on Ancient Egypt, remember that for the individual child in front of you, this is the first time the question has been asked.

5.4.4 Parents

Working with parents and other adult caretakers is part of doing reference work with children and young adults. Many children can't travel to the library on their own, and parents often want to continue to help their children once they arrive at the library. Some parents are an invaluable ally in the reference transaction. These parents are interested in their children's questions, eager to find appropriate material to answer them, and usually want to help the children learn how to get help and find resources at the library. However, problems arise in the reference interview in two situations that involve parents. The first occurs when the parent arrives at the library alone to get materials for a child's project and the librarian can't talk directly to the child or teen. This is an imposed query (5.3.1) made even trickier because now there are two filters standing between the librarian and the originator of the question: the child and the child's parent. The second problematic situation involves the overbearing parent. These parents arrive at the reference desk with a child or teenager in tow but completely dominate the interaction. Sometimes the young person utters not a single word, possibly even wandering off to another part of the library. Here is a list of strategies that you can use to make the adult-accompanied child a full participant in the reference interview while at the same time channelling parental involvement along productive lines.

- Smile at and establish eye contact with the child or young adult as well as with the parent so as to include the young person in the reference transaction right from the start.

- Make sure that you speak with the child or young adult throughout the entire reference interview. When a parent asks a question, redirect the reference interview to the child by using acknowledgment with him or by asking him the follow-up question. For example, in response to a mother who asks "Do you have any books about trucks for my son?" You can turn and directly say to the four-your-old "So, you're looking for some books about trucks."

- If possible separate an "overbearing" parent from the child. You can do this by offering to help the child find what they need while the parent is looking for her or his own materials. For example, a librarian might say, "Sure. I would be happy to help Mary. We've got a great current magazine collection right here. Perhaps you would like to look through some of these while Mary and I look for information on pioneers." Alternately, you could leave the parent doing a task related to a query, such as checking encyclopedias for relevant articles while you and the child or teenager do another task, such as searching the periodical index.

5.4.5 Children, Teens and the Virtual Reference Interview

Stephen Abram and Judy Luther (2007, 77) define the "Net Generation, or Net Gen,...as made up of people born between 1982 and 2002." The Net Gen is comfortable with information in a variety of formats including multimedia, expects to be able to access information from anywhere and at any time using a wide variety of devices and programs, and prefers to work in collaborative contexts. Studies indicate that children, and especially young adults, use virtual reference services sponsored by the library and other sources (Lankes, 2003; Kortz, Morris, and Greene, 2006). As members of the Net Gen, the children and young adults who use today's libraries have high expectations for virtual reference services. Many young people are tech savvy, but because of developmental differences, they also have special needs when it comes to the virtual reference interview.

To learn firsthand about the special challenges of the virtual reference interview, try out existing services. Three examples of well-established, specific virtual reference services illustrate the variety of approaches now being used to serve young people. *Ask an Expert*, *People's Network*, and the Internet Public Library's *Kidspace* and *Teenspace* all provide digital collections which a child or teen can search independently. They all also have virtual reference desks where questions may be asked and, in some cases, negotiated. For example, *Ask an Expert* tries to connect young people with a subject expert. Children complete and submit a form, receiving an answer via e-mail from the chosen expert within a week.

Many public libraries are now providing online reference services, usually collaboratively with one or more library systems (see section 5.8 and Chapter 6). In the United Kingdom, a consortium of more than eighty public libraries in England and Scotland called *People's Network* answers questions 24/7 either by e-mail or through real-time chat service. While not specific to children and teens, the site is accessible to young people using clear language and is an easy-to-navigate interface. Queries are generally answered within a day. If the user chooses the chat reference option, the interaction is synchronous, allowing for more extensive and rapid interaction with the responding librarian. Unfortunately neither of the forms used by *Ask an Expert* and *People's Network* do the job of incorporating essential elements of the reference interview on the form itself. Forms are more likely to elicit what the user really wants to know if they include questions such as: "It would help us provide more useful information if you could tell us what aspect of the topic interests you/how you plan to use this information."

The Internet Public Library (IPL), developed at the School of Information at the University of Michigan and now hosted by Drexel University, has through its *Kidspace* and *Teenspace* provided "Ask an *IPL* Librarian" reference service to children and teens since IPL began in 1995. Kids under thirteen complete a form that includes questions about age, grade at school, the date by which the information is needed, whether or not the query is related to a school project and, if so, the

Did You Know?

The new "Guidelines for Library Services to Teens, Ages 12–18," jointly created and adopted by RUSA and YALSA (2006), includes the following statement: "Online information and electronic communication is a way of life for most teens. They have come of age with the Internet, iPods, cable and satellite television, cell phones, etc., and these tools form a seamless part of their everyday lives." The document goes on to recommend incorporating "the use of social networking (for example, instant messaging, blogs and social Web sites) into service plans that are designed to provide reference services for teens." It also recommends the provision of "online reference services available 24/7 to accommodate teens' busy lifestyles and often unpredictable study and research habits."

ANALYZE THIS REFERENCE TRANSACTION

Case 28: Washington Confidential

In this excerpt from a live chat interview with a young adult from the Seeking Synchronicity Project (Radford and Connaway, 2005–2008), the user needs information for a research project for school. We know that teens value the anonymity of chat reference. In this interview, the user wonders just how confidential the service is and whether his address will be "broadcast to the world."

1	User:	what are natural resourses of washington?
2	Librarian:	Do you just need a list of resources? Or do you need information about the resources too? (*two closed questions*)
3	User:	I am doing a research project for school and I need just a long list or what our resourses are. could you help me you [Librarian Name]?
4	User:	sorry, typo
5	User:	Could you help me to find a list of Washingtons' supplied materials to the world?
6	Librarian:	Don't worry about the typos—I make them too! Let me see what I can find online. You may also want to check an encyclopedia and/or the World Almanac because I know they contain the kind of info that you're looking for.
7	Librarian:	Give me just a minute to do some searching . . . (*inclusion*)
8	User:	Thank you SO much!
9	Librarian:	I'm still searching. Thanks for your patience . . . (*inclusion*)
10	User:	pardon my spelling, it is resources.
11	Librarian:	I'm not finding a list online. Do you mind if I do some more searching both online and in our print collection, and send you an email to let you know what I find?
12	User:	alright
13	Librarian:	What's your email address?
14	User:	I would like to know if i will be on a mailing list, and if it would be brodcast to the world.
15	Librarian:	You won't be on any type of mailing list. The only people who will see your email address are me and perhaps some of my coworkers. That's it.
16	User:	So, it is strictly confidential?
17	Librarian:	Yes, it is strictly confidential. We actually all sign confidentiality agreements stating that we won't release customer contact information.

[Some further exchanges about contact information.]

| 27 | Librarian: | Is there anything else that I can help you with at the moment, [Patron Name]? |

Comment: In a goal-directed interpersonal interaction such as an interview or a group discussion, conversational turns can be sorted into two categories: task functions that get the job done (e.g., line 2 above), and maintenance functions that create a positive communication climate and provide reassurance and encouragement. In this interview, a large proportion of the librarian's talk falls into this latter category of maintenance (e.g., "Don't worry about the typos—I make them too!" "Thanks for your patience," and "strictly confidential") in response to the user's expression of apology ("sorry, typo") and anxiety ("I would like to know if i will be on a mailing list").

For discussion: In comparing a chat reference interview with an FtF interview, would you expect to see any differences in the frequency with which the librarian provides reassurance and encouragement? Why do you think so? Could a case be made for the opposite answer?

nature of the assignment (e.g., length of the report). Teens and adults complete a similar form. Although answers usually take about a week, queries are acknowledged and sometimes clarified with an e-mail sent within twenty-four hours. A study by Henley (2004) found that the responses received to ten queries posed to IPL by an imaginary sixth grader provided resources which were age appropriate, of good quality, and engaging.

The following list provides suggestions for conducting the virtual reference interview with children and teens (note that many of these same suggestions work with adults as well):

- A short friendly message sent at the beginning of an interaction builds rapport and helps young users to understand that they are interacting with a real librarian rather than an automated service or computer.

- Early in your interaction, try to determine a child or teen's age so as to adopt developmentally appropriate communication strategies.

- Use simple, clear language appropriate to the reading and cognitive abilities of the child or teen user.

- Accept that children are likely to make many spelling and grammar errors in their messages to you. Fagan and Desai (2002/2003, 142) note, "Misspellings are important only if they confuse the question at hand. It may help to say words out loud to figure out what they mean."

- Large blocks of text can be overwhelming for a child. Keep your messages relatively brief. Consider using larger size fonts. Use paragraphing and spacing to create manageable chunks.

- Avoid using library jargon. Difficult enough for children to understand when spoken, these unfamiliar terms become even more opaque when presented in text.

- Use emoticons and other exaggerated typographical symbols such as repeated punctuation traditionally associated with electronic communication (see 6.2.2). Not only do these help create a sense of informality and approachability but they are easier to understand for younger children with more reading and writing skills.

- Learn about "the mores, the etiquette, the lingo" and the interaction practices common in digital environments used by children and teens (Janes, 2003). While you may want to adopt these stylistic inflections only selectively in your virtual reference desk practices, understanding them will enhance your ability to respond to children and young adults.

- The younger the child, the more difficult for the child to wait for a response. Regular, brief updates about the status of the search are important for all users and essential when working with children.

Did You Know?
In one of the few research studies designed to capture the responses of teen users themselves to library chat reference services, Greene and Thompson (as cited in Kortz, Morris, and Greene, 2006, 10) reported that teens prefer chat over e-mail reference, value being able to remain anonymous, would like greater speed, and "enjoyed the casual nature of chat and the use of jargon, abbreviations and coded messages." Teens also said that they liked developing a personalized relationship with the librarian, wanted to be able to request a specific librarian, and would like an option to rate librarians.

- Quick responses (and the choice of a medium like instant messaging or chat reference that supports this) are essential for students whose assignment is, almost always, due tomorrow.

- Remember that the more anonymous and forgiving context of the virtual reference interview can seem less risky to children and teens with little or no experience using libraries. Hence the virtual reference transaction provides an excellent opportunity for positive first interactions with young people.

5.5 Interviewing Adults with Special Language-related Needs

Since the basis of communication is a common language, communication accidents are more likely to happen when you and the user do not share the same first language or dialect, or when the user has a speech or hearing disability. Cultural differences can also create barriers to communication. In your effort to understand what the user is saying, you might be sending other, negative messages (such as asking too many questions or infringing on personal space) that hamper communication, usually unintentionally. It is important not to make assumptions about intelligence or competence on the basis of language proficiency.

For people whose English language skills or ability to enunciate are not perfect, remember to listen patiently. Talk clearly and a bit more slowly than usual, but not louder. Above all, stay calm and be patient. Don't say to yourself: "I didn't understand a word of what he said—and I never will." Work through the strategies of acknowledgment, taking ownership, asking the user to write the question down, restating and paraphrasing the question. One of these will work in most situations.

1. Restate what you do understand (2.4.3). If you catch the word "book" or "information," respond with some acknowledgment such as: "You're looking for a book on...?" or "You need some information...?" This establishes your willingness to help, encourages the user to repeat or fill in the part you missed, and gives you a second chance to listen.

2. Take ownership of the problem. Say, "I'm sorry, I seem to be having trouble understanding people today. Could you tell me again?"

3. If you still do not understand what the user wants, ask him to write it down. Again, take ownership: "It would help me if you could just write the name (or topic) down on this paper." However, keep in mind that some people might not be able to write English.

4. You can also ask if the person came with someone else who might be able to translate. Even a young child can act as an interpreter and may be nearby in the children's room.

Did You Know?

Osa, Nyana, and Ogbaa (2006, 24) remind us that staff members who are themselves from other cultures might have problems overcoming cultural differences. Following training in which the importance of maintaining eye contact was emphasized, one employee found it difficult to do, explaining that it seemed too bold and to challenge the patrons: "I will want them to feel comfortable, not to feel as though I am challenging them to a duel."

Did You Know?

Do you consider raised voices to be a sign that a fight has begun? Not necessarily! In some cultures, an increase in volume is a sign of an exciting conversation among friends (Berlanga-Cortéz, 2000).

A QUICK TIP

Don't Overlook the Niceties

In North America we tend to be quite informal when using e-mail, but we can unintentionally offend people from other cultures who consider it rude to be addressed by their first name. Simply answering the question without polite small talk can offend anyone. Polite small talk in an e-mail is simply the written equivalent of acknowledgement (e.g., "Good afternoon; thank you for your question about...").

5. If all else fails, ask someone else to help. Sometimes another librarian will be able to hear immediately what the person is saying. Do this gracefully: "Maybe Mrs. Milne will be able to help. Let's just go over there and ask her." Often just moving with the user to a less public area will lessen tension or frustration for both of you and encourage the user to express the request in another way.

5.5.1 Cross-cultural Communication

Culture affects all types of communication. In this section, we point out a few of the communication accidents that can occur in the reference context directly as a result of cultural differences. If the number of "intercultural accidents" seems to be increasing, one reason why is that we are all encountering cultural differences more often now than before. We must therefore make a special effort to be aware of differing perspectives in order to avoid misunderstandings. First we need to educate ourselves about intercultural communication so that we are able to identify intercultural differences. Then we need a way of thinking about these differences that will enable us to develop intentional strategies for communicating effectively.

A good first step is to read as much as you can about the factors that affect intercultural communication and discuss them with knowledgeable people. The main differences between cultures are the different values and attitudes towards human relationships. McGuigan (2002) explained that if you overlook these differences, you might violate deeply held cultural values, and may inadvertently be perceived as arrogant or rude. These cultural differences usually manifest themselves in differences in body language, in sense of time and personal space, and in general rules for etiquette or "being polite" or showing respect. Some differences seem quite arbitrary; for example, the "thumbs up" gesture means "all right" in North America, but to some people from southern Europe, Iran, and South American it means the equivalent of the American obscene gesture of the "middle finger."

Most cultural differences are internally logical. Many are based on concepts of time, space and one's social position in any given situation. For example, in some cultures, being late is a mark of your importance because it shows that you are busy. Personal space is also often culture-specific: a distance of two feet between two people may be perceived as "too close" (read "pushy") by the British participant and "too distant" (read "unfriendly") by the Latino. Touching is fraught with subtle cultural, social, and gender differences. A "friendly" tap on the shoulder of a South Asian female student by a male Euro-American librarian will likely be considered quite inappropriate. In some cultures, space is perceived as communal, permitting people to jump queues. Conflict then occurs when a person with this view of space comes to a culture that rigidly observes the "first come, first served" rule. Directness or "getting to the point" is valued by North Americans as an indication of efficiency and honesty, but in some Asian and Middle Eastern cultures it is perceived as

---

Did You Know?
Personal space is culturally related and involves four zones for North Americans: the *intimate zone* (up to eighteen inches) is reserved for close, intimate relationships; the *personal zone* (one- and-a-half to three-and-a-half feet) is used for confidentiality; the *social zone* (four to twelve feet) is the normal conversational space; and beyond those, the *public zone* is used for walking across a room and for public speaking. In other cultures the zones exist, but their distances will vary.

(Berlanga-Cortéz, 2000; Garner, 2003)

A QUICK TIP

Use Inclusion
Especially with international students, explain *why* you are asking questions. Yvonne De Souza (1996) explained that international students may not be aware that it is part of the reference librarian's job to conduct a reference interview and may therefore interpret your questions as some sort of test. If you ask, "What have you done/ found so far?" the international user may be embarrassed to say, "Nothing," for fear of losing face. One less threatening way to ask this question might be, "Have you had a chance to get started yet?" Use inclusion (4.1.1) to explain why you are asking open or sense-making questions.

Conducting the Reference Interview

EXERCISE

Consider This Scenario

An international student approaches the reference desk. In a quiet and retiring manner, the student asks for help. The librarian on the other side of the desk tenses while straining to understand the questions through the heavily accented, soft-spoken voice of the student. The librarian becomes agitated, thinking why doesn't this student speak up? Why can't he speak English? The foreign student senses the librarian's distress, apologizes and leaves without getting the needed information. (Hoffman and Popa, 1986: 356–360)

For discussion: What cultural factors should the librarian have considered? How might the librarian have dealt with her own discomfort? What specific steps could she have taken to understand the question?

---

impolite, if not downright offensive. The tolerance for conflict varies between cultures—saying "No" directly may be seen as a sign of disrespect by people whose culture values harmony. Many of these cultural differences occur because cultures are of two types: "high-context" and "low-context." High-context cultures place importance on ambience, nonverbal signals, rapport, etc., while low-context cultures tend to ignore the things that are important to high-context cultures like some nonverbal communication. Low-context cultures may emphasize content, but accept smiles or nodding as clear indication of consent and approval (Berlanga-Cortéz, 2000).

Having given some examples of situations that call for cultural sensitivity, we must also point out that a little knowledge is a dangerous thing. As we learn more about different cultures, we are tempted to over-generalize behavior within a particular culture. Vast individual differences exist within any one culture—your own way of communicating may differ drastically from that of someone else from your culture. Communication accidents arising between two people of different cultures may not, in fact, have their roots in culture but may have resulted from other individual or situational factors. So there are no general "rules" for cross-cultural communication, except perhaps to assess each situation on its merits, and show respect for the individual. However, here are a few tips for using nonverbal and speaking skills with people of another culture:

- Use body language (2.4.2) that suggests approachability, respect and willingness to help—smiling, standing up, giving the user your full attention.

- Restate or paraphrase (3.2.4) the user's words to allow the other person to correct you.

- Do not assume that the user's smile means agreement—check it out.

- Recognize that the user's silence or lack of eye contact may mean agreement or demonstration of respect rather than lack of understanding.

EXERCISE

Observe Eye Contact

Eye contact carries different meanings in different cultures. Berlanga-Cortéz (2000) explained that in the African-American, Hispanic, and Asian cultures, *speakers* are expected to look at listeners directly in the eye, while *listeners* are expected to avert eyes to indicate respect and attention. On the other hand, in the Anglo-American culture listeners are expected to look at a speaker directly to indicate respect and attention and speakers are expected to avert eye contact (especially in informal speaking). Make your own informal survey as you speak with colleagues and library users. Do your findings agree with Berlanga-Cortéz? What are the implications of this finding on cultural difference for reference interview success?

- Keep your questions simple and wait for an answer.

- Observe the other's behavior patterns and try to model these. For example, if he makes eye contact, do the same. But if he looks down, this may be a sign of respect, so don't force it.

- Avoid touching people from other cultures and keep hand gestures to a minimum. Your hands should be in a relaxed and open position, not clenched.

- Avoid taking the mouse or keyboard from another person. Ask for permission if this is necessary.

- If you work in an area with a high concentration of people from a particular culture, you should read as much as you can about their customs and nonverbal communication patterns. Become more observant and seek to model their behaviors.

- Use inclusion (4.1.1) to explain why you are asking sense-making questions (3.2.3) about what the user has done so far or how the information will be used.

5.5.2 English Language Learners

In our increasingly multicultural societies, many library users do not speak English as their first language. Lack of fluency in English can create communication problems, but is not the only barrier to providing reference service. Many users come from countries where access to written materials is limited and where a library may simply be a large reading room with closed stacks. Questions, if asked at all, will focus on obtaining books from the stacks or on library holdings. Ziming Liu (1993, 28) notes that it's not just working in a second language that deters university students from developing countries from asking reference questions but also "the lack of attention to reference services in their home countries." Because the role of reference librarians is not always understood, "international students always feel that they are imposing or troubling the librarians with their questions" (Kumar and Suresh, 2000, 334). Nevertheless, language barriers are the major barrier for international students

---

A QUICK TIP

Write It Down

In Curry and Copeman's (2007) study, an international student rated very highly the librarian who wrote down keywords from the question on a piece of paper and showed it to her. This simple act confirms that the librarian understands the question and helps circumvent misunderstanding.

Conducting the Reference Interview

Did You Know?

Liu and Redfern (1997) did a research study of reference success at San Jose State University library where there was a 50.7 percent "minority" population (including Hispanics, Asians, African Americans, Native Americans, and Pacific Islanders). They found that successful reference outcomes for these students depended upon two factors: English proficiency and frequency of library use. Users with less successful reference outcomes seldom asked reference questions and *avoided* the reference desk. Why did these students avoid the reference desk?

- Lack of knowledge:
  They never think of asking reference questions.
  They do not do know what a reference librarian does.
- Fear:
  Of asking stupid questions
  Of their English not being good enough to ask the question
  Of not being able to understand the answers well enough

EXERCISE

Slow and Fast

An international student who asked for information on immigration described the experience as follows:

> I spoke slowly, "I am going to write a paper on immigration. Can you help me find some information on the topic?" She listened to me and asked what specific topic I wanted. She talked very fast and I couldn't recall exactly what she said. I felt that I was slow to answer but she kept going quickly. (From Curry and Copeman, 2007).

For discussion: What did the librarian do right? What went wrong? How could the librarian self-correct?

because variations in pronunciation, intonation, speech patterns, and enunciation of words hinder the reference librarian's ability to understand the question (Curry and Copeman, 2005).

Libraries can help by training library staff in cross-cultural communication (5.5.1) and by hiring staff members who can speak the dominant languages of the area served. In academic libraries, international students who are familiar with using North American libraries should be asked to participate in tours for new students. A large public library system needs to determine which branches have different language concentrations and provide appropriate staffing. But they must also keep aware of changes in the population. Particular cultural groups may move to new areas, and collections and services (and sometimes staff) must move with them.

Here are some suggestions for improving reference communication with English language learners.

- Be patient.
- Pay attention to speech patterns and listen to words, not intonation.
- Make no assumptions (3.2.2). Assumptions are sometimes made about the level of service needed before users have gotten past the first few words of their question.
- Avoid using library jargon and acronyms (to be avoided with any user but especially with English language learners).
- Speak slowly and don't raise your voice because users' lack of fluency in English doesn't mean they can't hear you.
- Avoid using complex sentence structure and vocabulary. But don't just assume that the user will necessarily understand all the everyday words that you choose instead. Hendricks (1991) points out that many English language learners have learned their English from textbooks and have never learned the everyday words.
- Avoid jokes. Garner (2003) points out that jokes and allusions are not international; they are often culture-bound and do not translate well.

- Don't ask negative questions such as, "Don't you want this book?" or double-barreled questions like, "Do you want to search yourself or do you want me to show you how?"

- Check often for comprehension. But don't just ask, "Did you understand?" Non-native English language learners who want to be polite and respectful may say yes, even when they have not understood.

- Remember that you have an accent too. Your own English accent might be quite different from the English that international students learned at school.

- Use visual aids such as handouts and provide users with written library guides or pathfinders appropriate to their questions.

(Adapted from Curry and Copeman, 2005; Garner, 2003; Greenfield, Johnston, and Williams, 1986; Janes and Meltzer, 1990; and Ormondroyd, 1989)

5.5.3 Interviewing People with Disabilities

Libraries have worked hard to eliminate physical barriers that in the past hampered access to libraries and library materials by people with disabilities. The Americans with Disabilities Act (ADA), passed into law in 1990, applies in most U.S. libraries in both public and private settings, and has prompted the reassessment of library facilities, collections, and services. Libraries elsewhere are also paying greater attention to removing physical barriers to library access. On January 16, 2001, the American Library Association (ALA) Council approved the "Library Services for People with Disabilities Policy." This policy states: "Libraries must not discriminate against individuals with disabilities and shall ensure that individuals with disabilities have equal access to library resources." While emphasizing facilities, collections, and adaptive devices, the policy does not explicitly address communication skills needed by staff members who respond to the information needs of persons with disabilities. Nevertheless helping library staff acquire appropriate communication skills is a crucial element in providing equal access.

The key, as with English language learners, is to respect the user and take every question seriously—possibly even more seriously than usual, since it can take more determination for a person with a disability to come to the library and approach a stranger with a request for help. A number of physical and mental conditions can make communication difficult. There are speech disorders, including problems of articulation, voice production and rhythm, which can be caused by a variety of factors including hearing impairment, head injuries, stroke, and cerebral palsy. Users with a mental illness may speak in a manner that appears inappropriate: incoherent or too loud, for example. Although the library literature sometimes refers to these users as "problem patrons," the Americans with Disabilities Act recognizes that mental impairment is a disability. The ADA defines mental impairments as "any mental or psychological disorder, such as metal retardation, organic brain syndrome, emotional or mental illness, and specific learning disabilities."

Did You Know?
Especially with users who are English language learners, it is easy for similar-sounding words to be confused or misheard. Dewdney and Michell (1996) provide many examples such as bird control/ birth control and laws/ lace. They advise asking a question like, "What would you like to know about lace?" If the user answers that he wants to know the laws regarding copyright, the librarian stands a good chance of repairing the miscommunication.

Did You Know?
E-mail, chat reference, and text messaging have made it possible for the hearing impaired to participate in reference interviews. Some deaf or hard of hearing users may welcome the choice of asking their question via chat or IM, if they know that these services exist. Text-based services are a natural solution to those with hearing impairments. Another source of text-based help is provided through use of a search engine such as ASK (www.ask.com) which encourages natural language questions.

Telephone-based technologies can still be used as well. Text telephones (TTY) and telecommunication devices for the deaf (TDD) provide a way for deaf and hard of hearing persons to communicate through the telephone. Using TDD, a hearing impaired person can type a message over telephone lines and receive a response from a TDD-equipped library staff member. Many libraries have TTY and TDD machines available for patron use. Computers that are voice compatible can be enabled to talk directly to TTYs. Also available are wireless messenger paging systems that allow the user to send and receive e-mail, TTY message, faxes, text-to-speech and speech-to-text messages, and a text message to one-way alphanumeric pagers.

People with hearing difficulties have different ways of communicating, depending on when the problem began. People who have been profoundly deaf from very early childhood have never heard spoken language and will often communicate using a sign language such as ASL (American Sign Language). For libraries serving such users, equitable access can be provided by hiring a staff member who can use sign language or by recruiting signing volunteers. Some who have been hearing-impaired from birth but have residual hearing might wish to communicate by speaking. Because their pronunciation may be non-standard, you need to listen carefully, use acknowledgment (2.4.3), ask for repetition when necessary, and sometimes ask the user to write down the question. Those with hearing loss in later life can speak without difficulty, but may have a problem understanding your response. Your library will provide services to users with a wide range of disabilities. The skills needed for helping these users can be learned through self-education and practice. Workshops are available through agencies and community groups, and Web-based programs are available as well. To get you started, see "Rhea Joyce Rubin's Tips for Serving Patrons with Disabilities."

RHEA JOYCE RUBIN'S TIPS FOR SERVING PEOPLE WITH DISABILITIES

Serving Patrons Who Are Deaf or Hard of Hearing

- Approach users so that you can be seen.
- Get users' attention before you start speaking.
- Ask users how they prefer to communicate and then accommodate the request.
- Do not assume a knowledge of sign language.
- Do not leave to find a person who can sign unless the patron requests it.
- Reduce background noise or move to a quieter location.
- Always face users as you speak and maintain eye contact.
- If you are using an interpreter, be sure to speak directly to the user, not to the interpreter.

- Speak at a normal pace, enunciating carefully; do not exaggerate your lip movements or mumble as this makes speech reading difficult.
- Keep your mouth visible —do not obscure it with your hands or by chewing gum or food.
- Be aware of the lighting. For example, do not stand in front of a light source because that makes it difficult to speech read or to pick up visual cues.
- If hard of hearing users have hearing aids or other assistive listening devices, give them an opportunity to adjust the equipment.
- If users do not seem to understand you, write it down

Serving Patrons Who Are Blind or Visually Impaired

- Do not yell or speak loudly to people with vision loss; most are not deaf or hard of hearing.
- Identify yourself and others with you. If in a group setting, remember to identify the person you are addressing.
- Have your voice show your welcome and helpfulness.
- Speak directly to users, not through their sighted companions. Do not touch or pet a guide dog on duty.

- When giving directions, use the clock face as your basis. For example, "The reference desk is at three o'clock from where you're facing."
- When guiding users, allow them to take your elbow; do not grab their arms or hands. Stand next to them and slightly ahead, then ask them to take your arm.
- Ask what you can do to help and which materials format/ communication method is preferred.

(Cont'd.)

RHEA JOYCE RUBIN'S TIPS FOR SERVING PEOPLE WITH DISABILITIES *(Continued)*

Serving Patrons with Learning Disabilities

- Give clear directions, checking for comprehension, and paraphrasing or repeating if necessary.
- Be patient. A person with a learning disability may need extra time to understand you or to complete a task.
- Be literal. Some people with learning differences have difficulty with tonal subtleties and with metaphors.

- If a form (e.g., library card application) needs completion, offer assistance if writing is a problem.
- Offer information in a variety of reading and comprehension levels and in non-print formats.
- Treat the person with respect. Often people with learning differences are treated as stupid, lazy, or developmentally disabled, or mentally ill.

Serving Patrons with Motor Impairments

- Keep clear pathways for people using wheelchairs and canes. A wheelchair (or scooter or walker) is part of the personal body space of its user. Do not touch it (or push it) without permission.
- Do not carry a user unless it is an emergency evacuation situation or the person requests it.
- Place yourself at the user's eye level by sitting or crouching.

- Speak directly to users rather than through their attendants.
- Do not assume speech or other disabilities.
- Do not assume they need information on disabilities.
- A person using a wheelchair is not "wheelchair bound," "crippled," or "handicapped."
- Ask the person how you can help.

Serving Patrons with Speech Disorders

- If you are unsure what the person is saying, repeat it back, asking for confirmation that you have understood.
- If you definitely do not understand what users are saying, tell them and ask how you can communicate more easily.
- Offer writing as an alternative means of communication. Note that some causes of speech difficulty also make writing arduous.

- Consider moving to a quiet, less public area. Stressful situations often exacerbate a person's speech difficulties.
- Be patient. A person with a speech difficulty may need extra time to communicate clearly.
- Do not finish users' sentences for them. This is insulting.
- Treat the person with respect. Often a person with a speech difficulty is treated as drunk, developmentally disabled, or mentally ill.

(From Rhea Joyce Rubin, *Planning for Library Services for People with Disabilities,* Chicago: ASCLA, 2001; used with permission)

A QUICK TIP

Develop Guidelines and Policies

In a survey completed by 136 academic libraries, Wiler and Lomax (2000) found that only 9 percent had a written policy covering service to library users with disabilities. To help you in preparing such policies, see ALA's (2001) "Library Services for People with Disabilities Policy." This document can be supplemented by various published guidelines for serving special populations. For example, ALA (1996) published guidelines for serving the American deaf community, and IFLA broadened these to apply internationally (Day, 2000).

A QUICK TIP

Beware of Spread

According to Wright and Davie (1991, 5), "spread" happens when you assume that a person with one disability also has problems in other areas as well. This can be observed when "people raise their voices in conversation with a blind person."

5.6 Interviewing Problematic People

Much literature exists on the so-called "problem" library user. Topics considered include such issues as who gets to define the problem, what categories of problems are typically found in libraries, and what methods of handling specific problems are recommended. When the focus is on definition, an important question becomes: Is the "problem user" a product of labeling (i.e., the system calls someone a problem who doesn't fit the system or obey its rules)? Is the problem an aspect of the user or does it arise interactively from the communication context? However defined, the problems encountered in libraries range from mild disruption of library routines to behaviors that are dangerous, criminal, or both. Some individuals get categorized as problem users because of their behavior, the concerns they raise for staff, or the effects they might have on other library users. An important first step is to identify the kind of problem you are facing. You also need to consider whether elements in the library system, including your own behaviors, are contributing to the problem. For many problems, you can adapt and use skills that we have discussed as useful in general for the reference interview.

Libraries categorize as problematic many different kinds of behaviors. Some users may be destructive, dangerous, or display antisocial or criminal behaviors. Some are angry and frustrated. Some, such as cell phone users,

---

EXERCISE

Active Listening

Anne M. Turner (2004) describes an "active listening" technique that involves listening between the lines and reflecting feeling (3.3.4). The idea is that you must first acknowledge or accept the other person's feelings so that then together you can get on to fixing the problem. This skill takes practice and may seem stilted and contrived at first. But it really works! Turner (2004: 37) provides the example of a complaining user and two possible responses:

User: What a crummy library! This is the biggest mess I've ever seen!

Staff: Yes, it could be better organized, but we do our best to make it work. If you really have a complaint, you can go to the director's office.

OR

Staff: It sounds like you've had a frustrating experience. Is there any way I can help you find what you need?

For discussion: The first response did acknowledge the person's complaint, but then went off course. What happened? Why is the second response better?

For practice with the skill: As a group training exercise, ask participants to write down on cards some examples of users' complaints that typically occur in their library setting. Take turns in pairs—one person plays the role of user with the complaint, reading from the card; the other person responds, using active listening. The rest of the group should listen and provide feedback on whether or not the response was an effective use of active listening. Take turns until each participant has had a chance to present a complaint and receive a response.

noisy teens, or argumentative seniors, are disruptive to other users. Other causes of concern in libraries are unattended children, the homeless, and people with mental illness (Sarkodie-Mensah, 2002). Not all difficulties presented can be solved through good reference interviewing techniques, of course, but many can. In this section, we concentrate on those common, garden-variety problems which are ameliorated by good communication skills.

Most people, as Rubin (2000) explains, enter calmly into a library transaction. They become angry, agitated, or upset when one or more of their expectations are not met. Users who arrive already stressed by tight deadlines, impatient, rushed, or irate become even more upset when they fail to get the help they need or if they are not treated courteously. Justina Osa (2002) notes that patron frustration often comes from getting the wrong information. And why is the user getting the wrong information? Too often the reason is that the reference interview has been bypassed.

In some cases, the so-called problem patron seems to be another version of the bad guy user (1.7). Osa (2002, 269) interviewed reference desk staff members at one university to find out how staff identified people as "problem patrons." Interestingly, 90 percent of the staff identified as problems those users "who want you to give them the right/best response but would not give you time to search for the best source of information." These library users allegedly wanted an answer instantaneously and became frustrated with any delay. This sounds to us like a situation that calls for the following skills: establishing contact (2.3); using one or more sense-making questions to determine the information need; listening attentively; and including the user in the search process. As we have been arguing throughout this book, taking a few minutes at the outset to find out what the user really wants to know saves time in the end. It prevents the frustrating situation in which the librarian looks fruitlessly through many, many sources, comes up with nothing, and leaves the user disappointed and angry.

The following reference interview techniques work in FtF situations to prevent or diffuse problems; not surprisingly they are the same ones that work in general:

- Use nonverbal attending skills (2.4.2) to establish contact: look up, smile, be welcoming, stand up, show through a smile or nod that you have seen people in line.

- During the interview, use appropriate eye contact—look at the person not at the computer screen. Maintain a polite tone of voice and open body language.

- Be an active listener (2.4.5).

- Focus on the problem, not on the behavior.

- Ask open and sense-making questions (3.2.1; 3.2.3).

- Use acknowledgment (2.4.3) and reflection of content (3.3.4); let the user know that you have heard and understand the question.

Did You Know?
Beth McNeil and Denise J. Johnson (1996) have identified three classes of problem patrons in libraries. Class 1 is the most serious—dangerous persons who commit or attempt to commit an act of violence (e.g., they are openly hostile, verbally abusive, or combative). Class 2 problems might become serious—who knows? These are persons who are disruptive to other users or staff (e.g., they may be drunk, narcotized, highly emotional). Class 3 individuals are annoying but harmless nuisances who may be unpleasant or obnoxious (e.g., they are talking loudly, laughing, malodorous, eating in areas where eating is prohibited, or taking up too much of the staff member's time). The good news is that events involving Class 1 problems are very rare while good communication skills usually are the best bet with the others.

A QUICK TIP

The Talker

Pat is alone at the reference desk, during a moderately busy time, and a line of users is waiting for help. A male library user waits in line and, when his turn comes, starts talking to Pat. He does not have a question but just seems to want someone to talk to. Pat explains politely that there is a line of users, but the man says, "I waited in line. Now it is their turn to wait." What should Pat do?

For discussion: How much time should Pat spend with this user? How can Pat disengage without becoming rude? What can be done with needy users who just need someone to talk to? What alternatives does Pat have?

ANALYZE THIS REFERENCE TRANSACTION

Case 29: "I hate this Web site."

This is the entirety of a live chat reference interaction from the Seeking Synchronicity Project (Radford and Connaway, 2005–2008). Is this a case of a problem user or a problematic situation?

1	User:	I want to learn how to have telekinetic powers
2	Librarian:	[A librarian will be with you in about a minute.]
3	Librarian:	[Librarian Name - A librarian has joined the session.]
4	Librarian:	will be things about it, but may not tell you how to do it
5	Librarian:	"telekinetic powers" gets 19,000 hits in google -
6	Librarian:	adding site:edu gets 141 - mostly things about stories that talk about it
7	Librarian:	"telekinesis" site:edu gets 1900
8	User:	I HATE THIS WEBSITE AND I WILL NEVER COME HERE AGAIN
9	User:	[patron - has disconnected]

For discussion:

1. Brainstorm all the factors that could have contributed to the user's response in lines 8 and 9, typing an all caps "FLAME" and abruptly disconnecting?
2. Would a reference interview have helped? If so how?
3. What could have been done to improve this chat communication?

- Use inclusion: explain what you are doing, let users see the screen you are working on, and invite them to come with you to the shelves.

- With frustrated or angry people, use reflection of feeling (3.3.4). You could say, "I know that this has been a very frustrating experience for you being referred from one place to another. Let's make sure we get to the bottom of your question...."

- With angry users who raise their voices, speak quietly. You will find that after a few conversational turns, the user is mirroring your tone and talking more softly.

Problematic situations also arise with telephone, e-mail, or chat reference. With the telephone reference interview, Ann Curry (1996, 184) notes that the inability of both the caller and the librarian to readily "assess the stress or confusion surrounding the other at the moment encourages false assumptions." A person phoning in "can be annoyed by background noise and the sense that the staff member is inattentive" unable to see "the long line of unserved and impatient customers forming as the telephone conversation continues." Curry also points out that the telephone provides the protection of "visual anonymity," leading many people to more aggressive behavior than they are capable of in person. Similarly the chat reference users cannot see what is going on in the physical library and may feel equally visually anonymous. See the following suggestions for dealing with rude and impatient users in chat encounters (most of which apply equally well on the phone). Remember that you have skills and experience in dealing with rude/impatient people in FtF encounters, and these skills can be just as effective in virtual encounters.

- Don't "mirror" rude behavior. Rudeness provokes further rudeness.

- Resist the urge to reprimand or admonish users for rude behavior or FLAMING, a response that tends to elicit further rudeness.

- Avoid jargon or language that will create a barrier or send the message that you are blindly following the rulebook.

- Apologize to the user as appropriate, a tactful gesture that can diffuse potentially rude behavior on line. You can say, "I'm sorry that you had to wait so long; our service is very busy today."

- When users are impatient ("Hurry, hurry!"), let them know *realistically* how long you think that the search will take. Present alternatives and let the user decide. Say, "I know you are in a hurry, but this will take about four to five minutes. Can you wait or would you like me to e-mail you when I find something?"

- If users complain about library service or another chat librarian, thank them for bringing their concern to your attention and promise to follow up. Regard a complaint as a gift, and as a way to improve service.

- Don't condescend to a person with a "simple question." (e.g., the Valentine's Day example in section 5.2.1). Something simple to one person is not simple to another. Treat all users with equal courtesy and respect.

- Don't take rude behaviors personally. Sometimes users are stressed by deadlines and other life problems. (Radford, 2004)

5.7 Interviewing Users with Consumer Health and Legal Questions

In 2007, the Pew Internet and American Life Project found that, even though many people have access to the Internet and use it heavily for medical and legal questions, many still ask such questions in libraries. Of 2,068 people surveyed, 46 percent of those with a health problem and 36 percent of those with a legal problem had used the Internet for information. 10 percent of those with a health problem and 10 percent with a legal problem used the public library to find information (Estabrook, 2007, 15). Extrapolated to the population as a whole, 10 percent is a lot

---

A QUICK TIP

Keep Your Cool

You may not be able to control the other person's behavior, but you can control your own. When an interaction becomes problematic, remember to breathe so your body knows you are not in a "fight or flight" situation. Speak in a calm, soft voice, even if the other person begins to talk loudly. An apology, even if you are not at fault, can defuse things. Focus on the problem and offer alternatives to bring the user into the process. If you do find that you are unable to remain calm, remove yourself by politely offering to "find someone else who can help." When you walk away, the user has a chance to take a breath and regain composure.

A QUICK TIP

Yes We Can

Rhea Rubin (2000) recommends that you stress what you and the library *can* do for the patron, rather than what you cannot do. Instead of saying, "I can't do X," say, "What I can do is Y." Instead of, "It's not our policy...," try, "Usually we..." Instead of saying, "You have to do X," say instead, "It would help if you did X." Instead of saying, "You don't understand...," try, "Let me clarify..."

Did You Know?
Consumer health questions are those that relate directly to a personal medical concern of the person asking for information or the person's relative or friend. They do not include questions from students doing research for a school report, health professionals, or someone doing work-related research.
(Healthnet)

Conducting the Reference Interview

of people coming to libraries to ask consumer health or legal questions. While many are using the Internet, Harris, Wathen, and Chan (2005, 152) found that "many people do not find health information on Web sites or telehealth databases useful, nor even think to use them." Similarly people often find it hard to search the Web for legal information. In a library, a staff member is available to help users frame their questions, navigate the Internet, and identify authoritative sources on or off the Web.

A librarian once told us that her least favorite reference questions concerned legal and health issues. Both types of queries undoubtedly present special challenges, especially for public librarians. Although they are unlikely to be specialists, they have to cope with unfamiliar terminology, complicated or inadequate resources, and tricky ethical issues (including the "information" vs. "advice" problem). In addition, users who need consumer health or legal information might be reluctant to disclose the problem to the librarian. Yet effective service requires the librarian to determine not only the subject and scope of the question, but also the user's expectations and requirements, including that of privacy. This section deals with the first problem the librarian encounters in legal and health information service—finding out what the user really wants to know. Of course, the actual search for legal and health information raises other problems owing to inherent difficulties of their respective literatures, but that's beyond our scope here. For more information, see RUSA's (2001) "Guidelines for Medical, Legal, and Business Information Services Responses."

Both the legal and the health reference interview follow the sequence of good reference interview in general: establishing a good communication climate, asking questions, verifying details of the reference query, and following up. But legal and health queries pose some special problems. First, users have often consulted their family and friends as well as the Internet before coming to you, so the library is sometimes seen as the last resort. Users with legal questions often seek advice because a friend told them that the library has legal forms (Olver, 2000). Users with consumer health questions may already have searched Google without finding what they were looking for. Second, most users have no idea of the huge scope of these subject areas. They commonly ask overly broad questions, such as "Where is your law section?" thinking they can find what they need by themselves, or they may request overly specific materials, such as "a book on plantar warts," when the information they need is likely in a medical encyclopedia or periodical article. Often they want very recent information such as new drug trials that they cannot find in a catalog, and so their initial question may be, "Can you show me how this catalog works?" Both the medical and legal literatures are constantly changing. Users might also have difficulty articulating their needs because of the specialized terminology in these fields. Consider, for example, the genealogy/gynecology mix-up (1.4.1).

The third and even trickier aspect of legal and health queries is that they often arise from personal needs involving sensitive or emotional factors. In particular, privacy and anonymity might be of great concern to the user. Consequently, certain interview skills described previously in this book

ANALYZE THIS REFERENCE TRANSACTION

Case 30: Pulling out the big words.

Here is a live chat reference interaction taken verbatim from the Seeking Synchronicity Project (Radford and Connaway, 2005–2008). The transaction seems to have turned into a duel of language and "big words." The specialized language of legal and medical questions poses an additional hurdle for communication.

1	User:	what if defendant has moved and order to appear to small claims court, sent via registered mail, does not reach the defendant? Will the court hold the hearing in absentia or plaintiff or the court wil exercise another way to serve the defendant?
2	Librarian:	[A librarian will be with you in about a minute.]
3	Librarian:	[Law Librarian [Librarian ID Number]- A librarian has joined the session]
4	Librarian:	you've either been talking to a lawyer or been reading black's law dictionary. Either way, notice must be effectuated. what I suggest is that you either go to your local county law library and look in the civil codes for service of process or go online to www.leginfo.ca.gov/calaw.html there are other ways to serve process besides personal service.
5	User:	what is "effectuated"?
6	User:	what is absentia?
7	Librarian:	you're the one pulling out the big words...effectuated means it must be done, completed, effected upon someone/thing
8	Librarian:	effectuate suggest actions not just that a thing need be done
9	Librarian:	you could always wait and see what the judge says - but even in small claims, the court will look to due dilligence (i.e. did you really earnestly try to serve the defendant or did you give up on the first attempt).
10	Librarian:	[Thank you for using the 24/7 reference. Please contact us again when you need assistance finding legal information.]
11	Note to staff:	COMP [Law Librarian [Librarian ID Number] - user has closed this session]

For discussion:

1. Where did this transaction take a wrong turn? What could the librarian have done differently?
2. In this transaction, the librarian bypasses the reference interview. What might the librarian have said instead at line 4?
3. Somewhere after line 6, the user disappears. What do you think about the ending of the transaction? What could the librarian have done earlier to repair the communication climate?

must be used with special care, or even avoided. For example, the skills of acknowledgment or restatement (2.4.3), which involve repeating or paraphrasing what the user has said, must be used very carefully in legal and health reference interviews. A person who whispers his question to the librarian does not want "Sex education?" or "You were arrested?" broadcast to the rest of the library or even to nearby staff.

Study carefully the following stages and skills needed for consumer health and medical questions to see how they differ from other types of interviewing.

1. Establish a good communication climate:

- Demonstrate positive body language such as initial eye contact, and smiling (or sympathetic nodding, depending on the user's state of mind) to reassure and encourage the user (2.4.2).

Conducting the Reference Interview

- Use encouragers (2.4.4) such as, "Mm-hmm," "I see," or "and then?" in a supportive tone.
- Listen (2.4.5) to show that you are interested and attentive. Don't interrupt unless the conversation gets way off track.
- Assure users that they are not alone: "A lot of people ask us about that type of thing."
- Use reflection of feeling, but very carefully. "So that's really worrying you" or "You sound pretty upset about this" may help establish rapport, but equally it might provoke an emotional outburst that is hard to handle.
- Use your intuition and experience to guide you in these situations. Sometimes a simple statement, "I'm here to help find some useful information" said in a calm, friendly voice can go a long way to reassuring the user.

2. **Find out what help is needed:**
   - Avoid premature diagnosis (3.2.2). Don't jump to conclusions about the use to which users will put the information, or whether users are simply pretending that they need it for a friend. People often ask questions on behalf of family members or friends who cannot come to the library. Find out whether the question is related to a personal concern or whether it's related to school or work—listen for clues (5.3.1). The person with a personal health question often needs specific information, whereas the student might need a broad overview.
   - Respect the person's privacy. If you suspect that the user may describe the query more fully in private, invite her to walk with you away from the desk or computers to a more private area.
   - Use inclusion (4.1.1). Explain why you need to know more about the query: "There are a lot of Web sites dealing with cancer so if you could tell me a little bit more about it, I may be able to find something more helpful."
   - Ask open questions (3.2.1) that users can answer in their own words (e.g., "What aspect of the law [medicine] are you looking for?" or "what is the original source of your question" rather than closed questions to which the user might not know the answer such as "Is that a bylaw?" or "Is that a bacterium or a virus?"
   - Ask sense-making questions (3.2.3) that leave users in control but still give them an opportunity to describe the important aspects of the information
   - To get at the situation, ask "Can you tell me a bit about how this problem arose?" or "Where did you come across this term?" or "What have you done so far to find out about this?" Answers to these questions may also help you to determine where users are in the search process, and whether they have already consulted a lawyer or doctor.

INITIAL AND NEGOTIATED HEALTH AND LEGAL QUESTIONS

The following question pairs, reported to us by public librarians, show why it is important to avoid premature diagnosis and to conduct a reference interview that gets beyond the initial statement of the question to the real need.

Initial question	Negotiated question
1. I'd like a book on becoming a lady.	Information on menstruation for a young girl.
2. I'd like to see the National Building Code.	I'd like to see a map of seismic zones in this region.
3. Where are your phone books?	An address for a California medical clinic.
4. Can you get me a book on cosmetic surgery?	Information on the risks of breast reduction.
5. Have you got New Jersey laws?	Was a song by Bruce Springsteen adopted as the official state song?
6. Books on schizophrenia and homosexuality.	Help in understanding a member of a family.
7. I want to read about the law.	How to get a "deadbeat dad" to pay child support.

- To get at the knowledge gap, ask, "What would you like to know?" and then "What do you already know about X?"

- To find out the intended use of the information, say, "If you can tell me a little bit about how you hope to use this information, I can help you better." The phrase "a little bit" is crucial with sensitive questions. These questions encourage users to describe in their own words what they want to be able to do as a result of the search. Sometimes the answer is "to figure out if what I found on the Internet is correct," "to make a decision," or "to know what the doctor's talking about." The kind of materials needed in each case will be different.

- Ask verifying questions to confirm your understanding: "You said this was German measles not red measles?" or "You mentioned a particular Supreme Court case in 1999?"

- Use closure (3.2.5) to redirect the focus back to the search when the discussion gets sidetracked into a long personal account. You can say: "Okay, I think I have enough to go on to find just what you need. Let's look at this Web site/ reference resource together." Keep the focus on solving the informational need, not the tale of woe.

3. **Establish boundaries:**
- Explain that you provide information, not advice or interpretation. Contrary to the beliefs of many librarians, users rarely use the library for a cheap source of professional advice. More often they want to prepare themselves for an appointment with their doctor or lawyer, or may just want to read more about what they have been told. Nevertheless, make it clear that the user should not solely depend on library or Internet materials, that these are always changing (and sometimes are inaccurate), and that the user should consult a professional for advice.

A QUICK TIP

Why? Where? What? What Else?

To understand legal questions, you need to find out *why* users want to know, *where* (in which jurisdiction involved—federal/province or state/local?), *what* situation they are in and what they would like to do about it, and *what else*. The best approach is to ask open questions and let users describe the situation in their own words. If you ask a series of closed questions, such as, "Is this civil or criminal law?" or "Is this a probate case?" the user quite often has no idea but says yes or no anyway, getting the search onto the wrong path.

A QUICK TIP

Read That Morning Paper

Users often come to the reference desk having read about a "hot case" in the newspaper and they are curious, wanting to read the actual case. Dilevko and Dolan (1999) recommend that all reference librarians keep current by reading a daily newspaper to anticipate these kinds of questions.

ANALYZE THIS REFERENCE TRANSACTION

Case 31: Not a made-up word

As a participant in the Library Visit Study, Jane sent this question by e-mail to a mid-size public library (using its Ask-A-Librarian adult form, which asked for name, e-mail address, and question) and got this response:

User: I was wondering if you could provide me with a definition of craniotherapy. Can you recommend any resources on the subject? Thank you very much!

Librarian: Hello, thank you for your enquiry. *Mosby's Medical Dictionary*, National Library of Medicine online, and 3 health databases had no reference to the term 'cranotherpy.' [*sic*]"
Regards.

Comment: Initially pleased with the quick response, and the fact that the librarian had listed the resources used, Jane said she would have liked the databases to be named. What bothered her more was the impersonality of the response:

> I did not expect to be treated like a close friend . . . but I expected that the person responding would, at the very least, provide their name. The response itself was rather curt and economical as well; I felt like I was being dispatched quickly. This was an important question—it was a question about a medical therapy, which means that the response from the librarian could have serious consequences. I expected the question to be taken seriously, and felt like it had not been. Finally, this was a term that I had come up with somewhere—it was not a made-up word. The response from the librarian implies that this term does not exist, because it is not in any of the sources they consulted. In a way, I felt like I was being called a liar and wasting their time with my question that had no answer.

After getting more information, Jane tried again in a return e-mail, this time asking about "cranial sacral therapy." The response was more personal (names used) and provided a sourced definition and additional information about using the library's health database to find additional resources. Jane said, "I felt a lot better after the second transaction. I felt like I had been taken seriously, and in a strange way, I felt validated because she was able to find information on the therapy. The feeling that I was wasting the time of the librarian was gone. . . [and] it took away the negative feelings that were generated by the first transaction." She was not sure, however, that she would want to return to this Ask-A-Librarian service again.

(Library Visit Study)

Discussion: The needed information was supplied, but only after a second request. If the user were not a participant in the Library Visit Study, it is unlikely that she would have tried again.

1. Look closely at the first response sent to Jane, and at Jane's comments on how this response made her feel. Could Jane's negative response been predicted and avoided?
2. Revise the librarian's first response to improve it. What questions could the librarian have included?
3. How did the fact that this was a consumer health question affect this transaction?

- Do not make referrals to specific practitioners. Instead, refer the user to a service (e.g., hospital, law society) that gives out names of doctors or lawyers who are accepting new clients.

- Do not use self-disclosure ("I had that kind of problem myself...") or talk about other individuals' personal problems. You can put the user at ease without comparing problems, which might in fact not be similar at all.

4. Close the interview part of the transaction:

- Give information about other search strategies. Let the user know that there are other routes to pursue, perhaps by offering a referral to another service or showing the user the links to other sources on the Web.

- Use closure (3.2.5) to end a conversation with an overly talkative user. People with personal problems sometimes just need to talk about it. But occasionally you'll have to say, "I've given you the best information we have, so perhaps you'd like to take that home and have a look at it," or "I wish I had more time to talk, but do call the community center—here's the number." If they persist, use the "broken record technique" restating your position in a firm, but gentle tone, "I wish I had more time to talk, but do call the community center." This approach might seem strange at first, but it does work.

- Always ask a follow-up question (4.1.3). If users were unable to get the help they needed, they should know that they can ask again, or ask for a referral to another service or site. After looking at some material, users may be better able to articulate their query. An all-purpose question you can use: "If this information doesn't help, please ask again and I can suggest some other places to try." Even if the user hasn't been willing to describe the information need completely (or at all), a follow-up statement helps to ensure the user doesn't give up looking for help.

A QUICK TIP

Use a Reference Form for Health and Legal Questions

A health or legal reference form or checklist that prompts you to ask key questions can be very helpful particularly for complex questions, or if you need to refer the question to another librarian or library. The form can also provide a list of resources useful for checking off what has already been tried to answer the question. Casini and Kenyon (2002) recommend that you ask users to write out requests in their own words. Allcock (2000) suggests that to ensure confidentiality you do not record users' names on the same paper or form; if you need names in order to call users back, keep that information elsewhere. Price, Urquhart, and Cooper (accessed 2008) discuss the use of a question form in answering health questions on the telephone

---

Did You Know?
With consumer health or legal questions, restate the question before starting to look for answers, and verify spellings of medical or legal terms. In providing an answer, cite the source completely and quote from the source verbatim. When calling people back with information, maintain confidentiality. Don't leave the answer to the question with a second party.

Did You Know?
Understanding the user's problem is often the greatest challenge. In two public library mail surveys—one directed to librarians who answer legal reference questions and one directed to librarians who answer health questions—researchers identified eight categories of problems. The most frequent problem for both groups, according to these librarians, was the user's inability or unwillingness to express the query clearly or completely. More than 40 percent of these librarians said they "often" or "very often" had difficulty understanding what the user really wanted to know (Dewdney, Marshall, and Tiamiyu, 1991, 191). A well-conducted reference interview is all the more important with consumer health and legal questions.

5.8 Implications of Consortial Reference

Collaboration has always been part of reference work. Pomerantz (2006) points out that librarians collaborate with users, with colleagues at the reference desk (McKenzie, 2003), and with colleagues elsewhere. They collaborate through referral to other libraries or to outside experts or agencies. Now the Internet enables collaboration through forums and blogs and through the forwarding of questions to Web-based AskA services such as Ask Dr. Math. Informal at first, online collaboration among libraries became more formalized in the mid-1990s. Asynchronous (e-mail) Ask-A-librarian services began to form into consortia in order to swap questions that could not be answered locally. By the late 1990s, libraries began to form consortia with other libraries that used the same software applications such as chat to offer virtual reference (VR). Consortial agreements among libraries require standards for exchanging questions, policies regarding who will be served, who will answer questions, and other administrative matters.

In our view, a serious shortcoming with most guidelines governing individual consortia is that they focus on administration and technology and are silent about the conduct of the reference interview (discussed in Chapter 8). But, as Pomerantz explains, the users don't care where the answer comes from as long as they get it, so to them the whole consortial arrangement is invisible. Users care that their real questions are answered. This means that the ultimate test of the success of collaborative reference is user satisfaction.

In order to get at the real question, the *first* librarian that the user encounters must conduct a proper reference interview, whether to answer the question immediately or to refer the question elsewhere. If the question is referred before the real question is determined, all subsequent time and effort will be wasted. Because VR is a costly endeavor, it is inefficient to add to these costs by simply moving questions around.

While the ALA/RUSA "Guidelines for Cooperative Reference Services" (Reference and User Services Association, Cooperative Reference Service Committee, 2006) make no mention of the reference interview, the focus is on administration and delivery of services, and there is no suggestion that it is the responsibility of the originating library to clarify the reference question. Some individual consortia have guidelines that do mention in a limited way the reference interview. For example, the QuestionPoint "User Guidelines" (Library of Congress) state, "General standards for reference services must meet the same qualifications as those endorsed by the library profession in pre-digital days." However, the only mention of a reference interview states that the Web form is used to facilitate the "reference interview" (the scare quotes seem to minimize the importance of the reference interview). Alison Morin (2004) describes the QuestionPoint "Global Reference Network Member Guidelines" as more behavioral in scope. However, we find no mention of the interview, and the focus is on quality and accuracy of answers (QuestionPoint). These member guidelines simply indicate that QuestionPoint follows the standards listed in *Facets of Quality for Digital Reference Services*, and these do mention the reference interview (see Virtual Reference Desk, 2003). The guidelines of more local or regional consortia also tend to give little attention to the reference interview. While individual librarians might be conducting initial reference interviews, we recommend that a complete reference interview should be mandated in guidelines and policies of all consortia.

Success of consortial reference is usually measured from the system perspective, rather than the user perspective (3.1.3). Evaluative studies have counted how many questions have been asked and answered, and have assessed whether or not test questions have been answered correctly. But we have little information on user satisfaction. One exception can be found in QandANJ, a statewide reference consortium that has collected a large quantity of user satisfaction data. At the end of the chat interaction, the user is invited to complete a drop-down survey. Bromberg (2003) reported that 20 to 30 percent of users filled out the brief survey each month and that QandANJ has consistently received high marks for satisfaction. Bromberg also keeps a large notebook of user comments from the surveys that has been used to show to legislators to justify funding requests. There is no way of knowing, however, whether the responses from the 20 to 30 percent are representative of the whole population of users or whether they come from users grateful enough for the answer received that they are willing to fill in the survey.

One aspect of reference transactions intrinsic to consortial reference that has been studied is referral. Kwon (2006) compared "correctness" of responses to questions that had been referred with user satisfaction data. In consortial reference, referrals are usually unmonitored, meaning that the librarian makes no effort to determine if the user actually does get the needed information (see 3.1.4). We know that unmonitored referrals often lead to unsatisfied users in FtF transactions (Dewdney and Ross, 1994) and see no reason to suppose that unmonitored referrals produce better results with virtual reference. Collaborative reference is intended to support referral of reference questions that cannot be answered locally. In most cases, these referrals are unmonitored. In Kwon's (2006) study of 420 chat reference transactions, 30 percent of questions were referred to collaborative reference service. None of these referrals was monitored. The satisfaction rate of these users was determined using a pop-up survey immediately after the transaction. This satisfaction rate was analyzed by type of answer received (complete, partial answer, no answer, referral, problematic ending). Kwon's study found that "users were far less satisfied with referrals than with completed answers and experience only about the same degree of satisfaction as users receiving either a partial answer or no answer at all" (2006, 14). Problematic endings occurred when there was an abrupt completion of the transcripts (for unknown or technological reasons), including the librarian's premature ending without proper closing remarks. Users were most dissatisfied with problematic endings. We would be interested in knowing how many of the problematic endings were the result specifically

GUIDELINES FOR LIBRARIANS PROVIDING VIRTUAL REFERENCE SERVICE IN CONSORTIA

Marie Radford and Lynn Silipigni Connaway (2008) have developed the following guidelines for VR consortia reference librarians.

Start off on the right foot.

Establish rapport early in the chat. Building rapport requires developing a more personal interactive experience for the user including using first names (or pseudonyms for the privacy-conscious)and refraining from using too many automated scripts. When users see scripts, they recognize them as computer generated, and are more likely to become impatient or rude. In order to promote good rapport, the librarian may also need to reassure a user who seems to be intimidated by the format or technology. The goal is to keep the user from feeling "judged by the librarian" and to focus on the user's informational need. When one user apologized to the librarian for making a typo (5.4.5, Case 28), the VRS librarian assured the user that typos were no problem by stating, "Don't worry about the typos—I make them too!" Rapport is not easy to establish with every user, and negative comments from a user should not be taken personally. Librarians can defuse the situation by staying detached from the negative interaction, demonstrating a sense of humor, and offering to follow up on the question by e-mail.

Dazzle 'em (from a distance).

VRS librarians should promote both a global and local presence. The cooperative nature of the staffing means that the chances of users connecting to one of their own local librarians can be quite small. Therefore, many users will go to their own library Web site, but be helped by a librarian with no connection to the users' library. In a telephone interview, one VRS librarian stated, "I think [VRS] is going to kind of contribute to the whole globalization that the Internet is doing; it's going to make it possible for anyone, anywhere to ask a librarian a question—a question of any librarian or any information person anywhere." Scripted or non-scripted greetings identifying the librarian, the librarian's location, and the nature of the cooperative service should be used. This type of greeting provides a perfect opportunity for VRS librarians to use the same interpersonal techniques to connect globally to local users and to build rapport with them in a virtual environment. This benefit may be more evident from the user's perspective than from the librarian's perspective. One user from the Midwestern United States who was seeking information from a librarian on the East coast of the United States asked, "How is the weather in Boston?" when the user realized the librarian was located thousands of miles away.

Overcome boundaries and heighten awareness of remote access issues.

Try to help users with resources at the users' own library, rather than with resources at the VRS librarian's institution. Librarians in cooperative VRS must provide links to their local library's databases and policy pages to allow cooperative VRS librarians to direct users to their own local sources. Librarians should not just send links to Web pages, but rather provide context and instruction to the user. Merely providing links to resources will often not suffice because some URLs are dynamic such as library catalog search results, and some databases will not be available to the user. The librarian may need to guide users beyond consortial limits, such as to other databases that are accessible to the user or to a local library that would provide access to the databases and resources.

(Cont'd.)

GUIDELINES FOR LIBRARIANS PROVIDING VIRTUAL REFERENCE SERVICE IN CONSORTIA (Continued)

Develop and share expectations.

It is crucial that all participants in a cooperative VRS have a shared vision for what the service offers, and for determining quality. Quality is defined both by accuracy in answering questions and by building strong interpersonal rapport with virtual users. Members of the cooperative must agree on how much help will be given (aim for generosity within staff/ time limits), so that a consistently high level of service is developed and consistently offered to users. All users —children, young adults, even rude or impatient people— should receive high levels of professionalism, courtesy and respect.

The reference interview is the key element in developing user expectations, putting the user at ease, and in determining the real question. Following a properly conducted reference interview, the librarian is able to tell the user what can be done during the online session and what may need to be sent for follow-up. In online chat, the reference interview all too often is bypassed. Librarians, however, should always ask at least one question, if only to repeat what the user just said. Users make typographical errors, and may not, in fact, mean what they just typed. As always, open questions work well because they allow users to explain what they need in their own words.

Exceed expectations—aim for excellent service and cultivate repeat users.

Show users new to cooperative VRS what the service can do for them by providing valuable information in a friendly and approachable way. The key value added to a virtual reference service is personal interaction with a knowledgeable information guide. Several minutes spent with a capable reference librarian can save many users countless hours spent on Google or other search engines. The way to ensure that valuable information has been provided is to ask the follow-up question, "Does this completely answer your question?" Sending this message signals the librarian's

interest in the user and tends to result in higher user satisfaction with the service. Once all needs have been met, VRS librarians should either send the scripted goodbye message provided by the user's library ("Thanks for using Maryland AskUsNow!"), or, if no script is available, thank the users for using the service and encourage them to return if they have more questions. This practice reinforces the name of the service and helps to cultivate repeat users. Users will come back and will spread the word to others when they have a positive experience.

Accentuate the positive.

Focus on what *can* be done to answer users' questions, avoiding negative words like "can't," "don't," or "but." Instead of offering a negative response to a homework question ("We cannot do homework for you"), turn the situation into a

teachable moment by helping users narrow down topics for their essays, demonstrate a database, instruct them on effective search terms, or on ways to evaluate resources for authoritativeness and relevancy.

Give the user the option to go beyond initial resources.

Providing professional search help is the value added by an online reference service. Many times, however, librarians simply push Web pages to the user in order to answer a question. It is important to provide context and instruction to the user, rather than just

sharing resources or merely sending Web pages. Librarians should provide enough guidance for the user to recreate the search if needed (include the name of links, indicating which one the user should click on, as well as the "click path").

(Cont'd.)

GUIDELINES FOR LIBRARIANS PROVIDING VIRTUAL REFERENCE SERVICE IN CONSORTIA *(Continued)*

Manage complex or multiple queries.

Researchers with complex questions or students seeking answers to multiple homework questions in the course of one chat session represent particular challenges to librarians, especially when the service is busy. Librarians can handle multiple student questions by recognizing common elements to the questions, by providing appropriate general resources for general questions, and by offering the user alternative ways to procure an answer (e-mail, phone, etc.). For complex queries, interaction between user and librarian is invaluable for negotiating the query, determining what steps the researcher has already tried and what resources have already been found.

Continue providing information if the user disappears.

Online users may disappear from a chat session for a variety of reasons, but it is important for the librarian to continue providing as complete an answer as possible. In many chat systems, if the user has left an e-mail address, then the entire session will be sent to that address automatically.

(Adapted from Radford and Connaway, 2008)

of lack of closing remarks. While the referred transactions were probably counted as successful by the librarians involved, users were probably less satisfied.

5.9 Annotated References

5.9.1 Telephone Reference

Adler, Ronald B., and Jeanne Marquardt Elmhorst. 2008. *Communicating at Work: Principles and Practices for Business and the Professions*, 9th ed. New York: McGraw-Hill. Good tips for using voicemail and other electronic media. Includes two chapters on interviewing.

Agosto, Denise E., and Holly Anderton. 2007. "Whatever Happened to 'Always Cite the Source'? A Study of Source Citing and Other Issues Related to Telephone Reference." *Reference & User Services Quarterly* 47, no. 1 (fall): 44–54.

Austin Public Library. Reference Services Policy. Telephone Reference Guidelines. Austin, Texas. Available: www.ci.austin.tx.us/library/refpolicy.htm (accessed October 4, 2008).

Bond, Elizabeth. 1953. "Some Problems of Telephone Reference Service." *Wilson Library Bulletin* 27: 641–44.

Dewdney, Patricia, and Catherine Sheldrick Ross. 1994. "Flying a Light Aircraft: Reference Evaluation from a User's Viewpoint." *RQ* 34, no. 2 (winter): 217–230.

Dilevko, Juris, and Elizabeth Dolan. 1999. "Reference Work and the Value of Reading Newspapers: An Unobtrusive Study of Telephone Reference Service." *Reference & User Services Quarterly* 39, no. 1 (fall): 71–81.

Duke, Deborah C. 1994. "Night Owl: Maryland's After-hours Reference Service." *Public Libraries* 33 (May/June): 145–148. The Night Owl toll-free service of the Enoch Pratt Free Library and Maryland's Library Resource

Centre is offered to Maryland residents Monday through Friday evenings until 11 p.m.

Durrance, Joan. 1995. "Factors That Influence Reference Success." *The Reference Librarian* 49/50: 243–265.

Gannett, Emily. 1936. "Reference Service by Telephone." *Library Journal* 61: 909–911.

Glaze, Violet. 2007. "Enoch Pratt Free Library's Telephone Reference Service. *Baltimore City Paper.* (November 28). Available: www.citypaper.com/news/story.asp?id=1489 (accessed September 8, 2008). This newspaper article describes the experiences of five librarians at Enoch Pratt who answer questions for the service.

Kern, Kathleen. 2004. "Have(n't) We Been Here Before?: Lessons from Telephone Reference." *The Reference Librarian* 85: 1–17. Kern compares the development and implementation of telephone and chat reference, noting that the similarities are greater than the differences. Includes a good history of telephone reference.

Lever, Katie M., and James E. Katz. 2006. "Cell Phones in Campus Libraries: An Analysis of Policy Responses to an Invasive Mobile Technology." *Information Processing & Management* 43: 1133–1139. Reports results from a survey of eighty-seven academic libraries, seventy-seven of which have established policies for cell phone use.

McCain, Cheryl. 2007. "Telephone Calls Received at an Academic Library's Reference Desk: A New Analysis." *The Reference Librarian* 47, no. 2 (#98): 5–16. Analysis of reference transactions at the University of Oklahoma over a two-year period (2004–2006) revealed that 21.4 percent of enquiries came from users who placed a telephone call to the reference desk

Naylor, Sharon, Bruce Stoffel, and Sharon Van Der Laan. 2008. "Why Isn't Our Chat Reference Used More?" *Reference & User Services Quarterly* 47, no. 4 (summer): 342–354.

Phone Pro—Leaders in Telephone Skills Training. 2007. Available: www.phonepro.org/ (accessed September 11, 2008). An example of telephone customer service training available online, with a number of free articles on customer service, culture and morale, and training and management.

Radford, Marie L., and Lynn Silipigni Connaway, (2005–2008). Seeking Synchronicity: Evaluating Virtual Reference Services from User, Non-User, and Librarian Perspectives. Funded by the Institute for Museum and Library Services, Rutgers University (NJ), and OCLC, Online Computer Library Center www.oclc.org/research/projects/synchronicity (accessed October 4, 2008).

University of Washington. Marian Gould Gallagher Law Library. Reference Services, 2008. Available: http://lib.law.washington.edu/ref/ref.html (accessed October 4, 2008). Telephone guidelines can be analyzed and compared with those in this book.

Walters, Suzanne. 1994. *Customer Service: A How-To-Do-It Manual for Librarians.* New York: Neal-Schuman. See pages 45–47 for helpful hints on training staff to answer the telephone properly.

Yates, Rochelle. 1986. *Librarian's Guide to Telephone Reference Service.* Hamden, CT: Library Professional Publications. 1986. Though dated, this book still provides useful suggestions

5.9.2 The Imposed Query

Bennett, Denise Beaubien, Pamela S. Cenzer, and Paul Kirk. 2004. "A Class Assignment Requiring Chat-based Reference." *Reference & User Services*

Quarterly 44, no. 2 (winter): 149–163. The authors' analysis of chat transcripts and student reports submitted as a result of an assignment requiring students to use a university library's chat service provides insight into dealing with both the instructors who impose queries and the students who may not be library users.

Chelton, Mary K. 1997. "Adult-Adolescent Service Encounters: The Library Context." Ph.D. dissertation. New Brunswick, NJ: Rutgers University. Examines the place of the adolescent as "social construct and individual agent within the context of library theory and practice."

Flowers, Sarah. 2008. "Guidelines for Library Services to Teens." *Young Adult Library Services* 6, no. 3: 4–7.

Gross, Melissa. 1995. "The Imposed Query." *RQ* 35, no. 2 (winter): 236–243. Deals with the theoretical and practical aspects of "secondhand" reference questions, where the inquirer is asking on behalf of someone else.

Gross, Melissa. 1998. "Imposed Query: Implications for Library Service Evaluation." *Reference & User Services Quarterly* 37 no. 3: 290–299. Explains why understanding the extent of imposed queries needs to be incorporated into reference evaluation in libraries.

Gross, Melissa. 1999. "Imposed Versus Self-Generated Questions," *Reference & User Services Quarterly* 39, no. 1 (fall): 53–61. Argues that librarians need to identify questions as either imposed or self-generated and provide special treatment for imposed queries.

Gross, Melissa. 2001. "Imposed Information Seeking in Public Libraries and School Library Media Centers: A Common Behaviour?" *Information Research* 6, no. 2. Available: http://informationr.net/ir/6-2/paper100.html (accessed September 11, 2008).

Gross, Melissa. 2004. "Children's Information Seeking at School: Findings from a Qualitative Study." In *Youth Information Seeking Behavior: Theories, Models and Issues*, edited by Mary K. Chelton and Colleen Cool (211–240). Lanham, MD: Scarecrow Press. Includes findings from Gross' previous studies of children's questions in school libraries.

Gross, Melissa, and Matthew L. Saxton. 2001. "Who Wants to Know? Imposed Queries in the Public Library." *Public Libraries* 40: 170–176. Reports on the first study of imposed queries at the adult reference desk

Gross, Melissa, and Matthew L. Saxton. 2002. "Integrating the Imposed Query into the Evaluation of Reference Service: A Dichotomous Analysis of User Ratings. *Library and Information Science Research* 24, no. 3: 251–263. Compares satisfaction measures for imposed and self-generated queries.

Kuhlthau, Carol. 2004. *Seeking Meaning: A Process Approach to Library and Information Services*, 2nd ed. Westport CT: Libraries Unlimited. Reports on the information search process of public, academic, and school library users, including students and information workers who are asking both imposed and self-generated questions.

Radford, Marie L., and Lynn Silipigni Connaway. 2007. "Are We Getting Warmer? Query Clarification in Virtual Reference." Presented at the Library Research Round Table, American Library Association Conference, Washington DC, June 21–27, 2007. Available: www.oclc.org/research/projects/synchronicity/presentations.htm#upcoming (accessed November 10, 2008).

5.9.3 Interviewing Children and Young Adults

Abram, Stephen, and Judy Luther. 2007. "Chips and Dips: Educating and Serving the Net Generation." In *The Whole Digital Library Handbook*, edited by Diane Kresh. Chicago: American Library Association.

Ask an Expert. Available: www.askanexpert.com (accessed November 1, 2008). Provided by Pitsco Innovative Education, a commercial publisher and producer of other educational goods, this Web site connects kids "with hundreds of real world experts."

Behrmann, Christine, and Dolores Vogliano. 1991. "On Training the Children's Reference Librarian." *Illinois Libraries* 73, no. 2 (February): 152–157. Describes the qualities of a good children's reference librarian and presents a model training workshop, including sample assignments.

Benne, Mae. 1991. "Staff Competencies." In *Principles of Children's Services in Public Libraries* (79–82). Chicago: American Library Association.

Bunge, Charles A. 1994. "Responsive Reference Service: Breaking Down Age Barriers." *School Library Journal* 44 (March): 142–145.

Burton, Melvin K. 1998. "Reference Interview: Strategies for Children." *North Carolina Libraries* 56, no 3 (fall): 110–113. Lists some special features of the reference interview with children, including the increased likelihood of ill-formed queries resulting from homophones and reconstructions (e.g., carnivorous/ coniferous forest; Rock Stew/ Stone Soup), the intermediating role of the parent; library staff's ambivalence over questions involving homework assignments; and the child's unfamiliarity with the library system and classification scheme.

Callaghan, Linda W. 1983. "Children's Questions: Reference Interviews with the Young." In *Reference Services for Children and Young Adults* (55–65), edited by Bill Katz and Ruth A. Fraley. New York: Haworth Press. Reprinted from *The Reference Librarian* 7/8 (spring/summer 1983).

Chelton, Mary K. 1997. "Adult-Adolescent Service Encounters: The Library Context." Ph.D. dissertation. New Brunswick, NJ: Rutgers University.

Chelton, Mary K. 1999. "Structural and Theoretical Constraints on Reference Service in a High School Library Media Center." *Reference and User Services Quarterly* 38, no. 3 (spring): 275–282. Finds that idealized standards for reference practice as articulated in the RUSA behavioral guidelines for reference service are not helpful to practitioners in school library media centers.

Dixon, Judith. 1996. "Are We Childproofing Our Public Libraries? Identifying the Barriers that Limit Use by Children." *Public Libraries* 35 (January/February): 50–56.

Fagan, Jody C., and Christina M. Desai. 2002/2003. "Communication Strategies for Instant Messaging and Chat Reference Services." *The Reference Librarian* 79/80: 121–155.

Gross, Melissa. 2000. "The Imposed Query and Information Services for Children." *Journal of Youth Services in Libraries* 13, no. 2 (winter): 10–17.

Henley, Caroline. 2004. "Digital Reference Services for Young Library Users: A Comparison of Four Services." *Library Review* 53, no. 1: 30–36.

Horning, Kathleen T. 1994 "Raising the Issue: Fishing for Questions." Wilson *Library Bulletin* 68 (May): 57–59.

Horning, Kathleen T. 1994. "How Can I Help You? The Joys and Challenges of Reference Work with Children." *Show-Me Libraries* 45 (spring/summer): 9–19.

Internet Public Library. *Kidspace.* Available: www.ipl.org/div/kidspace/ (accessed November 1, 2008).

Internet Public Library. *Teenspace.* Available: www.ipl.org/div/teen (accessed October 30, 2008).

Janes, Joseph. 2003. "Digital Reference for Teens." *Voice of Youth Advocates* 25, no. 6 (February): 451.

Jones, Patrick. 1998. "Reference Services." In *Connecting Young Adults and Libraries*, 2nd ed. 186–195. New York: Neal-Schuman.

Jones, Patrick, Michele Gorman, and Tricia Suellentrop. 2004. "Customer Service." In *Connecting Young Adults and Libraries: A How-To-Do-It Manual for Librarians*, 3rd ed. New York: Neal-Schuman.

Kortz, Laura, Sharon Morris, and Louise W. Greene. 2006. "Bringing Together Teens and Chat Reference: Reconsidering 'The Match Made in Heaven.'" In *The Virtual Reference Desk: Creating a Reference Future*, edited by R. David Lankes et al. New York: Neal-Schuman.

Kuhlthau, Carol C. 1988. "Meeting the Information Needs of Children and Young Adults: Basing Library Media Programs on Developmental States." *Journal of Youth Services in Libraries* 2 (fall): 51–57.

Kuhlthau, Carol C. 1991. "Inside the Search Process: Information Seeking from the User's Perspective." *Journal of the American Society for Information Science* 42, no. 6 (June): 361–371.

Kuhlthau, Carol C. 1994. "Students and the Information Search Process: Zones of Intervention for Librarians." In *Advances in Librarianship*, Vol. 18. San Diego CA: Academic Press.

Lankes, R. David. 2003. "Current State of Digital Reference in Primary and Secondary Education." *D-Lib Magazine* 9, no. 2 (February). Available: www.dlib.org/dlib/february03/lankes/02lankes.html (accessed November 1, 2008).

Loorie, Nancy. 1993. "Whose Homework Is It, Anyway? Helping Parents at the Reference Desk." *New Jersey Libraries* 26, no. 2 (February): 15–17.

Overmyer, Elizabeth. 1995. "Serving the Reference Needs of Children." *Wilson Library Bulletin* 69, no. 10 (June): 38–40. Uses examples from the San Francisco Bay Area regional reference center to focus on aspects of reference service to children, including resource sharing, online searching, telephone questions, and using the Internet.

People's Network. Available: www.peoplesnetwork.gov.uk (accessed November 1, 2008). Operated by the Museums, Libraries and Archives Council, the body responsible for public libraries in England.

Radford, Marie L., and Lynn Silipigni Connaway. 2007. "'Screenagers' and Live Chat Reference: Living Up to the Promise." *Scan* 26 no.1: 31–39. Reports findings of a study based on focus groups with high school students: young adults favor FtF reference when the librarian is kind and treats their questions seriously; they are not aware that live chat reference is available; they have security and privacy concerns because of their attitudes toward chat rooms; they would use chat if recommended by a trusted teacher or librarian.

Reference and User Services Association. 2004. "Guidelines for Behavioral Performance of Reference and Information Service Professionals." Available: www.ala.org/ala/mgrps/divs/rusa/resources/guidelines/guidelinesbehavioral.cfm (accessed October 22, 2008).

Reference and User Services Association (RUSA) and Young Adult Library Services Association (YALSA), American Library Association. 2006. "Guidelines for Library Services to Teens, 12–18. Available: http://yalsa.ala.org/guidelines/reference.guidelines.pdf via a link from http://wikis.ala.org/professionaltips/index.php/Teens_and_Young_Adults (accessed November 2, 2008).

Vaillancourt, Renee J. 2000. "The Reference Interview." In *Bare Bones Young Adult Services: Tips for Public Library Generalists*. Chicago: American Library Association.

Walter, Virginia A., and Cindy Mediavilla. 2005. "Teens are from Neptune, Librarians are from Pluto: An Analysis of Online Reference Transactions." *Library Trends* 54, no. 2 (fall): 209–227

Wanting, Birgit. 1986. "Some Results from an Investigation in Danish Libraries: How Do Children Ask Questions about Books in Children's Libraries?" *Scandinavian Public Library Quarterly* 19, no. 3: 96–101.

Wronka, Gretchen. 1983. "From the Firing Line: Practical Advice for Reference Service with Children in the Public Library." In *Reference Services for Children and Young Adults,* edited by Bill Katz and Ruth A. Fraley. New York: Haworth Press. Reprinted from *The Reference Librarian* 7/8 (Spring/Summer): 143–150).

5.9.4 Interviewing Adults with Special Language-related Needs

Abdullahi, Ismail. 1993. "Multicultural Issues for Readers' Advisory Services." *Collection Building* 12, no 3/4: 85–88. Addresses the role of multicultural readers' advisers and how they should be trained.

Adler, Ronald B., and Jeanne Marquardt Elmhorst. 1996. *Communicating at Work: Principles and Practices for Business and the Professions,* 5th ed. New York: McGraw-Hill. A business communications text with a strong multicultural focus.

Berlanga-Cortéz, Graciela. 2000. "Cross-cultural Communication: Identifying Barriers to Information Retrieval with Culturally and Linguistically Different Library Patrons." In *Library Services to Latinos: An Anthology* (51–60), edited by Salvador Güüereña. Jefferson, NC: McFarland. Discusses the impact of nonverbal communication on cross-cultural communication.

Brown, Christopher C. 2000. "Reference Services to the International Adult Learner: Understanding the Barriers." *The Reference Librarian* no. 69/70: 337–347. Examines the implications and means of overcoming language, culture, and technological barriers faced by international adult students.

Curry, Ann. 1996. "Managing the Problem Patron." *Public Libraries* 35, no. 3 (May/June): 181–188.

Curry, Ann, and Deborah Copeman. 2005. "Reference Service to International Students: A Field Stimulation Research Study." *Journal of Academic Librarianship* 31, no. 5: 409–420. Identifies barriers to effective reference service. Describes the results of a study in which a single proxy with heavily accented English asked the same questions on two separate visits to each of eleven college and university libraries. Unmonitored referrals and failure to follow up were the most common unhelpful reference behavior.

De Souza, Yvonne. 1996. "Reference Work with International Students: Making the Most Use of the Neutral Question." *Reference Services Review* 24, no. 4 (winter): 41–48. Provides suggestions on how to use sense-making questions with international students to avoid intimidating them.

Dewdney, Patricia, and Gillian Michell. 1996. "Oranges and Peaches: Understanding Communication Accidents in the Reference Interview." *RQ* 35, no. 4 (summer): 520–536.

Freiband, Susan Jane. 1993. "Developing Readers' Advisory Service for Library Users Whose Primary Language Is Not English." *Collection Building* 12, no. 3/4: 79–84.

Garner, Sarah Devotion. 2003. "Bridging an Intercultural Communication Gap at the Reference Desk: How to Have an Effective Reference Interaction with Asian LL.M Students." *Legal Reference Services Quarterly* 22, no. 2/3:

7–39. A thorough discussion of intercultural communication in which the recommended strategies and tips apply to many situations beyond the specific user group described.

Greenfield, Louise, Susan Johnston, and Karen Williams. 1986. "Educating the World: Training Library Staff to Communicate Effectively with International Students." *The Journal of Academic Librarianship* 12, no. 4 (September): 227–231.

Hall, Edward T. 1973, c1959. *The Silent Language.* Garden City, NY: Doubleday. The classic work on cross-cultural differences in communication. See also Hall's 1976 book *Beyond Culture*, New York: Doubleday.

Hendricks, Yoshi. 1991. "The Japanese as Library Patrons." *College and Research Library News* 52, no. 4 (July): 221–225.

Hoffman, Irene, and Opritsa Popa. 1986. "Library Orientation and Instruction for International Students: The University of California-Davis Experience." *RQ* 25: 356–360

Janes, Phoebe, and Ellen Meltzer. 1990. "Origins and Attitudes: Training Reference Librarians for a Pluralistic World." *The Reference Librarian* 30: 145–155.

Kumar, Suhasini L., and Raghini S. Suresh. 2000. "Strategies for Providing Effective Reference Services for International Adult Learners." *The Reference Librarian* no. 69/70: 327–336. Perceptions of international students of the major obstacles they face in using libraries in the United States.

Liu, Mengxiong, and Redfern, Bernice. 1997. "Information-Seeking Behavior of Multicultural Students: A Case Study at San Jose State University." *College & Research Libraries* 58, no. 4: 348–354.

Liu, Ziming. 1993. "Difficulties and Characteristics of Students from Developing Countries in Using American Libraries." *College and Research Libraries* 54: 25–31.

McGuigan, Glenn S. 2002. "When in Rome: A Rationale and Selection of Resources in International Business Etiquette and Intercultural Communication." *Reference & User Services Quarterly* 41, no. 3 (spring); 220–227. Describes the problems for business of intercultural miscommunication, and provides an annotated list of books that could be helpful for library staff.

Nebraska Library Commission. *The Nebraska STAR Reference Manual* (Statewide Training for Accurate Reference). Available: www.nlc.state.n .us/Ref/star/star .html (accessed October 1, 2008). The section entitled "Working with People" includes tips for working with people who do not speak English well, as well as information on Hispanic first and last names, and Asian naming systems.

Orange County Library System. Florida. Available: http://iii.ocls.info (accessed October 24, 2008).

Ormondroyd, Joan. 1989. "The International Student and Course-Integrated Instruction: The Librarian's Perspective." *Research Strategies* 7 (fall): 148–58. Provides rules for effective communication with international student in Appendix A.

Osa, Justina O., Sylvia A. Nyana, and Clara A. Ogbaa. 2006. "Effective Cross-Cultural Communication to Enhance Reference Transactions: Training Guidelines and Tips." *Knowledge Quest* 35, no.2 (November/December): 22–24. Directed at school librarians but provides useful information for librarians working in any type of library. Also available online on the ALA/AASL Web site, where it provides a link to a "Model Communications Behavior Checklist" that the authors developed for school librarians.

Reference and User Services Association. Reference Services Section. Library Services to the Spanish-Speaking Committee. 2007. "Guidelines for Library Services to Spanish-Speaking Library Users." Chicago: ALA. Available:

www.ala.org/ala/mgrps/divs/rusa/resources/guidelines/guidespanish.cfm (accessed October 24, 2008). Also available in *Reference & User Services Quarterly* 47, no. 2 (winter): 194–197. Emphasis of guidelines is on materials and programs; includes recommendations for staffing and staff diversity training.

Sackers, Nicole, Bess Secomb, and Heather Hulett. 2008. "How Well Do You Know Your Clients? International Students' Preferences for Learning about Library Services." *Australian Academic & Research Libraries* 39, no. 1 (March): 38–55. The results of this study showed that international students have a strong preference for in-person communication with the library.

Samovar, Larry A., and Richard E. Porter. 2001. *Communication between Cultures*, 4th ed. Belmont, CA: Wadsworth/ Thomson Learning. This textbook includes chapters on cultural identification and the use of language. See also from the same authors and publisher: *Intercultural Communication: A Reader* (9th ed., 2000), a research-based anthology of forty-two articles that help the reader attain intercultural communication competence. Both books are useful for staff discussion.

Sarkodie-Mensah, Kwasi.1992. "Dealing with International Students in a Multicultural Era." *The Journal of Academic Librarianship* 18, no. 2 (September): 214–216. Contains many practical tips on pronunciation problems, speech patterns, and taboo topics.

Sarkodie-Mensah, Kwasi. 2000. *Reference Services for the Adult Learner: Challenging Issues for the Traditional and Technological Era*. Binghamton, NY: The Haworth Press. Reprinted from *The Reference Librarian* 69/70. Includes four articles specifically on serving the international adult learner (including Brown, and Kumar and Suresh, above).

Shachaf, Pnina, Shannon M. Oltmann, and Sarah M. Horowitz. 2008. "Service Equality in Virtual Reference." *Journal of the American Society for Information Science and Technology* 59, no. 4: 535–550. Reports results of experiments in e-mail reference services of public and academic libraries. Users' names were manipulated to reflect different genders and ethnicities. No significant difference was found in service levels to the different groups.

Wang, Jian, and Donald G. Frank. 2002. "Cross-Cultural Communication: Implications for Effective Information Services in Academic Libraries." *portal: Libraries and the Academy* 2, no. 2 (April): 207–216. Focuses on cross-cultural differences that explain why library services are underutilized by international students.

5.9.5 Interviewing People with Disabilities

Many social service agencies, health organizations, and self-help groups publish pamphlets that increase understanding of specific disabilities and include tips for communicating. Ask your local organizations to provide you with multiple copies for your staff and your public. They may also provide speakers for staff training.

American Library Association. 1996. *Guidelines for Libraries and Information Services for the American Deaf Community*, edited by Martha L. Goddard. Chicago: Association of Specialized and Cooperative Library Agencies.

American Library Association. 2001. "Library Services for People with Disabilities Policy." Chicago: Association of Specialized and Cooperative Library Agencies. Available: www.ala.org/ala/mgrps/divs/ascla/asclaissues/library services.cfm. (accessed October 24, 2008).

Americans with Disabilities Act. *U.S. Code.* 1994. Vol. 42, secs. 12101–12213.

Dalton, Phyllis I. 1985. "Two-Way Communication." In *Library Service to the Deaf and Hearing Impaired* (24–33). Phoenix, AZ: Oryx Press. Discusses skills for working with groups and individuals, including American Sign Language and other systems.

Day, John Michael, ed. 2000. *Guidelines for Library Services to Deaf People*, 2nd ed. The Hague: IFLA. Available: www.ifla.org/VII/s9/nd1/iflapr-62e.pdf (accessed September 29, 2008).

Deines-Jones, Courtney, and Connie Van Fleet. 1995. *Preparing Staff to Serve Patrons with Disabilities: A How-To-Do-It Manual.* New York: Neal-Schuman. Tips, resources and front-line procedures for library staff to use with special classes of users with special needs. Also includes sections on readers advisory and the special needs of children and young adults.

Lenn, Katy. 1996. "Library Services to Disabled Students: Outreach and Education." *The Reference Librarian* 53: 13–25.

Mabry, Celia Hales. 2003. "Serving Seniors: Do's and Don'ts at the Desk." *American Libraries* 34 (1): 64–65. Provides several practical recommendations for helping older adults at the reference desk as well as statistics on disabilities for this population.

Nebraska Library Commission. *The Nebraska STAR Reference Manual (Statewide Training for Accurate Reference).* Available: www.nlc.state.ne.us/Ref/star/star .html (accessed October 1, 2008). The section entitled "Working with People" includes tips for working with people with hearing and visual difficulties.

Rubin, Rhea Joyce. 2002. "Serving People with Disabilities." Different Voices, Common Quest: ALA/OLOS Pre Conference. Available: http://72.14 .205.104/search?q=cache:mu_hA7Nvpg0J:www.infogrip.com/docs/people _with_disabilities.pdf (accessed September 24, 2008).

Rubin, Rhea Joyce. 2001. Planning for Library Services for People with Disabilities. Chicago: Association of Specialized and Cooperative Library Agencies. This planning manual includes a glossary of terms, guidelines for descriptive language use, and tip sheets for communicating with people with disabilities.

Tinerella, Vincent P., and Marcia A. Dick. 2005. "Academic Reference Service for the Visually Impaired: A Guide for the Non-specialist." *College & Research Libraries News* 66, no. 1 (January): 29–32 . Includes recommendations for communicating with visually impaired people.

Wiler, Linda Lou, and Elinor Lomax. 2000. "The Americans with Disabilities Act Compliance and Academic Libraries in the Southeastern United States." *Journal of Southern Academic and Special Librarianship.* Available: http:// southernlibrarianship.icaap.org/content/v02n01/wiler_l01.html (accessed September 24, 2008). Discusses findings of a survey completed by 136 academic libraries. Only 9 percent had a written policy covering assistance to library users with disabilities. The authors recommended that libraries not overlook the importance of changing attitudinal barriers toward individuals with disabilities.

Wright, Keith C., and Judith F. Davie. 1991. *Serving the Disabled: A How-To-Do-It Manual for Librarians.* New York: Neal-Schuman. Focuses on attitudes rather than technologies, but includes a chapter on what "going electronic" means for the disabled. Provides exercises, tests and staff development simulations.

Zipkowitz, Fay, ed. 1996. *Reference Services for the Unserved.* New York: Haworth Press. (Also published as *The Reference Librarian* 53, 1996). Includes articles on services to students with disabilities (see Lenn, above), battered women, and the mentally ill.

5.9.6 Interviewing Problematic People

Curry, Ann. 1996. "Managing the Problem Patron." *Public Libraries* 35, no. 3 (May/June): 181–188.

Hecker, Thomas E. 1996. "Patrons with Disabilities or Problem Patrons: Which Model Should Librarians Apply to People with Mental Illness?" *The Reference Librarian* 53: 5–12. Argues that those with mental illness should be treated as are other people with disabilities, not as "problem patrons."

Mabry, Celia Hales. 2003. "Serving Seniors: Do's and Don'ts at the Desk." *American Libraries* 34, no. 11 (December): 64–65. The increased longevity of today's library users means that we are seeing an increasing number of older people at the reference desk. This practical article provides sound advice on how to treat seniors with respect and avoid problems.

McNeil, Beth, and Denise J. Johnson. 1996. *Patron Behavior in Libraries: A Handbook of Positive Approaches to Negative Situations.* Chicago: ALA. Sixteen experts provide authoritative recommendations for dealing with negative situations in public and academic libraries, including how to handle: the homeless, the mentally ill, and specific populations such as young adults. Chapters focus on crime, legal issues, sexual harassment, and sexual behavior in libraries. Active listening and policy development and implementation are offered as solutions, and there is also an annotated guide to the literature on library users.

Osa, Justina. 2002. "The Difficult Patron Situation: Competency-based Training to Empower Frontline Staff." *The Reference Librarian* 75/76: 263–276.

Radford, Marie L. 2004. "Investigating Interpersonal Communication in Chat Reference: Dealing with Impatient Users and Rude Encounters." In *The Virtual Reference Desk: Creating a Reference Future* (23–45), edited by R. David Lankes et al. New York: Neal-Schuman.

Reed, Sally G. 1992. "Breaking Through: Effective Reference Mediation for Nontraditional Public Library Users." *The Reference Librarian* 37: 109–116. Focuses on two groups: the illiterate and newly literate, and those with mental illness.

Rubin, Rhea. 2000. *Defusing the Angry Patron: A How-To-Do-It Manual for Librarians.* New York: Neal-Schuman. Designed as a workbook rather than a textbook, includes preventative measures and strategies that help you deal with angry patrons along with examples, scenarios, exercises and self-tests that can be used in training.

Sarkodie-Mensah, Kwasi, ed. 2002. *Helping the Difficult Library Patron: New Approaches to Examining and Resolving a Long-Standing and Ongoing Problem.* Binghamton, NY: The Haworth Press. Also published as *The Reference Librarian* 75/76. Includes twenty-five articles (including Osa, 2002, listed previously) on problematic patrons of various types. Makes little specific mention of the reference interview, but there is much good advice on many aspects of the topic.

Smith, Kitty. 1993. *Serving the Difficult Customer: A How-To-Do-It Manual for Library Staff.* New York: Neal-Schuman. While much of the focus is on difficult staff rather than providing reference services to problematic people, there is solid information on understanding difficult people. Also includes guidelines for developing policies regarding user behavior.

Turner, Anne M. 2004. *It Comes with the Territory: Handling Problem Situations in Libraries.* Rev. ed. Jefferson NC: McFarland. Discusses some common "problems that plague us," provides practical advice, as well as guidelines and procedures that can be put in place.

5.9.7 Interviewing Users with Legal or Health Questions

Allcock, Jana C. 2000. "Helping Public Library Patrons Find Medical Information—the Reference Interview." *Public Library Quarterly* 18, no. 3/4: 21–27.

Baker, Lynda M., and Virginia Manbeck. 2002. *Consumer Health Information for Public Librarians.* Lanham, MD: Scarecrow Press. Provides guidance for public libraries that want to implement or improve consumer health information programs. Discusses information needs and information-seeking behavior of health care consumers, staff training, and reference interviewing.

Barnes, Newkirk. 2005. "Handling Legal Questions at the Reference Desk and Beyond." *Electronic Journal of Academic and Special Librarianship* 6, no. 2 (winter). Available: http://southernlibrarianship.icaap.org/content/v06n03/barnes_n01.htm (accessed October 1, 2008). Discusses the most common types of legal questions that the reference librarian will have to deal with (ready-reference, research, and referral), with examples. Strategies that you can use to probe the information need are provided.

Borman, C. Brandi, and Pamela J. McKenzie. 2005. "Trying to Help without Getting in Their Faces: Public Library Staff Descriptions of Providing Consumer Health Information." *Reference & User Services Quarterly* 45, no.2 (winter): 133–146. Staff perception of health interviews.

Casini, Barbara, and Andrea Kenyon. 2002. *The Public Librarian's Guide to Providing Consumer Health Information.* Chicago: Public Library Assn. While the focus is on materials and resources, there is discussion of the health consumer's behavior and information needs and the health reference interview, including tips for telephone and virtual as well as FtF interviews.

Condon, Charles J. 2001. "How to Avoid the Unauthorized Practice of Law at the Reference Desk." *Legal Reference Services Quarterly* 19, no. 2/3: 165–179. Includes strategies that can be used by reference librarians faced with legal questions.

Dewdney, Patricia, Joanne Marshall, and Muta Tiamiyu. 1991. "A Comparison of Legal and Health Information Services in Public Libraries." *RQ* 32, no. 2 (winter): 185–196.

Estabrook, Leigh. 2007. *Information Searches That Solve Problems: How People Use Libraries, the Internet, and Government Agencies When They Need Help.* Pew Internet and American Life Project and the Graduate School of Library and Information Science, University of Illinois at Urbana-Champaign. Available: www.pewinternet.org/pdfs/Pew_UI_LibrariesReport.pdf (accessed October 8, 2008).

Harris, Roma C., Nadine Wathen, and Donna Chan. "Public Library Responses to a Consumer Health Inquiry in a Public Health Crisis: The SARS Experience in Ontario." *Reference & User Services Quarterly* 45, no. 2 (winter): 147–154. Includes findings of a study in which proxies asked for information on SARS at sixty-nine public libraries by telephone or e-mail. Most respondents bypassed the reference interview—only 26 percent of those reached by telephone and none of the libraries reached by e-mail prompted the caller for more information.

Healthnet—Connecticut Consumer Health Information Network. *Guidelines for Providing Medical Information to Consumers.* 2000. Available: http://library.uchc.edu/departm/hnet/guidelines.html (accessed October 1, 2008). These useful guidelines can be used in training and re-training library staff to answer consumer health and medical questions.

King County Library System. *Please Ask Your Doctor: An Interview Guide to Use with Health Care Professionals.* Available: www.kcls.org/research/askdr.pdf (accessed October 1, 2008). A handout for library users.

Malmquist, Katherine. 1996. "Legal Issues Regarding Library Patrons." In *Patron Behavior in Libraries: A Handbook of Positive Approaches to Negative Situations* (95–105), edited by Beth McNeil and Denise J. Johnson. Chicago: ALA.

Medline Plus. Washington, DC: National Library of Medicine, last updated December 2007. Available: http://medlineplus.gov/ (accessed October 7, 2008).

National Network of Libraries of Medicine. Last updated June, 2007. "The Consumer Health Reference Interview and Ethical Issues." Prepared by Jane Lieberman, updated by Arpita Bose, and Gail Kouame. Available: http://nnlm.gov/outreach/consumer/ethics.html (accessed October 1, 2008). Outlines the special challenges of the consumer health interview.

Nebraska Library Commission. *The Nebraska STAR Reference Manual (Statewide Training for Accurate Reference).* Available: www.nlc.state.ne.us/Ref/star/star.html (accessed October 1, 2008). Includes guidelines on medical and legal resources with separate guidelines on medical and legal questions that include a worksheet to help you identify the patron need.

Olver, Lynne. 2000. *Legal Reference: Tips and Techniques* and *The Legal Reference Interview.* Morris County (NJ) Library and Highlands Regional Library Cooperative. Available: www.gti.net/mocolib1/demos/legalref.html (accessed October 1, 2008). These two items focus on the questions that need to be asked, rather than on librarian behavior.

Price, Toni, Christine Urquhart, and Janet Cooper. "Using a Prompt Sheet to Improve the Reference Interview in a Health Telephone Helpline Service." Available: http://cadair.aber.ac.uk/dspace/bitstream/2160/534/1/Eblip4_paper_v5_forCADAIR.doc (accessed October 10, 2008). Covers interviewing techniques for telephone questions in general and consumer health questions, and discusses the development, application, and effectiveness of a "prompt sheet" to aid staff responding to these questions. Includes typical health questions and responses to them.

Radford, Marie L. 2008. *Interpersonal Communication in Virtual Reference Encounters in the Library LAWLINE Consortium.* In *Virtual Reference Service: From Competencies to Assessment* (77–88), edited by R. David Lankes, Scott Nicholson, Marie L. Radford, Lynn Westbrook, Joanne Silverstein, and Philip Nast. New York: Neal-Schuman. Transcript analysis of law live chat reference sessions reveals interpersonal facilitators and barriers to successful interactions.

Reference and User Services Association. 2001. "Guidelines for Medical, Legal, and Business Information Services Responses." *Reference & User Services Quarterly* 41, no. 2 (winter): 111–113. Available: www.ala.org/ala/mgrps/divs/rusa/resources/guidelines/guidelinesmedical.cfm (accessed October 21, 2008).

Thomas, Deborah A. 2005. "The Consumer Health Reference Interview." *Journal of Hospital Librarianship* 5, no. 2: 45–56. Directed at hospital librarians providing consumer health information. Provides helpful suggestions for all librarians conducting consumer health interviews, with examples.

Trosow, Samuel E. 2001. "Jurisdictional Disputes and the Unauthorized Practice of Law: New Challenges for Law Librarianship." *Legal Reference Services Quarterly* 20, no. 4: 1–19. Explains the history of "unauthorized practice of law" legislation and considers how its enforcement might impact reference service.

Whisner, Mary. 2001. "Practicing Reference: Finding Out What They Really Want to Know." *Law Library Journal* 93, no. 4: 727–732.

Whisner, Mary. 2002. "Practicing Reference: Teaching the Art of the Reference Interview." *Law Library Journal* 94, no. 1: 161–166. Available: www.aall-net.org/products/pub_llj_v94n01/2002-10.pdf (accessed October 7, 2008). The focus is on training novice librarians. Appendix lists tips, with examples, on conducting legal reference interviews.

5.9.8 Implications of Consortial Reference

Bromberg, Peter. 2003. "Managing a Statewide Virtual Reference Service: How QandANJ Works." *Computers in Libraries* 23, no 4: 26–31. Details the genesis for QandANJ, the first statewide chat reference consortium. Discusses how the service works and how policies and procedures were established.

Dewdney, Patricia, and Catherine Sheldrick Ross. 1994. "Flying a Light Aircraft: Reference Service Evaluation from a User's Viewpoint." *RQ* 34, no. 2 (winter): 217–230.

Kwon, Nahyun. 2006. "User Satisfaction with Referrals at a Collaborative Virtual Reference Service. *Information Research* 11, no. 2 (January): 20 pages. Available: http://informationr.net/ir/11-2/paper246.html (accessed October 9, 2008). A study of chat reference transactions delivered through the Broward County public library system in Florida using a cooperative chat reference service.

Library of Congress. 2003."QuestionPoint User Guidelines." Available: www.loc.gov/rr/digiref/QP_best_practices.pdf (accessed October 10, 2008).

McKenzie, Pamela J. 2003. "User Perspectives on Staff Cooperation during the Reference Transactions." *The Reference Librarian* 93/84: 5–22.

Morin, Alison C. 2004. "Approaching Best Practices and Guidelines for Digital Reference." In *The Virtual Reference Experience: Integrating Theory into Practice* (185–198), edited by R. David Lankes et al. New York: Neal-Schuman.

Pomerantz, Jeffrey. 2006. "Collaboration as the Norm in Reference Work." *Reference & User Services Quarterly* 46, no. 1 (fall): 45–55.

QandANJ—New Jersey Library Network. Available: www.qandanj.org (accessed September 22, 2008). This is a statewide consortium that provides a chat reference service.

QuestionPoint. *Global Reference Network Member Guidelines.* Available: www.questionpoint.org/policies/memberguidelines.html#Quality (accessed October 10, 2008)

Radford, Marie L., and Lynn Silipigni Connaway 2008. "Exceeding Expectations: E-Reference Excellence in Collaborative VR." Public Library Association, Minneapolis, MN, March 25–29, 2008. Available: www.oclc.org/us/en/news/events/presentations/default.htm (accessed November 9, 2008).

Reference and User Services Association. Cooperative Reference Service Committee. 2006. "Guidelines for Cooperative Reference Services." Chicago: ALA. Available: www.ala.org/ala/mgrps/divs/rusa/resources/guidelines/guidelinescooperative.cfm (accessed October 21, 2008). Also published in *Reference & User Services Quarterly* 47, no. 1 (fall 2007): 97–100.

Virtual Reference Desk. 2003. *Facets of Quality for Digital Reference Service* Version 5. Available: www.webjunction.org/quality-standards/articles/content/438969 (accessed October 10, 2008).

The Reference Encounter in Virtual Environments

6.1 Introduction to Virtual Reference (VR)

The big change in reference in recent years has been the expanded variety and reach of services being offered through library Web pages. Now users have access round the clock to different Web-based Virtual Reference Services (VRS). According to the Reference and User Services Association (RUSA) of the American Library Association (ALA), "Virtual reference is reference service initiated electronically, often in real time, where patrons employ computers or other Internet technology to communicate with reference staff, without being physically present. Communication channels used frequently in virtual reference include chat, videoconferencing, Voice over IP, co-browsing, e-mail, and instant messaging" (RUSA, 2004). Once regarded as an "add on" service, VR (also known as electronic or digital reference) is now a basic service. Although some librarians still think of VR as "new," according to Bernie Sloan (2006) e-mail reference has already been in existence for over twenty years, live chat for over ten years.

In the late 1990s, live chat VRS emerged as a real-time synchronous alternative to e-mail reference. Slow at first, the adoption of live reference has accelerated as public and academic libraries formed consortial arrangements to offer round-the-clock service through shared staff (Sloan, 2006). Live chat services use sophisticated subscription-based software (including OCLC's QuestionPoint and Sirsi Dynix's Docutek). Such software allows for routing of questions for consortium collaboration, co-browsing of library databases and Web sites, customized scripts, and user queuing. Member libraries contribute staff hours and may opt to pay for reference librarian coverage during late night and/or weekends.

Instant Messaging (IM) reference using free commercial applications (such as AIM, Yahoo, MSN, or Google Talk) began appearing on library Web sites in the early 2000s. Penn State University Libraries and the University Library of the University of Illinois at Urbana-Champaign, among others, feature IM access to reference on their Web sites. *Library Success: A Best Practices Wiki* provides a long list of libraries in the U.S.

and world-wide that use IM for reference. This site also lists libraries offering SMS (Short Message Service, also known as phone text messaging) reference and even some that use the free Internet-based phone service Skype.

Moreover, Web 2.0 has encouraged innovative applications that feature greater interactivity with users and more user-generated content. Increasingly reference librarians have become early adopters of emerging technologies that promote reference such as streaming media, blogs, wikis, and social networking applications such as Facebook and MySpace (Maness, 2006) and podcasting (Bolan, Canada and Cullen, 2007). These non-traditional approaches push reference help and information to the user's desktop in familiar digital environments. This desktop access is especially attractive to younger users who are the digital natives and members of the "Net Gen" (Gibbons, 2007).

The goal of providing a range of reference modes, says Karen Schneider (2000), quoting Anne Lipow, is to "meet the users where they are, to seek them out, to market in language intelligible and attractive to our target communities, and to customize services based on the users' needs, preferences, and timetables." Of course, libraries have been serving users who were not physically present in the library for a long time through use of traditional delivery systems like telephone reference (5.2) and "snail mail" reference. However, increasingly tech-savvy library users expect quick access to resources and services from their desktops. User demand has provided a powerful reason to initiate VRS, which in turn has put a human face on the digital library. Having invested enormous amounts of money to provide Web-based resources, libraries have an obligation to help users access and effectively search these resources. Burgeoning courses and degrees in distance learning offered by colleges and universities have also accelerated user demand for desktop access. Typically, distance learners are off-campus students without the option of coming to the physical library. Although they may even live in other states or outside of the country, they still have the same need to access library resources and services as do students taking courses on campus.

In short, with desk-top access to electronic resources through the Web from home, office, or the local coffee wi-fi hotspot, people often don't need to visit a physical facility. Although today's online users may be located at great geographic distances from the library, or working at off-hours, this is not necessarily always the case. Several services report that VR use is heaviest during walk-in peak times. A number of users (perhaps as high as 25 or 30 percent) are actually present in the physical library. Judy Ruttenberg and Heather Tunender (2004), in a study at the University of California Irvine, found that 54.7 percent of the chats from 2002 to 2004 came from computers in campus buildings. They found that undergraduate chats more often came from within the library, while graduates came from other campus buildings. Users might choose chat, IM, or e-mail reference because it is more convenient to work from home, dorm, or office. Those within the library may not want to leave their laptops while they go to the reference desk, or risk losing their place at a computer workstation, or they may be English language learners, hearing impaired, or perhaps simply shy.

Does this trend to online use mean fewer reference interviews? The answer depends on what type of library you are working in. According to the National Center for Educational Statistics, reference questions in public libraries increased 18 percent from 1994 to 2004 while overall gate count increased 60 percent. On the other hand, academic libraries have reported that users are making fewer trips to the library in person, but often are engaging in a growing number of virtual reference queries, a trend that can be expected to continue (Kyrillidou and Young, 2006). The Association of Research Libraries (ARL) has reported that although many university libraries are reporting fewer face-to-face (FtF) questions, they are also indicating that the queries they do get are much more complex and time-consuming (Kyrillidou and Young, 2006). End users may be finding answers to easy, ready-reference questions (i.e., those requiring short, factual answers) by a quick Google search or through some other Web search engine. However, students with more in-depth research questions still need expert assistance. University libraries that have aggressively marketed their entire range of reference services are seeing a leveling off in the numbers of reference queries, or even some modest gains across all modes of service.

Despite all the hype about the entire universe of information being "at people's fingertips at the touch of a button and at the speed of light via the Web," we know that the complexity of today's informational landscape means that many people simply won't find the information they need without professional assistance. So to help online users navigate the information maze, libraries are experimenting with new ways of providing a traditional service—saving the time of users by connecting them with quality information. With either synchronous real-time encounters using chat and other IM software, or asynchronous e-mail, users can get their questions answered regardless of their location or the time of day.

With VRS, the library staff can transact the reference interview, refer the user to the online catalog and indexes, escort users through complex searches, provide library use instruction, evaluate sources, and deliver the required information in the form of Web sites, electronic journal articles, or entries in electronic reference tools. The whole process can be conducted online. At the end, the user has digital text or graphics that can be printed out or saved. For the user, this service offers clear advantages over telephone reference, where answers must be read over the phone or faxed, and where users are often advised to come to the library in person for anything that is not ready-reference. Seventy years after librarians first grappled with the best way to provide remote reference service using a relatively new technology—the telephone—we are now struggling with the problem of what combination of on-ground and VR services to offer at a time when budget cuts to libraries are coinciding with rising demand.

The VR interview requires a similar set of skills to those needed in FtF interviews, but there are some additional considerations that relate to the digital environment and to the bias of the technology. The fundamental

Referral

If you're sure you can't help the user, suggest another way of getting help. When the Internet Public Library (IPL) "Ask an IPL Librarian" service is closed for a holiday or some other reason, this message appears: "We are temporarily closed... [but] it's certainly not our intention to leave anyone stranded. There are lots of places you can go for help." A list of such places is then provided. A clever sign posted on a public library building in New Jersey that was closed for a holiday read, "The library building is closed today for the holiday, but our virtual library e-mail and live chat services are open 24/7/365." The URLs were clearly listed on the sign. What a great way to publicize the VRS and to assure users that they are not abandoned on holidays.

Did You Know?

Focus groups conducted by researchers at Illinois State University investigated low use of a chat reference service and found that upper-level undergraduates were unaware of reference services other than at the traditional reference desk. They did not know that the library offered e-mail or chat reference. They associated the name "chat" reference with "chatrooms," and said that they "would not likely have tried the service if they had encountered the term 'chat reference' because of negative associations with chatrooms" (Naylor, Stoffel, and Van Der Laan, 2008, 348). The authors concluded that "we will be wise to market the service differently and more carefully choose our terminology" (351). This study also found that students wanted a variety of reference services and desired more personalized assistance.

questions concerning the design of virtual reference services are often framed in terms of the technology. In fact, they have far more to do with the library's orientation to users and with the library's policies about service. In this chapter we focus primarily on communication with users. We examine the special features of the VR reference interview, which, unlike the FtF or telephone interview, is text-based, with all the constraints and advantages that text entails.

6.1.1 Setting the Stage

To have a successful virtual reference service, extensive work must be done behind the scenes. This work is the digital equivalent of setting the stage for an FtF question by paying close attention to making the physical environment and staff welcoming and approachable. In the brick-and-mortar library, this means using appropriate signage, positioning service desks and librarians where they are easy to find, and identifying the professional staff as the right people to receive the question (see 2.2). The digital counterpart to creating a welcoming physical environment is creating visible, easy-to-use Web links and well-designed, easily navigated Web pages. Just as the reference service in the physical library should not be hidden away in an out-of-the way area but be clearly marked and placed where users can find it, so the VRS should not be buried four levels deep in the Web site. VRS must be immediately available through highly visible links on the library's main page.

The bottom line is to make sure that users can easily see the options available to them for getting reference help. To facilitate point-of-need assistance, provide access to the array of VRS (including e-mail, chat, IM, etc.) from the top-level library Web page as well as from every other page, from the online catalog and even, if possible, from database pages. Since you want people to use the service, it should have a memorable name that clearly identifies it and is actively marketed and promoted. When advertising your VRS, make sure that users understand your policy on the kinds of help they can (and cannot) expect and, for e-mail, an idea of how long it will take for them to receive an answer.

You will notice that there are two kinds of information relating to VRS, each of which requires its own special treatment. First, there is information that *users* need to access and use the service; second there is information that *staff* need to do their jobs. The first category of information appears on your library's Web page. The second goes into your policy and procedures manual. When evaluating or suggesting changes to the library's Web page, keep in mind your audience. Ask yourself: what does a *user* need to know about our library's service? What questions will be in the minds of our user? Here are some things that a user wants to know:

- What is the "Ask a Librarian" service and who provides it?
- What is the format (e-mail, chat, IM, etc.)?
- Am I eligible to receive this service?
- What kinds of questions does this service answer?

- How long will it take to get an answer?
- What do I have to do to get this service?
- What kind of answer can I expect to get?
- How do I submit my question? (e.g., "Click here for e-mail question form" or "Click here to chat with a librarian.")
- How can I contact the library directly? (Be sure to prominently provide phone and fax numbers, street address, and directions. Some libraries now provide a link to Google Maps [http://maps.google.com/maps] or MapQuest [http://MapQuest.com].)
- What kind of privacy can I expect?

Here are some things that staff members need to know:

- Who is eligible to receive this service and what do users have to do to demonstrate eligibility?
- What is the procedure for answering users' questions? If e-mail questions are received centrally and routed to subject experts, who is responsible for the routing?
- What are the policies on how frequently e-mail is checked?
- What are the policies on how to negotiate questions?
- What are the policies on how much time to devote to questions, what kinds of answers are appropriate, and privacy?
- What are the policies of the live chat consortium, if your VRS is consortial?

Obviously there is some overlap between these two sets of questions. But even when the question is the same (e.g., who is eligible to receive service?), the text that provides the answer must be written differently to suit the intended audience. Staff members need much more detail. Users need to be told just enough to let them navigate the system. For example, users don't need to know about the procedures for handling questions within the library and routing, but for e-mail VR they should be told how soon to expect a reply. Staff members, on the other hand, need clear and detailed guidelines for internal use on such matters as consortial and local policies for answering chat questions. Staff need to know, for example, who checks e-mail and how often they check it; who is responsible for answering the question; and whether chat or IM questions are answered from the reference desk, in their office, from a designated workstation, or elsewhere.

In your explanation of the service for users, special pains should be taken to write in a friendly positive style that encourages users to use the service. Describing your VR service in this welcoming way must go hand-in-hand with the library's genuine commitment to the service. The description should come immediately after the user has clicked on the prominent "Ask a Librarian" link on the top level page of the library Web site.

A key question for users is, "Who is eligible to use the VR service?" Your library needs a policy and guidelines to define eligibility for use of

---

A QUICK TIP

A Click or Two Away

Don't let your service be a well-kept secret. The Seeking Synchronicity Project found out that the primary reason that people were not using their library's live chat VR was that they did not know it existed (Radford and Connaway, 2005–2008). Do not bury your live chat link, IM icon, or e-mail reference form. The user is unlikely to take the time to drill down many levels through your Web site to find your services. Your chat or IM link should be prominent and embedded throughout your Web site. Your e-mail form should be no more than two clicks away from the library home page: the first click should lead directly to a description of the service, and the second click should lead directly to the form. If you visit the Penn State University Libraries and click on "Ask! a Librarian" (http://ask.libraries.psu.edu/), you can quickly get to a menu that includes links to their chat, IM, e-mail, phone, visit a librarian, and FAQ pages. Their FAQ page features the top ten most frequently asked questions.

What's in a Name?

Your VR service should have a name that *clearly* identifies it, and prominently appears as a link on the top level of the library home page. Some names that libraries frequently use include the ever-popular "Ask a Librarian," "Ask a Question," and "Ask Us/Tell Us."

Some services incorporate the library's name into a catchy, memorable, but meaningful name. For example, the Hinsdale Public Library in Hinsdale, IL calls their service "Ask HPL." But *don't* call your service "Help," "Information," or "Virtual Service" because these names are confusing and ambiguous to users. Don't use the word "Reference" or "E-Reference" in the name, because many users have no idea what these terms mean in this context. In late 2008, the Internet Public Library's e-mail service changed its name to: "Ask an IPL Librarian," from the previous name of "Ask a Question" to highlight the value added by having librarians answering questions. Many businesses are now offering online chat customer services. The Lands' End Web site invites users to click "Get Live Help" (http://landsend.com), while Nordstrom's uses the even simpler "Live Help" (http://Nordstrom.com). These direct approaches leave no doubt as to how to get online help. Many consortial services have begun using "Ask" as a brand such as Maryland AskUsNow! and AskColorado. On the University of Washington Libraries' home page the VR button says "Save time! Ask Us" (http://library.wustl.edu/). It is important to make sure your "brand" lets users know that professional librarians will be answering their questions.

its live chat, IM, or e-mail reference services. With a few exceptions, including the Library of Congress's "Ask a Librarian" service and the Internet Public Library's "Ask an IPL Librarian" service, the vast majority of e-mail services are not prepared to welcome the entire planet. Some libraries have made the decision to concentrate resources on certain classes of users who will have priority and to answer questions from others only as time allows. In any case, you need to make your *eligibility policy clear* in all descriptions of the service.

In a public library, your service might be limited to card-holders, to local residents, or to residents of your state or province. Even statewide consortial chat services have limited staff resources and usually put limits on who can use their service. For example, according to its Web site, "QandANJ is a service for New Jersey residents and students." To ask a question of this statewide consortium, you must be authenticated through inputting your NJ library card number or bar code.

In an academic library, you might limit your service to faculty, staff, students, and alumni of your own institution. In state-funded institutions you might serve all residents of the state or province. For example, when you click on "Who is eligible to use this service?" on the FAQ page of Baruch College in New York City, this statement appears for their e-mail reference guidelines: "Students, faculty, staff, alumni of Baruch College and the CUNY Online BA community. Service will be extended to those outside the college community who have questions about special collections of the Newman Library."

In a special library, your service might be limited to internal clients, or it might include external clients or members. Special libraries may belong to statewide VR consortia and serve as subject experts when questions relating to their areas are received (such as medical or law libraries).

Table 6.1 considers how the important elements in the reference interview can be achieved in the different formats of FtF, live chat/IM, and e-mail. The same elements need to be present—e.g., approachability, avoiding premature diagnosis, asking open and sense-making questions, etc.—but the means of achieving them vary.

Some library e-mail services provide a well-developed question form for users to submit their questions, along with a description of the service offered and guidelines. Without a well-designed form that takes the place of a reference interview (see 6.3.2), it can require extra time and several back and forth messages to negotiate the question. Instructions should be included both in the description text and on the search form itself.

Once you have established your VR service, you should monitor it closely by tracking questions and answers. You might also want to provide a list of Frequently Asked Questions (FAQ) for users to access on their own from the library Web site. For example, if you often get the question, "How do I connect from home to the library's catalog and e-journals?" provide the answer to this question. If the user bypasses the FAQ page and asks you anyway, you can answer by providing a link to your FAQ answer in your response. One advantage of live chat VR is that a verbatim transcript is produced for every interaction. In this chapter, we have

Table 6.1. Comparing the FtF, Live Chat/IM, and E-mail Reference Interview

	Face-to-Face	Live Chat/IM	E-mail
Being Approachable	Locate the service desk in a prominent place. At the desk, look up, make eye-contact, use welcoming body language, and a pleasant expression. Do not bury your head in your work or the computer screen.	Display link to chat prominently on all Web pages. Let user know when questions can be submitted (or if service is 24/7).	Provide an easy-to find and well-designed form that is not overcrowded. Questions can be submitted 24/7.
Using Acknowledgement	Greet user in a personal and comfortable way, e.g., "Hi, may I help you?" Restate what you have understood of user's question. If necessary for a shared understanding, paraphrase.	Give user a personal greeting along with the scripted greeting. Use first names if possible, e.g., "Hi, Pat, that's an interesting question."	Send an automatic receipt thanking the user for the question and explaining when a response can be expected.
Avoiding Premature Diagnosis	Don't assume that the initial question is the real question. Don't prejudge the user's need based on status, appearance, or speech.	Don't assume that the initial question is the real question. Don't prejudge the user's need based on writing skills, use of chat-speak, spelling errors, typos, screen name, or level of question. Parents may be helping children with homework questions.	Don't assume that the initial question is the real question. Don't prejudge the user's need based on writing skills, spelling errors, typos, or e-mail address. Children may use a parent's e-mail and vice-versa.
Using Open or Sense-making Questions	Get the user to provide more information; assess the situation, gaps, and kind of help wanted.	Get the user to provide more information; assess the situation, gaps, and kind of help wanted. Ask a clarifying question before you start to search to save the user's as well as your own time.	Use sense-making questions on the form to find out the situation, gaps, or uses. If further clarification is needed, ask open or sense-making questions in your e-mail response, just as you would in person.
Using Inclusion	Explain why the user's answer will help you to provide a more helpful answer. Involve the user in the search. Turn the computer screen toward users so that they can see it, or let the user type while you guide the search. Ask for frequent feedback.	Use inclusive language such as "we," "us," "let's." Ask for frequent feedback, e.g., "Do you see the page I sent?" "Does this Web site look helpful to you?"	On the form, explain why the user's responses will help you provide a more helpful answer.
Paraphrasing Your Understanding of the Information Need	Rephrase the question as you understand it. Ask for confirmation before searching.	Rephrase the question as you understand it. Ask for confirmation before searching.	If clarification was necessary, rephrase the question as you understand it. Send something that you think will be useful but ask for confirmation before searching further.
Following Up	After providing answers or information, say, "If this isn't what you are looking for, come back and we'll try something else." If the user goes to another part of the library, ask him to come back if more help is needed. If you see the user later, follow up by asking, "Did you find what you needed?"	Ask users if the question/ information need has been completely answered/satisfied. Invite them to return to your VR service if more help is needed.	After providing an answer or information, say, "If this isn't what you are looking for, please e-mail us again." If you recommend e-resources, ask the user to get back to you if the source did not prove helpful.

Did You Know?

Many librarians worry about time pressure in live chat vs. FtF reference. They think all users are in a huge hurry and impatient. Transcript analysis of 850 chat VR sessions has found that sessions take an average mean time of 12.42 minutes with a median of twelve minutes. The minimum was found to be twelve seconds and the maximum to be seventy-one minutes. Studies of FtF reference session times have found the median to be twelve to thirteen minutes, about the same amount of time, so the message here is to relax in VR. Many users are coming to VR for convenience, not because they are in a hurry (Radford and Connaway, 2005–2008).

For comparison, services that are using the less formal IM platform rather than chat, are reporting a slightly shorter session length. Pam Sessoms and Jean Ferguson (2008) reported that their IM sessions (using AIM, Yahoo, and MSN) at Duke University libraries and the Davis Library at the University of North Carolina at Chapel Hill averaged eight to eleven minutes.

EXERCISE

Getting Rid of the VRS User

For this exercise, pick the Web site of your own library or of a library in your area. Imagine that you are a user who is unfamiliar with the services offered, and you are exploring the site for the first time. Count how many features of the chosen site have the effect of discouraging the user from asking an e-question. Give one point for each of the following:

1. No link to the VR service(s) is provided from the home page
2. The VR link is found with difficulty after clicking around for a while.
3. It takes effort or several clicks to find the VR link (it is small, hidden at the bottom of the page, or not immediately recognized by you as the correct link).
4. The description of the VRS gives priority to what the service does *not* do, not what it does do (e.g., we do *not* provide answers to X; we do *not* serve Y categories of users).
5. The page describing VRS states that for good service you should come in person to the library.
6. High-end equipment, extremely fast connectivity, use of certain browsers, or downloaded software is needed to make use of the service.
7. For e-mail services, there is no digital form provided on which to submit a question or the form looks very complicated and gives the impression that it would take fifteen minutes or so to fill out.
8. For chat or IM services, the hours of operation are very limited (e.g., 2 p.m. to 4 p.m. only on weekdays).

If you give the site a score of 3 or more, the site needs improvement to make it more user-centered.

---

included a number of examples of verbatim transcripts automatically generated during a live chat reference transaction. A systematic and non-threatening evaluation of chat sessions should be done with all staff on a regular basis. Matt Saxton (2004) of the University of Washington has suggested a collegial peer review system in the article "Show Me Yours and I'll Show You Mine! Implementing Peer Review." Saxton urges VR providers to meet regularly to compare their transcripts and to provide constructive feedback in a non-threatening manner.

6.2 Real-time Reference: Live Chat and IM

VR started with e-mail, but many libraries are now augmenting their e-mail reference service with a real-time live chat and IM. The increasing popularity, especially among young people, of chat and IM has prompted libraries to offer stand-alone chat services or to join consortia so that their users can reap the benefits of synchronous VR. National and international collaborative networks of linked libraries, such as

OCLC's QuestionPoint, now enable an insomniac user in California to ask a question in the middle of the night and have it negotiated in real time by a librarian who is on duty at the virtual reference desk in another part of the United States, or in Australia, England, or India. Improvements in hardware and software applications have made consortial VRS an affordable 24/7/365 service for thousands of libraries. Long established as a chat service, QuestionPoint now also features a "Qwidget" that brings a previously unavailable IM interface to consortium members.

Here are some advantages of providing synchronous live chat or IM VR as compared to e-mail:

- **Chat/IM services allow librarians to respond immediately.** With synchronous services, you can conduct your reference interview at a faster pace than is possible with e-mail. The time lag between turns is a matter of seconds and minutes, not hours or days. You can ask the user to provide clarification or supplementary information and expect an immediate response.

- **Chat VR technology allows you to send URLs or push Web pages, and also to co-browse databases with the user.** You can demonstrate to the user how to find something on the Web or how to enter search terms in databases. These features allow you to walk your user through the source to find the answers and to provide library use instruction. Although not yet widely used in VR, technologies such as the Voice Over Internet Protocol (VOIP) and Skype allow you to talk to and hear users while connected.

- **When the library is not open, VR can be provided by a librarian working from home or in some other time zone.** Consortium membership frequently includes coverage by a staff of professional librarians during the overnight or holiday hours.

- **Complete transcripts of each chat session can be e-mailed to the user and archived** so that a full record of the reference transaction is available, complete with URLs and instructions provided. The transcripts (when cleansed of personal information such as names, e-mail addresses, etc.) can also be used for evaluation and training for service excellence.

Of course, there are also some drawbacks to VR:

- **As with e-mail reference, chat software does not allow you to get nonverbal cues.** You can neither see nor hear the user. All you have to go on are the written words. You may infer impatience or frustration from the user's text, but the environment is impoverished in comparison with the opportunities for nonverbal cues offered in FtF interactions.

- **Real-time VR is labor-intensive.** If the service is part of your regular reference desk duties, you will find that it competes for attention with FtF users just like telephone reference. VR demand is unpredictable. If the questions come in while the desk is busy with walk-in users, it is difficult to juggle the requests and provide excellent service to each user. It is far better to staff an online service with dedicated VR librarians who are not also responsible for providing FtF or phone reference service.

- **Some librarians find it stressful to provide live chat or IM reference** because the online user who is waiting for your reply cannot see what you are doing or whether there is a long queue. You need to tell the users what you are doing, alert them if other users are in front of them, and ask them if they prefer to wait or to come back at another time.

- **As in the e-mail reference interview, communication in the chat or IM mode requires you to *type* each of your queries to your user.** Finally the answer and the source must be put into written form. You can type only so fast, and your haste can cause typos and spelling errors that you would be able to clean up, were you on e-mail. Luckily chat users are very forgiving of spelling mistakes and frequently do not bother to correct their own. Chat is more fast-paced than e-mail and requires typing speed as well as interpersonal skill.

6.2.1 The Synchronous Reference Interview

The principles for the reference interview remain the same, no matter what the environment. The VR interview is very similar to the FtF reference interview as discussed in Chapter 3. Here are some of the similarities bewteen live chat and FtF:

- **Happening in real time.** As in FtF conversation, the interaction is a rapid and back-and-forth exchange.

- **Similar time pressure.** In both FtF and live chat, slow times are mixed with times when a queue of users awaits your help. Some users are patient and willing to wait; others may be stressed, on a deadline, or under other time constraints.

- **Negotiating questions.** Like FtF users, VR users frequently start the interaction with a question or statement that does not adequately capture their real information need. For example, in Case 33, the user entered only the word "Physics" into the box requesting the chat question. The real question turned out to be "when you drive forward in a bumper car at high speed and then you slam into the car in front of you, you find yourself thrown forward in your car. Which way is ur car accelerating?"

- **Answering questions and providing information.** VR chat questions and information requests closely resemble those posed face-to-face. Academic chat services generally receive academic questions related to the university's curriculum and student assignments. Public library chat services get more homework questions from younger users, and more community-related or everyday life questions. VR consortia receive a blend (Radford and Connaway, 2005–2008).

- **Service excellence as goal.** Just as in an FtF reference, one goal is to provide users with quality information.

- **Building relationships as goal.** Surprisingly high numbers of VR users are repeat users. If users have received excellent service once, they are likely to return again and again.

- **Variety of users.** Today's VR users are a diverse group, reflecting the diverse society we live in. More older people are discovering VR, including live chat, especially when they have used chat to keep in touch with children and grandchildren.

The text-based nature of VR means that there are also very significant differences between VR and FtF reference, including the following:

- **More keyboard woes.** People who do not have good keyboard skills find it difficult to keep up with the fast-paced nature of chat or IM reference.

- **Lack of nonverbal cues.** All you have to go on is what the user has typed. With some services, you have the user's e-mail address such as JamesJ435!@yahoo.com. You might guess that this user is male, but you could easily be wrong. In FtF transactions you can immediately determine the person's gender, age, status markers (such as suit or briefcase), and other cues. Some VR users do spontaneously self-disclose personal information ("I'm in 8th grade"). If not, you can ask, "How would you like this information to help you?" which might elicit details about a class assignment or other context of use.

- **Limited knowledge of user.** Lacking nonverbal cues, you know very little about the user. In FtF reference, affiliation to your institution may be apparent (e.g., a user approaches the university reference desk wearing a school sweatshirt; a user accompanied by a child in a stroller walks up to the public library desk). In FtF situations, it is much easier to tell if the user is an English language learner. In a text-based environment, this important information is obscured.

- **Chat speak.** Today's users have adopted many shortcuts to cut down on keystrokes in chat. This can be a challenge if you are not familiar with these expressions. We probably all know that LOL is short for "laughing out loud," but did you know HAG is short for "have a good (day)?" To learn more, see the later section Chat/Texting Abbreviations and Shortcuts.

- **Lack of knowledge of available resources.** When you are providing VR service, you may be unsure whether or not the user is affiliated with your organization and eligible to access the e-resources in your collection. With an unaffiliated user, you are typically limited to free Web resources as sources to answer the question.

- **More disruptive technical problems** (especially abrupt endings and disappearing users). Technical problems are far more frequent in a virtual environment than in a physical setting, and when they happen they are more disruptive. In FtF settings, you can see when someone walks away; in cyberspace, they are just gone. You may be left to wonder if the system went down, if the software hit a glitch, or if the user simply turned her attention elsewhere. Virtual users may disappear suddenly because their doorbell rings, their kettle is boiling, or their dog wants to go for a walk.

- **Transcript produced.** At the conclusion of an FtF interaction, there is no artifact. At the end of a chat session, on the positive side, you have the transcript that is useful for evaluation, follow-up, and for collecting statistics.

It is important, of course, always to remember to use your basic interpersonal communication skills in live chat or IM reference. Just because you can't see the user, doesn't mean that there isn't a real live person out there. In a synchronous VR encounter, it is vital to realize that the most time is spent in searching for the information. The interpersonal niceties (e.g., a personal greeting and closing, acknowledgement of humor, providing empathy if the user is upset or has disclosed an illness) actually take very little time. The research-based recommendations below can be used for training to improve interpersonal communication in live chat. A list of guidelines for dealing with rude or impatient chat users can be found in section 5.6.

Recommendations for Facilitating Interpersonal Communication in Chat Reference Encounters

- Remember that your interpersonal skills and experience are transferable to the chat environment.

- Although the search process may occupy the majority of the time in a chat transaction, the interpersonal dimension is still vitally important.

- Maintain "word contact" with your user by typing short sentences and hitting send frequently at appropriate intervals to serve as an online mode of inclusion. If you are searching for a while, continue to send short reassurances (e.g., "searching...") so that users know you are still working on the information question and have not disconnected.

- Give a brief personal greeting after the script ("Hi!").

- Use the person's first name in your response; younger users especially like a personal approach. The use of personal names softens the anonymous environment, and may head off problems.

- When reading user's initial question, look for any self-disclosure or indications that the user is seeking reassurance (e.g., "Can you help me?") and provide an appropriate response.

(continued on p. 204)

The Reference Encounter in Virtual Environments

ANALYZE THIS REFERENCE INTERVIEW

Case 32: Relational Facilitators

Case 32 is a verbatim transcript from the Seeking Synchronicity Project (Radford and Connaway, 2005–07) that illustrates the effective use of facilitators. In preparation for your close reading of this transcript, look again at the section Recommendations for Facilitating Interpersonal Communication in Chat Reference Encounters.

1	User:	i need a good website about the accomplishments of mathrmatics during the islamic empire
2	Librarian:	[A librarian will be with you in about a minute.]
3	Librarian:	[A librarian has joined the session.]
4	Librarian:	[You have been conferenced with name of service]
5	Librarian:	(Name) welcome to (service name) I'm looking at your question right now; it will be just a moment.
6	Librarian:	Hi (name)—sorry about the delay there. This is (name), a librarian in (city)
7	User:	ok
8	Librarian:	Okay, we should be able to find something on that topic. Math and Islam. Just a minute or two while I search. Please let me know if there's anything specific in this area that you're looking for, okay?
9	User:	i don;t care about the delay i have plenty of time
10	Librarian:	Thanks for understanding. We just had a very busy spell on the service and I just finished up another call. Let's see . . . searching now.
11	User:	i just need any certan mathematicians or the accomplishments of mathematics during the islamic Empire
12	Librarian:	Okay, to start I'm going to send you an article linked from the Math Forum:
13	Librarian:	[Page sent]
14	Librarian:	It should show on your screen in just a few seconds. Are you able to see it? the title is Arabic mathematics : forgotten brilliance?
15	User:	thank you very much
16	Librarian:	Great—glad you can see it! There was one other article - did you want me to send it to you, or are you okay with just this one?
17	User:	yes plaese
18	Librarian:	Okay, just a sec.
19	Librarian:	[Page sent]
20	User:	i spelled please wrong
21	Librarian:	The title of this 2nd page I just sent was, "The Arabic numeral system"
22	User:	thank you
23	Librarian:	No problem on the spelling. :) Typing this fast it's giong to happen.
24	Librarian:	*going*
25	Librarian:	Okay, what do you think? Will these answer your questions?
26	User:	yes thank you
27	Librarian:	Great! Please do write us back if you need anything else.
28	Librarian:	Thank you for using (name service)! If you have any further questions, please contact us again. If you provided an e-mail address, you should receive a full transcript in a few minutes. You may click the "End Call" button now.

For discussion:

1. Identify as many instances as you can find of the librarian's effective use of relational facilitators. What evidence is there in the transcript that these instances helped to create a good climate of communication?

2. What happens when the librarian asks the open question, "anything specific in this area that you're looking for?"

- When an initial question looks complex, immediately let the user know how much time your search is likely to take (e.g., "I'm going to search sources X and Y which may take about five minutes"). Ask if the user has the time to wait while you search. Users sometimes expect instant answers because their mental model of searching may be a Google search. But often they are multitasking and may not mind waiting, so long as they know that you are working on their question.

- If you can see that the user is from a geographically remote place, you may want to make a comment on this right away (e.g., "How's the weather in Florida? It's snowing here in Maryland"). This alerts the user that a question about local information may have to be referred.

Strategies for Building Rapport

- As appropriate, be willing to self-disclose, to provide information about yourself, and to use "I" statements. This can mean doing the following:
  - Offering evaluations, advice, or value judgments in areas of professional expertise (e.g., "I think that you will have more success if you do X," or "I have used this strategy before and it works"). But remember, *never* self-disclose, or give personal opinion or advice for medical or legal questions (5.8).
  - Admitting lack of knowledge (e.g., "I'm not really sure what you mean by new technology. Could you give me an example?" or "I have not heard of the Crystal Skull. Can you tell me something about it?").
  - Asking for confirmation as needed (e.g., "Is this what you mean?").

- Acknowledge user self-disclosure (e.g., "I'm sorry you're not feeling well and are unable to travel to your library. Let me see how I can help." Then, at the closing, "feel better soon!").

- Be empathetic when users self-disclose difficulty or frustration (e.g., "It is frustrating when our technology doesn't work!").

- Include the user in the search process (e.g., "Let's try this," "We'll look here first," or "Would it be okay if we ...?").

- Indicate your approval as appropriate (e.g., "That's great!" or "Good for you!").

- Offer reassurance when users indicate that they are tentative or unsure of how to proceed. Realize that they can be fearful of your disapproval (if, for example, they have poor computer skills or are new to VR).

- Use encouraging remarks, praise, and enthusiastic remarks as appropriate.

- Humor also can be reassuring, as can the use of self-deprecating remarks (e.g., "I'm not the world's best speller either").

- Mirror the level of formality/informality of the users.

- If they use informal language, feel free to be less formal (as appropriate).
- Be deferential and respectful of all users.
- Use polite expressions as appropriate (e.g., "please," "thanks," "you're welcome," etc.).
- Apologize as appropriate (e.g., "sorry," "unfortunately," or "oops").

Compensation for Lack of Nonverbal Cues

- Mirror the users' style. If they use shortcuts, acronyms, abbreviations, and emoticons (smileys), feel free to do so also (as appropriate).
- You may see more "chat speak" in younger users; respond in kind if you are comfortable doing so.
- If you are not comfortable using emoticons, you can spell out non-verbal behaviors or use interjections (e.g., hmmm, oh, ha ha, grin).
- Use repeated punctuation for emphasis (e.g., !!!, or ??).
- Use ellipses to indicate more to come (e.g., still searching . . .)
- Be aware that the use of ALL CAPS can be interpreted as a reprimand or as shouting (e.g., "Don't EVER . . ."). It should be used sparingly, if at all.

Closing

- Always give a brief personal closing ("Bye!").
- In the closing, as in the greeting, be sure to respond to self-disclosure, enthusiasm, or polite expressions. If the user says, "This is a great service!" don't just send her the scripted closing. Give an appropriate response like, "Glad you think so, thanks!"
- Make sure you have answered the user's question(s) completely. Use a follow-up question to ask if the user needs anything else before signing off.
- Look for subtle cues that the user wants more help. In the statement, "Well, thanks for your help," or "Well, thanks anyway,'" the "well" hedge may indicate that they are settling for what you have provided, but really want more. (© Marie L. Radford and OCLC Online Computer Library Center, Inc., 2008)

Relational Barriers to Interpersonal Communication in Chat Reference

Relational barriers, or barriers to interpersonal communication, are even more problematic in VR than they are in FtF reference. Because you can't see the user's reactions, you might assume from the words exchanged that everything is fine. But trouble might be brewing. Avoid problems by steering clear of these relational barriers:

- Robotic answers
- Sending an inappropriate script (e.g., a welcome script halfway through)
- Negative responses that emphasize what *can't* be done

(continued on p. 208)

ANALYZE THIS REFERENCE INTERVIEW

Case 33: "This isn't helpful."

Case 33 is a verbatim transcript from the Seeking Synchronicity Project (Radford and Connaway, 2005–2007) that fortunately is far from typical. Providing a concentration of relational barriers, this interaction demonstrates how things can go awry when the interpersonal dimension is neglected. When a user says, "can i hav another librarian" (line 15), this is surely a bad sign. It should have (but didn't) prompt the librarian to change gears, and attempt to repair the communication accident. Take another look at the section Relational Barriers to Interpersonal Communication in Chat Reference as background for your close reading of this transcript.

1	User:	Physics
2	Librarian:	[Please hold for the next available librarian. If you would like a transcript of this session emailed to you, please type your full email address now.]
3	Librarian:	[A librarian has joined the session.]
4	User:	when you drive forward in a bumper car at high speed and then you slam into the car in front of you, you find yourself thrown forward in your car. Which way is ur car accelerating?
5	Librarian:	thank you for holding I was working with another patron.
6	Librarian:	Is this a homework question.
7	Librarian:	I'm not an expert on driving so I really can't answer that.
8	User:	can u find a website or something
9	Librarian:	I'm not sure what you are asking.
10	User:	when you drive forward in a bumper car at high speed and then you slam into the car in front of you, you find yourself thrown forward in your car. Which way is ur car accelerating?
11	User:	. . . .
12	User:	hello?
13	Librarian:	Is this a homework a homework assignment. what subject is it.
14	Librarian:	I really don't understand how I can answer that for you.
15	User:	can i hav another librarian
16	Librarian:	The information you gave you me does not help me find any resources to help you.
17	Librarian:	What do you mean by which way is your car accerlaerating. Are you sure thats what your assignment asks.
18	User:	yes
19	Librarian:	What subject is this question from?
20	User:	physics
21	Librarian:	Okay just one moment.
22	Librarian:	[Page sent]
23	Librarian:	This is one site that may help.
24	Librarian:	[Page sent]
25	Librarian:	[Page sent - LeapStart Learning Table. Learning Starts Here!]
26	Librarian:	this is another site that youmay try forhelp.

(Cont'd.)

ANALYZE THIS REFERENCE INTERVIEW *(Continued)*

Case 33: "This isn't helpful." *(Cont'd.)*

27	Librarian:	When we disconnect you will have these links in a transcript.
28	Librarian:	[Page sent]
29	Librarian:	This site looks to be very helpful.
30	Librarian:	[Page sent—The Physics Classroom]
31	Librarian:	[Page sent—The Physics Classroom]
32	Librarian:	[Page sent—The Physics Classroom]
33	User:	this isn't helpful
34	Librarian:	Well I really don't have any other resources that can assit you.
35	Librarian:	[Page sent—The Physics Classroom]
36	Librarian:	I cannot answer the question for you, I don't have the physics knowledge.
37	Librarian:	Maybe you will need to ask your instructor for a clear understanding.
38	Librarian:	[Page sent—The Physics Classroom]
39	User:	do u kno ne1 who does
40	Librarian:	[Page sent—The Physics Classroom]
41	Librarian:	Sorry I do not
42	User:	okay
43	Librarian:	I have a few patron that I ned to assist.
44	User:	ok bye
45	Librarian:	[Thank you for using (service name)! If you have any further questions, please contact us again.]
46		Note to staff: COMP [user has closed this session]

Comment: The librarian explains the failure to help by saying, "I'm not an expert on driving so I can't answer that," and later says, "I cannot answer the question for you, I don't have the physics knowledge." Is it really driving skills and physics knowledge that are needed here or some other skill? Librarians are not expected to be experts in the topics of users' questions. But they are supposed to have good interviewing and searching skills.

For discussion:

1. Identify all the librarian-initiated behaviors that became stumbling blocks to providing good service and a helpful answer. How many different *kinds* of barriers did you find? How many instances did you find of each kind of barrier? You could even create a checklist, e.g., negative responses, robotic answers, etc.

2. The librarian blames the user for not providing enough information (line 16). What questions does the librarian use to gather more information? What function is performed by the question, "Is this a homework question/assignment" (lines 6 and 13)?

3. How many times does the librarian provide negative statements on what *can't* be done? What effect does this negativity have on the user?

- Ignoring user self-disclosure or use of humor (If the user makes a joke, even if it is lame!, respond with a ;-) or "ha!")
- Failing to offer reassurance when the user seeks it
- Ignoring parts of questions or additional questions
  - When dealing with a several part question, let the user know that you will take the questions in order.
  - If busy, indicate that you will start with question one, and may have to answer the others by e-mail.
- Condescending to the user or being disconfirming.
- Negative closure
  - Premature closing—Make sure that you have answered all questions.
  - Abrupt ending—Let the user know you are going to close.
  - Disclaimer—Don't indicate that the question is unanswerable or problematic before checking; many things previously unavailable may now be accessible. Provide a good referral if you are unable to answer question.
  - Never ignore cues that the user wants more help, even if it means asking them to wait while you help others.

(© Marie L. Radford and OCLC Online Computer Library Center, Inc., 2008)

One challenge to consortial VR services is the difficulty in answering queries requiring locally based information. Users frequently assume that if, for example, they are in Baltimore clicking into the statewide Maryland AskUsNow! service, that the librarian is also in Baltimore. Because AskUsNow! uses the QuestionPoint service, their questions may be answered in San Francisco or even Australia. In analyzing QuestionPoint live chat transcripts, Radford and Connaway (2005–2008) found that questions about holdings or local procedures answered by the consortium rather than by the local chat service took the longest to answer (16.6 minutes per session, compared to a mean of 12.42 minutes for the entire sample). Nahyun Kwon (2007) found that in a collaborative chat reference service, "local questions were less completely answered compared to non-local, generic questions," and "patrons who ask local questions tend to be less satisfied with the service than the patrons who ask non-local, generic questions." More libraries are posting local information (such as hours of operation) and providing online access to their catalogs (to answer questions like: "Does my local library have this book?" or "How do I get a library card?"). Additionally, local community information is being posted on the open Web (to answer questions such as, "Where can I take English as a second language classes?" or "What local transportation services are available for my elderly mother?" As more local information is posted, this problem might lessen in time. It is a good idea to let users know if you are not in their local region. During the greeting, you can refer to this by saying something like: "Hi there Toronto, how's the weather there today? It is raining here in California." This friendly self-disclosure can build rapport with the user.

6.2.2 Boosting Accuracy in Live Chat Reference

Because live chat enables the close examination of transcripts, it is possible to determine levels of accuracy and ways to improve. Research by Marie L. Radford and Lynn Silipigni Connaway (2009) found that there are some important and relatively easy ways to improve VR accuracy for ready-reference questions. They looked at 850 randomly selected live chat reference transcripts containing 915 reference questions from approximately 500,000 QuestionPoint chat sessions that included consortial, academic, public, and special library users. A close analysis of the 27 percent (243) that were ready-reference questions found that 78 percent (141) of these were answered correctly. Radford and Connaway make the following recommendations to boost accuracy in live chat reference:

1. Answer the specific question asked in ready-reference queries. Accuracy could have been boosted from seventy-eight percent (141) to ninety percent (168) had the librarian confirmed that the Web page provided actually answered the user's question. In the twenty-seven instances of failure, the librarian pushed a general Web site on the broad topic that did not contain the exact information requested.

2. Clarify the question. Just as in FtF reference, understanding the real question boosts accuracy for all types of questions. Make sure that you understand the specific question and not just the general topic before you begin to search. One user typed a chat query requesting information on "diving lessons" for her fifteen-year-old daughter. The librarian assumed that the user meant "scuba diving" and searched for and pushed Web pages on that topic without asking for clarification (e.g., "What type of diving?") After wasting several minutes, the librarian was corrected by the parent who said she was actually intending to ask about "driving lessons."

3. Ask a follow-up question (e.g., "Did this completely answer your question?") This simple step has been shown to further enhance accuracy. Like FtF reference users, VR users are most satisfied when the librarian has asked a follow-up question.

4. Check the Web links. Always take the time to click on and open links before you push them to users. This step saves the user time and frustration. No one wants to be pushed a great-looking resource only to find that the link doesn't work.

5. Answer all the questions asked. For multiple questions, check to make sure that each and every question has been answered before signing off. Transcript analysis revealed that frequently VR librarians overlook a second (or third) question and answer only the first question asked. The librarian may be in a hurry to help other users in the queue, but the user finds it off-putting when obliged to log in again to re-ask the unanswered questions.

A QUICK TIP

Chat "Word Contact"

When typing in live chat or IM reference, you do not need to complete your sentence before hitting send. Finish part of your sentence and then end with the ellipsis (...) to indicate more is coming. For example:

"I'm searching for some information now…" [send]

"Still searching…" [send]

"Hmm, this is taking longer than I thought, can you wait another minute or two?" [send]

Using this "word contact" instead of the FtF "eye contact" is a form of inclusion that can help to reassure users that you haven't disappeared and are working to find information for them. Letting them know that you will take a minute or two will also cut down on "disappearing users" who log off abruptly if they haven't had a quick response or if they think that *you* have disappeared.

Did You Know?

It's not just users who have technical problems with chat software. Librarians do too (Lupien, 2006).

Figure 6.1. What Types of Chat Reference Questions Are They Asking?

The graph shows results from research that examined 850 randomly selected live chat transcripts containing 915 reference questions from approximately 500,000 QuestionPoint chat service sessions from 2005 to 2007. The largest percentage of questions, 32 percent (293), was for subject searches; a surprisingly high 27 percent (243) of the questions were ready-reference.

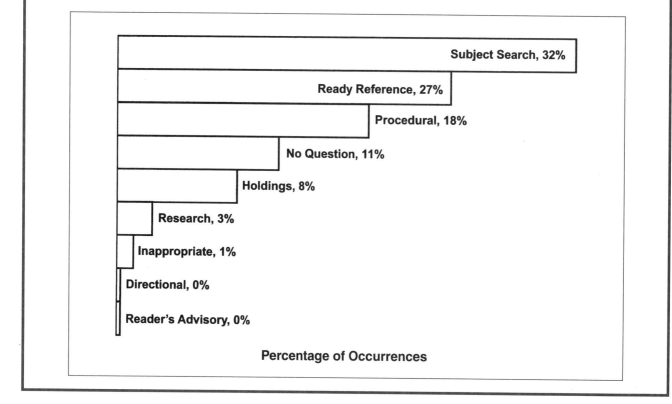

Subject Search, 32%
Ready Reference, 27%
Procedural, 18%
No Question, 11%
Holdings, 8%
Research, 3%
Inappropriate, 1%
Directional, 0%
Reader's Advisory, 0%

Percentage of Occurrences

Chat/Texting Abbreviations and Shortcuts

Because of the fast back-and-forth nature of live chat and texting, users have adopted numerous shortcuts that require fewer keystrokes and may use numbers to replace words or parts of words (e.g., b4 = before). Expect to see shortcuts when you are chatting online with users, especially younger ones. "Chat Speak" has become very common and no doubt will continue to grow in popularity. Feel free to use chat speak yourself in order to mirror their communication style of some of your users. In deciding when less formality is appropriate, take your cue from the user and use your common sense. If the user is formal and precise and doesn't use chat speak, neither should you. Here are some of the most common chat abbreviations:

*	Indicates a correction is being made, usually of a typo (e.g., sarry * sorry)
?	Indicates "I have a question"
asap	As Soon As Possible
b4n	Bye For Now

THREE MOST FREQUENT TYPES OF CHAT QUESTIONS

Here are some verbatim examples from the Seeking Synchronicity Project transcripts for the three most frequent question types:

- Subject Search:
  - "I am interested in hood gown colors that are used for graduate studies."'
  - "Where can I find indo about volcanoes and there eruptions and damage?"
  - "i am doing a project on Norway and later. i am going to the library, wut kind of reference materials can i use to find information
- Ready-reference:
  - "What is the name of the Spanish newspaper that is printed in Hartford? is it el extra news?"
  - "I am doing an biography on actor Brad Pitt, and I would like to know what age he graduated from high school. Could you find that info for me?"
  - "Who was Bentonville, NC named after?"
- Procedural:
  - "Can I get summer long term renewals online? How?"
  - "I tried to access the department of libraries online archives. It asked for my 14-digit barcode on my library card and my pin. I am not sure what my pin is or if I ever was issued one."
  - "Is there a way to look up an obituary listing on line from the Boston Globe in October 2004?"

A QUICK TIP

We Are Not Machines—Show Your Smile

Be sure to put a human face on the description of your VR service. Too often library Web sites emphasize resources, collections, and databases, but the staff members and their crucial work is invisible. Let your users know that a person, not a robot or knowbot, will be answering the questions. Joe Thompson, formerly with the Maryland AskUsNow! statewide VR consortium, encourages librarians to "show your smile" in live chat. Without nonverbal cues to help us do this, we have to use textual representations. One way is to type mood indicators such as <grin> or <g>; another is to type words such as "Ha Ha," or use smileys (aka emoticons). Here are the most frequently used emoticons:

:-) or :)	Basic smiley, used for a pleasant smile or joke.
;-) or ;)	Winking smiley, used for flirtatious and/or sarcastic remark.
:-(or :(	Frowning smiley, used to indicate person is sad, depressed, upset, or did not like last statement.

(From: *The Unofficial Smiley Dictionary*, 2008)

brb	Be Right Back
btw	By The Way
f2f or ftf	Face-To-Face
imho, imo	In My Humble Opinion, In My Opinion
jam	Just A Minute
jw	Just Wondering
k or kk	Okay
l8r	Later
lmho	Laughing My Head Off
lol	Laughing Out Loud
np	No Problem
r u there?	Are you there?
sec	Wait a second
tafn	That's All For Now
ty or thx	Thank You
u, ur	You, Your
w8	Wait

(Adapted from: ComputerUser.com's High-Tech Dictionary, 2001–to date, and Holson, 2008)

A QUICK TIP

Setting Expectations for E-mail

Unlike the case with live chat services, an insomniac still has to wait until the library opens to get an answer with e-mail. Moreover, the message might travel at the speed of light through fiber optic cables, but once it reaches the library a human being has to be assigned the question, find and evaluate the sources, and type out an answer. This problem of mismatch of service and expectations is frequently addressed by having the software send an automatic message to the user saying that you have received the question and will answer within some specified period such as twenty-four hours. Of course, users will then expect their answer or at least a clarifying question within that time limit. The New York Public Library's Web site uses this wording to set e-mail expectations; "We will make every effort to respond to your question within two working days. If we cannot quickly answer your question we will let you know."

6.3 E-mail Reference

Despite the proliferation of synchronous reference services including chat and IM, e-mail reference continues to be extremely popular and the most widely available choice for VR. Most libraries have been offering some kind of e-mail reference since the mid-1990s. Sloan (2006) provides a historical look at the development of e-mail and other forms of VR from their beginnings in the mid-1980s. Initially a service that was used by only a small minority of early adopters, e-reference has established itself firmly as a basic service with wide appeal.

Since the e-mail reference transaction is asynchronous and depends on the back-and-forth exchange of messages, users won't necessarily get an immediate answer. However, if the e-mail comes in when the librarian is checking it, the user may be pleasantly surprised. Lorri Mon (2008), of Florida State University, who has been actively involved as a volunteer for the IPL for several years, noted, "I have in fact answered many e-mail questions the moment they came in, by pasting in a standard answer within seconds. Chat would not be any faster than I was with my e-mail response, [chat] in fact would be considerably longer and more drawn-out."

Many users choose the convenience of e-mail because they can ask their questions when they think of them, at any time of the day or night, without taking the time to make a special trip to the library. As we have seen in Chapter 3, some reference staff have discovered ways of getting rid of users without actually helping them, such as advising them to search the catalog or to browse the shelves (e.g., "Our medical books are over there"). The nature of e-mail reference lowers the risk that a staff member will simply ask, "Have you done a Google search?" rather than finding a specific answer and sending it to the user.

Like live chat and IM VR, e-mail reference offers additional advantages to users with the following characteristics:

- Are shy and uneasy about asking questions in person, or who are too proud to ask.

- Do not speak English well enough to feel comfortable asking questions FtF or by telephone, but read and write English well enough to communicate. Transcription errors are avoided in the answer because the librarian writes the answer down, not the English language learner who may have difficulty hearing and writing down a spoken answer.

- Have constraints on mobility that prevent them from visiting a library in person. This group may well include a number of older users.

- Live at a distance from urban centers and large libraries. This group includes an increasingly large group of distance learners.

- Are members of less economically privileged groups who do not have access to computers at home. Since e-mail is asynchronous, users can check it when they are able to get to a computer.

In addition, some users choose e-mail because they are familiar with the technology, like it, and know what to expect. Live chat can be intimidating for people who have never used IM technology, or for those who lack fast keyboarding skills. Agosto and Hughes-Hassell (2005) found that urban youth are less likely to have continuous access to computers, and therefore choose e-mail much more frequently than do suburban youth.

E-mail reference offers advantages over FtF and live chat services for staff as well:

- When questions arrive electronically, there is more time for thought and reflection.

- Questions can be answered during less busy times or by librarians who are not working at the reference desk.

- It is easier to refer questions to the "resident expert," with the result that the expertise of the entire staff, including subject specialists, can be tapped as needed.

- The workload can be distributed among the staff.

Like live chat, e-mail software can capture transcripts of electronic questions and answers and store them in a database; it is easy to create a record that can be used for research and evaluation of reference services. The e-mail database can be also be used to develop FAQ files, which can anticipate questions that are commonly asked.

The drawbacks to e-mail reference all relate to its asynchronous, text-based technology and are the other side of the same coin:

- The text-based environment of e-mail, like chat and IM, lacks media richness and is impoverished because it strips away both visual and auditory cues (see O'Sullivan, 2000). You can't use eye contact or establish a connection through a welcoming tone of voice. The problem of interpreting the tone of an e-mail exchange is well-known for its role in creating flame wars in listservs. To compensate for the loss of nonverbal information in both e-mail and live chat, people now commonly use emoticons such as smileys :-), or add affect by spelling out facial expressions (e.g., <grin>), by using uppercase or asterisks for emphasis (e.g., DO NOT or *do not*), and by using "chat speak" including alpha or alpha-numeric shortcuts such as LOL for "laughing out loud," or G2G for "got to go" (see the section Chat/Texting Abbreviations and Shortcuts for more examples).

- Deprived of nonverbal cues, you can't tell whether the user is a child or a senior citizen, male or female. You can't see how fashionably the user is dressed, whether the user has a disability, or is member of a visible minority. An advantage is that you will be less likely to jump to conclusions based on assumptions derived from physical appearances. However, you still need to avoid making assumptions based on grammar, writing style, or spelling mistakes. For many topics, you will need to take extra steps to find out about the user's level of literacy and ability to make sense of specialized or technical information. *(continued on p. 215)*

Test Drive the IPL

The Internet Public Library (IPL) began as an experiment in providing virtual public library service on the Internet. It was started in 1995 in a graduate seminar at the University of Michigan School of Information and Library Studies under the direction of Joe Janes. IPL moved to Drexel University's College of Information Science and Technology on January 1, 2007, and now it is developed and maintained by a consortium of colleges and universities with programs in information science. The IPL provides both an e-mail reference service and a collection of free high-quality Web resources. Most of the reference questions the IPL gets are answered by graduate students from Masters in Information and Library Science (MLIS) programs around North America, supplemented by a team of volunteer librarians. Test drive the service at http://ipl.org/div/askus.

1. Ask a question at the IPL (if you haven't already done so) to see what the service is like from a user's point of view.

2. Examine the IPL site closely and become familiar with its resources. These can be very valuable when you are answering e-mail or live chat reference questions because the resources it lists are freely available on the Web and do not require a subscription as do proprietary indexes and full-text journal databases.

Conducting the Reference Interview

ANALYZE THIS REFERENCE TRANSACTION

Case 34: Typical e-mail questions

Bernie Sloan (2001) has provided a list of questions that users have asked in the "Ready for Reference" service, which was a live, 24/7 Web-based reference service piloted by eight academic libraries in the Alliance Library System in Illinois. Here are some of the questions:

- Do you know where I can find Chicago City Directories?
- I would like to find information on Trinidad and Tobago, don't want to use encyclopedias—any suggestions as to where to begin my search?
- Where can I find info about legislation concerning juvenile justice?
- I need sources (that are not magazines) dealing with environmental racism.
- I am giving a talk for a Mother-Daughter Banquet. My theme is "Sharing the Love of Story Across the Generations." I would like to open with reading a children's picture book that depicts the joy and value of grandmothers sharing their stories of life with their daughters and granddaughters. Or I would be interested in knowing some poetry on that topic.
- I need info on early television reporters.
- Where can I find data about the national deer populations over the past few years?
- Information on phentermine.
- I need help finding information on sexual activities among teenagers and young adults.
- Looking for information on Native American families.

Comment: Bernie Sloan (2001) notes, "People working with digital reference projects often discuss the concept of creating logs of questions to use to automate part of the digital reference process. The general idea is that, after a user asks a question, the question is automatically matched against a list of previously-asked questions to see if the question has already been asked and answered. If a match is found, that makes one less question a librarian will need to answer." Caleb Tucker-Raymond, Service Coordinator of L-Net—Oregon's Library Network has developed a database that does just that. When you click on the L-Net link to chat with a librarian, you get a message that gives you an estimate of how long you will have to wait, but also opens a search box that invites users to put their question in to see if it matches their FAQs as follows: "While you wait or before you ask, you can find *answers* to questions that have been asked before or *sites* librarians have used to answer other questions." Caleb Tucker-Raymond (2008) has reported that this new service is mostly geared to children's or YA homework questions, but he expects that the range of questions they can answer in this fashion will expand.

For discussion:

Analyze the user questions listed previously:

1. Do you think there are enough commonalties among these questions to make it feasible to automate the reference process?
2. Compare this list of questions with questions that are asked in person at the reference desk. What differences, if any, do you find?

- Unless you use a well-designed form to encourage users to provide appropriate contextual details about the information need (6.3.2), you are likely to need many back-and-forth e-mail messages. You cannot query the user while you are reading the question. Users who are infrequent e-mail users may take several days or a week to read your message asking for more information. The whole interview process may take considerable time before the question can finally be answered, by which time it might no longer be useful.

- Today's Web environment of speed and immediacy leads some users to have unrealistic expectations about an instantaneous answer. Input of the question can be 24/7, but for the most part, answering is done during normal hours, and usually takes from twenty-four to forty-eight hours.

- Unlike an FtF interview, which is usually completed in one encounter, the e-mail reference transaction is often distributed across a number of separate messages. Software is therefore needed that manages the traffic volume and links all the messages related to the same question, so that they can be read as a single thread or saved in a single folder.

- Providing a typed answer rather than a spoken answer for e-mail reference takes more time and depends on an additional set of skills, including writing skills and the use of correct spelling and grammar. A higher standard is becoming common for e-mail in comparison to the less formal chat sessions. In e-mail, it may take longer for you to type the response than to find the answer in the first place. Sometimes the response involves retyping information from print sources into the reply message. Cutting and pasting from e-resources, including Web URLs, can be done but often requires some editing. Careful and complete identification of the sources used must be included with the reply.

- Since everything has to be typed out, library use instruction is harder to provide via e-mail and may therefore get shortchanged because it might seem like simply too much effort to explain how the information was found and evaluated. Another shortcoming of the service is that it is prone to interruptions of the sort called "system vulnerability" in the literature. As one user put it, "If something is wrong with your e-mail system, then you're in trouble." Sometimes messages just disappear in cyberspace and the user may not receive the answer you have so painstakingly constructed.

What Kinds of E-mail Questions Do Users Ask?

Libraries that have reported on their e-mail service say that the following types of questions are common:

- **Requests for technology instruction**, troubleshooting questions, and questions about the system itself. Such questions often relate

---

A QUICK TIP

More Than a Search Engine
Sometimes users think that VR librarians are like Google or other search engines that will respond instantaneously. To provide helpful service to information seekers at their point of need, it is important go beyond what a search engine can do. On their own, Internet searchers can type a keyword into a search engine. But search engines can't do reference interviews that both present a more human face and help to clarify informational needs. What reference librarians can do (and search engines can't) is help users figure out what they really want to know, and also to establish a warm interpersonal relationship, even in a brief VR encounter. According to Elinor Mills (2006) of CNT News, "While the Web is good for offering quick results from a broad range of sources, which may or may not be trustworthy, librarians can help people get access to more authoritative information and go deeper with their research. . . . " For some people, if the answer isn't in the first few results it might as well not be there,' said Gary Price founding editor of the ResourceShelf blog (http://www.resourceshelf.com/). 'No matter how smart and helpful search engines get, they're never going to replace librarians.'"

to getting access to library resources from outside the library. These questions should be answered in a FAQ Web page which should be prominently displayed so that users can easily find it.

- **Questions on how to cite sources** using approved styles such as *The Chicago Manual of Style*, or those of the American Psychological Association (APA) or the Modern Languages Association (MLA). These are questions that the FAQ Web page can answer by providing links to the style guide sites.

- **Quick short-answer questions.** Many libraries have guidelines that ask users to limit their queries to short answers, and call or come in for more complex ones; other services do not stipulate what types of queries are permitted. See below for more on the "quick, short answer" problem.

- **Research questions.** Academic libraries often receive this kind of question. If these questions become too complex, the user is sometimes asked to make an appointment to meet with a librarian subject specialist. However, given the enormous expansion of courses offered to distance learners, academic libraries have a growing responsibility to provide reference service for research questions to users who cannot come to the library in person.

- **Genealogy questions.** Public libraries receive many genealogy questions from online users who are tracking down every lead in order to construct their family tree.

If you provide several sample questions for each of the categories, your users might better understand what kinds of questions are okay to ask from the perspective of the library system. These sample questions can be made accessible through a link from your service description. As many libraries have found, the strategy of saying, "We answer only ready-reference questions," or "We answer only quick short-answer questions" doesn't work. Who but a librarian knows what a "ready-reference question" is anyway? Moreover, as we have seen, even librarians often don't know in advance if a question is easy or difficult. Library users are even less likely to know what is quick and ready, and what's slow and difficult to find. Of course, as we have been saying throughout this book, the librarian doesn't fully know what kind of question it is until *after* a good reference interview has happened.

6.3.1 The E-mail Reference Interview

The reference interviewing skills discussed in Chapters 2 and 3 apply just as much in the digital environment as they do in FtF encounters. The goal does not change just because you are working through e-mail. You still need to establish a welcoming environment, make contact with the user, find out what the user wants to know, link the user to the system, and confirm that the answer provided is actually what was wanted. The challenge is to find a way to provide these standard functions in the text-based asynchronous environment of e-mail.

The key to conducting a successful e-mail interview is to take into account the bias of the medium. In FtF, live chat reference, or phone reference encounters—even very short ones—there is a good deal of turn-taking, but frequent turn-taking does not increase the total length of the transaction. Turns are often short, especially when minimal encouragers are used such as "umn-hmm," or "That's interesting" (2.4.4), and the user's responses are immediate. But with the e-mail interview, turn-taking introduces delays, sometimes up to several days to a week, depending on how frequently users monitor their e-mail. The literature on e-reference refers to this phenomenon as "high dialogue penalties." Quite simply, the fewer e-mail exchanges needed to clarify the real question, the faster the answer can be provided and the transaction completed. Moreover, when the negotiation of the question is stretched out over a prolonged series of e-mails, reference staff has increased work of linking the chain of messages and rereading earlier messages unless their software does this.

Many libraries have discovered that the secret to reducing turn-taking and its accompanying high dialogue penalties is to develop a form that structures the information provided by the user along the lines needed by the staff member to answer the question. The purpose of a good e-mail reference form is to provide a framework in which the user is prompted to take many turns at once. This means that the standard skills of welcoming the user, asking open and sense-making questions, using encouragers, and avoiding premature diagnosis all need to be incorporated into the form itself. The equivalent of turn-taking in the reference interview is achieved through the series of well-designed questions on the form. Whereas the FtF interview takes place as a series of exchanges extended in time, the questions on the form are extended in space.

Here are some tips to facilitate the e-mail reference interview:

- Provide a reference question form that users can access from the library Web page. If they e-mail you directly, use a standard response explaining why they will get a more helpful answer if they fill out the form. Your reply should include a description of the service and a link to the form.

- For questions that arrive when the library is closed, the software should be designed to send an automatic response saying, in effect, "Thank you for your electronic reference question. We will get back to you within 24–48 hours."

- Because you are using e-mail, you can't see those uncertain looks or signs of discouragement or impatience. All the messages that the user receives—from the initial form to the automatic response on receipt of the question to your individualized answer—must be friendly and welcome further communication.

- On the electronic form, ask the user to double check their e-mail address. Explain why.

- In your first individualized reply, acknowledge the question by restating what you understand the user has asked for (see 2.4.3).

Did You Know?
Participating in the Library Visit Study at The University of Western Ontario, 150 MLIS students asked questions of chat and e-mail services at public and academic libraries over a five-year period (2003–2007). Seventy-four students used public libraries and seventy-six used academic libraries. While most students (112) used e-mail services, only thirty-eight used chat services. Analysis of use and type of forms encountered by students shows that 12.7 percent of all libraries used no e-mail reference form at all, while only 9.3 percent of all libraries used a detailed form (see 6.3.2). Detailed forms were used at almost the same rate by academic (9.2 percent) and public (9.5 percent) institutions. Most libraries (78 percent) used a minimal form, with public libraries (79.7 percent) slightly more likely than academic libraries (76 percent) to use a minimal form. Academic libraries were more likely than public libraries to use no form at all, thus 14.5 percent of academic libraries versus 10.8 percent of public libraries assumed that users were able to provide sufficient information about their questions without any guidance or probing by the library. Only 12.5 percent of e-mail services used a detailed form, and none of the chat services did. Ten percent of e-mail services and 21 percent of chat services used no forms at all.

Brush Up on Clarity and Brevity of Your Writing

In e-mail VR, a crucial skill is being able to write clearly in an appropriate style that is correct but not too formal. In your answer, you need to start with a friendly greeting, summarize your understanding of the user's question, provide a concise answer, include sources, and end with a follow-up inviting the user to get back to you if the answer was incomplete.

Did You Know?

Describing the early days of the Internet Public Library reference service, Nettie Lagace (1998) reported that when users presented incomplete statements of their informational need, librarians preferred to "send answers 'fast,' pulling together a package of material that might, or might not, be what the user needs, bundling it in an e-mail message, and sending it." However, the temptation to bypass the reference interview and proceed by guesswork is no more likely to work in the electronic environment than it does in FtF encounters.

If your form has been well-designed, you should be able to send some kind of answer in your first reply. But even with the best of forms, often some crucial piece of information will be missing. Supposing the user has said, "I am working on a sociology paper that needs references for the immigration patterns of Welsh immigrants 1870s–1890s. Any suggestions?" Your response might acknowledge the question by saying, "I understand that you want information on immigration patterns of Welsh immigrants 1870s–1890s. I have assumed that you are specifically interested in the pattern of immigration from Wales to the United States. Here are the URLs for two sites that provide information on this (be sure to name the sites and indicate how to find the information). If this information isn't helpful or you want Welsh emigration or immigration in general, please let me know what specifically is missing that you still need to know about."

- Suggest that users phrase their request in their own words. Encourage them to give some kind of context for the search (e.g., "It's often helpful if you tell me a little bit about how you plan to use this information so that I can find the most helpful materials"). You don't want to spend a long time looking for the exact, most up-to-date figures on literacy in Saudi Arabia when all they want to know is whether or not more than fifty percent of the population can read.

- Use inclusion (4.1.1) right on the form itself to explain to the users why you are asking for certain kind of information.

- Find out what the real question is before you try to answer it. A well-designed form should eliminate many of the too-general initial questions. (e.g., an actual e-mail question to a military academy library was "I need information about World War II.") But if the user's initial question is still unclear or too broad, there is no point in taking a scatter-gun approach to providing an answer, barraging the user with information in the hope that somehow some of it will be relevant. This approach doesn't work in FtF reference, and it won't work in the digital environment. It is better to respond with a small amount of information plus a request for clarification. Make sure that you ask in the same e-mail *all* the questions that you need to get answered.

- Always include a follow-up question (4.1.3) with your response such as: "If this answer isn't helpful, please e-mail us again."

- Keep back and forth messaging to a minimum. If you find that routinely you need to send multiple messages before you understand the question, analyze the exchanges to pinpoint the problem. Is your library's form not working as well as it should?

- Make sure your library's list of FAQs is updated regularly and easily located on the Web site.

- Always end by thanking the user for the question and inviting him/her to return again when the need arises.

SOME SAMPLE SCRIPTS FOR E-MAIL

For referring users to the library FAQ:

You can find the answer to your question on the library FAQ page. The URL is www.xxx.com If you need additional information, please let us know specifically what is missing that you still need to know. That way we can help you better. For more information, you can also consult the XX library reference service in person or by telephone [provide telephone reference number].

For acknowledging the question:

This is to let you know that we got your question on topic X and will be getting back to you within one working day. Thanks for contacting the "Ask a Librarian" service of the Y Library.

For negotiating the question:

I'm not familiar with X. What else can you tell me about this subject?

What specifically would you like to know about X?

It would help me locate exactly what you need if you could tell me how you plan to use this information.

For providing an answer:

Thank you for using [name of service]. We hope the following information will help you.

For follow-up:

If this information is not what you need, please let us know what specifically is missing so that we can help you further.

No matter how fast you type, you will feel that it's not fast enough. Here is where pre-formatted scripts come in. They work like boiler-plate in a lawyer's pre-formatted form covering a situation that frequently recurs in a law practice. You can format these messages in advance and send them to your users as needed. But you need to be careful when using a script that it is a relevant response and not just another way of getting rid of the user.

EXERCISE

Anthropological Strangeness

This exercise is for librarians who are engaged in providing VR. Imagine that you are an anthropologist from Mars who is studying the communication that takes place during a VR exchange. Select at random three reference questions received at your information service. Examine all the messages sent to each of these three users.

- From the point of view that you have adopted of outsider to the library system, what do you notice about the nature of the communication exchange?
- What, if anything, does this exercise suggest about ways to improve communication with users?

Designing Space

Naturally you want your Web pages to be attractive, uncluttered, easy-to-read, with clear instructions. But how do you achieve this? Read Edward Tufte, the acknowledged authority on the visual display of information. He has written a dazzling series of books that set out principles for making information accessible to users in data rich displays that are uncluttered. In his fourth book, *Visual Explanations* (Tufte, 1997: 146–150), he turns his attention to what's wrong with Web pages: interfaces based on a tedious series of binary choices; interfaces featuring clunky icons that require labels ("why won't just the words do?" he asks); pages that are too cluttered with too many pixels devoted to big buttons having no informational value, or to distracting animations. Tufte recommends an evaluation of an interface by calculating the proportion of space on the screen devoted to informational content in comparison with the space devoted to computer administration, or system debris, or distracting analogies.

6.3.2 Using Forms

In the evolution of e-mail reference service, the first stage was often to provide a simple "mail to" e-mail address. The users sent a question to the reference department using the regular e-mail message space. The main drawback of such a primitive system is that online users resemble FtF users: unless prompted, they do not provide enough information about themselves or about the question (1.4). While e-reference users probably won't say, "I need everything on transportation," they still tend to ask initial questions that are too broad. As we have been emphasizing throughout this book, most users do not understand what information librarians need to know in order to answer their question. The user's mental model of how bricks-and-mortar libraries work is apt to be sketchy; in the case of e-reference, users may think that a computer is finding the answer for them. Hence the next stage is to provide a form that substitutes for the reference interview by structuring the information so that the librarian can understand what the user really wants to know. A well-structured form helps cut down on back-and-forth e-mail exchanges that can result when the librarian needs more information in order to answer the question, exchanges which often add to user frustration.

If you design your own form or adapt one used in another library, you need to be even more conscious of the difference between a systems-based approach and a user-based approach than you are in the FtF reference interview. Unfortunately, many forms consist almost entirely of questions that relate to system requirements. Often the e-reference form requests substantial demographic information, and asks for limitations by geographic area, language, time period of published sources, and format of the preferred answer. It then prompts the user by saying something like, "In the box below describe the topic of your search." Some forms provide even less direction to the user on what information to provide about the information need, being content to provide a box with a heading like "Your question?" or "Your message?" or "Type your question."

HOW WELL WELL-DESIGNED FORMS ASSIST USERS

Here are some comments from participants in the Library Visit Study (2006, 2007):

- The Web form is a forum or venue for the patron and the librarian to conduct question negotiations that can yield quality answers.

- By listing possible details to include, the librarian gives the user some vocabulary with which to speak.

- The instructions provide the user with some guidance as to what is appropriate in a virtual reference question, while providing the library with the essential information to begin a search on the topic of concern.

- I was surprised at the manner in which these forms assist the users—on how best to design their request for information in order to properly arm the librarian to return a relevant answer for them.

(Library Visit Study)

In describing the early years of the Internet Public Library (IPL) reference service, Nettie Lagace (1998) reported that many questions to the IPL consisted of "two or three keywords, with few clues specifying information." This problem, she said, prompted a revision of the form. The IPL e-mail form has since gone through several additional revisions.

A well-designed form will eliminate problems before they occur and provide the right framework for finding out what the user really wants to know. The questions you ask will vary somewhat by type of library, but in all libraries the form needs to ask questions that tap the situation, gaps, and uses that are the context for the query. The core of the form should ask about the context of the user's question, what the user wants to know about the topic, and how the requested information will be used. Whether you are redesigning your library's already existing form, are designing the form from scratch, or are using another library's form as a model, there are some basic rules of that can help you. The tips below will help you evaluate good and bad forms:

Some Tips for Creating Question Forms

- **Use one standard form throughout the system.** Some academic libraries have forms for each departmental library in the system, but students are often unaware of how the library system works and might choose an inappropriate library for their question. Standard forms can be rerouted to any library or subject librarian. In the Library Visit Study, one library had a well-designed form when the user clicked on "Ask a Librarian" and an almost useless minimal e-mail form that popped up during the hours that the chat service was not staffed. The users who find both forms are confused because they don't know which one to use.

- **Name the form.** You can simply extend the name of the service (e.g., "Ask a Librarian Question Form"). By giving the form a name, you can more easily direct users to it or refer to it when responding to their questions.

- **Provide essential instructions and advice** for completing the form on the form itself. Don't make the user click to another page to get necessary information. Be concise.

- **Keep the form clean, functional, typographically simple, and easy to read.** Don't use busy wallpaper designs in the background or animated flash graphics that compete for the reader's attention. These irritating bugaboos also make the Web page take longer to download.

- **Use boxes for each part of your form**, which the user fills in. Indicate clearly which boxes are *not* optional, such as the address to which they want the answer sent. Some software provides the capacity to prevent the user from submitting the form until the required boxes are filled in.

- **Keep the form as short as possible** so that it doesn't take so long to fill out that it becomes a formidable barrier to users. Look at every question on the form and ask yourself, "Why do I need to know that?" If the answer is, "Well, I'm not sure but Library X's form asks

A QUICK TIP

If You Know

Avoid asking users for information that they are ill-equipped to give you. For example, we dislike the question "If you know the subject, enter it here" because this actually requires that users know the LC subject heading verbatim, which they seldom do. Another problematic request is, "Please select the most appropriate library for your question," with a list such as the Betty and Billy Blaisdell Library, the Woolley Business Library, the Stevenson Library, and so on.

EXERCISE

Evaluating Your E-mail Reference Form

Students participating in the Library Visit Study at The University of Western Ontario evaluated e-reference forms used in a range of public and academic libraries over a five year period (2003–2007). Use their criteria to evaluate the e-mail reference form in your library or a library nearby. The students identified a good form as one that asks questions designed to get answers to the following:

- **Eligibility:** The "who" and "where" questions that allow the library to determine whether the user is eligible to use this service and to provide a context for the question.
- **History of the question:** What have you done so far? What is the most useful source you have found so far?
- **Gaps:** What would you like to find out? Describe your interest in the topic.
- **Uses:** How do you plan to use this information?
- **Features of the perfect answer:** For example, "The perfect answer would be an e-mail address and/or telephone number for an expert on topic X that I could contact," "The perfect answer would be an introduction to topic X written for non-specialists," or "The perfect answer would be a list of the best Web sites on topic X."
- **Time constraints:** What is your deadline for a reply?

for this and so maybe we should ask for it too," then delete it. Be equally ruthless with all that demographic information that routinely gets added. You will need some way of screening users, if your service policy puts restrictions on the types of users eligible to receive the service, but if you don't plan to use the information for anything, don't ask it. Demographic information doesn't help you understand what the user wants to know. On the other hand, a minimalist form (e.g., one that only requests name, e-mail address, the question) puts all of the responsibility on the user to formulate his question in such a way that anybody can understand exactly what he wants to know.

- **Aim for a form that doesn't take more than one screen**, if possible. The form should not look like a census form that will take half-an-hour to fill out. With a compact form, you and the user can see the whole thing at once and recognize immediately that necessary information has been left out. One Library Visit Study participant commented about a too-long form, "By the time I finished reading the form, I was dissuaded from using it simply for its length and degree of knowledge and willingness anticipated in providing responses for each [of thirteen boxes]."

- **After you have designed the form, analyze it.** How many of your questions are system-based questions in comparison with questions that ask users to describe the answer wanted in their own words? Does the form include questions that are unnecessary for providing relevant answers, but have been included anyway so that you can

EXERCISE

Comparing in Person, Phone, E-mail, and Live Chat Reference
This exercise will give you some experience with a variety of types of reference interactions from the user perspective.

- Come up with a reference question that is meaningful to you. Choose four different libraries having a reference department or librarian-staffed VRS. Live chat and e-mail VRS are very easy to find on the Web. If you like, you can use the IPL for the e-mail format and the Library of Congress (LOC) "Ask a Librarian" site for live chat. The LOC service is freely open to all, but be aware that this service has limited hours and days of availability. Ask the same question four times (one time at each library) as a "surrogate user" in four different ways: in person, by phone, by e-mail, and by chat. If your question is a real question, then you are ethically entitled to do this, and you will be able to evaluate the helpfulness of the answers received in terms of your own real-life situation.

- Analyze each interaction by asking yourself the following questions:
  - Are all the components of a good reference interview present in each format?
  - How do the formats compare in efficiency (e.g. did you get the correct answer in a reasonable time frame)?
  - How do the formats compare in the quality of the interpersonal interaction (e.g., how did the interaction make you feel about the way the librarian treated you as a user)?
  - Which format did you like the most and why?
  - What are the strengths/weakness of the different modes?
  - How did phone, chat and e-mail encounters compare to FtF reference?
  - Were you satisfied with each service and would you use it again?
  - What recommendations for heads of reference departments would you make, based on your experiences?
  - What else did you learn from this exercise?

A QUICK TIP

We're Not Nosy; It's Our Job

When designing your form, adapt best practices. A good place to start is the Internet Public Library (IPL) reference question form (**http://www.ipl.org/div/askus**) which we think is one of the best. One big strength of this form is that it asks the sense-making question "How will you use this information?" followed by this explanation: "understanding the context and scope of your information needs helps us to deliver an answer that you will find useful."

easily create reports that break down users by category (e.g., male/female; undergraduate/graduate student/staff/faculty)? Try to rewrite the system-based questions or delete them.

- **Devote your greatest attention to refining the part of your form that elicits the information needed.** This part is the electronic equivalent of the reference interview. A box that says, "Type your question here" is *not* good enough. You can help the user understand what kinds of details you need by providing a link to an example of a form that has been filled out in a way that makes the context of the question clear.

- **Provide a link to sample questions that list examples of the types of questions that can (and cannot) be answered.** But don't do this unless you are quite sure that you would *never* answer such a question. On the other hand, simply listing types of questions, without examples, might discourage users who are unsure if their question is *allowed* to be answered.

- **Test your form by recruiting a novice user to help you.** Get the user to try filling out the form to ask a question, while you observe difficulties, if any. Revise and test again.

- **Acknowledge that you have received the question and will respond within a specified time period.** After the user has clicked the submit or send button, be sure that your service responds automatically with a clearly worded message indicating that you have received the question and will respond within a specified time period.

- **Don't limit your FAQ page to facts about the system.** You can eliminate the need for some routine questions by providing the answers to Frequently Asked Questions as well.

- **Address privacy concerns** by letting the user know what happens to the data after the question has been answered. On the form itself and/or in the description of the service, you can include a button (e.g., "Concerned about privacy?" or "Policy on privacy") that opens to the explanation.

6.4   Trends in Virtual Reference

Newer VR initiatives are radically changing reference through the use of new technological developments such as Web 2.0, appearance of virtual 3-D worlds, cell phone use that has enabled text messaging, and the evolution of social networking sites such as Facebook. Driven by librarians' desires to meet today's users (especially younger ones and distance learners) where they live (in cyberspace), a growing number of libraries are experimenting with new reference configurations. Increasingly the traditional reference desk is augmented by a hybrid suite of online options making this an exciting time for reference departments. Marie L. Radford (2009, 108–110) notes that "rapid and remarkable advances are taking place in a variety of library settings across the United States and beyond. These changes involve the merging and morphing of a large range of reference modes." Some of these trends and new initiatives are discussed in the following section.

6.4.1   Merging and Crossover of Virtual Reference Modes

One major trend in reference services is the merging and crossover of reference modes. In the FtF reference encounter, the interaction traditionally began and ended at the reference desk. Now it is common for an encounter to begin in one format, perhaps live chat, and continue by e-mail, phone, or even FtF. This trend is prompting libraries to re-examine the ways in which the encounter is conceptualized and enacted. It also requires rethinking how reference statistics are counted.

Joe Janes (2003) of the University of Washington has advocated that we embrace the idea that "It's all reference!" and treat all the different types of reference services as a unified whole. This means that even the solo librarian in a small library no longer has to work alone and be expected to know the answer for every question. Help is now available through a variety of modes from librarian colleagues and other experts. The first recourse should be the colleague in the next office. But beyond the available people in your own building, you can call others when needed (or e-mail, chat, IM, text, Tweet, etc., if you prefer). For example, one librarian in the middle of a live chat encounter reported using the phone to go the extra mile in an interview conducted for the Seeking Synchronicity Project:

> Someone needed to know if a library had a particular volume of a journal. . . . the first thing I did was go to the library's catalog and look there, and it turned out that the information was not there, and then I just kind of picked up the phone and called that library and found the information that way. And sometimes I feel that it isn't all or nothing, it doesn't have to be completely online. I could have just looked up the phone number and given it to them, but I went the extra part to call it for them and make them a satisfied customer!

This option of mixing modes is not always possible, depending on the time of day when the chat inquiry arrives or whether there is a queue. Many times, however, it is possible and may be quicker than doing a long (possibly fruitless) search on your own. Be sure to practice inclusion by letting the chat user know what you are doing, and how much time you estimate that it will take. Users are generally patient when they know you are working to get them the best possible answer (e.g., "I'm going to look in the *Academic Search Premier* journal index to see if I can find an article on your topic. This will probably take a few minutes. Can you wait?").

As new technological developments expand the range of VRS modes available, greater collaboration and increasing involvement in VR consortia can be expected. Future software enhancements will result in routing systems that will allow the referral of the more difficult questions to subject experts with specialized skills. Users are generally willing to wait for quality answers from subject specialists if you give them the option (Radford and Connaway, 2005–2008).

6.4.2 Emerging Virtual Reference Initiatives

The explosion in the popularity of cell phones and other portable handheld devices (such as Palm Pilots and other PDAs, and Blackberrys) is transforming communication patterns. "What's old is new again," with telephone reference service returning as an important mode (5.2). A growing number of libraries are implementing reference services that use the platform of SMS (Short Message Service) or phone text messaging. Present text-messaging technology allows for short, quick encounters. SMS is already being used to send URLs, give directions, and answer quick questions. These reference interactions may start as text messages and, if they are complex, may crossover to a phone call, e-mail or FtF visit.

Did You Know?
Diane Granfield and Mark Robertson (2008, 51) used surveys and focus groups to explore the help-seeking preferences of students at two large urban universities in Toronto. They found that VR users considered these services to be significant and that VR has a special appeal to graduate students who are more likely to be working outside of the library building. Granfield and Robertson list these implications for planning of academic reference services:

- Virtual reference services should not be staffed by scaling back at the physical reference desk. The reference desk remains an important and prominent service even for those users who are already exposed to VR services.

- Libraries should respect and accommodate the use of VR within library facilities. VR users consider VR an important service point even from within campus libraries.

- VR services need to be promoted more heavily to reference desk users. These users do not generally seem to be very aware of the option of using VR when off campus.

- VR services need to be promoted more heavily to graduate students. VR seems to accommodate the behavior of graduate students who tend to work outside of the library.

TEXT MESSAGING AT HINSDALE PUBLIC LIBRARY

Hinsdale Public Library (HPL) in Illinois has been doing IM reference since the summer of 2006. With IM service gradually growing in popularity, the library then added text messaging in July of 2008. Mike Oetting, reference librarian at HPL, had discovered on a blog posting instructions for using the AOL (America Online) gateway. These instructions made it possible to offer text-messaging reference as an adjunct to IM reference at no cost to the library. In a phone interview in September of 2008, Mike Oetting said that HPL was excited to embrace new ways to reach library users and is continuing to adopt new technology. The HPL Web site offers the following easy instructions and examples of questions that are appropriate for this mode. HPL invites all types of questions, but does have a caveat for more complex questions:

askHPL via SMS text messaging

Alternatively, you can text us your question from a cell phone. Just...start your question with "askhpl:" For example;

askhpl: is the book Into the Wild by Krakauer in the library?

askhpl: when does the library close on Saturday?

What kind of questions can I send to ASK HPL?

Any question that you might ask at the library. If it is a very complex question, we recommend that you come to the library in person or call us. (Hinsdale Public Library)

This wording is reassuring and welcomes all types of questions but recommends alternatives if the question is complicated. Software is currently being used by libraries that converts reference text messages to e-mail and back again for easier typing and cutting and pasting of URLs. Future technological developments (including more cell phones with QWERTY keyboards) will surely result in more advocates for reference service by text messaging.

(From: *Library Success—A Best Practices Wiki*)

The enormous popularity and rapid spread of texting for the younger generation means that these services will grow. According to *Library Success: A Best Practices Wiki*, text-messaging reference services are being offered at all types of libraries throughout the world. In the United States, public libraries offering the service include the Orange County Library System in Florida and Hinsdale Public Library in Illinois; academic libraries providing text-messaging reference services include Yale Science Libraries in New Haven CT and the library at American University in Washington DC. The Krupp Library at Bryant University, Rhode Island, launched its text-messaging (SMS) service in September of 2007. With active marketing and promotion to their students, they received 420 SMS reference queries in the fall semester ending in December 2008.

What kind of SMS queries did the Krupp Library get? According to Kohl and Keating (2008: 106), "Most questions that we received were academic or ready-reference questions." Here is a sample:

"I'm looking for the case *Brady v. Brown, 51f. 3d 810* can you help me find it?"

"I'm writing a paper on Congress. Could you please tell me the percentage of the Senate that needs to vote yes for a bill to get passed?"

"I have to write a paper on phytoremediation. Where is a good place to start looking. I want to prove or disprove that with phytoremediation we can remove toxins from soil to have a positive impact on the surrounding ecosystems."

Kohl and Keating (2008) are advocates for SMS as an outreach tool that adds to the array of services available. They note, "By choosing to text message with our users, we offer further proof that librarians are current, relevant, indispensible—and it doesn't hurt if they think we are hip too" (p. 118).

The growing Web 2.0 suite of applications have opened up other new models for reference services which tap into younger users' interest in social networking sites (SNS), such as MySpace (www.myspace.com/) or Facebook (www.facebook.com/) or in 3-D worlds such as Second Life (http://secondlife.com/). *American Libraries* reported in September of 2008 that Facebook is the fastest growing and largest social network in the world "with a 153 percent increase in unique visitors in June 2008 over June 2007. . . . Social networks received more than half a billion unique visits in June 2008, up 25 percent from the year before" ("Facebook Fastest-Growing Network," 2008, 32). MySpace was ranked second with 117 million visitors, but had a much smaller growth rate of 3 percent. The enormous popularity of these sites has encouraged many libraries, especially academic institutions, to host Facebook or MySpace pages, including Penn State University, New York University, and Brooklyn College. Through these social networking sites, reference information can be pushed to young users. The reference encounter in these venues is similar to the e-mail reference encounter and requires similar interview skills.

Future growth can be expected in avatar-based reference in virtual worlds such as Second Life (SL), which has been in existence since 2003. Many universities have rented space in SL and constructed islands for development of academic applications using avatars. Avatars are 3-D computer representations of people that can move around and speak to one another using chat text. In 2006, Kitty Pope, Barbara Galik, Lori Bell, and other staff from the Alliance Library System, a consortium of 259 Illinois libraries, began an experimentation and exploration of library and reference services within SL. In 2007, approximately 200 SL volunteer reference librarians handled 6,769 reference queries from avatars on Information Island. The majority of questions received at this virtual service desk were about how to navigate in SL. Newbie avatars frequently get lost or disoriented and there is no "help desk" in SL. The volunteer librarians initially used QuestionPoint, OCLC software to chat back and forth with users' avatars that "walked" up to the service desk so that the reference interview on Info Island is similar to IM or live chat.

What kinds of reference questions are being asked in Second Life? At the Reference Desk on Information Island in Second Life, both e-mail

Did You Know?

In 2006, Laurie Charnigo and Paula Barnett-Ellis surveyed 126 academic librarians regarding their perceptions and attitudes toward Facebook. They found that 114 of the 126 librarians surveyed were aware of the "Facebook phenomenon." Although "some librarians were excited about the possibilities of Facebook, the majority" (54 percent) "appeared to consider Facebook outside the purview of professional librarianship" (Charnigo and Barnett-Ellis, 2007, 23). They conclude, "By exploring popular new types of Internet services such as Facebook instead of quickly dismissing them as irrelevant to librarianship, we might learn new ways to reach out and communicate better with a larger segment of our users" (31).

Did You Know?
A post to the Digital Reference listserv advertised a non-credit course entitled the "Virtual World Librarianship Course." The course promised to be a "hands-on course that will introduce you to providing reference services and building collections and exhibits in Second Life, to planning programs and events, and to the skills needed for the twenty-first-century librarian in a virtual world." The course takes place on Info Island in Second Life (since that time, Info Island has expanded into Info Continent.) Do you think the substantial learning curve is worth the payoff for the investment?

and live chat reference help are available to people whose avatars come to the desk. While most questions asked regard how to maneuver around Info Island or Second Life itself, or how to find events to attend in SL, regular reference questions are also asked. Here are verbatim sample e-mail questions with the answers provided by the Second Life reference desk volunteer librarians.

Example 1

SL User: I seem to be all on my own on this island; how can I get to a more populated area please?

SL Librarian: Hello. Are you new? We have many events which you can check on the event calendar at www.secondlife.com by logging in and selecting events from the drop down menu. We also have many more people on at night than during the day. Also if you go to your search tab at the bottom and open it up at the top you will see a list of the most popular places. If you tell me what kinds of things you are looking for, I would be glad to point you to places, or add you to the Second Life library list where you will get an update on our activities. I hope this helps. Thank you for stopping by.

Example 2

SL User: Thanks in advance for your help and groundbreaking work on Second Life. I would like to understand the ethnic composition of the Pacific U.S. states including Alaska on a per state basis as part of a consumer product research study for employee benefits. Ideally it would be great to know the ethnicity, ages, marital status and sex along with employment status. By employment I am very interested to know if there is an appreciable difference in kind of employment by ethnicity. Example would be if one group tended to work in small business and another in big business. This would affect the kind of benefits they would be likely to be eligible for.

SL Librarian: Hi. The best resource for the information that you are looking for would be the U.S. Census. You can find very detailed information on most of the areas that you are looking for at: http://www.census.gov/population/www/index.html.

(Examples courtesy of QuestionPoint, OCLC Online Computer Library Center, Inc. and Second Life Information Island Reference)

Some librarians, such as those at Penn State University, are experimenting with SL reference services. McMaster University Library in Hamilton Canada initiated a reference pilot study from May 1–July 31, 2007 to see if reference service providers in SL required "onerous" staff training. They found that SL reference was very similar to FtF encounters and that "a reference interview is still required to assist users" (Buckland and Godfrey, 2008, 8). They also found that interaction is enhanced by gesture and images that are lacking in text-based VR and by the anonymity of avatars that "allows individuals the freedom to ask questions without fear or embarrassment" (p. 8). If, as expected, the technology evolves to include Voice Over Internet Protocol (VOIP), information provision in SL will approach more closely the FtF mode.

Jack M. Maness (2006) discusses integrating Web 2.0 technologies into library reference services to "deliver personalized information systems to students and scholars" (p. 139). Other Web 2.0 applications include: streaming media, blogs, wikis, photosharing services, gaming, vod and podcasting. He believes that these technologies, which are evolving rapidly, will make library services more user-centered. He notes, "Almost certainly the time will soon come when Web reference is nearly indistinguishable from face-to-face reference" (p. 141).

The reference encounter in virtual environments is a likely candidate for staff training and continuing education. While true that the basic principles of the virtual reference interview are surprisingly similar to the FtF interview, there are significant differences that must be mastered.

6.5 Annotated References

6.5.1 Bibliographies and Discussion Groups

Library Success: A Best Practices Wiki. Available www.libsuccess.org (accessed September 22, 2008). According to the introduction section of this site's home page, "This wiki was created to be a one-stop shop for great ideas and information for all types of librarians. All over the world, librarians are developing successful programs and doing innovative things with technology that no one outside of their library knows about. There are lots of great blogs out there sharing information about the profession, but there is no one place where all of this information is collected and organized." This wiki provides lists of U.S. and worldwide libraries that use IM, SMS, Skype and other technologies for reference (see Reference#Libraries_Offering_SMS_Reference_Services). This interactive site encourages all interested parties to join the community and to add to the wiki.

Reference Renaissance Conference Web Site. Available: www.bcr.org/referencerenaissance (accessed October 20, 2008). Includes handouts and presentations for most of the sessions. Print proceedings will be edited by Marie L. Radford and R. David Lankes and published by Neal-Schuman in 2009.

Virtual Reference Bibliography. 2009. Available: http://vrbib.rutgers.edu (accessed April 8, 2009). Hosted by Rutgers University and directed by Marie L. Radford, this site continues the digital reference services bibliography maintained from 2000 to 2004 by Bernie Sloan. It contains over 700 entries from the original bibliography plus over 200 new items published from 2004 to the present—all searchable.

6.5.2 Virtual Reference

Abels, Eileen G. 1996. "The E-mail Reference Interview." *RQ* 35, no 3 (spring): 345–358. Suggests a systematic approach to interviewing remote clients and provides a model for the e-mail interview, including a search request form to initiate the process.

Agosto, Denise E., and Sandra Hughes-Hassell. 2005. "People, Places, and Questions: An Investigation of the Everyday Life Information-seeking

Did You Know?

"Slam the Boards" is a movement by librarians, led by Bill Pardue of Arlington Heights Memorial Library in Illinois. It is an attempt, says Pardue, to get reference librarians to provide answers on popular "Answer Board" sites like Yahoo Answers, WikiAnswers, AskVille, etc. We also make it clear that the questions have been answered by librarians. This gives us the opportunity to demonstrate our question-answering skills to users who may not realize that librarians provide reference services." Slam the Boards has been happening on the tenth of every month beginning in September 2007.

(Answer Board Librarians)

Behaviors of Urban Young Adults." *Library & Information Science Research* 27, no. 2: 141–163.

Answer Board Librarians "Slam the Boards!" Available: http://answerboards .wetpaint.com/page/Slam+the+Boards!?t=anon (accessed October 20, 2008).

Arnold, Julie, and Neal Kaske. 2005. "Evaluating the Quality of a Chat Service." *portal: Libraries and the Academy* 5, no. 2: 177–193. Available from Project Muse: http://muse.jhu.edu/journals/portal_libraries_and_the_ academy/v005/5.2arnold.html (accessed December 19, 2008). Quantitative study of a university chat reference service found that correct answers occurred 92 percent overall.

Baruch College of the City of New York. Newman Library. Ask-a-Librarian. Frequently Asked Questions about E-mail Reference. Available: http:// newman.baruch.cuny.edu/help/faqs_email.html#answer_01 (accessed September 22, 2008).

Bolan, Kimberly, Meg Canada, and Rob Cullin. 2007. "Web, Library, and Teen Services 2.0." *Young Adult Library Services* 5, no. 2: 40–43.

Bromberg, Peter. 2003. "Managing a Statewide Virtual Reference Service: How QandANJ Works." *Computers in Libraries* 23, no. 4: 26–31. Describes the successful initiation and management of the first statewide live chat reference consortium. Use greatly expanded when the service went to twenty-four hours, seven days per week.

Buckland, Amy, and Krista Godfrey "Gimmick or Groundbreaking? Canadian Academic Libraries using Chat Reference in Multi-User Virtual Environment." *Libraries without Borders: Navigating towards Global Understanding.* Proceedings of World Library and Information Congress, 4th IFLA General Congress and Conference. Québec, Canada August 10–14 2008. Session 158 Reference and Information Services. Available: www.ifla.org/IV/ ifla74/papers/158-Buckland_Godfrey-en.pdf (accessed December 19, 2008).

Charnigo, Laurie, and Paula Barnett-Ellis. 2007. "Checking Out Facebook .com: The Impact of a Digital Trend on Academic Libraries." *Information Technology and Libraries* 26, no. 1: 23–34.

ComputerUser.com (2001– to date). *High-Tech Dictionary.* Available: www .computeruser.com/resources/dictionary/chat.html (accessed September 22, 2008).

De Groote, Sandra L. 2005. "Questions Asked at the Virtual and Physical Health Sciences Reference Desk: How Do They Compare and What Do They Tell Us?" *Medical Reference Services Quarterly* 24 no. 2 (summer): 11–23. Discusses research into user behavior in health sciences reference. Found that undergraduate students favored live chat reference, graduate students favored e-mail, and faculty/staff preferred to interact with librarians via FtF encounters or by phone.

De Groote, Sandra L. 2005. "Quantifying Cooperation: Collaborative Digital Reference Service in the Large Academic Library." *College & Research Libraries* 66, no. 5 (September): 436–454.

Diamond, Wendy, and Barbara Pease. 2002. "Digital Reference: A Case Study of Question Types in an Academic Library." *Reference Services Review* 29, no 3 (fall): 210–218. Analyzes categories of questions received over a two year period (August 1997 to May 1999) in a medium-sized academic library. Suggests that an "Answer Checklist" can stand in for a reference interview in the digital environment and remind librarians to reply in a systematic way.

"Facebook Fastest-Growing Network." 2008. *American Libraries* 39, no. 8 (September): 32.

Gibbons, Susan. 2007. *The Academic Library and the Net Gen Student: Making the Connections*. Chicago: American Library Association.

Granfield, Diane, and Mark Robertson. 2008. "Preference for Reference: New Options and Choices for Academic Library Users." *RUSQ* 48, no. 1: 44–53. Discusses results of focus groups and surveys of students at two urban universities in Toronto. Includes survey.

Graves, Stephanie J., and Christina M. Desai. 2006. "Instruction via Chat: Does Co-browse Help?" *Reference Services Review* 34, no. 3: 340–357. Discusses two studies of chat and IM transcripts which found that users welcome instruction, whether they ask for it or not, and generally are satisfied with the instruction they received via chat/IM.

Hinsdale Public Library. Available: www.hinsdalelibrary.info/ask/askhpl.htm (accessed September 22, 2008).

Holson, Laura M. 2008. "Text Gap UR 2 Old (Or RU?)." *New York Times*, March 9, Bu 9.

Internet Public Library. Ask an IPL Librarian. Available: www.ipl.org/div/askus (accessed September 22, 2008).

Janes, Joseph. 2003. *Introduction to Reference Work in the Digital Age*. New York: Neal-Schuman.

Johnson, Corey M. 2004. "Online Chat Reference: Survey Results from Affiliates of Two Universities." *Reference & User Services Quarterly* 43, no. 3 (spring): 237–247. Survey of two universities found that initial awareness and use of chat reference was low but respondents forecasted that the service would be heavily used in the next ten years. Found that FtF reference was still popular and preferred as first option if seeking reference help.

Kern, M. Kathleen. 2008. *Virtual Reference Best Practices: Tailoring Services to Your Library*. Chicago: ALA Editions. This book provides general guidelines for implementing VR and integrating it into traditional reference services. It contains checklists of important issues, sustainability plans, activities and discussion points for decision making. There is a one-page summary of current research as well as provides sample policies.

Kohl, Laura, and Maura Keating. 2009. "A Phone of One's Own: Texting at the Bryant University Reference Desk." *College & Research Libraries News* 70, no. 2 (February): 104–106, 118.

Kwon, Nahyun. 2007. "Public Library Patrons' Use of Collaborative Chat Reference Service: The Effectiveness of Question Answering by Question Type." *Library & Information Science Research* 29, no. 1: 83–84.

Kyrillidou, Martha, and Mark Young, comps. 2006. *ARL Statistics*, 2004–05. Washington, DC: Association of Research Libraries.

Lagace, Nettie. 1998. "The Internet Public Library's 'Ask A Question' Worldwide Reference Service." *Art Documentation* 17, no. 1: 5–7.

Lankes, R. David et al., eds. 2004. *The Virtual Reference Experience: Integrating Theory into Practice*. New York: Neal-Schuman.

Lankes, R. David et al, eds. 2006. *The Virtual Reference Desk: Creating a Reference Future*. New York: Neal-Schuman.

Lankes, R. David et al. 2008. *Virtual Reference Service: From Competencies to Assessment*. New York: Neal-Schuman.

Lee, Ian J. 2004. "Do Virtual Reference Librarians Dream of Digital Reference Questions? A Qualitative and Quantitative Analysis of E-mail and Chat Reference." *Australian Academic & Research Libraries* 35, no. 2 (June): 95–110.

Library of Congress. "Ask a Librarian." Available: www.loc.gov/rr/askalib (accessed September 22, 2008).

Lipow, Anne G. 2003. *The Virtual Reference Librarian's Handbook*. New York: Neal-Schuman.

L-Net—Oregon's Library Network. Available: www.oregonlibraries.net (accessed September 22, 2008).

Lupien, Pascal. 2006. "Virtual Reference in the Age of Pop-Up Blockers, Firewalls, and Service Pack 2." *Online* 30, no. 4: 14–19.

Maness, Jack M. 2006. "Library 2.0: The Next Generation of Web-based Library Services." *LOGOS: Journal of the World Book Community* 17, no. 3: 139–145.

McClure, Charles R., R. David Lankes, Melissa Gross, Beverly Choltco-Devlin. 2002. "Statistics Measures and Quality Standards for Assessing Digital Reference Library Services: Guidelines and Procedures." Available: quartz.syr.edu/quality (accessed December 18, 2008). Manual developed to assist in the development of statistics, measures, and quality standards for evaluating and improving digital reference services. Pdf of complete manual includes all data collection forms and the list of quality standards.

Mills, Elinor. 2006. "Most Reliable Search Engine Tool Could Be Your Librarian." CNT News, September 29. Available: http://news.cnet.com/2100-1032_3-6120778.html. (accessed September 12, 2008).

Mon, Lorri. 2008. Personal e-mail to Marie L. Radford, September 11, 2008.

National Center for Educational Statistics, Public Libraries in the United States, Fiscal Year 2004. Appendix A. Available: http://harvester.census.gov/imls/pubs/pls/pub_detail.asp?id=3# (accessed December 19, 2008).

Naylor, Sharon, Bruce Stoffel, and Sharon Van Der Laan. 2008. "Why Isn't Our Chat Reference Used More?" *RUSQ*, 47, no. 4: 342–354. Report of focus groups with upper level undergraduates at Illinois State University that found the students wanted both more personalized reference services and a variety of reference service types.

New York Public Library. 2008. "Ask NYPL." www.nypl.org/questions/#email (accessed October 20, 2008).

Nilsen, Kirsti. 2006. "Comparing Users' Perspectives of In-Person and Virtual Reference." *New Library World* 107, no. 3/4 (1222/1223): 91–104. Includes findings from The University of Western Ontario Library Visit Study comparing 261 FtF with eighty-five virtual reference interviews in public and academic libraries. A report of earlier data covering forty-two virtual reference interviews was published online in 2004 as "The Library Visit Study: User Experiences at the Virtual Reference Desk." *Information Research* 9, no. 2 (January). Available: http://informationr.net/ir/9-2/paper171.html (accessed December 22, 2008).

Nilsen, Kirsti, and Catherine Sheldrick Ross. 2006. "Evaluating Virtual Reference from the Users' Perspective." *The Reference Librarian* no. 95/96: 53–79. Includes a listing of the features of the virtual reference services and staff behavior that helped and those that were unhelpful to participants in the Library Visit Study.

OCLC. QuestionPoint—24/7 Reference Services.2008. Available: www.question point.org (accessed September 22, 2008).

Oetting, Mike. Telephone interview with Marie L. Radford, September 9, 2008.

O'Sullivan, Patrick B. 2000. "What You Don't Know Won't Hurt Me: Impression Management Functions of Communication Channels in Relationships." *Human Communication Research* 26, no. 3: 40–58.

Pennsylvania State University Libraries. 2008. Available: www.libraries.psu.edu/psul.html (accessed September 22, 2008).

Pope, Kitty, Barbara Galik, and Lori Bell. 2007. *Alliance Second Life Library End of Year Report 2007*. Alliance Library System and Alliance Second Life Library. Available: www.alliancelibraries.info/slendofyearreport2007.pdf (accessed March 31, 2008).

QandANJ New Jersey Library Network. Available: www.qandanj.org (accessed September 22, 2008). This is a statewide consortium that provides a chat reference service.

QuestionPoint. 2008. 24/7 Reference Services. Available: www.questionpoint .org (accessed October 20, 2008).

QuestionPoint. 2008. Introducing Qwidget. Available: http://questionpoint .blogs.com/questionpoint_247_referen/2008/01/introducing-qwi.html (accessed October 20, 2008).

Radford, Marie L. 2006a. "Encountering Virtual Users: A Qualitative Investigation of Interpersonal Communication in Chat Reference." *Journal of the American Society for Information Science and Technology* 57, no. 8 (June): 1046–1059.

Radford, Marie L. 2006b. "Interpersonal Communication in Chat Reference: Encounters with Rude and Impatient Users." In *The Virtual Reference Desk: Creating a Reference Future* (41–73), edited by R. David Lankes, et al. New York: Neal-Schuman.

Radford, Marie L. 2009. "A Personal Choice: Reference Service Excellence." *Reference and User's Services Quarterly* 48, no. 2: 108–115. Discusses the changes in reference services, challenges, and possibilities for reference excellence. Makes numerous recommendations for service improvement.

Radford, Marie L., and Kathleen M. Kern. 2006."A Multiple-Case Study Investigation of the Discontinuation of Nine Chat Reference Services." *Library & Information Science Research* 28, no. 4 (winter): 24–42.

Radford, Marie L., and Lorri Mon. 2008. "Reference Service in Face-to-Face and Virtual Environments." In *Academic Library Research: Perspectives and Current Trends*, edited by Marie L. Radford and Pamela Snelson ALA/ACRL. Publications in Librarianship #59, Chicago: ACRL. This chapter reviews the research on VR and FtF reference in the academic library setting from 1990 to 2007. It highlights important findings and implications for practice. Contains an extensive bibliography and a list of future trends in reference.

Radford, Marie L., and Lynn Silipigni Connaway. 2005–2008. "Seeking Synchronicity: Evaluating Virtual Reference Services from User, Non-User, and Librarian Perspectives." Institute for Museum and Library Services, Rutgers University (NJ), and OCLC, Online Computer Library Center. Grant Web site available: www.oclc.org/research/projects/synchronicity (accessed September 22, 2008).

Radford, Marie L., and Lynn Silipigni Connaway. 2007. "Screenagers" and Live Chat Reference: Living Up to the Promise." *Scan* 26, no. 1 (February): 31–39.

Radford, Marie L., and Lynn Silipigni Connaway. (in press 2009). "Getting Better All the Time: Improving Communication and Accuracy in Virtual Reference." In *Creating a Reference Renaissance: Current and Future Trends*, edited by Marie L. Radford and R. David Lankes. New York: Neal-Schuman.

Reference and User Services Association. 2004. "Guidelines for Implementing and Maintaining Virtual Reference." Available: www.ala.org/ala/mgrps/ divs/rusa/resources/guidelines/virtrefguidelines.cfm (accessed December 19, 2008).

Ronan, Jana Smith. 2003. "The Reference Interview Online." *Reference & User Services Quarterly* 43, no. 1 (fall): 43–47.

Ruttenberg, Judy, and Heather Tunender. 2004. Mapping Virtual Reference Using Geographic Information Systems (GIS). Available: http://helios.lib.uci.edu/question/GIS-ALA2004/ (accessed October 6, 2008).

Saxton, Matthew. 2004. "Show Me Yours and I'll Show You Mine! Implementing Peer Review." Virtual Reference Desk. 6th Annual Conference, November 8–9, 2004, Cincinnati, OH.

Schneider, Karen G. 2000. "The Distributed Librarian—Live, Online, Real-Time Reference." *American Libraries* 31, no 10 (November): 64. Argues that libraries need to collaborate to offer 24/7 online real-time reference or lose their market share to commercial Web-based services.

Sessoms, Pam, and Jean Ferguson. 2008. "Adding Instant Messaging to an Established Virtual Reference Service: Asking "r u there?" In *Virtual Reference Service: from Competencies to Assessment* (37–50), edited by R. David Lankes et al. New York: Neal-Schuman.

Sirsi Dynix. Docutek. www.docutek.com (accessed September 22, 2008).

Sloan, Bernie. 2001 "Ready for Reference: Academic Libraries Offer Live Web-Based Reference: Evaluating System Use." Available: http://web.archive.org/web/20070217200932rn_1/people.lis.uiuc.edu/~b-sloan/ready4ref.htm (accessed December 19, 2008).

Sloan, Bernie. 2006. "Twenty Years of Virtual Reference." *Internet Reference Services Quarterly* 11, no. 2: 91–95.

Tucker-Raymond, Caleb. 2008. "Models for Using Digital Reference Transcripts to Create Digital Reference Tools." Libraries in the Digital Age (LIDA), June 2–7, Dubrovnik and Mljet, Croatia.

Tufte, Edward. 1997. *Visual Explanations: Images and Quantities, Evidence and Narrative.* Chesure, CT: Graphics Press.

University of Illinois at Urbana-Champaign. University Library. Ask a Librarian." Available: www.library.uiuc.edu/askus (accessed September 22, 2008).

The Unofficial Smiley Dictionary. Available: http://w2.eff.org/Net_culture/Net_info/EFF_Net_Guide/EEGTTI_HTML/eeg_286.html (accessed September 22, 2008).

van Duinkerken, Wyoma, Jane Stephens, and Karen L. MacDonald. 2009. "The Chat Reference Interview: Seeking Evidence Based on RUSA's Guidelines: A Case Study at Texas A&M University Libraries." *New Library World* 110, no. 3/4: 107–121.

Walter, Virginia A., and Cindy Mediavilla. 2005. "Teens are from Neptune, Librarians are from Pluto: An Analysis of Online Reference Transactions." *Library Trends* 54, no. 2 (fall): 209–227.

Ward, David. 2004. "Measuring the Completeness of Reference Transactions in Online Chats." *Reference & User Services Quarterly* 44, no. 1 (fall): 46–56.

White, Marilyn D., Elaine G. Abels, and Neil Kaske. 2003."Evaluation of Chat Reference Service Quality." *D-Lib Magazine* 9, no. 2 (February): 1–13. Reports results from a pilot study of public and academic chat reference that evaluates service quality from the user's point of view.

The Readers' Advisory Interview

7.1 Introduction to the Readers' Advisory Interview

The readers' advisory interview is focused on helping readers find materials they want to read, listen to, or view for pleasure. In the revival of readers' advisory (RA) work that has happened since the early 1980s, the emphasis has been on fiction. More recently, however, the literature on RA has recognized that people also read nonfiction for pleasure, especially genres with a narrative shape such as history, biography, memoirs, travel, true adventure, and true crime (Wyatt, 2007; Moyer, 2008). RA is not just for printed books, but also includes audiovisual formats such as audiobooks and films. While in this chapter, for convenience we refer to "books," it should be understood that the same RA interviewing skills can be used with users wanting nonprint formats for leisure. Whatever the format desired, essentially the RA transaction is a matchmaking service. The RA interview resembles the reference interview in requiring similar communication skills: first set the stage by being approachable, and then use appropriate skills of questioning and listening. However, the RA interview differs from the reference interview in one important way— the requirement to engage readers in conversations about books. In the course of the RA interview, readers must be encouraged to talk about the kinds of books they enjoy and conversely do not enjoy. The readers' advisor needs to learn how to listen with a tuned ear to clues about reading taste revealed in the comments that readers make about their experiences, positive and negative, with books.

The crucial importance of effective readers' advisory services is undisputed. Surveys of users repeatedly find that the vast majority of people who visit a public library do so specifically to get books. As Francine Fialkoff (1998, 58), editor of *Library Journal*, has noted, "All the surveys we've seen, conducted by librarians as well as non-librarians, indicate that there is virtually no service library users value more highly than the ability to match a book with a reader, or to answer the question,

'What do I read next?'" In this chapter we consider what library staff can do to understand the kinds of books users enjoy, and the kind of reading experience they seek.

There are two elements in effective readers' advisory work: the behind-the-scenes work, sometimes called "passive strategies" (but passive only in the sense of not involving direct contact with the user), and the direct person-to-person interaction of the RA interview. So-called passive strategies include putting spine labels on books, shelving books in separate genre collections such as mysteries or science fiction, creating bookmarks and annotated book lists, and setting up attractive displays that are constantly replenished. This behind-the-scenes work sets the stage for the RA interview.

In RA transactions, you need above all to create a climate that encourages readers to talk about books and authors. A good open question that works for readers' advisers is, "Can you tell me about a book you've read recently and really enjoyed?" followed up by a further probe, "What particularly did you like about it?" The ability to listen and distill the essence of what users say is a crucial skill for all reference interviews, but is especially challenging in the RA context. The readers' adviser has to pay close attention to what the reader says about a complex set of book appeal characteristics such as plot, characters, setting, pacing, preferred type of ending, literary quality, reading difficulty, and length ("quick reads" versus "fat books")—in short, the "feel" of the desired reading experience.

In addition to the skills needed for reference work in general, the readers' adviser should know something about reading and popular genres of fiction. In RA work, there is seldom a single right answer; there are usually many books that would suit the reader. But there are also many wrong answers—books that would *not* be appropriate for that particular reader. The role of the readers' adviser is to help narrow down choices to a manageable number of suggestions that match the reader's stated interests and tastes. Does this mean that readers' advisers need to have read every book that they recommend? No, not any more than reference librarians working in other domains are expected to have all the answers in their heads. That's what reference tools are for. Fortunately, the number of excellent RA tools, including electronic resources, has grown enormously in recent years (RUSA, 2004; Moyer, 2008).

But are these tools being used? In an ongoing, unpublished study, Catherine Ross and Jennifer Noon now have more than 500 library visit transactions in which MLIS students at the The University of Western Ontario visited public libraries between fall 2002 and fall 2008 and asked for help in finding "some interesting books to read." Over this six-year period, staff members' use of professional RA tools has increased, though still is not consistently practiced. In 2002, staff members used *no* tools in fully half of the RA library visits. In the other 50 percent of cases, the most commonly used sources were RA print tools (mentioned in 31 percent of visit accounts), followed by book displays (12 percent), and lists of bestsellers and award-winning books (6 percent). By 2008, tools were used 75 percent of the time, with a corresponding increase in

"FIFTY THOUSAND CORRECT ANSWERS"

From an interview with Joyce Saricks:

Ross: You have written a whole book on how to do readers' advisory work. But could you boil it down? What are some of the most important tips for readers' advisers?

Saricks: You have to be a good listener. You've got to be able to get readers to talk to you. Duncan [Smith] is right—it's a conversation. You've got to listen so that you can hear what they are saying about what they like. There's no way around the fact that you have to read—read reviews, read books, talk to readers. Pump the readers for things that they're reading. You have to build that knowledge.... The other thing is to remember it's fun. It's not like a reference question where there may be only one correct answer to the question. There are fifty thousand correct answers to the request, "Give me a good book." So readers' advisers need to know that readers' advisory is about setting up relationships, that it's fun, and that readers love it....

The readers' advisory interview is also structured because you are listening for them to tell you about their experience such as, "This book didn't please me because it just took me too long to get into it." You are listening to the positive and to the negative and you are making mental choices. You're eliminating parts of the collection or adding parts of the collection in as you talk to them. At the end you sum up and say, "It sounds as if this is what you want." I think it's a conversation, but there is structure to it.

Did You Know?

Ross's (2004) study of avid readers who read for pleasure found that the single most important strategy for picking books was to choose a book by a known and trusted author. Said a Salman Rushdie fan, "It's like finding a gold mine and following the vein when you find a good author like that" (14). Second to choosing by author, the next most popular strategy was to use genre to identify the kind of experience promised by a book. Genre was often used in conjunction with author.

the variety of types of tools used. The growth in electronic resources was noticeable, with the following resources used: the library catalog (mentioned in 25 percent of visit accounts), NoveList (29 percent), lists of bestsellers and award-winning books (16 percent), Web pages (11 percent), bookmarks (11 percent), and RA print tools (10 percent).

This improvement is encouraging, but the fact that staff members chose *not* to use any reference sources in one quarter of the RA library visit transactions remains problematic. Reporting on what happened when her students in the MLS program at Queens College, New York, went undercover to complete a surrogate user assignment, Mary K. Chelton (2003) strongly criticizes the widespread tendency for staff members to rely on personal reading experience instead of professional tools. She comments, "At an absolute minimum, librarians who may be asked RA questions should be familiar with the following resources: *Fiction Catalog*, Fiction_L (online discussion), *Genreflecting*, NoveList (a database), *Reader's Guide to Genre Fiction*, and *What Do I Read Next?*" (38–39).

Despite the growing awareness of the importance of RA work, it remains an area that many reference librarians find unfamiliar, difficult, and anxiety-inducing. One reason many librarians feel unequipped to provide RA help is that, as Dana Watson (2000) reports, only fourteen of the fifty-six master's degree programs accredited by the American Library Association offer courses in readers' advisory services. Jessica E. Moyer (2005), who reviewed the teaching of RA skills in selected LIS programs in the United States, Canada and Europe, found that opportunities for MLIS students to take courses on readers' advisory services happen

It's Not about You

When Catherine Ross in 2007 interviewed super-readers Cindy Orr, Nancy Pearl, Joyce Saricks, and Sharron Smith to get their tips on RA, they said, among other things: "Realize that it's not about you; it's not about the last book you read and loved." "Listen to how the readers describe their favorite books. Do they emphasize character, language, setting, or story?" "Remember that there is no one right answer." "Keep a reading log" of your own reading in which you identify elements in the book that might appeal to other readers.

mostly in programs lucky enough to have faculty members with a keen interest in RA work (e.g., Briony Train and Judith Elkin at the University of Central England Birmingham, and Bill Crowley at Dominican University). Nor has RA work been given as much research attention as other areas of reference, with the result that we don't know enough about the way that the RA interview is actually conducted in libraries. The few research studies to date that have focused on the RA transaction have found that when readers ask for suggestions for good books to read, staff members tend not to use their professional skills consistently.

Kenneth Shearer (1996), Pauletta Brown Bracy (1996), Anne K. May (2001; 2002), and Mary K. Chelton (2003) are four researchers who have used unobtrusive methods to study what happens during the RA library visit. In these studies, students in MLIS courses on RA posed as users to find out what really happens during the RA encounter. All four researchers reported the same problems: staff members too often fail to conduct an interview; they often rely on personal reading as their only source; they use few reference tools apart from the catalog (helpful only for a known author or title); and they do not follow up. In Shearer's (1996) study, students were instructed to say initially, "I enjoyed *To Kill a Mockingbird* and would like something else like it. Can you help me?" Shearer (1996) found that an RA interview in which the advisor asked what the user liked about the book happened less than 25 percent of the time. His conclusion is that "the RA transaction is *not* about how similar the text of Book A is to the text of Book B." It is "about relating Reader A's experience with Book A to the likelihood that Reader A would value the experience of reading Book B" (1996: 19). This research finding means that readers' advisers have to talk to readers and pay close attention to what they say about the kinds of reading experiences they value.

Four years after the Shearer study, four graduate students in the Queens College Graduate School of Library and Information Studies visited the fifty-four districts of the Nassau County, New York library system and posed an RA question at each location (May, 2001). Using a variant of Shearer's methodology, the participants in this study browsed the fiction stacks for up to five minutes awaiting an offer of help. If no help was volunteered, they approached the service desk closest to the main entrance and requested "a librarian who can recommend a good book." If the staff member asked what the reader had recently read and enjoyed, the script required them to "offer up *Memoirs of a Geisha*," which they had all read in advance (May, 2001, 127, 133). Again it was striking that the staff members often seemed caught off guard in a domain where they felt ill-equipped to serve. May (2001, 134) reports, "One librarian remarked, 'You know, this is the query the reference desk dreads,' and another muttered under her breath, 'I hate this question.'" May et al. (2000, 40–43) report that the findings of an unobtrusive study of RA service in the Nassau, New York library system "underscored that a non-methodical, informal, and serendipitous response was the norm to a patron's request for a 'good read.'"

Especially troubling in all four of these unobtrusive studies was the prevalence of a strategy of negative closure (3.1.5) in which the librarians used their own lack of personal interest in a particular author or genre as a reason for not providing any help. When reference staff was asked for help in finding a book similar to one the user had previously enjoyed, a common response was to say something along the lines of, "I'm sorry but I've never read author X," or "I'm not very familiar with African-American authors [or science fiction, or YA fiction, or regency romance], but maybe if you just browse over there you'll find something." Underlying these reported problems with the RA transaction is a common factor. Librarians, by and large, do *not* view RA as an area in which they can appropriately use their professional skills and training.

With regular reference questions, librarians have received professional training and know what to do: conduct a reference interview, consult the appropriate reference tools, and provide an answer that is supported by authoritative sources. They would not consider it appropriate to respond to a question about, say, the current population of Sydney, Australia, by saying, "I'm sorry but I don't know much about Australia—I've never been there." It is understood that the professionalism of the reference librarian does not depend on personal interest in the user's topic. Professional commitment to helping users motivates reference librarians to find answers in reference sources, irrespective of the topic. They do not rely on whatever information happens to reside in their own heads. As Duncan Smith (2000) has pointed out, if a user asks for information on starting a small business, it is not acceptable for a reference librarian to say, "You know, I started a small business once and this is how I did it." Why, he wonders, can it be supposed that an acceptable answer to an RA question could be, "You know, I read a book that you might like to read." Although the user *might* like to read the book most recently enjoyed by the librarian, it is also quite possible that the user's tastes and interests are very different from the librarian's. The readers' adviser should not rely on a lucky coincidence of tastes, but should use professional skills first to find out about the advisee's reading interests and, second, to use reference tools to find suitable books that match those interests.

Success in RA work depends on learning and systematically using a cluster of skills that can be acquired rather than on some inborn knack that lucky people are born with but others can never learn.

7.2   Setting the Stage for Readers' Advisory Service

Setting the stage is even more important for RA work than for other kinds of reference. As we saw in section 2.1, users with reference questions are often diffident about asking their question at the reference desk, but at least they usually know that reference help is available. In contrast, readers looking for good books to read think of libraries, especially public libraries, as a storehouse where they can get books to read. However, they rarely think of librarians as experts on pleasure reading who can help them choose books. When asked why they wouldn't ask a

---

A QUICK TIP

Tailor Your Pitch

According to Heather Booth (2005), teen readers come to the library with the prior experience of having received unsolicited advice from authority figures on books they *should* read. Therefore readers' advisers need to work extra hard to get out the message that they are there to help YAs find enjoyable books or media, that nothing is required, and that anything they enjoy reading is okay. She recommends providing a description of what the book is about, based on their own interests.

A QUICK TIP

Signage

Let users know that the library is the right place to ask for advice about what to read next. Put up signs that read:

- Fiction Desk
- Fiction Services
- Looking for a Good Book to Read? Ask Us for Suggestions.

Conducting the Reference Interview

Did You Know?

During RA interviews, it can help to have an aide-mémoire to help jog your memory about authors and titles. As you talk to users about what kind of mystery stories they enjoy, you can show them the section on mysteries in Herald's (2006) *Genreflecting*, and use the categories provided to help narrow down whether the reader wants police procedurals, hard-boiled mysteries, mysteries with an anthropological interest, etc. Or you can use electronic RA resources such as EBSCO Publishing's NoveList. For a free trial of Novelist, contact **novelist@epnet.com**. With this online RA resource, adults and children can find new titles by genre, setting, characters, or subject, as well as find titles with similarities to titles they have read and enjoyed.

librarian for suggestions about reading, users are apt to say that librarians wouldn't know what they liked, or that librarians might try to improve their reading tastes, or that librarians were too busy to bother with requests for pleasure reading.

In Ross and Noon's RA Library Visit Study transactions, users said that some staff members gave out signals that they were "unapproachable," "too busy," or "wanted to get rid of me." Users were also diffident about "bothering" librarians with questions about pleasure reading, an area that observably is often given short shrift in comparison with informational and factual questions. This means that a library wanting to get into the business of providing RA service needs to promote the service and let users know that it exists. No one requests a service that is invisible. But when users are encouraged to ask for help in choosing books and are satisfied with the help they get, they become repeat customers. Saricks notes in *Readers' Advisory Service in the Public Library*, "Only when readers have been helped and are made comfortable coming to the desk do we find substantial numbers of readers asking us directly for assistance" (2005, 86).

The first step is to create a physical environment that says, in effect, "In this library, we care about your reading interests and want to help you find books that you would enjoy. This is the place to come, not just for factual information, but for the delights of story." Libraries need to change the public's mental model of the library so that they see it as a place to get advice about books to read and about the large variety of media to listen to or view. Public libraries have much to learn from bookstores when it comes to creating a welcoming environment for readers. A good start is to provide comfortable chairs for reading near the fiction stacks. Readers' advisers need to be situated near the fiction collection so that they can be prepared to offer help. Clear and readable signs should advertise the existence of RA service by saying something like "Wondering what to read next? Ask us for suggestions." Create enticing displays that showcase books and booklists on a focused theme, replenishing the books as they are borrowed.

One good way to give prominence to RA as professional service is to assemble a collection of relevant tools and make them available for users too. Don't hide your professional RA tools away where only librarians can find them. Readers will enjoy using them on their own, once they discover that RA tools exist to map their favorite genre from mysteries and horror to romance and inspirational fiction. Create an RA corner stocked with core tools such as *Fiction Catalog* (Wilson), *What Do I Read Next?* (Gale), *Genreflecting* (Herald and Wiegand, 2006), *Readers' Advisory Guide to Genre Fiction* (Saricks, 2001), *Book Lust* (Pearl, 2003), and *More Book Lust* (Pearl, 2005). RUSA's Collection Development and Evaluation Section (CODES) Readers' Advisory Committee has developed a very useful list, "Recommended Readers' Advisory Tools" (RUSA, 2004). Put a sign on the shelf that reads, "Guides for Finding the Next Book to Read."

Readers need help in narrowing down the book choices to a manageable number because of the phenomenon that Sharon Baker (1986) calls "overload." Fiction readers come to the library knowing the names of five or six favorite authors, hoping that one of these favorites has written a new book and that the new book will be on the shelf. When disappointed, readers resort to "browsing," defined by Baker as looking for something without a clear idea of what it is that you are looking for. Experienced readers have developed effective strategies for browsing, based on their broad familiarity with books, their knowledge of authors and genres, their ability to read the cues on book covers, their memory of reviews or recommendations by friends, etc. But less practiced readers are daunted by the alphabetic arrangement of fiction and quite often end up choosing books at random and then being dissatisfied with the reading experience. A beginning reader who had trouble finding new books of interest said, "I go to the library and stand there for hours. So I end up picking just at random. I pick some books up, bring them home, and end up taking them all back. You read the first couple pages, and the author goes on and on about some long description. It's just so boring and you don't really get any excitement out of it" (Ross, 2001, 9).

Research shows circulation increases when libraries adopt the strategies that Baker (1986) describes as helping browsers cope with overload: separating popular genre titles into separate sections; putting genre labels on the spines of books; providing annotated lists; creating book displays; systematic weeding. Like the layout of the bookstore, the physical arrangement of the fiction collection should help readers choose books. In addition, when these strategies are pursued, the library itself becomes a prop for the RA conversation, which we discuss next.

7.3 Conducting the Interview

The RA interview is indispensable in the process of matching book to reader because, as we have seen, the term *good book* is relative. For readers this term means "a good book for me; a book that matches my mood right now; a book that suits my level of reading ability; a book that satisfies my particular needs and interests." Readers may say that they are looking for a "well-written" book, but they mean written to maximize the effects that they enjoy. Some want a book that reassures them, makes then laugh, or lifts their spirits, while others want a book that surprises them, challenges them, unsettles their preconceived ideas, or opens their eyes to dangerous new possibilities. It doesn't work to have a ready-made, generic list of "Good Books" such as *Passage to India*, *Middlemarch*, or *No Country for Old Men*. Nor should readers' advisers recommend their own personal favorites unless they have reason to believe that the user has the same reading tastes (e.g., "I've just read Kate Atkinson's *One Good Turn* and absolutely loved it. You'll love it too."). You can't tell whether a reader will enjoy a particular book by considering the text alone because the book is only half the equation. The other half is the reader's mood, interests, and skill as a reader. That's why it's important to have a conversation with the reader about his or her experience of books. For many avid readers, talking about books is an enjoyable experience in itself, and an extension of the pleasurable reading experience.

Did You Know?
Up to 85 percent of people who come to the library searching for good books to read use browsing as a strategy. Once the reader starts to browse within a range of books, the cover and the clues provided on the book itself become important. One reader interviewed by Ross explained, "When you're as genre-specific as I guess I am, and read as voraciously as I do, you're looking for some quick identifiers on what's a good book. It'll take me ten minutes to go in [to the science fiction section], get five books, and leave because I'm just so familiar with the genre in general" (2001, 14). The "quick identifiers" most frequently mentioned by readers in Ross's study were the cover, the blurb on the back, and the sample page.

Conducting the Reference Interview

ANALYZE THIS REFERENCE TRANSACTION

Case 36: In the mood for challenging and quirky?

User: I was wondering if you could suggest some good books for me to read.

Librarian: What do you usually like to read? (*open question* that gets the user to talk about past reading preferences)

User: I enjoy contemporary fiction. Two writers that are among my favorites are Nabokov and Kundera.

Librarian: Um-hmmm [nods, smiles, and pauses].

User: And also I like contemporary Canadian fiction. In fact, today I'd like to find an interesting book by a new Canadian author that I haven't read yet.

Librarian: Okay, the best place to start is this book; it lists all the important Canadian authors. [Goes to a nearby stack, finds Smith and O'Connor's *Canadian Fiction: A Guide to Reading Interests* (2005), opens it, and shows the user the table of contents.] Another good starting point is this bulletin board where we post reading lists, reviews, upcoming events, and lists of award-winning books. In your case, the Giller Prize Shortlist and the Nominees for the Governor General's Literary Awards list could be helpful in suggesting authors. (library use instruction using *inclusion*) What particular elements in a work of fiction are important to you? (*open question*)

User: I like challenging, quirky books. One that I really liked was Robertson Davies's *Fifth Business*.

Librarian: Okay, here are some books I could suggest. Although Jane Urquhart's *The Stone Carvers* is on both shortlists, you might not find it so interesting since it doesn't have the quirkiness that you seem to enjoy. But you might want to try Gail Anderson-Dargatz's *A Recipe for Bees* and Ann-Marie MacDonald's *Fall on Your Knees*, which is also on the Oprah list. And another thing that might help you when you are browsing for Canadian books: all the books in the fiction section by Canadian authors have a maple leaf sticker on the spine.

User: Thanks, I really appreciate all your help.

(Library Visit Study)

Comment: In this interview, the questions "What do you usually like to read?" and "What particular elements in a work of fiction are important to you?" worked well because they got the reader to talk about her experience with books. A big plus in this transaction is the way that the readers' adviser was able to go beyond her own personal reading by using a reference tool and the lists posted on the bulletin board as props in the interview.

   The user gave this transaction the highest possible rating and commented that the librarian's "informal, relaxed attitude made the experience of searching for a book enjoyable, and, more important, non-threatening.... I find this kind of behavior helpful because it is analogous to the experience of pleasure reading itself.... In contrast, recommending too many books, relying too heavily on personal opinions, and not listening to what the user is saying would have been very detrimental. Essentially, the readers' advisory service should offer an informative, congenial invitation to reading."

FACTORS THAT AFFECT READERS' BOOK CHOICES

The following list, adapted from Pejtersen and Austin (1983; 1984), shows what factors readers take into account when they look for a fiction book to read.

Subject—What is the book about?

- What kind of *action* occurs in this book? Does the plot involve a conflict between two matched opponents, the uncovering of a mystery, the coming of age of the central character, a quest or journey, the gradual development of a love relationship, etc.? Is the action interior and psychological or is it external, involving a lot of activity such as fights and chase scenes?

- What kinds of *characters* are featured in this book— a mother and daughter, a fellowship of elves, a strong woman who overcomes setbacks, a runaway, a private eye, pirates, vampires, members of a religious community, terrorists, an extended family, etc.? What sorts of relationships take place between characters?

- What is the *theme*—love, war, survival, revenge, coping with illness, the conflict of good and evil, discovery of identity, etc.?

Setting:

- *When* does the story happen—past, present, or future? Time periods often offer clues to genre preferences, with the past associated with historical fiction or fantasy, and the future associated with science fiction.

- *Where* does the story happen—on another planet, a high school, a village in Kashmir, an advertising agency in Manhattan, the American frontier, a nursing home? Geographic settings also provide clues to genre preferences, with bestselling melodrama associated with wealth and glamour and the frontier associated with the Western or the family saga.

Kind of reading experience offered by the book:

- Does the reader *learn something* from this book? For example: I learned so much about Islamic family life in postwar Cairo (or bee taxonomists, or the fashion industry in Paris, or how to break a horse).

- Does the reader *feel something* as a result of reading this book? (e.g., It made me feel happy/sad/ hopeful about human goodness. I was alarmed about the proliferation of land mines that maim civilians and children. It scared me. It made me laugh. It reassured me and confirmed my values. It was like comfort food. It challenged me to reassess my beliefs.) Does the book have a happy ending? What is the mood engendered by reading this book?

Accessibility:

Accessibilty includes both intellectual access (can the reader understand it?) and physical access.

- What r*eading skills* are demanded by this book? Does this book use literary conventions that may be unfamiliar—stream-of-consciousness narrative method, an unreliable first-person narrator, flashbacks, postmodern reflexiveness, literary parody?

- How *predictable* is it? The more conventional and formulaic the book is, the more the reader already knows about the content of the book, and the easier it is to read. Depending on mood, sometimes readers want easy, predictable, safe reads and sometimes they seek challenging, unpredictable, risky reads.

- How *accessible* is the book physically in terms of size and heaviness? In terms of the size of the type?

Not all of these factors will be salient for all readers. A reader with strong arms and good eyesight could find the physical characteristics of the book irrelevant. A reader might not care where the book is set, as long as it depicts strong, independent-minded female characters. On the other hand, a reader may refuse to read anything with too much sex and violence in it, or anything with confusing Russian names in it, or anything set in historical times. To find out which factors matter to an individual reader, ask open questions. The list in "Some Questions for Readers' Advisers" suggests some questions to choose from the next time someone says, "Can you recommend a good book?"

The soul of an RA interview is the talk about books. The primary question recommended by Joyce Saricks is, "Tell me about a book you've read and enjoyed. Or one that you've hated" (Saricks, 2005). The key is to get readers talking about their own engagement with a

Virginia's Williamsburg Regional Library (WRL) has been a pioneer in developing a form-based readers' advisory program called "Looking for a Good Book." Readers are invited to fill in a reader program, which librarians will use to create a customized reading list to be sent back within a week. The form itself advises, "The more information you provide, the more likely it is that we can suggest books you will like." The elaborate form, which substitutes for an interview, asks among other things for genre preferences, desired tone/ mood (e.g., happy ending), and appeal factors (e.g., focus on characters/ focus on action and events, etc.) and requests a listing of five favorite books and five favorite authors. Other libraries are following suit. Salt Lake County Library (SLCL) in Utah was inspired by hearing Barry Trott talk about forms-based readers advisory programs at PLA 2006 in Boston and developed its own similar service. "Launched with no publicity at all, we just added it to the Web page quietly one day and boom, it took off," said Trish Hull, manager of SLCL's Magna Library.

SOME QUESTIONS FOR READERS' ADVISERS

To initiate a readers' advisory interview:
- Is there a special book you are looking for?
- Are you finding what you're looking for?

To get a picture of previous reading patterns:
- So that I can get a picture of your reading interests, can you tell me about a book/author you've read and enjoyed?
- What did you enjoy about that book (author/ type of book)?
- What do you *not* like and wouldn't want to read?
- What elements do you usually look for in a novel (nonfiction book/ biography/ travel book)?

To determine current reading preferences:
- What are you in the mood for today?
- What have you looked at so far? [to a person who has been looking unsuccessfully for reading material]
- What did you *not* like about these books that you looked at?
- If we could find the perfect book for you today, what would it be like? (What would it be about? What would you like best about it? What elements would it include?)

To understand the function of the book:
- What kind of reading experience do you want to find?
- What do you want to get from this book? What do you find satisfying?
- What would you like this book to do for you?

To follow up on a recommendation:
- If you find that these books weren't to your taste, get back to me and we can suggest something else.
- What else can I help you with?

book. The features of the book that readers choose to talk about are important clues to reading tastes and preferences. Listen very closely. Does the reader talk about fast-paced action and excitement? Does the reader emphasize the relationships that develop between or among characters? Is setting important? Is the reader looking for something that is soothing and comforting or challenging and quirky?

Saricks points out that most fiction readers "are usually not looking for a book on a certain subject. They want a book with a particular 'feel'" (2005, 40). When asked to talk about a book they've enjoyed, readers mention being drawn into the story, or they talk about factors such as strong, empathetic characters or intriguing settings or an upbeat tone—elements that Joyce Saricks calls "appeal factors." For Saricks, the important appeal factors of a book are its pacing, characterization, storyline, and frame, or the particular atmosphere or tone that the author constructs. *Readers' Advisory Service in the Public Library* provides a list of useful questions that can be used to identify each of these appeal factors.

For example, to identify pacing, Saricks recommends asking, "Is there more dialogue or description?" To identify characterization, she suggests asking, "Is the focus on a single character or on several whose lives are intertwined?" Readers' advisers need to train themselves to listen carefully for clues to what the particular reader is looking for in a good book, whether it's plot, or setting, or character, or language, or some combination thereof.

Here is an example of the integration of skills in the RA interview:

User: Can you recommend a good book?

Librarian: You're looking for a book to read for enjoyment? (*acknowledgment* to confirm the reader's purpose)

User: Yes, I'm going on vacation and want a few books for cottage reading.

Librarian: Okay. To give me an idea of the kind of thing you like, can you tell me about a book that you've read recently and enjoyed? (*closed question* that functions as an *open question*)

User: I've just finished Barbara Kingsolver's *The Poisonwood Bible* and loved it.

Librarian: Uhhuh (*encourager*) What was it you loved about that book?

User: The way the family life was developed over time, and the relationship between the parents and the three sisters. I also liked the fact that the book was set in Africa. I felt that I was learning something about African life and politics. I like to learn about different places.

Librarian: Okay. And are there types of books that you definitely would *not* like?

User: I don't like predictable books, which is why I don't want to waste my time reading those authors that just churn out the same book over and over.

Librarian: What sort of books are you in the mood for now?

User: I'd like to read some new authors—writers who could really surprise me with something unexpected. Amaze me!

Some Quick Tips for the RA Interview

- Remember that you are trying to understand what the *reader* thinks is a good book. Don't fall into the trap of recommending the last book that you enjoyed, unless you have reason to think that the reader shares your reading tastes.

- Be careful with the term "well-written." When readers say that they are looking for a well-written book, they might *not* mean a book that has a high degree of literary value, such as a recent Man Booker Prize winner. Readers are more likely to mean well-written to achieve the particular experience they are looking for—e.g., a well-written horror story scares the reader; a well-written romance depicts the growing

---

A QUICK TIP

In the Mood

Pleasure readers often say that they are looking for a book that matches their mood (Ross and Chelton, 2001). Whichbook.net is a UK-based Web site that makes book recommendations based on matching book and reader's mood. You are asked to fill in a short form in which you indicate what you want on a series of dimensions: happy/ sad; funny/ serious; safe/ disturbing; expected/ unpredictable; larger-than-life/ down-to-earth; beautiful/ disgusting; gentle/ violent; easy/ demanding; no sex/ sex; conventional/ unusual; optimistic/ bleak; short/ long. Try it out at **http://www.whichbook.net/**

A QUICK TIP

LibraryThing

In live chat VR, sometimes all that is available to help with RA questions is the open Web. Communal recommender services, such as LibraryThing (**www.librarything.com**) can be very helpful in providing tailored lists of books. LibraryThing employs user tags rather than Library of Congress Subject Headings which are notoriously poor for finding fiction. In December 2008, the most tagged vampire book at LibraryThing was Stephenie Meyer's Twilight series. In the site's discussion group Librarians Who LibraryThing, questions such as, "What do you recommend to Twilight fans?" receive thoughtful and useful answers.

The Five Book Challenge

Read five books in a new genre every year to get an understanding of the genre. This is the five book challenge first issued by Ann Bouricius (2000) in her *Romance Readers' Advisory* and expanded by Joyce Saricks (2001) in *The Readers' Advisory Guide to Genre Fiction*. For fifteen different genres, Saricks suggests five authors and titles that are good starting points for exploring a genre. To really expand your background, start by reading in the genre that you have read the least and have always thought you didn't like. The experience may surprise you.

relationship of two characters that the reader cares about; a well-written thriller is a page-turner; a well-written western is evocative of the place and time of the Old West. Check out what they mean by asking, "Can you tell me about a well-written book that you've enjoyed recently?" They might say Michael Ondaatje's *Anil's Ghost*, but then again, they may mention a genre book.

- Do not be judgmental or try to get readers to change their reading tastes. A reader who enjoys a category romance will definitely not welcome a comment like, "Why waste your time on that when you can be reading a really good book like *Jane Eyre*?"

- If you are in a library small enough for you to get to know readers, talk to them about their reading. Ask them what they liked or didn't like about the books they are returning. Show an active interest.

- Put RA tools close to the fiction collection where users can find them and where you can use them, along with the user, in order to explore reading preferences and narrow down choices of authors or books.

EXERCISE

Practicing the Readers' Advisory Interview

Here are two role-play scenarios to help you practice the readers' advisory interview. In pairs, one person takes the role of the librarian, who must find out what sort of book the user would like, and the other person, who acts the part of the user, is given one of these scripts. Switch roles for the other script. After each role-play, the actors should discuss how they felt about the interview, then invite comments or suggestions from observers. To expand this exercise, create additional scenarios that profile different kinds of readers, e.g., a reader of literary fiction, an adolescent boy who has just gotten turned on to reading by the Harry Potter books and wants other fantasy books that are "just the same," a reader of historical fiction preferably featuring naval or land battles, etc.

1. You like popular fiction and generally try to read what is on the bestseller list. In the past you have particularly enjoyed Sidney Sheldon, Robert Ludlum, and Ken Follett. You enjoy books that have a quick pace and are suspenseful, but you don't like anything with a historical bent. You approach the readers' adviser with this statement: "I'm looking for something good to read. I've checked your bestseller list but I can't seem to find any of them on the shelves."

2. You are a grade twelve student and your English assignment requires that you read one novel by each of three different authors that deal with a similar theme. You have decided to choose books that deal with YA problems—like drugs, pregnancy, or street kids. You approach the readers' adviser with this question: "Where are your books about teenagers?"

(Thanks to Heather Johnson, London Public Library, London, Ontario, for this exercise)

EXERCISE

The Perfect Book

The following seven statements are accounts provided by avid readers when they were asked to describe what they considered to be the "perfect book." For each of the statements:

1. identify the appeal factors that the reader looks for in a book (what do you think are the most important clues, in each case, to the reader's preferences?);

2. use RA tools to come up with a list of five books that you would suggest to the reader that he or she might enjoy; and

3. if you are doing this as a group exercise, compare your lists with others and discuss the reasons for your choices.

A. Most of the books I read are British and written by women, for example, Fay Weldon, Barbara Pym, Miss Read. I like books that present family life, probably because I'm looking for security. I'm honestly interested in how people react under different conditions—how they get through life and face their problems. In fiction, you understand that things are tough for people, but they seem to be solved so easily. Things seem to work out. It doesn't work that way in real life. Maybe that's why I like reading about families, written from a woman's point of view. (female reader, age 31)

B. For a book to somehow touch me, I have to feel that whoever wrote it is sincere. And to me, in a novel especially—but even in a work of biography or history—there has to be something in it that tells me that the author, if not loves, then at least appreciates and is somehow able to understand the people that he or she has chosen to write about. There has to be some kind of grounding in reality for me. Even if the book is a total fantasy, like the devil coming to Moscow [in *The Master and Margarita*], I have to feel that there is a strong element of reality and a strong feeling that the author understands what it means to be alive. That's what a book needs to have to hold my attention. You know, in The *Invisible Man*, Ralph Ellison talks about how he and his little brother—this is a black writer in the South—how he and his little brother learned how to fish by reading novels by Ernest Hemingway. I've always enjoyed that. They'd go page by page and figure it out step by step. (male reader, age 26)

C. I like books about the life of a family—good, clean fiction without all the four-letter words. And not filled with sex, which is not necessary. A book can be written so that you can imagine it without putting it in plain words. I'm reading a good book right now that is really "high society," and it's all about all the fancy clothes they have to wear to their big parties. I also like those stories set in hospitals—doctor and nurse stories. (female reader, age 75)

D. It would be long. I like books that are long because they're good and meaty. You get your value for your money. It would be about 500 to 800 pages. It would have lots of adventure in it. It would be suspenseful. It would have some instructional material in it. It would be very descriptive of places and people. During the book, there would be descriptions of how the people used to do things, or the way things are done now or the way things are made—that sort of thing. The Tom Clancy books are good because they combine science fiction and instructional material right in them. (male reader, age 51)

E. Why don't we look at a book that I really thought was great and maybe that will tell me what I like? Well for instance, *The Far Pavilions*. I like books that can tell me details of cultures and religions that I'm not familiar with. I like lots of sort of nonfictional detail immersed in fiction. I'm very fond of that. I like to immerse myself in a different time space. Perhaps that's why I like the India stories so much, because it is so different. So I guess the perfect book for me takes me to a different time and space. But then there's another element too, when I think of *The Bridges of Madison County*, for instance. I just loved that book because it was about a real person, my age, and it was a beautifully crafted book in the literary sense. But it was about a person my age who had some feelings and so on, that she had to deal with. It also involved her family. So I guess I like to read about women I can identify with, in a historically based novel or real life. (female reader, age 46)

(Cont.d.)

EXERCISE *(Continued)*

The Perfect Book *(Cont'd.)*

F.   I would like to have a novel based on fact, that actually happened in the world. But put it into a novel form, so that there are fictitious characters in the book. I want to be able to relate the book to an actual country, a world, a situation that took place, an earthquake, or a fire, or a bombing, or an incident in a war that you know of or have heard of. *The Bridge on the River Kwai* is probably the movie that has stuck in my mind more than anything else. But, if you actually read the book *On the Kwai River* in Burma, it's not the exact situation of the movie, although some things are the same. There was a railway built, it was built by slaves, it was built by prisoners of war that the Japanese had. That's the type of book that I like. (male reader, age 60)

G.   It would have to have strong characters, both good and bad. There's no use having strong heroines and weak villains because it doesn't make for an interesting book. One of the neat things about the *Sherlock Holmes* mysteries is that Moriarty is such an opponent. He matches Holmes move-for-move and word-for-word. The characters would be the most important thing. And it would have to have a good plot, something that followed and made sense, with a bit of suspense, even if it wasn't necessarily a mystery book. Even in a romance, you don't want to know what's going to happen, where the relationship's going. Those would be the main things—and a few interesting subplots, because they usually spice the book up, but not so many that you get confused. (female reader, age 26)

7.4   Annotated References

7.4.1   Evaluation of the Readers' Advisory Transaction

Bracy, Pauletta Brown. 1996. "The Nature of the Readers' Advisory Transaction in Children's and Young Adult Reading." In *Guiding the Reader to the Next Book* (21–43), edited by Kenneth D. Shearer. New York: Neal-Schuman. Adapting the method used by Shearer (1996), Bracy discovers that advisers frequently made unwarranted assumptions instead of conducting an interview.

Chelton, Mary K. 2003. "Readers' Advisory 101." *Library Journal* 128, no. 18: 38–39. Reflecting on the "service mistakes" that her students encountered when they asked for RA help, Chelton makes six recommendations: beware of turning to the OPAC before finding out what the user wants; know about appeal factors; get beyond personal experience; follow through; improve interpersonal communication; and mine hidden tools.

May, Anne K. 2001. "Readers' Advisory Service: Explorations of the Transaction." In *The Readers' Advisor's Companion* (123–148), edited by Kenneth D. Shearer and Robert Burgin. Littleton, CO: Libraries Unlimited. Provides details of the library visit script and observational worksheet used in the May et al. 2000 study and comments on shortcoming in conducting the RA interview and using professional tools.

May, Anne K., Elizabeth Olesh, Anne Weinlich Mitlenberg, and Catherine Patricia Lackner. 2000. "A Look at Reader's Advisory Services." *Library Journal* 125, no. 15 (September 15): 40–43. Reports the results of an unobtrusive study of readers' advisory service provided at the fifty-four public libraries of the Nassau, New York library system.

Shearer, Kenneth D. 1996. "The Nature of the Readers' Advisory Transaction in Adult Reading." In *Guiding the Reader to the Next Book* (1–20), edited by Kenneth D. Shearer. New York: Neal-Schuman. Reports what happened in fifty-four public library transactions when students in Shearer's graduate course in an MLIS program at North Carolina Central University asked for help with finding a good book to read that was similar to one they had enjoyed earlier.

7.4.2 Indirect RA Services

Armstrong, Nora M. 2001. "No Thanks—I'd Rather Do It Myself: Indirect Advisory Services." In *The Readers' Advisor's Companion*, edited by Kenneth D. Shearer and Robert Burgin. Littleton, CO: Libraries Unlimited.

Baker, Sharon L. 1986. "Overload, Browsers, and Selections." *Library and Information Science Research* 8 (October–December): 315–329. Advocates ways to help browsers narrow selections using such techniques as book lists and book displays.

Baker, Sharon L. 1993. "Booklists: What We Know, What We Need to Know." *RQ* 33, no. 2 (winter): 177–180. Demonstrates how to write book list annotations that are interesting as well as informative.

Baker, Sharon L. 1996. "A Decade's Worth of Research on Browsing Fiction Collections." In *Guiding the Reader to the Next Book*, edited by Kenneth D. Shearer. New York: Neal-Schuman. Provides practical tips for helping browsers.

Moyer, Jessica E. 2008. *Research-Based Readers' Advisory*. Chicago: American Library Association. Chapter 10, "Cataloguing, Classification, and Browsing" summarizes relevant research on fiction classification, genrefication (shelving fiction books by genre), and browsing.

Saricks, Joyce G. 2005. *Readers' Advisory Service in the Public Library*, 3rd ed. Chicago: American Library Association. Chapter 6 on promotion provides an excellent discussion of segregated genre collections, book displays (e.g., stocking a "Good Books You May Have Missed" cart), creating bookmarks on sturdy stock card with a narrowly focused list of authors and titles (e.g., "Locked Room Mysteries"), creating annotated reading lists with a targeted appeal (e.g., "Gentle Reads or Novels with a Touch of Science"), and booktalking.

Saricks, Joyce G., and Nancy Brown. 1997. *Readers' Advisory Service in the Public Library*, 2nd ed. Chicago: American Library Association.

7.4.3 Readers' Advisory and Reading

Burgin, Robert, ed. 2004. *Nonfiction Readers' Advisory*. Westport, CT: Libraries Unlimited. A valuable collection of articles on nonfiction and pleasure reading that expand to nonfiction the concepts of genre and appeal factors previously used mostly in the context of fiction.

Chelton, Mary K. 1999. "What We Know and Don't Know about Reading, Readers, and Readers' Advisory Services." *Public Libraries* 38, no. 1 (January/February): 42–47. Summarizes research on reading and readers, along with suggestions about the implications of this research for public libraries.

De la Peña McCook, Kathleen, and Gary O. Rolstad, eds. 1993. *Developing Readers' Advisory Services: Concepts and Commitments*. New York: Neal-Schuman.

Jones, Patrick. 1992. *Connecting Young Adults and Libraries*. New York: Neal-Schuman. Includes a useful section on talking with young adults.

Moyer, Jessica E. 2005. "Adult Fiction Reading: A Literature Review of Readers' Advisory Services, Adult Fiction Librarianship and Fiction Readers." *Reference and User Services Quarterly* 44, no. 2 (spring): 38–47. Reviews articles, books, theses and reports published from 1995 to June 2003 on fiction classification, browsing, user studies, and adult readers' advisory service.

Moyer, Jessica E. 2008. *Research-based Readers' Advisory*. Chicago: American Library Association. Chapters illuminate key topics such as nonfiction RA, audiovisual RA, book groups, the RA interview, and others from two perspectives: Moyer's review of the research literature and the view from the field provided by librarians on the front lines of RA work. Brings together in one convenient place summaries and an evaluation of the key works on readers' advisory.

Radway, Janice. 1994. "Beyond Mary Bailey and Old Maid Librarians: Reimagining Readers and Rethinking Reading." *Journal of Education for Library and Information Science* 35, no. 4 (fall): 275–96. Written originally as a talk for librarians, this article summarizes research on reading as a context for arguing for a new way of thinking about pleasure reading.

Ross, Catherine Sheldrick. 1991. "Readers' Advisory Services: New Directions." *RQ* 30, no. 4 (summer): 503–18.

Ross, Catherine Sheldrick. 1995. "'If They Read Nancy Drew, So What?': Series Book Readers Talk Back." *Library and Information Science Research* 17, no. 3 (summer): 201–36. Research results based on interviews with readers suggest that series books can be allies in the making of readers.

Ross, Catherine Sheldrick. 2001. "Making Choices: What Readers Say about Choosing Books to Read for Pleasure." *The Acquisitions Librarian* 25: 5–21. Analyzes 194 open-ended interviews with avid readers in order to understand how readers choose as well as reject books.

Ross, Catherine Sheldrick, and Mary Kay Chelton. 2001. "Reader's Advisory: Matching Mood and Material." *Library Journal* 126, no. 2 (February 1): 52–55. Draws out the implications for readers' advisers of Ross's research on the factors that influence readers' decisions when choosing a book to read for pleasure.

Ross, Catherine Sheldrick, Lynne (E.F.) McKechnie, and Paulette M. Rothbauer. 2006. *Reading Matters: What the Research Reveals about Reading, Libraries, and Community*. Westport, CT: Libraries Unlimited. By providing a road map to research findings on reading, audiences, genres, and the role of libraries in promoting literacy and reading, this guide offers a rationale for making pleasure reading a priority in the library and in schools.

Saricks, Joyce G. 2001. *The Readers' Advisory Guide to Genre Fiction*. Chicago: American Library Association. Written by one of the world's best readers' advisers, this overview of fifteen genres and their appeal to readers is a tremendous resource for readers' advisers. Each chapter contains a section on the readers' advisory interview for the particular genre under discussion.

Saricks, Joyce. 2005. "At Leisure: Writing a Reader Profile; or, What I Like and Why." *Booklist* 102, 3 (Oct. 1): 35. Tips for readers' advisers on how to understand their own reading interests.

Shearer, Kenneth D., and Robert Burgin, eds. 2001. *The Readers' Advisor's Companion*. Littleton, CO: Libraries Unlimited. Sixteen articles by researchers and noted practitioners, including Wayne Wiegand, Duncan Smith, Joyce Saricks, Robert Burgin, Roberta Johnson, and Glen Holt.

Smith, Duncan. 1993. "Reconstructing the Reader: Educating Readers' Advisors." *Collection Building* 12, no. 3/4: 21–30. Smith's article is one of a number of very useful articles in this special theme issue of *Collection Building* on readers' advisory.

Smith, Duncan. 1996. "Librarians' Abilities to Recognize Reading Tastes." In *Guiding the Reader to the Next Book*, edited by Kenneth D. Shearer. New York: Neal-Schuman. An interesting and informed demonstration by three experienced readers' advisers of how to analyze a reader's response to "Tell me about a book you've read and enjoyed" and make book suggestions.

Smith, Duncan. 2000. "Talking with Readers: A Competency Based Approach to Readers Advisory Service." *Reference & User Services Quarterly* 40, no. 2 (winter): 135–142. Describes a training manual, *Talking with Readers*, that Smith and others associated with NoveList developed for the Minnesota Division of Library Development and Services. The key competencies identified are a background in fiction and nonfiction; an understanding of readers; the appeal factors of books; the readers' advisory transaction.

Watson, Dana, and RUSA CODES Readers' Advisory Committee. 2000. "Time to Turn the Page: Library Education for Readers' Advisory Services." *Reference & User Services Quarterly* 40, no. 2 (winter): 143–146. Summarizes what is being taught in readers' advisory-related courses at fourteen of the fifty-six ALA-accredited master's programs and recommends that other programs do more to provide RA training.

Yu, Liangzhi, and Ann O'Brien. 1996. "Domain of Adult Fiction Librarianship." *Advances in Librarianship*, vol. 20: 151–189. A review of the literature on adult fiction provision in libraries, emphasizing studies from the UK and including work focusing on understanding fiction readers, browsing, fiction representation and retrieval systems, books promotion, and readers' advisory.

7.4.4 Readers' Advisory Interview

Booth, Heather. 2005. "RA for YA: Tailoring the Readers' Advisory Interview to the Needs of Young Adult Patrons." *Public Libraries* 44, no. 1: 33–36.

Chelton, Mary K. 1993. "Read Any Good Books Lately? Helping Patrons Find What They Want." *Library Journal* 118, no. 8 (May 1): 33–37. An excellent short introduction to RA skills.

Fialkoff, Francine. 1998. "New Twists on an Old Service." *Library Journal* 123, no. 17 (October 15): 58.

Johnson, Roberta S., and Natalya Fishman. 2002. "The History of Fiction_L." *Reference & User Services Quarterly* 42, no. 1 (Fall): 30–33.

Moyer, Jessica E. 2008. *Research-based Readers' Advisory*. Chicago: American Library Association. In chapter 8, Moyer summarizes the sparse literature on the readers' advisory interview, calling it an essential but understudied transaction.

NoveList RA News. "Lessons Learned in Form-based Readers' Advisory." Available: www.ebscohost.com/novelist/uploads/topicFile-170.pdf (accessed April 2, 2009).

Pejtersen, Annelise, and Jutta Austin. 1983–84. "Fiction Retrieval: Experimental Design and Evaluation of a Search System Based on Users' Value Criteria." Parts 1 and 2. *Journal of Documentation* 39, no. 4 (December): 230–46; 40, no. 1 (March): 25–35. As a preliminary to designing their classification system for fiction retrieval, the authors analyzed three hundred user/librarian conversations as the basis for identifying the dimensions of fiction books that are important to readers.

Saricks, Joyce G. 2001. *The Readers' Advisory Guide to Genre Fiction*. Chicago and London: American Library Association. Contains sections on the readers' advisory interview tailored for each genre.

Did You Know?
Roberta Johnson started the RA listserv Fiction_L in 1995 when she was readers' advisory services librarian at the Morton Grove Public Library (Johnson and Fishman, 2002). It has been a space for readers' advisers to build community, post questions, and share reading lists. You can find booklists on such topics as "romance with vampires for teens," "mysteries set in hot climates," and "desert island books." Dorothy Broderick has said, "Real librarians read Fiction_L." Check it out at: **www. webrary.org/rs/rsmenu.html**

Saricks, Joyce G. 2005. *Readers' Advisory Service in the Public Library*, 3d ed. Chicago: American Library Association. An indispensable guide that covers reference sources, appeal factors of books, promotion, passive strategies, and training. Contains a chapter on the readers' advisory interview which is defined as a conversation about books.

Williamsburg Regional Library. Looking for a Good Book program. Available: www.wrl.org/bookweb/RA/index.html (accessed April 2, 2009). A form-based readers advisory service.

7.4.5 Guides and Tools for Readers' Advisers

After you have read Joyce G. Saricks's (2001) article, "The Best Tools for Advisors and How to Integrate Them into Successful Transactions" in *The Readers' Advisor's Companion* (Littleton CO: Libraries Unlimited), you will find these sources helpful.

American Library Association's Readers' Advisory Committee, Collection Development Section, RUSA. 1996. "Readers' Advisory Reference Tools: A Suggested List of Fiction Sources for All Libraries." *RQ* 36, no. 2 (winter): 206–29. This bibliography of recommended tools for readers' advisers is a good starting point.

Barron, Neil, Wayne Barton, Kristen Ramsdell, and Steven A. Stilwell. 1990. *What Do I Read Next? A Reader's Guide to Current Genre Fiction*. Detroit: Gale Research. An annual publication.

Berman, Matt. 1995–96. *What Else Should I Read? Guiding Kids to Good Books*. 2 vols. Littleton, CO: Libraries Unlimited. Helps students in grades three through eight find books by subject, author, and genre.

Bouricius, Ann. 2000. *The Romance Readers' Advisory: The Librarian's Guide to Love in the Stacks*. Chicago: American Library Association.

Herald, Diana Tixier. 2003. *Teen Genreflecting: A Guide to Reading Interests*, 2d ed. Westport, CT: Libraries Unlimited

Herald, Diana Tixier. 2006. *Genreflecting: A Guide to Reading Interests in Genre Fiction*, 6th ed. Westport, CT: Libraries Unlimited. Invaluable for readers' advisory work, lists authors and books, grouped by genres, themes, and types. New since the fifth edition are essays on the social nature of reading, the history of readers' advisory, the readers' advisory interview, and serving today's reader.

Herald, Diana Tixier. 2007. *Fluent in Fantasy: The Next Generation*. Westport, CT: Libraries Unlimited.

Johnson, Roberta S. 2001. "The Global Conversation about Books, Readers, and Reading on the Internet." In *The Readers' Advisor's Companion*, edited by Kenneth D. Shearer and Robert Burgin. Littleton, CO: Libraries Unlimited. A compact and informative introduction to the art of getting the most from Internet resources.

LibraryThing. Available: www.librarything.com (accessed December 24, 2008). Communal book cataloging (tagging), recommending, and reviewing Web site that employs user tags instead of library subject headings. Available free on the open Web.

Morton Grove Public Library's Webrary: The Reader's Corner. [Morton Grove, Illinois]. This Web site is a gold standard for online readers' advisory help, including links to book lists, book blogs, book lists, and the archives for Fiction_L. Available: www.webrary.org/rs/rsmenu.html (accessed April 2, 2009).

Moyer, Jessica E. 2008. "Core Collection: Electronic Readers' Advisory Tools." *Booklist* 104, no. 21 (July): 10–11. Provides an annotated list of recommended electronic RA tools including subscription databases and free Web-based tools.

NoveList [online]. EBSCO Publishing. Created by Duncan Smith, NoveList is a subscription Web–based readers' advisory database and resource that provides access to 150,000 fiction titles and over 4,000 custom created articles and lists. In 2008, NoveList Plus was launched with access to 50,000 "readable nonfiction titles." Readers can find new titles by genre, setting, characters or subject. Available: www.ebscohost.com/novelist/.

Pearl, Nancy. 2002. *Now Read This II: A Guide to Mainstream Fiction, 1990–2001.* Westport, CT: Libraries Unlimited.

Pearl, Nancy. 2003. *Book Lust: Recommended Reading for Every Mood, Moment, and Reason.* Seattle, WA: Sasquatch Books.

Pearl, Nancy. 2005. *More Book Lust: Recommended Reading for Every Mood, Moment, and Reason.* Seattle, WA: Sasquatch Books.

Quinn, Mary Ellen. 2008. "Core Collection: Readers'-Advisory Guides." *Booklist* 104, no. 21 (July): 8–9.

Radford, Marie L., and Lynn Silipigni Connaway. 2005–2008. "Seeking Synchronicity: Evaluating Virtual Reference Services from User, Non-User, and Librarian Perspectives." Institute for Museum and Library Services, Rutgers University (NJ), and OCLC, Online Computer Library Center. Grant Web site available: www.oclc.org/research/projects/synchronicity (accessed September 22, 2008).

Ramsdell, Kristin. 1997. *What Romance Do I Read Next?* Detroit: Gale Research.

Reader's Advisor Online. A subscription database based on Libraries Unlimited's excellent Genreflecting Advisory Series. Available: http://readersadvisoronline.com (accessed December 26, 2008).

Readersadvisory.org is a Web site developed by RA practitioners to share ideas and RA resources. Available: www.readersadvisory.org (accessed December 26, 2008).

Reference and User Services Association. 2004. Collection Development and Evaluation Section Readers' Advisory Committee. "Recommended Readers' Advisory Tools." *Reference & User Services Quarterly* 43, no 4 (summer): 294–305. An annotated list of RA tools for a core collection and an expanded collection, with sections devoted to genres (e.g., horror, inspirational, mystery, romance, science fiction, and fantasy), to audience (e.g., young adult) and to services (e.g., book discussion).

Smith, Sharron, and Maureen O'Connor. 2005. *Canadian Fiction: A Guide to Reading Interests.* Westport, CT: Libraries Unlimited.

Wyatt, Neal. 2007. *The Readers' Advisory Guide to Nonfiction.* Chicago: American Library Association. Describes the key categories of nonfiction that appeal to pleasure readers.

Establishing Policy and Training for the Reference Interview

8.1   The Library Context

Throughout this book, we have stressed that a reference question is an informational need that arises in the context of the user's day-to-day life. A reference interview is a structured conversation that links the user's world to our information systems in a way that makes sense to the user. As we have said in our discussion of Brenda Dervin's sense-making theory (3.2.3), information seeking occurs within this larger context of the user's situation, the specific information that the user wants to know in that situation (the gap), and the specific goal that the user wants to achieve in the situation (the uses to which the information will be put). Situations in which people need information are diverse and numerous. A person may want to write a speech, find a research topic, make an important personal decision, cope with a legal, health, or family emergency, prepare for a career, apply for a job, find comfort or consolation, find relaxation in a hobby, or simply find out more about something to satisfy a curiosity. In each situation, the gaps in the user's understanding—that is, what the person wants to know—differ from one individual to the next and can't be predicted from the situation alone. For this reason, a well-conducted reference interview is a crucial element in the process of linking the user's information need to the store of information.

In this final chapter, we raise for discussion some of the issues that affect information service providers within the library system and we place particular emphasis on institutional policy and training. It is not enough for an individual librarian to want to provide excellent service to users through conducting effective reference interviews and linking users to sources. The library as an institutional system must support the individual librarian through the articulation of policies that support service goals and through the provision of training.

8.2 Institutional Policy and the Reference Interview

8.2.1 Typical Policies

The librarian at work operates within a system that provides guidelines and constraints in the form of written policy. This policy is usually drawn from a broader mission statement (e.g., to serve the informational needs of residents of X county, or to serve the students and faculty of educational institution Y, or to serve the employees of company Z), and from a set of legal statements approved by the governing body. Parts of a library's policy, and the law that governs it, are usually based on even broader professional guidelines such as "freedom of information" and the right of the user to have access to information service.

The content of library policies will differ depending on the type and size of the library. Because part of the mission of academic libraries, for example, is to educate students in the finding of information, library use instruction will be a more important component than would be the case in public libraries. Public library policies themselves may take different approaches according to the type of user—students working on a project may be encouraged to learn how to find information themselves while older adults wanting information on homecare may be given the information and helped to make contact with appropriate local services. In special libraries, the level of service is generally higher, with the librarian providing not only directions but also copies or summaries of the material, all within very tight time frames. Policies of library consortia attempt to ensure equivalent service across the consortial membership.

In addition to general library policies, some libraries have policies specifically covering the delivery of reference services—in person, by live chat, e-mail or other electronic means, by telephone, and by post. A written reference policy is important because it helps to set service priorities, establish standards and levels of service, ensure consistency in staff response to similar situations, provide a basis for staff training and evaluation, and clarify goals and objectives (Easley, 1985; and, for examples, see DeMiller, 1994, and Brumley, 2004).

All of these policies have two intended audiences—the library users and the library staff. Usually, two different kinds of policy statements are produced—a shorter statement for library patrons and a longer policy manual for staff. Policy statements written for library users list a library's policies with respect to nature of the collections, services available to them, expected user behavior, and any necessary limits on service. These policy statements sometimes refer to library association guidelines, such as the American Library Association's Library Bill of Rights and its Freedom to Read Statement.

Libraries also have written policies and procedures manuals exclusively for staff members that cover, among other things: standards of service, levels and limits of service to users, priorities of service, and the operation of the library. Staff manuals may also include recommended procedures that ensure consistency in practical service delivery, as well as guidelines to staff reference behavior. These staff manuals also often refer to library association guidelines, such as the ALA Code of Ethics and sometimes to specific state or provincial legislation as well. The staff policy and procedures manual, which is more detailed than the statements designed for users, not only serves current employees but is used to train new recruits and to evaluate staff. Both the public and the staff documents should be reviewed regularly to ensure that they remain current. Sometimes older policies become outdated, and new unwritten policies develop that should be incorporated into the written documents. In particular the rapid growth of virtual reference (VR) services needs to be matched by the development of policies that reflect the whole range of reference modes provided.

Reference department policy statements directed at users should be available to walk-in users and also be published on library Web sites. Among the many advantages of posting a reference policy on your library Web site are that you can refer to it from your library home page or from other appropriate pages in your site and provide links to it, and that you can provide links from the posted reference policy to relevant sections of your own Web site as well as to the various library association statements that you wish to highlight for users. In this way, the policy document itself can be more concise.

In contrast to policy statements, reference department staff manuals, which are not considered public documents, are often mounted on library Intranets requiring password access. This limitation to an internal audience is appropriate, as staff manuals provide a great deal of detail that is not of general interest to the public. The focus of many staff manuals is system based, with names and addresses of people, information about buildings, forms, and other internal information. Some have links to training modules or to performance standards.

8.2.2 What Should Be in the Reference Service Policy?

Typically, a reference department policy statement for staff consists of two main parts, one general and one more specific. The general statement usually shows how reference department activities fit into the library's overall mission statement. It covers the basic service goals, philosophy, and ethics of the reference department. This section might include a separate mission statement for different kinds of reference service (walk-in, virtual, and telephone), explain the purpose of reference guidelines, and describe the general role of reference staff. A more specific section usually deals with guidelines for reference service to library users, such as desk service guidelines, question guidelines, online searching, and loan of reference materials (Antone et al., 1994).

VR policies usually indicate audience (who may use the service), level of service (question restrictions), and privacy policy. Statements on acceptable and unacceptable user behavior in the VR environment are less common (Kern and Gillie, 2004). While VR policies should be a natural extension of existing policies, they do not typically include mention of

Conducting the Reference Interview

the reference interview. Because interviews are often overlooked in VR interactions but are critical for providing a helpful answer (Chapter 6), they should be specifically mentioned in VR policies and guidelines.

The Dorchester County Public Library in Maryland has a Web site with a clearly stated reference policy and procedures manual available to the public. It includes a section on "Courtesy and Interest" and another on the "Reference Interview" (see Exercise—Policy Discussion). In addition to the sections quoted in the exercise, the policy provides some guidelines on such topics as walk-in and telephone inquiries, leaving the information desk, and evaluation. There is, however, no mention of the need for an interview in response to e-mailed reference questions nor of staff responsibility to interview users who submit questions through its live chat service offered through a statewide consortium, Maryland AskUsNow! The Dorchester County PL policy notes that as part of evaluation, "Library staff members will be observed by the department head on the use of the Model Reference Behaviors. Observations will be included on the employee performance evaluation."

The problem with many reference staff manuals is that often the reference interview is taken for granted but invisible. Sometimes it is not mentioned at all or is mentioned only in passing in a subordinate clause such as, "After you have conducted a reference interview..." Quite often there is no discussion of the interview process itself, no list of model behaviors, and usually no explicitly stated requirement regarding reference interviews. Even the RUSA (2000) "Guidelines for Information Services" do not explicitly mention the reference interview. Guideline 1.1 states, "The goal of information services is to provide the information sought by the user," but it does not indicate how the librarian determines that information need. The RUSA (2004) "Guidelines for Implementing and Maintaining Virtual Reference Services" simply notes that "standard guidelines of reference service (such as reference interviewing, exchange of questions between services, et al.) should prevail." The RUSA (2004) "Guidelines for Behavioral Performance of Reference and Information Services Professionals" *do* emphasize the behaviors necessary in a good reference interview. Nevertheless, the reference interview seems to be assumed in most library policies, rather like breathing. This is not good enough. We believe that the reference interview should not only be mentioned explicitly, but should also be *required*. One simple thing that all libraries could, and should, do right away is to add a paragraph to their reference policy along the lines of the following:

A reference interview must be conducted with every user who asks an information question. This means that at the traditional reference desk, when a user asks, "Where are your books on transportation?" you should not just say, "Our books on transportation are over there; I'll show you where you can look," but also add, "We have a lot of materials on this topic. Is there a specific aspect of transportation you are interested in?" This means that in a VR situation, when a chat user says, "I'd like to find information on diving lessons for my fifteen-year-old daughter," you should ask, "Is there a particular type of diving you are interested in?" *before* sending e-sources to the user.

Establishing Policy and Training for the Reference Interview

Why require a reference interview? After all, it could be argued that most librarians have learned about interviewing in their professional education and are able to judge when an interview is needed. However, as we have emphasized throughout this book, in practice, staff members bypass the interview about half the time and in such cases usually provide less than satisfactory service. The "diving" example (p. 209) was from an actual VR question—as it turned out, the user really wanted information about *driving* lessons, not *diving* lessons. As a result of bypassing the reference interview, the librarian wasted valuable time looking for the wrong information when a quick probe could have clarified the user's request (Radford, 2006).

A truly effective information service can be achieved only when reference interviews are routinely conducted by all staff members, even if the reference interview consists of the minimal "Are you finding what you are looking for?" or "If you don't find the information there, please ask again." If the policy statement explicitly requires a reference interview, staff members will grow more attuned to assessing whether people are really finding out what they want to know. The more reference interviews librarians engage in, after proper training, the better they will be able to serve library users. As staff members begin to use reference interviews consistently and skillfully, they will come to realize the value of the process. There is a final advantage to requiring staff to conduct reference interviews. When there is an explicit statement requiring its use rather than, as at present, a tacit assumption that somehow interviews just happen, management is more likely to pay attention to the reference interview. This emphasis in the policy means a greater likelihood that training will be provided and that interviewing skills will be evaluated.

Sample Guidelines for Reference Behavior

Guidelines for reference behavior are readily available on the Internet (see the Annotated Readings at the end of this chapter). One of the best, "The Maryland Model Reference Behaviors," can be found on the *Ohio Reference Excellence on the Web* site (see Ohio Library Council), which includes model reference behaviors for in-person and remote services (our version of the model behaviors is found later in this chapter). Another excellent set of guidelines is RUSA's (2004) "Guidelines for Behavioral Performance of Reference and Information Services Professionals." Other guideline documents, such as RUSA's (2003) "Professional Competencies for Reference and User Services Librarians," refer to the behavioral guidelines rather than repeating them. Guidelines for reference services for specific types of questions (e.g. medical, legal), and types of users (e.g. teens, users with disabilities) are available as well. See Chapter 5 for a discussion of these types of questions.

In concert with the explosion of VR services, there continues to be a growing number of sound guidelines being developed for the virtual environment (Morin, 2004). While most guidelines for VR make only passing mention, if any, to the reference interview, the "IFLA Digital Reference Guidelines" include a detailed section on the practice of digital reference that provides specific phrasing that can be used in virtual

---

EXERCISE

Can You Improve on This Statement?

One public library reference policy includes only the following statement. How might it be improved?

Reference Interview: The reference interview is used to help define customer needs and to answer customer questions. Staff will begin reference transactions with verification of customer needs. The structured discussion that follows should clarify questions to be answered and the best way to provide the customer with information requested. Staff will provide a full citation of the resources used or recommended to the customer. Staff will also make referrals to other XX Library units or outside agencies as needed. The reference transaction will conclude with verification that the information need has been met.

YOUR POLICY MANUAL SHOULD INCLUDE THESE ELEMENTS

- A statement that the reference interview (at least a brief one) is mandatory
- A short explanation of the value of the reference interview and why it is required
- A listing of reference behaviors that elicit information from users
- A reference to guidelines such as the Maryland Model Reference Behaviors or RUSA's (2004) "Guidelines for Behavioral Performance of Reference and Information Services Professionals" (The complete text of these guidelines should be available in print form either as an appendix or as a separate document.)
- A statement that the guidelines will be used for purposes of training and evaluation

encounters. With the expansion of distance education, guidelines for serving off-campus students via digital means have been developed (see Jones, 2004, for a comparison of several guidelines produced by ACRL and other associations).

RUSA's most recent version of guidelines for cooperative reference apply to any type of cooperation through any modes of communication. These guidelines focus on administration, delivery, and evaluation. There is, however, an important omission: no mention is made of the responsibility of the requesting institution to ensure that the forwarded question is, in fact, the real question. Guidelines from individual consortia and collaboratives tend also to focus on systems-based issues of administration and technology rather than on user-based issues of reference communication. QuestionPoint's "24/7 collaborative polices and procedures" manual does, however, include a section on performance standards that identifies the reference interview as critical to the success of chat sessions and provides some guidance on clarifying the user's request. (See section 5.8 for more discussion of policies for consortial reference.)

8.3 Training Staff in Reference Interview Skills

A library that truly believes in its mission as an information service must hire managers who value and support the front-line staff who deliver the service. Providing staff training as a part of professional development is an essential ingredient of staff support. By helping reference workers develop the skills they need to do their jobs well, staff training also enhances job satisfaction and professional growth. Contrary to what some managers and even some new librarians believe, reference librarians do not spring fully-formed from library school. Nor does prolonged experience in itself ensure that librarians are providing good service—lengthy experience repeating behaviors such as the "without-speaking-

BEFORE TRAINING, ASK THESE QUESTIONS

Before developing any training proposal, first ask yourself these questions:

- To whom are the events of the training program geared? Professionals only? Support staff? New staff? A mix?

- Is in-service training designed for a particular library more appropriate than mixing staff from different types of libraries?

- What are the goals of the overall training program (i.e., all events)? What are the objectives of a specific training event? How will you know whether these objectives are achieved?

- Is the content of each session manageable? Is there sufficient time for trainees to learn without being overwhelmed? If skills are taught in a series of events, is there enough time between events for trainees to practice on the job? Are sessions scheduled closely enough together that trainees will not forget too much between sessions?

- What provision is there for participants to evaluate the training event itself? What are you trying to evaluate—participants' general satisfaction with the trainer's approach? New knowledge learned by participants? The trainer's success in teaching new skills? The learner's ability to use the skills? Effect of training on performance? These are all different outcomes and require different means of evaluation.

- What specific recommendations are there for follow-up training and reinforcement of the new skills?

- What evaluation instruments are recommended? Are these designed primarily to provide feedback and support? Are they tied to job performance ratings? (Two separate strategies might be designed, for these two different purposes.)

she-began-to-type" maneuver, or strategies of negative closure can scarcely be considered an advantage (see 3.1.1).

In the Library Visit Study (see 1.3), users sometimes attributed unsatisfactory service to the librarian's indifference, but is this the case? The decisive question here is: Could reference librarians have provided satisfactory answers if their lives depended on it? If the answer is yes, then the problem to be addressed is the librarian's attitude toward the user. However there is evidence in the Library Visit Study that at least part of the problem might lie elsewhere. Users who had received less than satisfactory service often said things like, "He looked puzzled," "She looked annoyed," or "The computer screen was being used as a shield." It seems that sometimes professional staff feel overwhelmed and defensive, in which case the answer may be in-service training that gives staff the tools to do the good job they would really like to do. In particular, libraries should examine the type of support they provide to new staff, including orientation according to accepted guidelines for public service behavior.

Training should be ongoing and available throughout the staff member's career. It must not be left to chance but be an explicit objective in the library's policies. In budget planning, administrators should earmark funds to regular training activities for both new and experienced employees. Even if employees leave a particular library system, their training is transferable to other settings and enriches the profession as a whole. In addition to library-funded training programs, individual librarians must take responsibility for their own continuing education through memberships in library associations and attendance at training sessions that these associations provide. The following sections give an overview of ways for using this book and other training materials for independent and group training. For a more complete discussion of the theory and practice of training library staff, read Chapter 10 in *Communicating Professionally* (Ross and Dewdney, 1998).

8.3.1 Independent Learning

Reference service policy ideally includes "off-desk" time for staff to upgrade their skills and continue their education through reading or using distance-education programs. However, in practice other duties and demands often encroach on the time available, which is one reason that we have written this book in a modular format that can be read in short periods. It is possible for an independent learner to work his way through this book, focusing on learning one skill at a time, and practicing each new skill with library users and noting the results. For example, a list of general-purpose open questions can be taped to the desk as a reminder, or a name tag worn as an experiment for a shift or two. Some of the suggested exercises can be done alone. Self-study training specific to reference interviewing is readily available online. Among the best sites are Ohio Library Council's *Ohio Reference Excellence on the Web* and the Nebraska Library Commission's *Statewide Training for Accurate Reference*. Reference interview training for support staff is available at Librarysupportstaff.com. Since the reference interview is an act of communication, self-study can only go so far. A better way of learning is to practice with others—perhaps with other staff at first—with the support of a skilled trainer.

8.3.2 Group Learning

A successful way of training staff in reference interview skills is to work in small groups using the microtraining method described in 2.4.1. The essence of this approach is identifying and defining the unique skills or behaviors that facilitate any interview, observing each skill as modeled by others, reading about the skills and its underlying concepts, practicing the skill in a supportive environment, using the skill with real library users, and finally, teaching the skill to others. Allen Ivey, who developed microtraining, calls this the "Learn, Do and Teach" approach. The most difficult stage is fine-tuning the new skills and integrating them seamlessly into existing behavior. Check out section 4.2 for proven tips on integrating skills. It is natural for trainees to feel awkward at first. The key is practice—trying the skills out first in non-threatening or simple situations and gradually increasing confidence with experience. In any group training, a leader with professional knowledge of group dynamics is essential. This book can be used by experienced leaders to introduce new skills and approaches. In-group sessions can be supplemented not only with reading but also through peer-coaching, so that trainees can continue to get feedback, evaluation, and support.

There are many ways to set up the necessary training for staff. Many of the basic skills, such as listening, paraphrasing and asking open questions, apply to all kinds of interview situations, and general training is available either online or in classes at local colleges. Group trainers who are focusing on the reference interview can use the online self-study programs recommended in section 8.3.1. *Ohio Reference Excellence on the Web*, for example, allows for supervisor input and feedback. Library associations are active supporters of continuing education and skilled leaders often offer workshops at professional library conferences. Outside of conferences, some library associations provide on-going training programs, increasingly working together to do so. One example is the Education Institute, a partnership of library associations providing online and audio courses as well as audio and Web conferences. In addition, individual libraries can organize in-house workshops and other training activities. See Hirko and Ross (2003) for suggestions on VR training.

To be truly effective, training must be ongoing rather than a one-shot event, and must be explicitly relevant to information service. A regular series of workshops for new or for more senior employees can be arranged for individual libraries or groups of libraries. Library managers proposing to hire a trainer should always check out his or her qualifications and obtain references from other organizations that have used this trainer. Whether or not the library uses a professional consultant or relies on its own staff as trainers, objectives must be specific and must take into account that a broad training program will need to include many events at different times and for different types of staff.

It is often effective to use an approach to training that combines outside training with in-house support for practice, peer coaching, and follow-up. The first step may be to invite an outside expert to provide staff training in reference skills and reinforce the point that skills can be learned. One value in bringing in the outside person is that it signals the fact that the library system takes reference training seriously and is willing to invest in staff training. Another advantage is that trainees might be more open and less self-conscious with a trainer who is not also a supervisor.

The next step should then be on-going reinforcement of skills within the library system itself, using peer coaching. Peer coaching can be a very effective approach as long as the environment is professional, supportive, and not threatening. When practicing new skills, trainees need to feel that it's okay to make some mistakes at first; that success is measured when each attempt comes a bit closer to the desired behavior; and that asking for feedback is a helpful element when mastering a skill. Peer coaching focused on the reference interview makes reference staff members more aware of their communication behaviors. Writing on the use of peer coaching to improve the reference process, Huling (1999) identified feedback as the most important facet of training, but she noted that most reference librarians and managers are not practiced in the art of providing feedback. It *is* a skill that can be developed with practice. See "Guidelines for Feedback" for some suggestions.

Did You Know?
The training method used affects how long we retain what we have learned. The "Learning Pyramid" suggests that trainees retain only 5 percent of what they hear in lectures and 10 percent of what they read, but they will retain 75 percent of what they practice by doing and 90 percent if they teach others. Trainees forget what they have learned in as little as twenty-four hours, without continual practice and follow-up sessions. The Learning Pyramid is most often attributed to the National Training Laboratories in Bethel Maine, but Atherton (2008) explains that even NTL has no idea where it comes from and cannot trace the original research. However, even if the research that supports the percentages is lost (or never existed), the pyramid is, as Atherton points out, "intuitively accurate." It can be used as a guideline in planning training sessions.

GUIDELINES FOR PROVIDING FEEDBACK

If you are called upon to provide feedback in a peer coaching or other training situations, here are some guidelines:

- **Start first with one or two positive comments**, even when the overall performance was not very good. Find something good that you can praise. You could say to the interviewer, "You did a good job of creating a welcoming climate by looking up and smiling," or "You showed a real interest in the user's question." Feedback that is entirely negative discourages further effort. The person getting the entirely negative feedback is apt to think, "What's the point of trying? I'm *never* going to be any good at this."

- **Be specific.** Focus on concrete instances of behavior, not generalities. Don't say, "Your interviewing skills need brushing up." Better to say, "I noticed that you asked two closed questions: 'Is this for a school project?' and 'Do you need magazine articles?' but you didn't find out what specifically the user wanted to know. An open question might have worked here, such as, 'What particular aspect of environmentalism are you interested in?'"

- **Be descriptive** rather than simply providing a global evaluation. Saying something is excellent or terrible is not very helpful. Especially when you are making suggestions for improvements, it is important to stick to observable facts and behaviors. You shouldn't make comments like, "That last reference interview had problems," or "When you were negotiating that interview, you didn't use inclusion." Instead, you could say, "When the user asked his question, I noticed that you walked away to get the information he needed, but you didn't tell him what you were doing. I thought the user seemed confused about whether he should follow you or not."

- **Be realistic.** Suggest improvements that are within the capability of the person. Improvements are usually made one step at a time. An interviewer who has relied for years on the "without-speaking-she-began-to-type maneuver" could be encouraged to look at the user, smile, and use acknowledgment.

- **Limit your suggestions** for improvements to the most important one or two areas. It's better for the trainee to focus on one skill at a time. Once one skill is mastered, other areas can be focused on.

- **Suggest rather than prescribe.** In most situations, it works best to suggest a change tentatively, as in, "You might want to ask an open question here."

- **Consider the needs of the receiver of your feedback.** Provide the amount of information that the receiver can use, rather than everything that can be said. Before giving feedback, you could ask, "Which particular areas would you like feedback on?" The trainee may want to focus on a specific skill, such as asking open questions or using a follow-up.

- **Seek out opportunities to offer sincere praise** (people will recognize and resent insincerity). People work and learn better when their value is recognized and acknowledged.

- **Create a climate that is positive and encouraging**—that's the key to providing helpful coaching.

Before you start on a peer coaching program, you need to agree on a set of behavioral guidelines and pick specific behaviors for immediate attention. You may wish to use the "Model Reference Behaviors Checklist,"

MODEL REFERENCE BEHAVIORS CHECKLIST

The user's initial question (record the user's words verbatim):

What the user really wanted (as clarified in the interview):

Model behaviors: Put a check beside each behavior that the staff member displayed during the interview. For verbal skills, record as accurately as possible what the librarian says.

SKILL	OBSERVED (check if present)	LIBRARIAN'S WORDS (record verbatim)
Being approachable		
The staff member miles or has a pleasant facial expression		
The staff member looks up		
The staff member makes eye contact		
The staff member gives a friendly greeting		
The staff member is at eye level with the user		
Establishing a comfortable environment		
The staff member speaks in a pleasant tone of voice		
The staff member appears unhurried and willing to take time with the user's question		
The staff member maintains a distance that seems comfortable to the user		
Showing interest		
The staff member puts aside competing activities		
The staff member maintains appropriate eye contact		
The staff member makes short encouraging comments such as "Um-hmm," "That's interesting," or "Yes?" to encourage the user to say more		
The staff member gives full attention to the user		
The staff member doesn't just point to distant resources but goes with the user		

(Cont'd.)

MODEL REFERENCE BEHAVIORS CHECKLIST *(Continued)*

Model behaviors *(Cont'd.)*

Put a check beside each behavior that the staff member displayed during the interview. For verbal skills, record as accurately as possible what the librarian says.

SKILL	OBSERVED (check if present)	LIBRARIAN'S WORDS (record verbatim)
Listening		
The staff member foes not interrupt		
The staff member uses acknowledgment or restatement		
The staff member clarifies		
Asking questions		
The staff member asks open questions		
The staff member uses probes such as "What do you mean by X?"		
The staff member checks that his/her understanding of what the user wants is correct		
Informing		
The staff member speaks clearly		
The staff member lets the user know what s/he is doing (inclusion)		
The staff member checks if answer is understood		
The staff member offers help in using and evaluating a source		
The staff member cites source used		
Following up		
The staff member asks, "Does this completely answer your question?" or equivalent question		
The staff member encourages the user to come back if the answer provided is not adequate or complete		

(Adapted from Dyson, 1992)

adapted from the very successful checklist used in Maryland. Work in pairs and take turns, with one person conducting the interview and the partner observing the interview and recording what happened. The checklist becomes a useful tool for providing feedback. In the VR environment, almost all of these behaviors have equivalents that should be used (8.3.3).

8.3.3 Training for Virtual Reference

Typically, VR training is done in MLIS programs and on the job. Training can be done by one-on-one mentoring or by hands-on workshops and can be provided by in-house staff or in cooperation with vendors. In addition, vendors can be used to "train the trainer" as a first step in in-house training. Statewide or regional consortia offer online training—one example is the "Anytime, Anywhere Answers" project in Washington State (Hirko and Ross, 2004). Training for the VR interview can include reviews of reference negotiation techniques and the microskills covered in this book, use of peer coaching, analysis of chat transcripts, hands-on reference scenarios, and activities such as secret-patron exercises and use of the "Recommendations for Facilitating Interpersonal Communication in Chat Reference Encounters" (6.2.1). Students in MLIS programs are increasingly being prepared for VR work though their reference courses (Harris, 2004). Many of these courses require students both to ask and answer questions in order to experience VR from both the users' and the staff perspective. Hirko and Ross (2004) recommend the use of such "real-world and simulated environments that exemplify the issues and practices of digital reference."

Chat reference has the inherent advantage of providing a printed transcript of the reference transaction. For training purposes, you can use a selection of transcripts from your own library or from other libraries—transcripts that for privacy have been cleansed of identifying information. Close examination of real-life cases of successful and unsuccessful reference interviews can be especially effective in a group situation where all participants can read the same transcripts. Reading over the transcripts together elicits discussion about reference interview skills along with other aspects of each transaction. Alternatively, trainees can be asked to use an evaluative worksheet to analyze a number of chat transcripts. Using this method, Ward (2003) identified follow-up and closure skills as areas needing more training. E-mail interviews can also be assembled and evaluated in a similar manner. Trainees can ask questions at public and academic library using chat or e-mail and submit copies of the e-mail exchanges or chat transcripts for analysis. Kovacs (2007) recommends learning activities in which trainees practice and observe chat and e-mail reference, either by using real-world library services or by role-playing with colleagues.

Training participants in "secret patron" exercises used in the Anytime Anywhere Answers curriculum confirmed the common problem of bypassing question negotiation. Hirko and Ross (2004) stressed the importance of good training to improve chances that the reference interview actually happens. In particular they recommend "secret patron"

Did You Know?
At The University of Western Ontario, students in an advanced reference course are required to ask a reference question at a Canadian academic or public library that offers e-mail or chat service. Each student "visits" a different library and asks a question that is unrelated to his or her course work and that is of personal interest. The students' perception of these VR visits have been compared with in-person visits as described in various Libary Visit Study articles (see 6.5.2 for articles by Nilsen, and Nilsen and Ross). Each student is required to answer about ten questions as "volunteers" for the Internet Public Library. The students identified this opportunity to as a powerful learning experience. Many other MLIS programs offer similar opportunities for their students.

Did You Know?
Training for VR requires review of traditional reference skills along with the necessary focus on technology. It has been found that even experienced and gifted reference librarians often forget to do simple things such as greeting users, clarifying ambiguous questions, and even fail to communicate with users for extended periods—things they would never do in FtF reference (Ronan, Reakes, and Cornwell, 2003).

Did You Know?
Training can increase confidence in the ability to conduct a virtual reference interview. In one study, none of the participants rated their ability as very high before the workshop and 12 percent rated it as very low. Following the workshop, 80 percent rated their ability as high or very high, and none rated it as very low (Abels and Ruffner, 2006).

A QUICK TIP

Planning VR Staff Training

All reference staff should receive similar training, if they are expected to provide similar quality service.

Centralized training is recommended to ensure consistency and minimize gaps in training.

Training sessions need to be focused and relevant to have the most impact.

Provide a variety of training mechanisms to accommodate various learning styles.

(Kawakami and Swartz, 2003).

EXERCISE

Understanding the User's Perspective

Think of a question for which you really want an answer and ask it using the VR service (chat, instant messaging, e-mail, or other digital means) of a public or academic library. If your question is a real question, then you are ethically entitled to do this. Think about your expectations and your perceptions of the service you receive. Note, in particular, whether a reference interview occurred and, if so, how it might have been improved.

A QUICK TIP

Training-Evaluation

Exit questionnaires are an easy, but not completely reliable, method of evaluating the training event. Good questions to ask are: "In what ways did this workshop help you? Not help you?" so that trainees can be specific. Ideally, participants should be surveyed again six weeks after an individual training event to assess the durability of the training.

exercises to help library staff members to understand what it feels like to be a virtual reference patron. They noted that learners had a strong reaction when they themselves received impersonal and curt treatment and in turn were determined to avoid perpetrating such behavior themselves.

Multiuser electronic environments such as Second Life presents new challenges for training, as librarians create library-related "information islands" where reference service is offered (see 6.4.2). A pilot project at McMaster University in Hamilton, Ontario investigated whether answering reference questions in a virtual world required burdensome, special staff training. As described by Buckland and Godfrey (2008), reference interviews can be readily conducted within the virtual world. Conversation, even without voice, flows easily because the use of avatars encourages behavior similar to real-life behavior. The learning curve with respect to the technology is steep. Buckland and Godfrey suggest that librarians who are adept at conducting the reference interview in real life do not need additional reference training to conduct successful interviews in the virtual world. The skills are transferable. However, the same experienced librarians who bypass the reference interview in FtF and chat encounters are likely to bypass the reference interview in virtual worlds. Therefore training for virtual world librarianship should be explicit about the need for a reference interview, must emphasize general reference interview techniques, and must draw attention to specific adaptations needed for effective communication in the virtual environment.

When training staff for chat and for virtual world interviews, use the recommendation in section 6.2.1 along with the model reference behaviors listed earlier in this chapter.

8.3.4 Evaluation of Training

Evaluation should be built into the design of any training program so that you might improve future training. You can use a number of measurement techniques to evaluate of effectiveness of training. Some methods of evaluation involve self-reports, such as trainees' assessments of the following: overall satisfaction with the training; satisfaction with, or preferences for, specific training techniques; levels of confidence in both FtF and virtual reference interviews (Abels and Ruffner, 2006). Other evaluation methods measure the ability of trainees to perform specific skills through the completion of hands-on exercises, or through successful performance of the skills in a role-played situation or on the job. The technology of VR allows for pre- and post-training assessments by evaluation of chat reference transcripts collected before and after training. Hirko and Ross (2004) provide a number of assessment checklists that can be used to evaluate VR competencies.

8.3.5 Resistance to Training—and Some Answers

Some staff question the usefulness of training for the reference interview. Here are some common objections that trainees raise together with our answers.

Establishing Policy and Training for the Reference Interview

1. **Good communication skills are inborn and cannot be learned.** It's true some people seem to have a "talent" for communication, but they probably learned it from modeling others. Most of us have to learn systematically how to do effective interviews. A large body of research now shows that people *can* change their communication behavior through training. We are beginning to get some solid evidence that a good reference interview is positively correlated with good search outcomes.

2. **Reference interviews are rarely necessary, and so training is a waste of time.** We hope by now to have convinced you otherwise. If not, please take another look at Chapter 1 and the myth of the face value rule. Of course it may seem silly to interview the user with books to check out who asks for directions to the circulation desk. However you could easily say, "It looks like you found what you were looking for. Let me know if there is anything else you need." Many questions requiring an interview do begin as directional questions. At the very least, training teaches you to offer the user an opportunity to describe her informational need more clearly and more completely so that you can provide better service. If you are using the appropriate skills and she doesn't accept your invitation, that is her choice. If all that is learned from training is to ask follow-up questions such as, "If that doesn't help you, please ask again," using this additional skill alone would bring about a big improvement in typical reference service.

3. **It takes too long to use these skills. We're too busy to repeat what users are saying or ask open questions.** In that case, you are probably also too busy to be going off into the stacks (or mining the Web), looking for something that isn't required, wasn't asked for, and won't help the user. Have you ever seen users surreptitiously leave materials behind when you were sure your long search yielded the very best sources? We are not claiming that time spent doing an interview *always* shortens search time—sometime you can guess and be lucky—but often it does.

4. **Using microskills is manipulative, not genuine—it's like requiring retail staff to say "Have a good day!"** We're assuming that librarians entered the profession because they have a genuine desire to help people find the information they need. Using appropriate skills makes that desire explicit to the user, much as using correct grammar and spelling enhances your ability to communicate in writing.

5. **The trouble with conducting a good reference interview is that you then have to find the materials that will help the user.** So true. But that's why we have librarians. At least you know, after the interview, what you're looking for and you may well save your own time as well as the time of the user. We also advocate training programs that will help librarians find the best sources—we just think they should know what the question is first.

Did You Know?

Microtraining works. Many studies by Allen Ivey have shown that people can learn microskills fairly easily. In a controlled experiment, Elaine Jennerich found that prospective librarians could learn basic microskills within a short time. Using a pre-test, post-test research design in a public library setting, Patricia Dewdney found that, after three training sessions, librarians trained in microskills used acknowledgment and encouragers more often, and asked more sense-making and open questions. The habit that librarians seemed to find hardest to break was asking too many closed questions.

(From Ivey, 1994; Jennerich, 1997; and Dewdney, 1986)

8.4 Annotated References

8.4.1 Policies and Guidelines for Reference Staff

American Library Association. "Code of Ethics." Chicago: ALA, 1997, amended 2008. Available: www.ala.org/ala/aboutala/offices/oif/statementspols/codeofethics/codeethics.cfm (accessed November 4, 2008).

American Library Association. "Freedom to Read Statement." Chicago: ALA, 1953, amended 1972, 1991, 2000, 2004. Available: www.ala.org/aboutala/offices/oif/statementspols/ftrstatement/freedomreadstatement.cfm (accessed November 4, 2008).

American Library Association. "Library Bill of Rights." Chicago: ALA, 1948, amended 1961, 1967, 1080, 2006. Available: www.ala.org/ala/aboutala/offices/oif/statementspols/statementsif/librarybillrights.cfm (accessed November 4, 2008).

International Federation of Library Associations and Institutions. "IFLA Digital Reference Guidelines." The Hague: Reference and Information Services Section, IFLA, 2004. Available: www.ifla.org/VII/s36/pubs/drg03.htm (accessed November 4, 2008). Designed to create common standards for libraries around the world, these guidelines promote best practices in virtual reference

Reference and User Services Association. "Guidelines for Behavioral Performance of Reference and Information Service Professionals." 2004. Available: www.ala.org/ala/mgrps/divs/rusa/resources/guidelines/guidelinesbehavioral.cfm (accessed November 4, 2008).

Reference and User Services Association. "Guidelines for Cooperative Reference Services." 1998, revised 2006. Available: www.ala.org/ala/mgrps/divs/rusa/resources/guidelines/guidelinescooperative.cfm (accessed November 4, 2008).

Reference and User Services Association. "Guidelines for Implementing and Maintaining Virtual Reference Services." 2004. Available: www.ala.org/ala/mgrps/divs/rusa/resources/guidelines/virtrefguidelines.cfm (accessed November 4, 2008).

Reference and User Services Association. "Guidelines for Information Services." 2000. Available: http://www.ala.org/ala/mgrps/divs/rusa/resources/guidelines/guidelinesinformation.cfm. (accessed November 4, 2008).

Reference and User Services Association. "Professional Competencies for Reference and User Services Librarians." 2003. Available: www.ala.org/ala/mgrps/divs/rusa/resources/guidelines/professional.cfm (accessed November 4, 2008).

8.4.2 Additional Readings on Reference Policy

Antone, Allen et al. 1994. "Information Services Policy Manual: An Outline." *RQ* 34 (winter): 165–172. This useful guide, prepared by ALA's RASD Management of Reference Committee, provides a framework for developing a reference policy manual, covering all topics that might be covered in a comprehensive manual.

Brumley, Rebecca. 2004. *The Reference Librarian's Policies, Forms, Guidelines, and Procedures Handbook, with CD-ROM.* New York: Neal-Schuman. Contains over 475 reference policy statements covering all aspects of in-person and virtual reference. Selected from more than 180 academic and public libraries, these policies are described as "among the best real-world examples in use today."

DeMiller, Anna L., compiler. 1994. *Reference Service Policies in ARL Libraries.* Spec Kit and Flyer 203. Washington, DC: Association of Research Libraries,

Office of Management Services. Provides examples of policies from university libraries.

Dorchester County Public Library (Maryland). *Reference Policy.* Available: www .dorchesterlibrary.org/library/refpolicy.html (accessed November 4, 2008).

Easley, Janet. 1985. "Reference Services Policies." *Reference Services Review* 13, no. 2 (summer): 79–82.

Jones, Marie F. 2004. "Internet Reference Services for Distance Education: Guidelines Comparison and Implementation." *Internet Reference Services Quarterly* 9, no. 3/4: 19–32.

Kern, M. Kathleen, and Esther Gillie. 2004. "Virtual Reference Policies: An Examination of Current Practice." In *The Virtual Reference Experience: Integrating Theory into Practice* (165–184), edited by R. David Lankes et al. New York: Neal-Schuman.

Morin, Alison C. 2004. "Approaching Best Practices and Guidelines for Digital Reference." In *The Virtual Reference Experience: Integrating Theory into Practice* (185–198), edited by R. David Lankes et al. New York: Neal–Schuman.

Nebraska Library Commission. *The Nebraska STAR Reference Manual (Statewide Training for Accurate Reference).* Available: www.nlc.state.ne.us/Ref/star/ star.html (accessed November 4, 2008). A thorough training resource.

QuestionPoint. 2008. 24/7 Reference Collaborative Polices and Procedures. Available: www.questionpoint.org/ordering/cooperative_guidelines_247 rev3.htm (accessed November 4, 2008).

8.4.3 Additional Readings on Training

Abels, Eileen G., and Malissa Ruffner. 2006. "Training for Online Virtual Reference: Measuring Effective Techniques." In *The Virtual Reference Desk: Creating a Reference Future* (49–73), edited by R. David Lankes et al. New York: Neal–Schuman.

Atherton, J. S. 2008. *Learning and Teaching; Misrepresentation, Myths and Misleading Ideas.* U.K. Available: www.learningandteaching.info/learning/ myths.htm (accessed November 4, 2008).

Buckland, Amy, and Krista Godfrey. 2008. "Gimmick or Groundbreaking? Canadian Academic Libraries Using Chat Reference in Multi-User Virtual Environments." *Libraries without Borders: Navigating towards Global Understanding.* Proceedings of World Library and Information Congress, 4th IFLA General Congress and Conference, Québec, Canada, August 10–14. Available: www.ifla.org/IV/ifla74/papers/158-Buckland_Godfrey–en.pdf (accessed November 4, 2008).

Dewdney, Patricia H. 1986. "The Effects of Training Reference Librarians in Interview Skills: A Field Experiment." Unpublished doctoral dissertation. London, Canada: The University of Western Ontario.

Dyson, Lillie Seward. 1992. "Improving Reference Services: A Maryland Training Program Brings Positive Results." *Public Libraries* 31, no. 5 (September/October): 284–289.

Education Institute. 2008. The Partnership. Provincial and Territorial Library Associations of Canada. Available: www.thepartnership.ca/partnership/ bins/index_ei.asp?cid=83&lang=1 (accessed November 4, 2008).

Harris, Lydia Eato. 2004. "Software Is Not Enough: Teaching and Training Digital Reference Librarians. In *The Virtual Reference Experience: Integrating Theory into Practice* (109–120), edited by R. David Lankes et al. New York: Neal-Schuman. Discusses virtual reference training in LIS schools, and design of a digital reference course at the University of Washington.

Hirko, Buff, and Mary Bucher Ross. 2004. *Virtual Reference Training: The Complete Guide to Providing Anytime, Anywhere Answers*. Chicago: ALA. This well-reviewed and very useful guide outlines the curriculum and lessons learned in the "Anytime, Anywhere Answers" component of Washington's Statewide Virtual Reference Project that ran from 2001 to 2006. The book provides numerous exercises and learning activities as well as training tips and assessment tools. Although the Anytime, Anywhere Answers project ended in 2006, a five week online training program is still available online at: http://vrstrain.spl.org/orientation.htm (accessed November 4, 2008). The third week of training focuses on the reference interview.

Huling, Nancy. 1999. "Peer Reflection: Collegial Coaching and Reference Effectiveness." *The Reference Librarian* 66: 61–74. Focuses specifically on using peer coaching to improve the reference interview, and provides a number of suggestions.

Isenstein, Laura. 1992. "Get Your Reference Staff on the STAR Track." *Library Journal* 117, no. 7 (April 15): 34–37. Good example of a skills-based training program. Describes a program for training reference staff to use open questions, paraphrase, and follow-up in which reference staff increased their success rate from 60 to almost 80 percent.

Kawakami, Alice, and Pauline Swartz. 2003. "Digital Reference Training and Assessment for Service Improvement." *Reference Services Review* 31, no. 3: 227–236.

Kovacs, Diane K. 2007. *The Virtual Reference Handbook: Interview and Information Delivery Techniques for the Chat and E-Mail Environments*. New York: Neal-Schuman. Identifies communication competencies needed for successful reference interviews, and includes learning activities that can be used for independent learning or incorporated into group training.

LibrarySupportStaff.com. Reference Trainng and the Art of the Reference Interview. Available: www.librarysupportstaff.com/reftrain.html (accessed November 4, 2008). In addition to reference training, this site provides links to many staff training and development resources.

Ohio Library Council. 2000 (last updated 2008). *Ohio Reference Excellence on the Web*. Available: www.olc.org/ore (accessed November 4, 2008). An excellent Web-based training program, with support for supervisors doing their own one-on-one training.

Ohles, Judith K., and Julie McDaniel. 1993. *Training Paraprofessionals for Reference Service: A How-To-Do-It Manual for Librarians*. New York: Neal-Schuman. A guide for librarians who need to create, implement and evaluate reference training programs for paraprofessionals.

Radford, Marie L. 2006. "Encountering Virtual Users: A Qualitative Investigation of Interpersonal Communication in Chat Reference." *Journal of the American Society for Information Science and Technology* 57, no. 8: 1046–1059.

Ronan, Jana, Patrick Reakes, and Gary Cornwell. 2002/2003. "Evaluating Online Real-Time Reference in an Academic Library: Obstacles and Recommendations." *The Reference Librarian* 79/80: 224–240.

Ross, Catherine S., and Patricia Dewdney. 1998. *Communicating Professionally*, 2nd ed. New York: Neal-Schuman. See Chapter 10 on training and development, with an extensive bibliography.

Second Life. Available: http://secondlife.com/ (accessed November 4, 2008).

Ward, David. 2003. "Using Virtual Reference Transcripts for Staff Training." *Reference Services Review* 31, no. 1: 46–56. Describes use of chat transcripts in an academic library for training graduate assistants. Includes the Reference Interview Evaluation Sheet used by trainees.

Index

A

About the Authors

The authors are all faculty members who have taught reference in various universities in Canada and the United States, and who have conducted field research on what happens when real users ask questions in libraries, either face-to-face or through electronic mediations.

Dr. Catherine Sheldrick Ross teaches graduate courses in reference services, readers' advisory work, and research methods in the MLIS and PhD programs at The University of Western Ontario. She has presented more than fifty workshops to library professionals in the United States and Canada. Together with Patricia Dewdney, she has written two editions of *Communicating Professionally* (Neal-Schuman, 2nd ed., 1998) and is a four-time winner of the Reference Services Press Award. She has published extensively in the areas of reference services, readers' advisory, and the ethnography of reading for pleasure. With co-authors Lynne (E.F.) McKechnie and Paulette M. Rothbauer, she has published *Reading Matters: What the Research Reveals about Reading, Libraries, and Community* (Libraries Unlimited, 2006).

Dr. Kirsti Nilsen is currently an independent researcher and writer. She has taught introductory and advanced courses in reference, government information, collection development, special libraries, and information policy in the MLIS programs at both The University of Western Ontario and the University of Toronto. She is the editor of the latest edition of the *Guide to Reference Materials for Canadian Libraries* (University of Toronto Press, 8th ed., 1992), and was co-author with Catherine Ross and Patricia Dewdney of the first edition of *Conducting the Reference Interview*. In addition, she is the author of *The Impact of Information Policy* (Ablex, 2001) and co-author of *Constraining Public Libraries: The World Trade Organization's General Agreement on Trade in Services* (Scarecrow, 2006).

Dr. Marie L Radford is Associate Professor at Rutgers SCILS. Prior to joining the Rutgers faculty, she was Acting Dean and Associate Professor of Pratt Institute's School of Information and Library Science. Her research interests include interpersonal communication in reference service (both traditional and digital), evaluation of digital resources and services, cultural studies, and media stereotypes of librarians. She was a co-editor of *Virtual Reference Service: From Competencies to Assessment* (Neal-Schuman, 2008) with R. David Lankes and others. Her latest book is *Academic Library Research: Perspectives and Current Trends* (Association of College & Research Libraries, 2008), co-edited with Pamela Snelson. Radford is active in library and communication associations, including ALA, ALISE, and RUSA. Her Web site can be found at: http://www.scils.rutgers.edu/~mradford, and her blog at http://librarygarden.blogspot.com/.

To contact the authors, send an e-mail to ross@uwo.ca.